On Becoming Human

On Becoming
Human

A Journey
of 5,000,000
Years

Arthur Niehoff

THE HOMINID PRESS ～ BONSALL, CALIFORNIA

ISBN 0-9643072-1-9
Library of Congress Catalog Card No: 94-92303

Book design and typography: Joel Friedlander
Illustration: Jan Imbrescia

Manufactured in the United States of America

Publisher's Cataloging in Publication
(Prepared by Quality Books Inc.)
Niehoff, Arthur H., 1921-
    On becoming human : a journey of 5,000,000 years / Arthur
Niehoff.
    p. cm.
    Includes index.
    ISBN 0-9643072-1-9

    1. Anthropology. 2. Social evolution. 3. History.   I. Title.
GN281.4.N54 1995   303.44
                        QBI94-1792

Contents

What the Book is About

The intention of this book is to be "intriguing, informative, and fun"—a comment made by a publisher in reference to another book of mine on anthropology. And I have to confess at this point that I am so hooked on this field that I cannot write about anything else. So the reader will know that I am dedicated but not fanatic.

Anthropology cannot help being intriguing because it deals with humankind in all its variety—a favorite subject of most readers. But it is also informative in several ways. First, it gives the broadest picture of humankind that any subject can. It can give us a grasp on some of the most remote corners of our world and help us to understand many seeming inexplicables. It helps answer interesting questions like: Why do men of most cultures avoid their mothers-in-law? Why do men wear clothing made to follow the contours of the body while women more often wear tubular garments (dresses)? And why do Americans think they have achieved the highest form of government in history?

I think there is no doubt that anthropology is basically intriguing and informative. But how is it fun? I must admit that though it has long been my opinion that the subject matter of anthropology lends itself naturally to pleasurable thoughts, I have been surprised periodically that students have had a less-than-fun experience in an anthropology class. So I have devoted most of my energies in teaching to presenting this most fascinating subject in an interesting fashion. If there was ever any criticism from a student that would seriously bother me, it was that the subject I was teaching was boring. And although I admittedly have many deficiencies, being boring was never one of them, especially in presenting anthropology. In fact, I once wrote an essay entitled, "Anthropology is a Ball."

But some, particularly the self-perceived erudite, believe that this subject, being an "ology," is very serious business. I have no quarrel with that point of view, and I have surely benefited from it in learning the subject. Most of the practitioners of the subject, like the practitioners of other "ologies," have been rewarded primarily for treating it very seriously and for having produced learned works on specialized topics. They have built the edifice of theory and description which is the basis of the science.

We can use much of this knowledge seriously. Mankind has got by with unabashed ethnocentrism as long as we know, right up through the nineteenth century. Being "johnny-come-latelies" in the Western European Tradition, we Americans have continued in this mode up through World War II. Our supreme victory over the enemy forces proved our martial superiority. But we also conceived ourselves as superior in most other ways. And even when we tried to help others, we invariably tried to make them similar to us. And that is what ethnocentrism is, the judgement of the people of one culture that it is central or superior to all others, and taking action on this belief. This is a point of view that practically all cultures we know anything about have espoused. Almost all tribal cultures were ethnocentric until they were taken over. A dominant culture, if it doesn't eliminate the weaker ones, almost always tries to impose its way on them, always in power control, and frequently in other aspects of the culture. The most recent dominants have been the Western Europeans, who have had no equals in ethnocentric imposition.

But dominance, like everything else, is temporary. If one looks through history, one sees that, with the possible exceptions of Egypt and China, cultural dominance lasts only a few hundred years. As we approach the twenty-first century, there is every indication that the cultural dominance of Europe and America, which has lasted for a little less than 500 years, is fading. If we take the United States by itself, the dominance has been less than 100 years. The ethnocentrism of European man no longer prevails and as we move into the twenty-first century, it will become even less. In other words, it will be increasingly less likely that Euros will be able to impose their way, whether in social, economic, or political forms, technology, or religion.

What does this have to do with anthropology? Until the sciences proliferated, from the sixteenth century on, humankind operated on a basis of centrism, from geocentrism to homocentrism—from earth centeredness to man centeredness. One of the last pervasive forms has been ethno-centeredness; that is, the belief that one's own culture is central and is superior to all others. Even though ethno-centeredness has been under attack since the rise of the non-Euros in the twentieth century, it is still a potent force. Americans still think their religion and their political, economic, and family system are the best that have emerged. Unfortunately, many others think the same of theirs, and no longer accept us as dominant. So cultural relativism, the idea that there are different ways to solve human problems, has come to the fore. Pure unabashed ethnocentrism, or even subtly-hidden forms, will no longer do. And what subject has devoted more time and energy to cultural relativism and multiculturism than anthropology?

To make a long story short, it is my opinion that, one way or another, more of the ideas of cultural anthropology will have to be a part of the thinking man's make-up in the twenty-first century and perhaps beyond. The only other option I can imagine would be a single culture for all mankind, imposed in my imagination by superior aliens. But until that happens, we will more than ever before need to know about other ways, and anthropology seems a natural focus for this learning.

So I will present anthropology as intriguing, informative, and fun. There are plenty of textbooks which fulfill the first two functions. And that is okay too. But I, like many others, have learned from teaching that the fun aspect is often sadly missing. Most of us academics got the fun from assigning corollary books. Thus, we assigned a text which covered all the basics, but also a book or books of a more imaginative tenor. I have used quite a variety through the years. And now I have written my own book to serve such a function, to be used along with a standard text.

But as I have already indicated, I am also aiming at another audience, that of the general reader who likes to learn things but likes to have pleasure at the same time. Even before I got into anthropology, I was doing some creative writing, and I have continued, a little or a lot, in the years I have been practicing anthropology. In the process, I became thoroughly convinced that creative writing and anthropology make a natural combination. This was a fortunate discovery for me, because when I retired, I could devote myself completely to this kind of writing, thus satisfying two basic needs: to continue to practice anthropology, and to engage in creative writing.

So I am writing this as a crossover book—a work that encompasses two kinds of audiences. In this case, the crossover is from a text to a trade book. The result is an informative book that is fun to read.

Actually there is less crossover than might be imagined. Although there are two types of reader, the general public and the anthropology student, the readership would not differ that much, except by age.

So what else can I say that will make this book meaningful? First, I must emphasize that, although by describing the high points of the cultural way I will be doing history, it is anthropological history which is different in two ways from the standard treatment. In the first place, following the anthropological way, it will describe the way of life of the ordinary person, unlike the "big man" approach to history. We get infatuated with the details of the leaders in history to the point where we forget that the leaders, like all others, are a part of the way of life shared by everyone of the same culture. Thus, we in the West are currently observing the anniversary of Columbus. But Columbus was a member of an expanding, ethnocentric culture, Western European, with a very self-righteous religion, Christianity, and a very exploitative technology. Those of Columbus' culture shared most of his values, even if there might have been a difference of degree. So if it hadn't been for Columbus, there would have been someone like him, and the same is true of the conquerors of Mexico, Peru, and the Pueblo peoples. The Spanish, and later other Euros, were producing so many fierce warriors because the cultural way was encouraging their development, not because more were being born. And that is what we anthropologists have always been interested in, the cultural matrix; and this is so with all pivotal occurrences of history. The great man treatment tells us who and at exactly what point an event occurred, but the cultural way, the matrix, tells us what evolved overall. Anthropology tells us that it doesn't matter who invented the wheel or the alphabet as much as what the cultural context was. We inherited them because they were accepted in their day just as much as because they were invented.

The second difference from traditional history is that anthropology is concerned with all peoples during all times and in all places; it does not limit itself to a particular cultural tradition. Neither China nor Western Europe are the centers of the cultural universe. In our study of man's way we begin in Africa, then move on to Asia, then to Europe, and finally the New World. And we do it for all times since man was upright. Thus the cultural way did not begin with the ancient Greeks or the Han Chinese, but rather with Australopithecus in Africa.

An explanation about the book's format may be useful. It is hoped that opening each chapter with a narrative of events brings to life the most important occurrences in man's history. And the question and answer section in the second half of each chapter was meant to reproduce a seminar, a type of learning experience which has been used at least since Socrates, and which continues in colleges across the country. As a professor, I have given many of these.

But more explicitly, it brings back a memory of a conversation I had years ago with an old colleague of mine while we were travelling from Lagos to Ibadan, Nigeria. I asked Everett Rogers what the best class he had ever had was, and he responded without hesitation, "It was with Professor John Useem (an anthropology professor at his university)."

"And what was so special about it?"

"He gave us reading assignments and at the first session, he walked to the front of the class and said, 'any questions?'

"No lecture at all. Nothing more. We all sat stunned. And sat and sat, for an interminable length of time. Our fidgeting increased. And finally some brave soul put up his hand and said, 'Professor Useem, I do have a question.'

"And after that, it opened like a flood."

So let us begin with Squint, the primate who stood upright.

On Becoming Human

1

Out of Africa

Squint

Four million eight hundred sixty-four thousand three hundred and twenty-eight years ago, a small naked person crouched over the carcass of a partially decomposed zebra. His name meant nothing to Squint, since he and his kind were unable to name things or people, or to understand such names. (The name Squint, and the others which follow, was given according to the common practice of ethologists, who are watchers of animals in the wild. For precise identification, they give descriptive names to the individual animals they are studying.) Squint and his fellows had a series of sounds which they emitted, depending on the circumstances, but nothing approaching the complexity of a language. However, Squint was a man because he walked upright most of the time, the defining characteristic of *Homo*.

Squint waved the flies off the right hindquarters of the carcass while trying to tear a piece loose. The animal had been dead for two or three days, and it was high. This made it easier to tear chunks off, and made the meat easier to chew. The smell did not bother Squint. He was used to two or three day old carcasses, usually those of animals killed by lions. In fact, he preferred the taste to that of freshly killed meat, not that he got much of that.

3

He worked a fair-sized piece loose, but then had to hunch over and chew through the gristle. Reaching up with his right hand he took the piece of meat from his mouth and raised his head to listen, his face dripping with the juices of decomposition. He heard the sound of footsteps in the dry leaves under the acacia tree, and quickly recognized that they were made by small feet, probably those of a jackal. Tearing another piece of meat from the strip, he began chewing. The footsteps came closer, and he stood up, his rock in his hand.

He was about three and a half feet tall, very dark skinned, almost black. He was covered with body hair—less than a chimpanzee or a baboon, but more than an elephant or a hippo. As the footsteps came closer, he clutched the rock tensely, at the same time turning slightly toward another tree, ready for a quick retreat. A small narrow nose poked through the brush and he relaxed. The jackal posed no threat. For a moment he thought of hurling his stone at it, but then changed his mind. Good throwing rocks were not easy to find. He had found this one at the bottom of a wash where it had fallen from an outcrop.

Still holding his piece of meat, Squint climbed to the top of an old anthill to see farther. It was midday and hot, so not many animals were grazing, though he did see a few wildebeests and some impala in the distance. They were feeding quietly and didn't seem particularly nervous. If there were any big cats or wild dogs around, they would be sleeping. Not far away was the largest acacia in sight. He figured lions were probably resting under it. Several vultures perched in the top of the acacia where they had gone when Squint had chased them away from the carcass, but he couldn't see any lions. They must have fed well, he thought, probably from the carcass. It was unusual for a lion group to get two animals at once, though it sometimes happened, most often when the lions found a mother with her young one, as they had this time.

Squint climbed down from the anthill and turned seriously to the carcass. He had had little to eat for a couple of days—some wild figs, roots, and seeds, and a couple of lizards, all of which he had eaten on the spot. So the zebra meat was welcome. He ate fast to get as much as possible before the others arrived.

Since it was not a heavily wooded area, the others were not making their contact call, so he stood up periodically to look toward the distant hill from which he had come. It wasn't long before he saw a figure come across the ridge, watching carefully. The others must also have figured there were lions around. Squint ate faster, swallowing

4

pieces so large he could scarcely get them down. But he was used to gulping food, particularly meat, and since he still had most of his teeth, he could even chew it a little.

As the figure came closer, he recognized it as his ally, Gimp. The two of them had learned to team together to assert dominance. There were younger and stronger males, but they had not learned to cooperate well, so they were squeezed out of first choice of meat and females.

Gimp came into the clearing, saw Squint, and headed straight for the carcass. Squint stood up, holding a piece of meat in his hand. The others slowed down to let Gimp come up to Squint, and stood in a circle a few feet back from the carcass. They gesticulated toward the stinking, fly-covered pile, repeating the eat sound, "Gorp, gorp, gorp," but none stepped forward to touch it. Gimp reached over and touched Squint's arm. At first, Squint paid no attention, though he did not shake his ally's hand off. He tore a mouthful off and began to chew it, then suddenly handed the piece to Gimp, who also took a bite from it. The others squatted down and watched, though one, a big young male, approached the carcass and touched it carefully with a stick. Squint growled and the younger male moved back.

Squint and Gimp ate until they were full and then Squint began to twist what was left of one hindquarter. Gimp watched for a moment and then began to twist a piece loose also. The others were rapt in their attention, saliva running down their chins. A couple of times one of the younger ones came forward, but moved back quickly when Squint and Gimp growled.

The two got their pieces loose and moved a short distance away, constantly brushing away flies. The others now moved in and squatted down, to begin tearing and chewing. One or another would periodically stand up and look around, particularly in the direction of the big acacia tree. A small ring of vultures and jackals had collected, but they kept their distance. Whenever one would move too far forward, one of the men would throw a rock or stick at it.

Squint and Gimp lay in the shade, belching every once in a while. But as comfortable as they appeared, they still got up frequently to look in the direction of the lions. Finally Gimp barked, "Nying, nying," and pointed. It was the warning call for ground predators, usually lions, leopards, or wild dogs.

Despite how much he had eaten, Squint was quickly on his feet. A female lion was moving toward the carcass. By this time all the others from the band were standing and watching, most with strips of meat in their hands or mouths. The lion kept moving toward them, not crouching in a hunting posture. She was evidently still full from what she had eaten earlier. But she kept coming. The whole group started to move away in the direction of some trees. Some of the jackals moved in to snatch at the carcass. Squint and Gimp started to move away too, first without the meat chunks, but then Squint picked up his, and Gimp followed his lead. They hurried to join the others, who were by this time almost on the ridge. When they got there, Squint looked back and saw the lion had been joined by another about the same size and both were gnawing on the carcass. The group of bipeds moved away, Squint and Gimp still carrying their pieces.

All the men were less than four feet in height, and though they walked upright most of the time, they used their arms for support whenever they were near a tree or rock. Several carried sticks, sometimes using them for support, sometimes poking them into holes or clumps of brush. Whenever a locust or other large insect would fly or run out of a clump, the man who had scared it out would try to knock it down with his stick or hand, and immediately tear off the wings or carapace and eat the small creature.

From time to time, one of the other males came close to Squint or Gimp and stared at the chunks of meat, but a low growl was enough to make him retreat.

The men's hands were quite capable of grasping insects or other things, as the thumbs were completely opposable to the fingers, unlike the feet which lacked opposable toes. In this sense they differed from chimpanzees who could grasp objects with their feet as well as with their hands. The heads of the upright creatures were much like those of chimpanzees, though a little larger. However, there was no true forehead or chin. The head just slanted back in front, top and bottom.

The six hominids had been on the move for three days, going south toward the base of the high mountain, always on the lookout for something to eat. They had left the main band at the campground near the big water. Though there was food in the vicinity of the campground, it was mostly vegetal, seeds and roots. Most of the grazing animals had moved away, looking for better grass, so there was very little meat, either what they killed themselves or that killed by predators.

But the group of six had found little meat. Once Gimp had spotted a newborn gazelle in the grass and the group had closed in on it, killing it easily, but it was not enough to go very far.

In a more wooded area they had come across a small group of chimpanzees feeding. Several females held babies by one arm or carried them on their backs. Chimpanzees could not stand upright for long and they always had to use at least one arm for support when they moved.

The group of six bipeds had stood at the edge of the clearing, watching the knuckle-walkers intently, particularly the mothers and infants. Squint had moved forward in a crouch, clutching his stone tightly, using small trees and brush for cover. The others had fanned out, keeping their eyes on him while keeping out of sight. They had all moved cautiously, knowing that the chimpanzees' vision was as good as their own. Finally Squint was close enough to a female carrying a baby. He crouched, ready to lunge. Just as he was tensing his muscles for the leap and snatch, he heard a great roar next to him and a very large male chimpanzee raised himself out of the nearby brush. The animal tore a large branch from a nearby tree and slammed it on the ground, roaring, all his hair standing on end. As the noise increased, several other heads appeared.

Squint wasn't sure the male had seen him, but he knew he was aware there was a possible danger nearby and was ready to protect the females and young. Squint or any of the other bipeds had been prepared to snatch an infant from a frightened female, but none of them was about to challenge a big male, and particularly one backed by several others. The only weapon Squint had was his rock, hardly enough to challenge a group of defensive male chimpanzees. Besides, by this time the female with the baby had disappeared. Squint did likewise, moving back very slowly in crab fashion. None of the males had attacked, and the men had continued on their way.

Like most of their efforts to kill something, this one had ended in failure. One simply went on. Sooner or later, they would catch and kill something.

Once the group had found a full-grown impala in the fork of a tree. It had been partially eaten and had been put there by a leopard to keep the wild dogs and lions from eating the rest. The men had checked the vicinity carefully, and had not found any trace of the cat. But just as Gimp had got the carcass loose, the leopard came running in full snarl. Gimp got down in time and they all ran. The cat, concerned only with protecting the carcass, had not followed.

The biggest prey they had managed to find was a cutting-grass, an African version of a wood-chuck. Apart from that, they just picked up little things as they passed, supplementing them with wild fruit, seeds, and roots. Until they had found the zebra kill, it had been like most other hunts.

Returning was faster than going, since the group was not searching hard for things to eat. By going straight, they made it in one day. Even so, the hindquarters Squint was carrying seemed to get heavier all the time. The continuing interest of the others in his and Gimp's pieces told him that they would be quite willing to help finish it on the spot. Although that would make travelling easier, Squint, and evidently Gimp also, was not willing to allow that.

Squint couldn't clearly understand exactly why he was so intent on getting back to the campground by the water, but he did know it had something to do with the female, Digger, and perhaps even with the young one she carried, little Squealer. One of the ways Squint had to make trekking less boring, especially when he wasn't on the lookout for food, was to create pictures in his mind. He didn't have words to describe things, only the images of things he had seen. Now, the image of the chimpanzee carrying the infant in one arm flashed in his mind, quickly followed by the image of Digger carrying the child in both arms. His lips pulled back in a slight grin as he thought about it— Digger did not need to support her body with one arm, and so could carry the little one in both arms. As he thought about it, he realized that she also carried other things in both arms, particularly the basket containers that she put together to carry seeds or fruit. He suddenly realized that he had never seen chimpanzees carrying such containers or much of anything, and he realized why—they never had both arms free. Then another image pictured itself—little Squealer did not hold onto his mother's body hair so tightly. For that matter, she had much less to hold onto. Squint passed his hand across his chest, which was hairy.

And so his thoughts went forward to the campground, to wondering if they would make it that night. They would have to stop when it got dark. There was no way they would take a chance with all the night hunters, not to mention the bodiless heads he and the others had seen lately. It would be simple enough to stay out another night. There were enough trees around for them all to climb up and make nests for the night, like the chimps. But he wanted to get back to the campground, which made him quicken his steps.

The afternoon wore on, bringing them closer to the camp. Gimp and Squint hurried, though most of the others lagged. They evidently had little pulling them toward the camp. Squint kept getting the image of Digger in his mind.

They came to a place under a tree where someone had been cracking nuts on a flat rock, scattering the shells about. Squint veered in that direction and studied the ground as he passed, hoping to see some pieces of nuts on the ground. He found none and realized he was hungry. Briefly, he thought of putting the piece of zebra meat down and tearing a piece off, but decided against it. He knew it wasn't far now to the camp, and he wanted to carry the piece back. He looked over at Gimp who was also still slogging along with his piece.

When they came to the river bed, dry at this season, Squint knew the campground near the water hole was just a short way downstream. The river was full during the rainy season, and now, in the dry season, the only place that still retained some water was near the campground. There was enough human activity there to keep most animals away, but occasionally one would come to drink, and it was possible to make a kill or to find the kill of a four-footed predator and take advantage of it. And it was important for the group to have water available. Squint quickened his steps, hearing the footsteps of Gimp not far behind.

They heard the sounds of voices before they saw anyone—the babble of different calls, the eating sound, the play sound, and the mother call. They heard no fright or excitement calls. Squint knew that one of the older children would be perched in a tree on the lookout for predators. The child would probably see the returning hunters soon and cry out with the non-danger recognition call. Then it came, the long, drawn-out "Hoo-o-o."

Squint was first to enter the camp, then Gimp, and then the others came straggling in. The campground was simply a grassy place interspersed with trees. There were dusty paths criss-crossing, usually from one shelter to another. These were simple affairs of crossed branches covered with leaves. Like the baskets, these shelters were made by the women. They were only used during daylight when there was a lookout stationed in one of the trees. At night everyone went up into the sleep-nests like the chimpanzees.

Women, children, and a few older people appeared when the hunters entered the clearing. They came near to stare at the men and particularly at the two with chunks of meat. As they came, they emitted their contact call. A few made the eat sound. The four hunters without meat drifted off to touch various camp people or to crawl into leaf shelters. The young female with upstanding breasts, Moonface, came up to Gimp. She put her hand out carefully, not touching his chunk of meat, but only his free arm. He did not growl. She lifted his hand to her lips. He stood still. She put his hand on her crotch. He pulled his hand back and smelled it. She was not in heat but sightly damp. He was aware that she was generally like this. The majority of females in the group who were not pregnant or nursing babies came into heat a few days each month, but a few, like Moonface and Digger, seemed to be ready most of the time.

One of the other hunters stood nearby watching the exchange. He put his arm toward the female and Gimp growled. The other looked toward Squint, then let his arm fall. Gimp pulled a piece of meat from the chunk and handed it to the female. She put it in her mouth and began chewing. When she finished, she reached over to touch the chunk again. Gimp did not growl, but offered her more. She turned, and getting on her hands and knees, offered her bottom. He studied her, and even put his face up to smell but did not mount her. Instead he began to step around her. She got up and followed him.

Squint did not see Digger right away so he went over to the leaf shelter she had built before he left. No one was there. He crawled in and put the chunk of meat into one corner. At least it was dark enough that most of the flies did not follow. He saw a couple of leaf baskets in one corner and picked one up. It had a layer of cracked nuts on the bottom. He took a handful and ate hungrily. The other basket contained a variety of plant products, mostly roots. He took a small root of the spreading-bush plant and chewed it slowly. One of his back teeth was sensitive. He could eat partly-decomposed meat with little trouble, swallowing it in fair-sized chunks, but some plant foods were more difficult.

He was about to go to the water for a drink when he heard the footsteps and mother-cluck of Digger. She came to the entrance, and seeing him squatting and still chewing, emitted the recognition call, though much lower than the boy had when he saw the hunting party approaching. She was carrying the child with both hands.

Digger was slightly smaller than Squint, just as dark, though with less body hair. Her head hair fell in a tangle even though it was wet. Evidently she had washed it. She was naked like all the others. Her breasts also were upstanding. The baby must have been her first.

She squatted next to him and reached for the basket of nuts, picking a good one and handing it to him. Though he had already eaten some, he took the one she offered and ate it.

He watched her gaze as she noticed the chunk of meat in the corner. She put her hand on it carefully, and he pulled it over to tear off a piece. Then instead of putting it in his mouth, he handed it to her. She put the baby down on a pile of leaves in the corner, then squatting down, began eating the meat while Squint ate nutmeats and roots. After a while he patted his stomach and farted. She did the same.

After the nuts and roots, he felt like a drink of water. He got up and went to the stream. At a distance he could see a female surrounded by several males, including a couple of juveniles. A couple of the larger ones were threatening the others, but none had the courage to mount her, even though she would frequently assume the position. Squint momentarily had the urge to enter the group—he was fairly sure he could drive off the juveniles and bluff the older ones. But suddenly the image of Digger came into his mind, and he turned back to the stream, scooped up some water in his cupped hands, and drank.

When he got back to the leaf shelter, the baby was asleep and Digger was on her back at one side. He lay down beside her and extended his leg over one of hers. She turned toward him and held out her arms.

Later all three climbed into a large tree nest which Digger had built and where they slept together during the night. He took pleasure in the warmth of her body early in the morning. When he awoke, he saw that three nests were scattered in the grove. He couldn't spot Gimp among the early risers, but he noticed that the others were all sleeping alone or were mothers with young ones.

It was getting warm as Squint headed toward the outcrop where he had picked up the stone the previous day, and where he knew there were others. He passed a group of women digging for roots on the side of a hill. Each had a stick, one end of which had been made more or less pointed. They were crude and did not dig very well, but in spite of that the women managed to make little piles of roots. Every once in a while one of the women would dig up a wiggling grub and pop it into her mouth.

Usually the men travelled in small groups, but now Squint was alone. Gimp had come by earlier, but after he had groomed Squint a short while, he had left. This was fine with Squint, who had no intention of hunting. Of course, if he came across something by chance, dead or alive, he would try to get it. But that wasn't likely since the rock outcrop was not far and all the human activity kept most of the animals further out. As he walked, Squint ruminated on the pleasure

11

of being groomed. To have another person go over your hairiest parts and methodically pull the hairs apart, picking out grains of sand, pieces of dirt or lice, was a pleasure second only to eating. Digger had groomed him for a long while after sex the previous night, and he remembered it with particular pleasure. It seemed to Squint that women were much better at grooming than men.

When he came over the rise above the outcrop, he was pleased to find no one else there. Generally, he and the other men would pick up whatever seemed suitable—globular rocks which were useful for pounding things like nuts or other rocks, or slivers of rock which would slice through meat or skin. Any shape could be thrown at an animal, but round ones were best for that. He had noticed another quality of rocks. Round ones tended to be granular, and if you hit one against another, they would crumble or come off in particles, but if you hit the shinier ones together, they would break off in flakes or slivers. The shiny, flake type were good for cutting.

There were plenty of rocks in the wash below the outcrop and Squint began to sort through them. He picked up round rocks until he found one that fit well in his hand. He tapped it tentatively against a much larger one, knowing that if he hit it too hard, it could break into pieces. As he worked carefully, small pieces broke off at the point of contact at each strike. Then he picked up some of the shiny, sliver-like stone and whacked one piece against another. Flakes would come off at each whack. He picked up one that looked especially sharp and cut his finger. Dropping the stone, he sucked the oozing blood. He tried again and again. He would get a stone almost to a good cutting shape, then take one more whack and watch it shatter. He was starting to get angry. Finally he got one with a good cutting edge on one side but rough enough on the other so he could hold it without cutting himself. He picked it up and started back towards the campground.

Squint saw a group of vultures circling in the distance. Then he saw a cluster on the ground fighting over the carcass of some fair-sized animal. He looked around to see if some predator was nearby, but saw nothing. He guessed it was some wounded or old animal that had fallen by itself, and the vultures had closed in. He hurried toward them. When he got near enough, he waved his arms and yelled. The vultures stayed until he got very close, but then lifted off, screaming, to a nearby tree.

He could just make out the carcass as that of a wildebeest. It had not been dead long enough to start stinking, but there wasn't much left. The vultures had even pulled apart most of the bones. Squint pulled at pieces that were left. Finally he got hold of a thigh bone with a little meat left on it. He pulled, but it wouldn't let go. The leg bone was still attached to the hip bone and also a piece of skin held the two together. Suddenly he remembered the sliver rock he was still carrying and, squatting, he sawed through the gristle holding the bones together and then the skin. He yanked and the piece was free. It wasn't much meat but all of a sudden he was too elated to care. He held the piece of sliver rock up in the air and yelled, "Yaa," meaning more or less, "I did it."

He picked up the remnant piece of meat and the sliver rock and turned toward the camp. He was scarcely to the top of the outcrop before the vultures again settled on the remnants.

~

Q: *It seems from what you have described that anthropologists know a great deal about the primitive people of long ago. How could such precise information be deduced from the evidence that was left; for instance about the people's sex life, the kind of language they used, and the color of their skin?*

A: This is a matter that needs to be cleared up early. The real evidence that we have of these people is quite limited. We have to face the fact that all sciences, and particularly the historical ones, are based on limited information, and the further back we go, the more limited it is.

Q: *You mean a lot of things you describe you don't know, like their language, skin color, and sex life?*

A: Well, we do and we don't—the usual academic cop-out. We are now talking about archeology (the study of past cultures) and paleontology (the study of past physical remains). And what we have to study are a few old bones and artifacts. All the rest has vanished due to the ravages of time. For instance, when we go back almost five million years, we do not have the whole skeleton of any person. The fossil type I am trying to describe is known as *Australopithecus* and until 1974 all we had to base our ideas on were some skulls and a few fragments of other bones. Then Dr. Johanson found most of the bones of one small person which he named Lucy, although that too is a moot point, as it is very difficult to know the sex of a fossil as different from modern man as *Australopithecus* was. And other physical characteristics, like skin color and body hair, are impossible to know from looking at a fossil skeleton.

Q: *But I saw the reconstruction of a fossil man in a museum and it was all hairy. Did they make that up?*

A: That's a good observation. You probably also noticed that the skin color was dark. And you ask, "Why, if we don't have any direct evidence?" The answer is "inference." We infer that these guys were hairy and dark skinned because of indirect evidence. In this case, it's of two kinds. Dark skin is the normal skin color for all varieties of men right up to modern times. Dark skin protects man from the harmful rays of the sun. You know as well as I do that we are very concerned these days about skin cancer. But one thing the medical people do not mention very often is that skin cancer is a white man's disease. The dark-skinned people of the tropics are not plagued with this problem, the reason being that their skin protects them from the ultra-violet rays. They evolved where the sun was strong and natural selection took care of the rest.

Q: *But why then do some of us have white skins—and so cancer?*

A: You know that white skins, which is not descriptively accurate anyway, since Europeans and those of European descent have light tan or cream-colored skins, evolved in northern Europe, and it is only because they spread all over since Christopher C. discovered the New World, that we now find them everywhere. You may know that the highest incidence of skin cancer in the world is in Australia. I read a commentary by a knowledgeable medical researcher recently who said it was no wonder there was so much skin cancer there. After all, Australia is mostly tropical desert, which means there is a lot of strong sunlight. And modern Australians are mostly pale-skinned immigrants from cloudy England and Ireland. They had no need for dark skins in their murky homeland, but in the glare of Australia such light skins are a liability. The original inhabitants of Australia, the aborigines, had quite dark skins, and they needed no body covering at all. Actually light colored skins give people some advantage in cloudy northern regions, but for conditions in the world generally, the primary need is to protect the skin from the sun's rays, and dark skin does that best.

Q: *So you are saying because* Australopithecus *lived in the tropics, and because dark skin is normal for people generally, that it is safe to infer that he was dark skinned?*

A: Right, and most of mankind afterwards. But there is another bit of evidence to make our case stronger. Our closest relatives, the monkeys and apes, are all dark skinned. A few species have infants with light skins but these get darker when they grow up. And since we evolutionists believe that man and then monkeys and apes have a common ancestry a few million years back, we can safely infer that our distant ancestor, who was much closer to the ape in his genealogy, must have been dark also.

Q: *Hmmm, interesting. Inference based on comparison. And you say that much other knowledge about* Australopithecus *and paleontology generally is also based on inference?*

A: Yes. If we were to restrict our generalizations to what we know from direct evidence, we would have little information indeed. So we infer. And that leaves us with a dark-skinned ancestor. The same would be true of body hair, because all our closest relatives, the monkeys and apes, are hairy. The inference about their sex life is a little more complicated and there may be an element of homocentrism in it. That is, we are trying to explain how our primitive ancestor was like us in this respect, even though the apes generally were not.

Q: *I can see very clearly that from the fossil record it would be difficult, if not impossible, to say anything about the creature's sex life. That must be a pretty complicated explanation.*

A: Yes. And in fact it is quite recent. It tries to explain several things at once, but particularly why the human female is the only member of the Primate order (the monkeys, apes, and man) who is sexually receptive all the time. You see, the female monkeys and apes, and here we will talk about the chimpanzees, who are supposed to be our closest relatives, only come into heat a few days each month when they are not pregnant; and generally they do not have sex any other time; but the human female is sexually receptive all the time, even when pregnant. Why? The answer is to provide a reward for the male to cooperate with her in various ways, but particularly to help raise the children. In other words, it is an explanation for the origin of the human family.

Q: *What do you mean by cooperate? What did Squint do? It seems to me that Digger was doing everything to take care of the child.*

A: I never said that *Australopithecus* had a modern, American-type family where the father was expected to do anything the mother did, except give birth and nurse the baby. But when you compare this little group with that of the chimpanzees, the contrast is evident. For that matter, even the existence of the father-mother-baby group, what we social scientists call the nuclear family, doesn't occur among the chimpanzees. They have what is called a multi-male band, in which males join females only temporarily, when they are in heat. Squint and Gimp, however, even kept pieces of meat for their women, carrying them all the way back from the hunt to give to them. And the women gave their men some of the roots and nuts they had gathered. This is sometimes called the campground theory. You may remember that Squint and Gimp came back to the campground by the water hole, where the women and children were, instead of eating their rotten pieces of meat and then bedding down for the night somewhere else.

Q: *Yes, I remember that. But I had thought it was normal with the chimpanzees also.*

A: No, what we have seen among the chimpanzees is that each individual eats whatever he or she finds or catches, the males more often eating meat, and the females whatever roots, berries, nuts, etc. they find. In fact, the chimpanzees don't even give anything to their young. The young ones have to watch their mothers to learn how to find their own food. But hand-outs just do not occur.

Q: *But the mothers must love their young since they nurse them.*

A: Sure, but they simply aren't programmed genetically to share food. The theory is that food sharing came later, when humankind took over. Anyway, we must go on to discuss some of the other things that you may have observed in the little drama on *Australopithecus*.

Q: *There were a lot of things that weren't totally clear. Should I start asking?*

A: Sure, why not? That's why this old professor has been provided.

Q: *Okay, let's start with language. It was said that Squint never knew his own name because the communication system was not complex enough to name things and people. But those little upright people did communicate, didn't they?*

A: Yes, they did so far as we know, though as you can easily guess, there is no direct evidence for this either.

Q: *I could see that a language with no writing system would leave practically no evidence in the archeological record. Is this another inference?*

A: Correct, just like so much else concerning those distant relatives. We are pretty sure they had what we call a sign system which is a much simpler communication system than language. They couldn't name things or people but they could make sounds which expressed a general idea, like the boy calling out "Ho-o-o" when he saw something approaching the camp. He did not have a word to say it was a man or woman, but he could say that something was coming that wasn't dangerous. The same was true of the contact call which enabled people to stay together, or the growl when they didn't want someone else taking their meat. This is the same kind of communication system the chimpanzees and other animals have. In fact, that is why we believe that the early bipeds had this kind of system, because all the apes and monkeys did. True language came much later. After all, there is no behavior which sets off *Homo* from other animals more than language. So, what next?

Q: *I was a little surprised that Squint and the others did not kill their own food, but instead fed off the left-overs of other animals. Was that typical?*

A: That is another idea that archeologists and paleontologists have come up with lately—the scavenging theory, that very early man really wasn't able to kill big animals easily, so he depended mostly on the kills of other predators. Thus the zebra, and later the remnants of the wildebeest that Squint came across.

Q: *Yes. I can see that in a way—how was that little three-and-a-half-foot punk going to run down a zebra and kill it with his bare hands the way a four-footed predator such as a lion or a wild dog would? But Squint was making stone tools. Couldn't he use some of them for hunting, like spear points?*

A: Maybe. But actually we think these came later. The first stone tools, like the one Squint made, were for cutting up meat. And here for the first time we have some direct evidence—the earliest stone tools which were those found by members of the Leaky family in East Africa.

Q: *What about the other primates, the chimpanzees, for instance. I take it they did not hunt?*

A: Almost all the monkeys and apes ate meat when they could get it. So in that sense we got our taste for meat from our primate ancestry. The baboons and chimpanzees in particular hunted other animals even though the majority of their food was from vegetal products. But they never hunted any big ones. Their favorite prey was babies, usually antelopes and other monkeys. But they weren't capable of killing a zebra or wildebeest.

Q: *What about the big apes, like the gorilla? Couldn't they kill a large animal?*

A: I suppose they could, if they could catch it. But frankly the gorilla, and the big Southeast Asian ape, the orangutan, were quite slow. They had grown so massive that they didn't need to be fast to escape from predators, but as a consequence they couldn't catch other animals either. The gorilla, for instance, has never been seen to hunt any other animals. The King Kong reputation of the gorilla is a consequence of the perception of the animal by early European explorers, and it wasn't correct. But to get back to *Australopithecus*, the dinky biped. He is not thought to have been capable of killing anything large and in good physical condition, but like quite a few other animals, he mainly fed off the kills of the big four-footed predators.

Q: *One other thing about his eating habits bothered me: eating partially decomposed, uncooked meat. Wasn't that bad for his health?*

A: Not really. He couldn't eat cooked meat, because so far as we know, *Australopithecus* did not control fire. But the process of decomposition makes meat more tender. In a way it serves the same purpose as cooking. All the big meat eating animals eat decomposed meat. In fact, they may prefer it. I remember a hunter in Laos who would shoot a young buffalo as bait and then wait several days until a tiger would come to feed on the rotten meat. In fact, even civilized people eat decomposed meat. It is called aged beef and is left in a room just above freezing for several days or weeks to let the bacteria and fungus grow on it. It was the highest priced meat sold from the slaughter house where I worked when I was young, sold to the highest priced restaurants. In recent times we have become so obsessed with sanitary procedures that we have forgotten a lot of worthwhile natural processes.

Q: *It doesn't sound very good to me but what you say makes sense. But to go on, I was interested in seeing that the hunters worked in a group as later on we see that the women did also. It seems they were very social animals.*

A: Yes, that's true. But humans were not exceptional in that respect. Many, perhaps most, varieties of animals are naturally social. Staying together has many benefits and all the monkeys and apes do it, with only one exception, the orangutan, so it should be expected that the first bipeds would also. As a matter of fact, the hunting group described in the drama was modelled after a combination of the hunting groups of chimpanzees and those of some surviving hunting peoples as observed by anthropologists. Both hunted in groups, the chimps fanning out to search for colobus monkeys or antelope in a small area, and hunting parties of such groups as the !Kung of Southwest Africa would range farther, sometimes staying out for several days. In both cases they would cooperate in running the prey down and also in sharing meat. In fact, this is one of the only times when chimpanzees were observed to share something with others. So it seems that the human custom of sharing things is linked to the custom of eating meat. Vegetal products gathered by chimpanzees and other monkeys were not often shared.

Q: *I did notice that sharing did not mean equal treatment, however. Squint and the others clearly had different status from one another. Isn't that true?*

A: Yes, the idea of equal rights in a social group is only an ideal, never a reality, whether human or non-human. As you may know, all human societies that have loudly proclaimed equal rights were operating on a basis of unequal rights, the ancient Greeks and modern Americans being outstanding examples. In both cases the concept of equality referred to those in power. And I am afraid that, too, is a product of our primate inheritance. All the monkeys and apes have systems of dominance, usually depending on physical strength or ability to establish alliances. Mankind, undoubtedly including *Australopithecus*, has done the same, and even used the same methods of enforcement: physical strength (in modern states wielded by police) and social manipulation (establishing alliances). We must assume the early hominids had systems of dominance also. You got meat according to your dominance position, or your sex. And that hasn't changed much, either. Females still trade sex for gifts.

Q: *The ape-men ate insects all the time it seems.*

A: Sure. Insects are known to be nutritious. All the other primates ate bugs when they found them. Ms. Goodall, the chimpanzee lady, made a great to-do about the way her chimps "fished" for termites. But all the other primates did this also. Insects are plentiful and easy to catch. Many modern cultures teach their people to eat insects. As a matter of fact, if history had taken a different direction, we might have become insect eaters ourselves, instead of eaters of beef, pork, and chicken. After all, the insect is farther down the food chain and a better converter of vegetal products than cattle or pigs. Besides, they have a higher reproductive capacity and a shorter life span. So if mankind had domesticated grasshoppers and crickets instead of cattle and pigs, we would have more protein on the table at less cost and in shorter time. I always thought it would make a good subject for a science fiction story.

Q: *In the physical description of* Australopithecus, *two things impressed me: his smallness and his clever hands. Could you comment on these?*

A: There is nothing special about his size. The earliest bipeds were smaller than later hominids, that's all. They were about mid-size for a primate, much smaller than a modern gorilla, quite a bit larger than a rhesus monkey, and not too different in size from their closest relative, the chimpanzee. Through evolutionary history *Homo* got larger, though overall this was not any special evolutionary advantage. As you may know, northern Europeans were fairly large but in the long run no more effective in cultural competition than smaller Asians.

The hands are another matter, however. As you may remember, these small people were described as having opposable thumbs. This permitted them to use tools effectively. That was how Squint could make the cutting tool and the women their leaf baskets and digging sticks. Through time these got better and new artifacts were added. And it was all due to that "clever" hand. As you may remember, I said the chimpanzees gathered termites with a simple tool. Chimps also used rocks to crack nuts and also probably some other kinds of tools. Their main problem was that their hands were not free from locomotion. They were semi-erect quadrupeds, and had to support their bodies with all four limbs. But even some other animals used simple tools. However, only *Homo* with free hands and opposable thumbs, went wild in making tools, undoubtedly the base for his culture. Physical anthropologists have theorized that the ability to make tools was the primary stimulus for brain growth. Although *Australopithecus* stood upright, his brain was not much larger than that of the chimpanzee. We believe that the upright posture which freed the hands for tool invention and use stimulated the brain so that in four million years the descendants of *Australopithecus* developed brains three times larger and a lot more complex. So it was uprightness, then handedness, then braininess.

Q: *It seems that the bipeds did not recognize their relationship to the chimpanzees. Otherwise, they would hardly have tried to catch a young one. I assume they intended to eat it.*

A: I am sure they did. After all, the village people of all the monkey and ape areas of the world, except India, have killed off their local primates, usually to eat them. And certainly the chimpanzee populations have been severely depleted by African villagers. I did a field study in Nigeria years ago in what had been prime chimpanzee country. By 1970 there were no wild chimpanzees except in some distant, small national parks. I never saw one. Anyway, since the surviving chimpanzees will hunt any other kind of monkey for food and would probably have tried to get little *Homo* types also, there is no reason to believe that *Homo* wouldn't do the same.

Q: *Anyway, the male chimpanzees defended the female and the young one. Would* Homo *have tried to do the same?*

A: Probably. As you saw later, the newly formed human group, the nuclear family, was already cooperating more than the chimps did.

Q: *The thoughts of Squint about his woman as contrasted to the chimpanzee were quite interesting. That was real thought, wasn't it?*

A: Well, yes, and though it is literary license to imagine what kind of mental process our hero was going through, there is no reason to believe he was incapable of thinking. And comparison is one of the simplest methods of description we know of. And what he was thinking about is important. That is based on another theory worked out by archeologists: the carrying hypothesis.

Q: *Yes?*

A: Well, as I explained earlier, the tool hypothesis is one used to explain how mankind started using his noggin and thus evolved the largest brain in the kingdom and the system of survival we call culture. In a sense you can think of this as the macho explanation of history, since the tool maker throughout has overwhelmingly been the male. Another explanation of humankind's erectness could be considered the feminist version, the carrying hypothesis. That is, erectness, however it happened, freed the hands not just to make tools, but to carry things. And what was the most precious burden throughout the history of mankind? The Kiddo, what else? Actually, in the end excessive numbers of children became a liability, but not in Squint's day.

You know by now that the chimpanzee infant, and all the other monkeys and apes, had to hang on to mama to survive. Oh, she used one arm from time to time to support the little one, but she couldn't use two arms for carrying him if she was moving. All the other primates walk on all fours, some like the apes are semi-erect, but still they have to support themselves, and if they are moving fast, that means all four. So the infant has to hang on with his own grasp. So with *Australopithecus* we get a type that has both hands free to hold the young, even when moving fast.

Q: *And would that affect the development of the brain?*

A: Well, you can't say that exactly, but it did do a couple of things that might have contributed. First, it made it easier to keep junior around longer. The infant could have more time to learn and after a while this had to be important. Much later, language emerged and that certainly depended on the infant being in close contact with a speaker. Who better than a carrying mother? And of course carrying things became important for the general build-up of a culture's technology. Foodstuff, building materials, weaponry, and fire all had to be carried from place to place. And the chief carrier throughout most of human history has been the female. So there you have the carrying hypothesis in a nutshell. If I didn't tell you before, I will now, that anthropology is continually interested in behaviors which seem to be of little consequence but make the difference between being human and not.

Q: *Thanks, it's interesting. And to go on, I have a little question that still intrigues me. In the drama they worry about sleeping out at night because of predators and bodiless heads. Were there really such things—bodiless heads, I mean?*

A: In the first place, most of the primates are active in the day, diurnal we say. They really have to be concerned with their safety at night. And it should come as no surprise that *Homo* is also diurnal. You may think that you are a night owl because you stay up late at night cracking the books, but in actuality that is only because your technology creates daytime conditions. Nowadays it is done with electricity, but even with nothing more than a fire, village people could transform the night to a limited extent. But before the beginning of electric light, humans went to bed when it got dark. And before men had fire, they must have acted like the other daytime animals, going to places of safety when it got dark—thus the tree-nests.

And about the bodiless heads, no, I don't think there were any. But many cultures have dreamed up fearsome creatures to inhabit the night, from bodiless heads to vampires. One cannot know if the southern ape man (*Australopithecus*) had enough imagination to dream up such a nightmare, but who is to say he didn't? Somewhere along the stream of evolution, humans dreamed up all kinds of weird creatures.

Q: *The campground seemed like a pretty simple place—paths, a few huts. Hardly even any garbage. Is that all they had?*

A: I'm afraid so. But let's face it, they lived a pretty simple life. I mean, this was the beginning of culture, the human way. The Africaners were living pretty much like their closest relatives except they were starting a simple technology and as we will see shortly, they were modifying their social pattern. And even the campground was a new idea. The chimpanzees and the other apes had sleeping areas where they would go when day was ending, but the permanency was more limited. It is believed to be quite significant that at least two of the Australopithecine hunters came back to share their rotten meat. And the reason there wasn't any garbage is that they didn't produce much.

Q: *What about the others, why didn't they participate? When they got back, they just seemed to drift off. There were no females to join them, right?*

A: It was a time of transition. Some females were becoming sexually receptive all the time, while the majority were still like the chimps, receptive only a few days per month. And the majority of males were still like male chimps, that is, they were relatively promiscuous with females. As you may have noticed, Squint was showing some jealousy. This seems to become more important as pair bonding becomes the norm. If everybody, male and female, gets some, as is typical of chimps, why get jealous? Of course there wasn't absolute freedom in sex, as you may have noticed in the group by the water hole. Generally speaking, dominant males saw to it that they mated with females in heat though before and after, others also got to mate. One of the surprising things about chimps is that even the juveniles got their turn. At least they learned that way. But Squint and Gimp were the wave of the future, and they even got to sleep with their mates at night. The happy family.

Q: *And what Squint did the next day was how they got started making tools, right?*

A: Yes, as best we can make out. Squint went to what archeologists call a quarry, a place where plenty of suitable rocks were available. The earliest tools were made from hard stone that would chip or flake when struck with another stone. Early man could get a good cutting edge this way, and later on, points to make weapons. That is what Squint was doing.

Q: *But he was having quite a bit of difficulty, wasn't he?*

A: Yes, but that was one of the first inventions. And nobody ever said inventions were easy. The inventor has to visualize something, then try to create it. Moreover, trial and error are built in. Flint, chert, or quartzite, the kinds of stone Squint was using, are hard and flaking requires skill. Otherwise, the inventor ends up with shattered pieces rather than a neat tool with a good cutting edge. Flint knappers of more recent times have left piles of chip and flake debris at such quarry sites.

Q: *So that was the beginning?*

A: Yes. Not much different from the chimps, but at least three things set man apart: a new posture—uprightness—with sensitive hands; a new social pattern; and the beginning of tool making. Man was heading out on the way of culture. Now let us go several thousand miles away, into the north, and see how Squint's descendants made out.

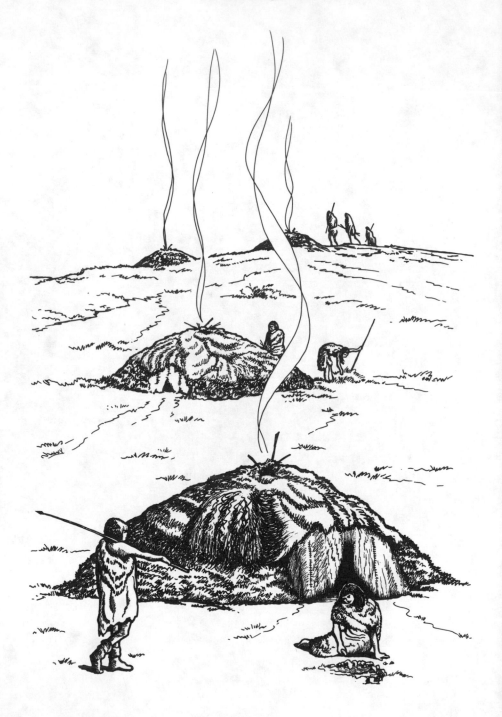

2

North by Northeast

Flower

The midwinter sun had just come up in Northeast Asia, not too far from where the city of Beijing would be located some 800,000 years later. A dusting of snow whitened the landscape, and grazing animals were scattered across the plain.

The woman called Flower awakened shivering. Anxious to avoid facing the reality of the cold morning, she pulled the fur robe up under her chin, then pulled her legs up, trying to make herself more compact. Her movement disturbed the man sharing her sleep robe, and he pulled on it. She looked toward the fireplace and could see no red embers. Sliding out from under the sleep robe, she stood up, pulling her body robe as tightly around her as she could and hunching her way around the other bodies until she could peek through the entrance. She pulled on her moccasins which were stuffed with dry grass. Her warm breath condensed into a little cloud.

(The personal names in the dramatization of Peking Man are derived from physical characteristics or special events. We do not know that these people named individuals, but since it is necessary to identify individuals in a drama, and presuming that they had a pre-language capable of naming things, we followed the practice of tribal people worldwide and gave individuals names of personal characteristics or natural events or things.)

Her dark brown face was peering out of a skin-covered hut just tall enough for a person to stand up in the middle. It was what in later ages would be called a bee-hive shape and a little like what the Central Asians called a yurt, a portable curved house, carried on the backs of women or animals from one campground to the next, in the never-ending effort to keep up with the herds of game. There were seven of these structures in sight.

Sometimes they stayed in caves which were usually much larger, often big enough for several families, but which had different kinds of problems. Caves were usually very drafty, and hard to warm. They were also frequently wet or at least damp, so the people would get coughs and colds. Also, they usually had to drive out other animals before they could move in. The worst were the bear people who could defend their territory against the upright people with little trouble, unless they were greatly outnumbered. The men could attack them in groups, using spears with fire hardened tips or, better yet, fire-wands.

Flower suddenly remembered what she was supposed to do, and quickly stepped outside and grabbed an armful of sticks from the pile she and her daughter had built up the day before. She knocked off the snow that had fallen during the night and hurried back inside, pulling the flap closed once she was inside. It was dark, though there was a smoke hole in the middle of the roof. She squatted next to the ashes and scraped with a stick to find embers still warm with fire. Finally she found one. She could have got an ember from one of the other huts, though it was early and most of the people would still be sleeping. She pulled a handful of thin dried grass stems from the place where she had put them between the skin cover and frame of the hut. She had particularly gathered them to restart fires. Pushing the coal onto the middle of the tinder grass, she put her mouth close and blew as hard as she could. It took a lot of blowing, but when she could see a tendril of smoke, she turned the coal around and around to favor the tiny flame. When the flame became clearly visible, she put the burning ball to the ground and methodically began adding sticks. The fire grew. Flower relaxed, rubbing her smarting eyes. She hunkered down and rubbed her hands together in front of the fire.

Flower shook Nosey's shoulder until the child awoke. Nosey groaned and rubbed her eyes. Flower used the sound for fire and pointed. Nosey scrunched out from under her sleep robe and came over to squat down, immediately beginning to feed sticks to the fire, sticks she had helped gather.

Flower went outside and surveyed the camp and surroundings. Smoke was coming out of one of the other huts and she could hear bodies stirring and voices groaning or making meaning sounds. The people did not have a true language but they did have a system of two to three hundred meaning sounds which they used to refer to one another, to things in the environment, or to states of being or becoming, like "sleep," "eat," "go," "stay." They always used these meaning sounds alone, never combining them to make more complex meanings. Still they could get across quite a few ideas.

Flower, standing erect in front of her hut, was a little over five feet tall, though already a little hunched from the burdens she had carried from camp to camp and around each campground. Her robe was wrapped as tightly as she could get it around her body, hiding most of it. On her uncovered head, long strings of brown hair fell to below her shoulders. She would cut it when it got longer than that, using one of the chipped stone knives, as was the custom of her people.

Flower's head was about two-thirds the size of the head of modern man, almost twice that of *Australopithecus*. Of course, since Flower was considerably bigger than Squint, her head would naturally be bigger; but it was larger even in proportion to her body. She had little in the way of a chin or forehead, both slanting noticeably. Her face looked like she was in her late thirties or early forties, although that was hard to know for sure, since it was so deeply weathered. There was practically no hair on her face, however.

Flower walked out of the camp to the stream bed in back where she was sure to find running water, even if under a skim of ice. She squatted on a flat rock and broke the ice with another rock she had picked up. Plunging her hands into the clear running water, she scooped it up over her face, trying to keep from getting it on her robe. A couple of splashes was enough to get her eyes wide open but hardly enough to get much dirt off. The people didn't clean themselves thoroughly in winter. It was too cold. In the short summer, they didn't mind the water, some of them immersing themselves completely in the sun-warmed pools. But they would even go without their robes in warm periods, wearing only a skin loincloth.

After a brief cleaning, Flower cupped her hands and scooped up water to drink. The cold water hurt her teeth.

She heard footsteps and looked around. Green Eyes was coming, also wrapped tightly in her robe. She had a limp which was a result of damage to her left foot when she had fallen from a tree as a child. Apart from that, she looked much like Flower except her eyes were green.

Green Eyes squatted next to Flower and said the word for "water," whereupon she began to scoop it up. She did not bother to splash any on her face, which was not unusual. In the winter some of the people did, others didn't. Flower stood up, ready to return. Before she could leave, Green Eyes spoke again, this time using the word for meat. Flower thought she noticed the rising inflection of a question, but couldn't be sure because some people used it, other did not. Green Eyes repeated the word and pointed back toward camp, then opened her mouth and pointed her bunched fingers. Flower gazed at her and then waving her arm in an arc toward camp, said, "Come."

Flower thought she knew what was on Green Eyes' mind. The other woman had to have seen her hanging the strips of meat on the limb next to her hut. And though it was Big Mouth who had been the first to come back for the women, the hunting party had been made up of five men, including Pass Wind, Green Eyes' man. Big Mouth had been excited, and it seemed a little angry, when they were walking back to the overhang. The group had come to this campground especially because of that overhang. They had used it before to drive grazing animals, using flapping hides and burning embers to frighten them over the edge. When they fell, the animals almost always hurt themselves, usually breaking their legs. Then the men down below would finish them with either spears or chipped stone knives. The campground was just over the hill from the overhang and it was no problem to send someone to get some of the women to help cut up the meat.

Big Mouth was probably the best hunter in the group and Flower knew that he would be the one to organize the hunt. If someone stepped out of line, for instance frightening the animals the wrong way, it would be Big Mouth's responsibility to control him. It wasn't that Big Mouth was in charge, simply that he was the best hunter and the others knew that. And Flower knew that Pass Wind tended to go off on his own more than the others. He wasn't the best to have along on a group hunt.

As Flower followed Big Mouth back to the overhang, he kept picking up stones and sticks and throwing them down and muttering words like "call" and "come" and "go" and "animals" and "run" in an angry voice. It was impossible to figure out exactly what had happened and of course with the kind of communication system they had, it was impossible to explain exactly. She would have to figure it out when they got there.

Big Mouth

He felt uncomfortable walking ahead of the other men but no other would walk in front of him, even Pass Wind. Big Mouth had not wanted Pass Wind along because one person who didn't work for group needs was enough to spoil a hunt. And there weren't that many animals around, a herd of shaggy brown horses off in one direction and a scattering of antelope on the edge of the herd. Moreover, the animals were edgy. It was probably because of the wolves the people had seen when they had come.

Big Mouth was wrapped in the same kind of skin robe as Flower and the others. They all wore moccasins stuffed with grass to protect their feet from the cold. The people had learned long ago that a good way to lose toes or even feet was to walk around in the winter with poor foot coverings. Fingers, too, could be frozen and some bands used hand coverings. Others, including Big Mouth's band, just kept their hands tucked inside their robes to keep them from freezing.

The band had had little enough to eat. Game was not as plentiful as they had hoped and their luck at the hunt had not been good. Big Mouth had thought their luck would change when they had found the hairy mammoths at the edge of the marsh on their way to the campground. The animals had been far enough away that they wouldn't have seen the travellers and Big Mouth had immediately scrunched down and begun moving away at an angle, waving at Flower and the children to follow. The other family groups followed suit, even Pass Wind and his woman. Big Mouth and the others stood up as soon as they were out of sight. They stopped just below the stone outcrop. Big Mouth climbed to the top and peered over. The mammoths were feeding on branches of the trees at the edge of the marsh. He was sure there was a skim of ice on the bog but a mammoth's foot would certainly break through that. It might be thick enough to hold the weight of a man so it was a good place to get one of the animals stuck where it could be hamstrung and hacked to death.

The ridge went around in a curve, with the bog at the bottom where it had formed from the run-off. There were four men, Big

Mouth, Pass Wind, Shortie, and Talker. Big Mouth touched Talker and said, "Come."

Big Mouth had his stone ax in one hand, his spear in the other. Shortie had both also, but the other two only had spears. Big Mouth started out, Talker following. Big Mouth thought the other two would wait. Everyone had hunted enough to know that a group didn't drive animals until they were blocked in. And mammoths were risky anyway, as big as they were. Sometimes they would stand and fight. The most the men could count on was that one would panic and go into the bog where he would get stuck, rather than running along the edge of the marsh. Once the men got an animal in the muck, they could try to drive it in deeper, and when it was hopelessly trapped they could try to close in on it, always watching out for the others. With luck, the animals would move into the bog in fright or confusion.

Big Mouth and Talker moved cautiously even though they had the ridge between them and the animals. It was almost automatic with Big Mouth, which was why he invariably came home with the most game. He threw up a few dry grass stems to be sure the wind was not blowing from them to the mammoths. Now and then he looked back to see Shortie and Pass Wind crouched below their outcrop. He could see Pass Wind anxiously peer out several times. He shook his head but continued on.

When Big Mouth and his partner were about half way to the next outcrop, a place which was natural for a blocking attack, he heard the yelling, first from Pass Wind, then from Shortie. He looked back quickly and saw the two running down the hill, yelling and throwing rocks. He couldn't believe it at first because he and Talker were too far away to help. They couldn't possibly get to the bottom and on the edge of the bog before the mammoths would make a run for it. He looked down the hill at the animals. They had stopped feeding and had their trunks up, trying to get a scent of the attackers. Big Mouth knew their sight was poor. They trumpeted and started moving away from the bog and toward the place where Big Mouth and Talker would have tried to block them.

There wasn't anything else to do, so Big Mouth stood up and started running down hill also, even though he felt sure he could never get down fast enough. He was counting on the slim hope that in their panic and confusion, the animals would turn back. Then maybe one of them would go into the bog. But it didn't work that way. When they saw Pass Wind and Shortie running down and yelling, the mammoths

32

just continued in the same direction but faster. Although Big Mouth made all the noise and commotion he could in running toward the animals, it was no use. They lumbered by long before he could get ahead of them. Big Mouth slowed down and soon stopped, to be joined by Talker, who was also panting. Big Mouth poked the tip of his spear into a hole in the thin snow as if to assure himself that he could at least catch a small rodent. But his face was angry when he looked toward Pass Wind, who was by this time approaching with Shortie. Big Mouth muttered, "scream" and "run" several times. When Pass Wind reached them, he pointed toward the mammoth group, by then small dots in the distance, saying, "go." When no one responded, he pointed to himself and the others and said, "men."

Big Mouth said, "No," and stood up, preparing to go back to join the rest of the band, disgusted to have lost game even before setting up camp.

Now, days later, all this was going through Big Mouth's mind even as he trekked toward the overhang. Ever since the group had located themselves at the campground, he had been doing all he could to keep away from Pass Wind, but it didn't seem to help much. Pass Wind did not seem to realize how angry he had been about the mammoth affair, but what could be done? It was so difficult to say "no" outright and even the refusal to follow the mammoths further after their break-out had been hard to do. And now here he was in the front of another hunting party, and despite all he had done to discourage him, Pass Wind was along. The picture of Pass Wind screaming and running down the hill toward the mammoths kept repeating itself in Big Mouth's mind.

By this time the group was close enough to the overhang that they all started to crouch and moved cautiously from one hidden place to the next to keep from spooking the animals. There were eight men but as they got nearer to the overhang, two angled off to go to the bottom. They were the butchers for when the animals would fall off. Pass Wind started to go with them but Big Mouth motioned to him, saying, "Come."

Big Mouth did not have any real right to give directions, he wasn't truly in charge, but he just couldn't seem to help himself. His family and the rest were so hungry, even an antelope would make a difference. So insofar as he could, he would try to see that this wouldn't be a fiasco.

Pass Wind looked at Big Mouth in puzzlement but did stay back. He would not go with the butchers. Big Mouth pointed forward where the rest of the men were going, and said, "Go."

Pass Wind followed the others and ultimately found himself at the end of the line, the other three opposite, the two lines making a V, the point at the drop-off. Big Mouth was at the point of the V, the last position before the drop-off. They waited. Then they heard yelling, and looking back, they saw the first of the horses moving toward them, back and forth nervously, seeming to sense the entrapment. The men on the sides of the V were flapping skins to keep the animals moving and to prevent their dashing to one side. The numbers were few enough that a big bunch would not form to the rear to push the forward animals over. It was even possible that some animals could turn and dash back through the herd after seeing the drop-off. But they kept coming as the drivers kept up their din. Big Mouth could not see Pass Wind but he assumed that however independent he usually was, this time the man was doing his job. Six drivers were not all that many if one weren't doing his job. The animals did come though, and faster when they saw the second and third man on each side. Then they were grouped and coming in close and Big Mouth could do nothing but yell and flap. One horse even veered close enough that Big Mouth jabbed it with his spear point. Then the forward animals saw the drop-off and there was pandemonium. They dug in their hooves, and eyes bulging, tried to turn around. Most could still manage it, though several got close enough that they lost their footing on the down side. Big Mouth jumped up on his side while Cutter, his counterpart, did the same, both yelling and wielding their spears. A horse was struggling on the edge and Big Mouth ran straight at it, ramming his spear into it as hard as he could. It screamed and lunged away from the pain, losing its footing completely, falling with loose rocks over the edge. Big Mouth quickly glanced over and saw one of the butchers running toward where it would fall, his stone ax upraised. Almost at the same time Big Mouth saw two scrambling antelopes slip over the edge. Then there was too much space for maneuvering, and no matter how much yelling and flapping Big Mouth and the others did, the remaining animals turned and raced away from the edge in a cloud of dust.

The V-men quickly went around to the side where it was possible to scramble down. Big Mouth saw that one butcher had already killed the horse. Also one of the antelope was down and still, blood running from its throat. The other antelope had a broken leg but was trying to run on three. Big Mouth ran over and bashed it with his stone ax.

The butchers quickly got busy skinning the animals and cutting them into pieces. Pass Wind came up and squatted down by the carcass of the horse as if to begin helping to cut it up. Big Mouth squatted next to him and pushed him back, not enough to make him lose his balance but a little rough nevertheless. Big Mouth pointed to Pass Wind and himself and repeated several times the words, "camp" and "women."

Pass Wind frowned but did not begin butchering. And when Big Mouth got up, he did also. Big Mouth immediately started back but Pass Wind did not follow. Instead he moved to the top of the outcrop to watch.

At the campground Big Mouth got three women, wives of the hunters, plus Flower, saying repeatedly, "meat," "come," "cut."

In the distance he saw Green Eyes and he could have steered the group in her direction but did not. He knew everyone would get some meat but taking her along for the butchering would only make it seem that Pass Wind had been a part of the killing group. and Big Mouth had his doubts. He had the feeling that Pass Wind had done little to drive the animals. He had never been much good in group hunts.

Flower

Flower and the other women had finished skinning and cutting up the carcasses, using the skins to wrap and carry the pieces of meat. The men had cut poles from which to hang the skin and meat bundles and helped carry them back to camp. Pass Wind had disappeared when Big Mouth came back with the women and did not come into camp until late that evening. By that time everyone had received some of the meat and the rest had been cut into strips and hung on nearby branches for quick freeze-drying. Green Eyes had been given a piece too. It was a small piece, and not much for two adults and a child, Flower knew, but since Pass Wind hadn't even been there when the women had been brought back to finish the butchering, she thought that something had gone wrong. She knew he had gone with the others but she also knew that Big Mouth had been angry with him since the failure to entrap the mammoths.

But Green Eyes was now asking for more meat. Flower knew it was not good to be selfish in a small band, but the best hunter and his family had some rights. Flower decided to give Green Eyes some bones of the horse that had some flesh still on them. She could roast them and let Pass Wind and the girl gnaw on them. Afterwards she could split the bones so they could suck out the marrow. So she took Green eyes back to the tree where the bones had been wrapped in an antelope skin and placed in a fork where the wolves couldn't reach them. Green Eyes stared at the meat strips but said nothing. She took the bones and headed toward her hut.

Flower carried some of the meat and the frozen skin into her hut to heat so the meat could be eaten and the skin softened for tanning later. The sun was bright in a clear sky and it would be warm enough later for her to stretch the skin on a framework she would make. She could scrape the skin then rub in the brains she had saved. She was pleased to find that Nosey had a good fire going, and was now squatting next to it, feeding it sticks. Flower hung the strips of meat on the crosspiece over the fire where they quickly began to sizzle.

Big Mouth and Jumper, the boy, had moved their sleeping places closer to the new fire, their heads still covered by their robes. It wasn't long, though before Jumper stirred, soon followed by Big Mouth. Then Jumper poked his head from under his robe and rubbed his eyes as he stared at the fire. He shifted his eyes toward the sizzling meat and got up. He was wearing his regular robe. Reaching down, he put on his moccasins. He looked to be about eight or ten years old, although it was hard for an outsider to be sure. He squatted in front of the fire and first warmed his hands, then took a piece of meat off the stick and began to chew. Big Mouth went out to wash his face and get a drink of water before he began eating. The hut filled with eating and pleasure sounds, smacking of lips, sucking, grunting, and belching. Once when Jumper reached for a piece that Big Mouth was going to take, the father emitted a growling sound and Jumper pulled his hand back.

Flower poured a little pile of nuts on the ground from the ones she had got the day before from a squirrel's cache. There was little enough for the women to get during the winter, which was why meat was so important. Among the main items they could find during this time were seeds and nuts stored by small animals. Flower and Nosey had been lucky enough to find three nests with nuts and seeds which they put into their skin bags to carry back. In between chewing pieces of meat, everyone munched on nuts. Big Mouth suddenly exclaimed, "Aah!" and spit in his hand. A piece of tooth came out, followed by a small pebble. He reached into his mouth to finger the spot where it had broken off but then went on, chewing on the other side.

One after another, the group made its way outside as the day became warmer. The hut was built just south of a stone outcrop which kept the cold wind off. As the sun climbed higher, its rays began to warm the rocks. The group had picked this spot knowing they would be here a few days, and this would be one of the warmest places in the area. Big Mouth found himself a protected corner among some rocks and squatted to finger his broken tooth. Jumper squatted nearby, pulling his robe tight because it was still cold, no matter the protection. But soon it became warmer and where the heat reflected off the rocks, the snow even disappeared. Big Mouth sat until the ache went out of his bones. Like most of the people in their thirties and older, he had pain on cold mornings. He got up for his bundle of chipped stone, bringing it into the sunlight where he began to retouch some flake tools.

Flower used skin thongs to tie together a frame of sticks she had put behind the hut the day before. Afterwards she unwrapped the skin and stretched it on the framework, scraping off the pieces of fat and thinning it. Then she rubbed the brains into the stretched skin. Carrying her processed skins to a place in the shelter of the rock, she sat down and began methodically chewing a piece of antelope skin. When it had become soft, she put it on a flat rock and cut pieces that could be fitted together to make a moccasin. Using a thorn tool she punched holes into the edges and ran skin cord through them, pulling pieces together. She had learned this painstaking work from her mother, and she would start teaching Nosey soon. At the moment Nosey was off playing with a couple of other girls.

It was almost midday when Flower finished fitting and doing the final sewing of the moccasins for Jumper. Satisfied with her morning's work, she let her mind wander. She thought of the cave and the people meat, especially the brains. It was a long trek and they would surely be hungry when they arrived at the cave, but it would be worth it. After all, they didn't often get people meat. They could leave the boy and girl in camp with her father, who was in another hut, along with his other woman. Flower's real mother had died when she was having another baby, so Flower couldn't remember her well. But her father was still fairly active and even had most of his teeth.

Flower went over and touched Big Mouth on the shoulder. He was dozing but awoke quickly. She pointed in the direction of the cave, saying, "Go, meat." He stood up, his stone ax in hand, and understood. He looked around. "Boy, girl, father," she said, and fell into position behind him as they started off.

There was evidence of much animal activity in the front of the cave, particularly hyena tracks. They went in carefully. Any kind of predators could be waiting inside, but they feared bears the most. Some leg and arm bones were on the ground. She picked one up. It was well chewed on the ends and already fairly dry. She dropped it. As they went further in, the air became warmer and damper. They went around a corner beyond which was a larger ante-room. She heard running feet, the creatures were coming straight toward her and Big Mouth. He raised his spear and two foxes came racing by, keeping to one side as they passed. Big Mouth laughed. It could have been something much bigger and more dangerous. There was little left when they got to the ledge.

Big Mouth

The day they had killed the other men, they had been out all day and had seen nothing but a few animals at a great distance when Cutter pointed to a plume of smoke in the distance. From then on everyone was cautious. They had seen signs of other people ever since they had got to the new campground, but this was the first clear indication. There were six men in their group. When they had got close enough, they could see three of the other people, one of them small. It was probably two men and a boy. When they got closer they could see that the men wore skin caps. Still they were certainly a kind of people. There were always bands in the countryside and usually one kept away from them because one could never be sure what they would do. But two men and a boy could not easily protect themselves from a group of six. Besides, the men of Cutter's group were hungry and cold, and the fire looked attractive. Someone must have carried a burning ember to make the fire. The main band couldn't be too far away, and that was why there had been such a scarcity of animals.

After watching long enough to assure themselves there was no one else around, the group had spread out in a fan. Pass Wind was not along so the men attacked silently in a line. The group around the fire jumped up but when they saw that they were outnumbered by strangers, they ran. Big Mouth caught the boy first, then Cutter speared one of the men while Jumper bashed the other with his ax.

They butchered the boy first, knowing he would be the most tender, and hung pieces of meat over the fire. They particularly relished the organs. The meat was similar to that of a young pig. Afterwards they cut up most of the other two men and used their robes for wrapping the chunks of meat and bone. They took off the heads last, then dragged the remains of the carcasses further into the cave and put them on the ledges. Big Mouth pushed the heads into a crevice and wedged them in with a fair-sized rock. Then they took the cut up pieces back to the campground where most of the people got some.

And now Big Mouth was back with Flower. Even before they got to the ledge, he knew that something had gotten to the carcasses. There were too many chewed bones lying around. Nothing was left on the ledge. Whatever had dragged them down, the wolves and hyenas had done the rest, tearing apart and cracking everything. They really should have come back the next day, though it had been so cold they thought the meat would last and Big Mouth had thought the ledges were high enough. He was wrong. He went straight to the crevice. The rock was still in place though there were claw marks on it where something had tried to pry it loose. The heads were still there!

Big Mouth took the head of one of the men and the boy by the hair and Flower took the head of the other man. Big Mouth had put the heads deep enough into the cave that they weren't frozen. He did not bother with the skin or any other part but went directly to where he knew the best meat was, the inside. Putting the skull upside down, he took his stone ax and methodically began to crack the bone around the hole in the base. He found a stick and jammed it inside to pry the grey matter loose. It dropped on the rock over which he was working. Both he and Flower began to eat. Brain, particularly after a few days, was tender and did not need cooking or any other processing to make it edible.

~

Q: *That last sequence must surely have been speculation, wasn't it? I mean what normal person would eat someone else's brains? Of course there are some deviants who would, but I hope the people in these accounts were normal for their time. So the real question is why put it in if it really didn't happen?*

A: There could be a reason. Anthropology has long been known to have considerable shock effect. After all, it is a subject which begins by putting aside the values of any particular culture, and especially those of the dominants. And it is thought that shock can induce learning.

Q: *Well, we've all heard about culture shock, but usually it is described as something that happens when someone is subjected to the customs of others, like when traveling in a foreign land. But generally it is described as making one uncomfortable, not helping the person learn something.*

A: It is true that culture shock does usually make one uncomfortable but that in a way may help teach—at least what anthropology tries to teach, that there is no absolute right and wrong, no universal values or proper way to do things. I take it what bothered you was the cannibalism, right?

Q: *Yes, and you have still not answered my question—why describe the cannibalism if it was only speculation? After all, how could anyone know that this kind of ancient man would eat someone from his own species? The account did imply that men of the central band were the same as the men they attacked and killed, didn't it?*

A: Yes, it did. But unfortunately, it isn't speculation, at least not very much, nothing like the speculation required for all kinds of other explanations. Like the kind of language those people spoke. We have no direct evidence for that. Or even something so material as skin clothing or shelter. The only reason we think those people had those things is that we can't imagine them surviving without them in that climate. But the belief that they were cannibals was based on some real evidence. As you must know, the theories about ancient men are based primarily on fossil bones. I already mentioned the *Australopithecus* skeleton called Lucy. There were quite a number more, primarily skulls and other material found in a cave near Beijing (Peking). In fact, when I was a student, they called him Pekinensis. It has only been in the last fifteen to twenty years that they put him into the new fraternity *Homo erectus*. A large number of skulls found in that cave had holes in the *foramen magnum*, the bottom of the skull, broken wider all around to make it larger and presumably to get the brains out.

Q: *But I thought the account implied that other animals were feeding off the bodies. Some of them could have chewed the holes open couldn't they?*

A: Sure, except that teeth make one kind of mark and tools make another. The holes in these skulls looked like they had been broken open with a stone implement. That sounds like man, doesn't it?

Q: *I guess so, but it also sounds terrible. And not that it makes that much difference now, but how do they know the men of Big Mouth's band killed the strangers? And how do they know they ate other parts of the people they killed?*

40

A: Well, actually they don't. There aren't any other bones that have been cracked like the skulls. We just assume they ate the other parts. Also we have no direct evidence that they killed the strangers. But it seems unlikely that they just happened across the carcasses of men killed by other animals and then ate their brains.

But we don't have to strain our imaginations to believe that *erectus* or some other kind of ancient man practiced cannibalism. And I am not here talking about some weirdo who captures victims in a modern city and in secret ritually consumes some parts of them and who when caught is treated like a total deviant. I am talking about the socially approved practice of cannibalism. As you may know, when European man spread throughout the world, following the Discovery and Conquest, many societies approved of cannibalism. Probably the main areas where cannibalism as a culturally-approved act was found were the Americas, Africa, and New Guinea, what came to be called Papua and West Irian. Probably the champions in respect to the numbers of people eaten were the Aztecs though the name itself came from a people called the Caribs of the Caribbean Islands, named "canibalis" by Christopher himself. Socially-approved cannibalism offended the European sensibility and for the next five hundred years the pale skins worked against it and succeeded in eliminating it in one society after another, frequently wiping out the people or their cultures at the same time. This is not to say that cannibalism was a particularly barbaric practice, though the Euros thought it was. They of course were burning multitudes of people at the stake during the Inquisition, enslaving Africans on a mass scale and dumping them into the ocean when being attacked by anti-slavers, using child labor on a mass scale, forcing opium on a population of hundreds of millions, and finally developing wars of mass destruction in which millions were killed in order to maintain or inaugurate one or another dynasty or political system. And of course they developed some quite pernicious and indiscriminate weapons like poison gas, the high-altitude bomber, and the rocket. I am afraid that I and most other anthropologists would find that eating a few thousand, or even hundreds of thousands of people, like the Aztecs did, would hardly compare to the horrors of mass destruction such as those of the Civil War, the Hundred Years War, the Napoleonic Wars, or World War I or II. But of course people tend to rationalize the practices of their own culture while they criticize other people's practices. So when Euroman took control, he came down hard on cannibalism as well as many other practices which were different from his own, usually claiming they were uncivilized. This is called ethnocentrism, an attitude you will often hear about in anthropology.

Q: *So I take it you think it was normal for* Homo erectus *to kill and eat innocent people?*

A: No, I didn't say that. But I would consider it as "normal" as bombing innocent people, as airplane combatants almost invariably do. You might have noticed that the people that were killed were from another band. This was generally the case with cannibals. If one killed and ate people, it was usually people from other societies or groups, just as modern societies approve of killing people from other societies in warfare but forbid killing within their own borders. The Aztecs, those much-maligned cannibals of pre-Hispanic Mexico, conducted war on other tribes, largely to capture people to ritually sacrifice and eat. I do not remember having heard of them ever eating another Aztec.

But there was another kind of cannibalism which was ritualistic. That is, people ate others or parts of others, not as meat, but for ritual reasons. They ate human flesh in order to get power, usually the strength of the person they were eating. The headhunters of Borneo were examples. And with this kind of cannibalism, one might even eat parts of an insider, even a relative, probably someone who had died a "natural" death. Although the people of New Guinea were widely known as gustatory cannibals—people meat was called "long pig"—they also practiced ritual cannibalism. A notorious nerve disease called Kuru was ultimately traced by Western researchers to be the result of women and children eating parts of their dead ancestors at funeral ceremonies. Culturally approved cannibalism was practiced by quite a few peoples before Westerners came on the scene; so if *H. erectus* ate a few people, or just their brains, it's no big deal anthropologically speaking, is it?

There's another matter, however, which though not so important, I do know from previous classes does bother some students. That is eating brains. American culture is quite fond of meat eating for a settled society. *Erectus*, as members of hunting societies, had to depend heavily on meat in the winter. We, as members of a cultivation society, can get along very well with no meat at all. But we still eat a lot of meat because our ancestors came from cold northern Europe. However, we eat striated muscle meat, whether ground or sliced. Most of us don't like identifiable organ meat much. And that includes brains. Of course, we do eat this kind of meat also, but not in recognizable form. Most organ meat comes to us ground up and otherwise processed, in hot dogs, bologna, and as lunch meat slices. Before the age of advanced food processing, we ate brains and other organ meats in their natural form. My mother, who was of German ancestry, used to fix brains frequently, mixing it with scrambled eggs. Nowadays, in the age of hamburgers and steaks, a lot of us have never eaten brains and find the idea unpleasant.

But we should leave poor *erectus* in peace with his cracked skulls. The only reason Euros get so perturbed about it is because they do not have that practice and they have thus stopped many others from following it. And let's face it, though *erectus* may have been the ancestor of all modern humans, he certainly was no Euro.

Q: *What about the title of the little drama, why "North by Northeast"?*

A: *Australopithecus* began his upright way of life in Africa, near the equator. A lot of things that would be crucial in a colder climate were not necessary there; he did not have fire, he made no shelters and he wore no clothing.

Q: *That would be natural, wouldn't it, since he was presented pretty much as an ape who became upright. And that's where the apes are, and were, I presume?*

A: Right. All the other primates, the monkeys and apes, live in the tropics or sub-tropics. They don't need to have techniques to keep warm. The only exception in modern times is the Japanese snow monkey which did manage to adapt to a climate which, though not frigid, did get cold enough for snow. All the rest of the apes and monkeys live in warm or hot zones.

Q: *And then we see that after three million years, the descendant of* Australopithecus *is living in a cold place and he has fire and clothing and builds shelters.*

A: Correct. Some time in that long interval man escaped from the tropics. He went from Africa to Eurasia, North and Northeast. Of course many of his type stayed behind in Africa. And as we have seen, this migration required innovations for temperature control. Human technology, culture, was on a roll. Because of this, *H. erectus* and later *H. sapiens* had an immeasurably larger part of the world to exploit. As we know now, by the twentieth century all land areas of the world were being used by man.

Q: *When you look at a map and realize where the major populations live today, you could say that man became a temperate zone animal, no?*

A: Well, actually not. It is true that most great populations ended up in places that have winters: China, Russia, Western Europe, and America. Even so, these people, and all others, remained tropical animals biologically. They simply created tropical conditions in the envelope they put around their bodies. Even the Eskimo, who live in one of the coldest climates in the world, created a tropical envelope for themselves in their very efficient skin clothing, subterranean houses and little seal oil fires.

And all of this was started some time between Lucy and *H. erectus pekinensis*. If stepping on the moon was a great step for mankind, building a fire and sewing up a skin garment was just as great in the distance it took mankind.

Q: *Hmm. And I noticed that the woman's role in all this was very important.*

A: It certainly was. As you may know, historical explanations usually follow the trend of the times and until recently it has been fashionable to emphasize the role of man the hunter. After all, hunting is an exciting business and it's what men have done throughout history. Furthermore, the writers of history have primarily been men. So what would be more natural than that they would describe hunting exploits as the basis for later human achievements.

But times have changed. We are now in the age of feminism and it has become fashionable to emphasize the woman's role. And despite the fads in history, this is one trend that was long overdue. Woman has been very important, even apart from her vital role in bearing the young. Male history writers have certainly skewed history. As we have seen, even in the earliest stage of culture, the era of *Australopithecus*, the woman's role was very important because she was the gatherer of wild plant products. And from what we can interpolate from what happens with modern hunter-gatherers, the solid base for food supplies was the gathering activities of the woman. This wasn't so true of *erectus*, at least in the winter, because there just wasn't enough vegetal food to be gathered. But there we see the female stepping in to be the vital element for keeping people warm. We know from studies of the Eskimo, who were one of the few peoples who lived almost entirely on products of the chase, that the female's role in making a water-tight seam was vital. Without this, the Eskimo hunter could not function most of the time and everyone would starve. And of course the female through the nomadic phase of history was the shelter builder and fire keeper also. She served other very important human functions, probably being the primary language teacher to infants, which came to be vital for the continuance of the group. And through the whole nomadic period of man's history, nine-tenths of his existence, the female was the carrier of burdens. So apart from weaponry, the goods of the group carried from place to place went on the backs of the women. So modern ladies should be happy with this little historical correction.

Q: *If hunting was secondary in importance, why does it occur so often in the dramatizations?*

A: Well, part of it is probably still male bias. I am sure I have some yet, even though I have long given up hunting and even gave up eating meat. But then, too, hunting makes more exciting drama than picking nuts and berries. How could you get an exciting incident like that mammoth hunt or the drive over the overhang if all you did was dig out wild roots? But also people in cold areas are forced to depend more on flesh food than people where there is much plant growth, the warm zones. The heaviest meat eaters we knew of among tribal man was the Eskimo. And they relished plant food. But for most of the year it was unavailable except in the guts of the animals they killed, and they ate that with gusto. The *erectus* female probably did what she could to gather vegetal food but pickings were slim in the long cold winter. So they had to eat much meat.

Q: *I had another question about the woman's role. Though they had fire, they didn't seem to use it for cooking as much as for heating. Is that true?*

A: Sure. The idea that fire was primarily used for cooking seems very deeply entrenched. In fact, it reminds me of a bit of mythological history I heard from my mother, who knew very little real history but like most people, was always ready with an explanation. She told me seriously that the way fire was discovered to be useful was when a Chinese farmer had some pigs under his house, and the house caught fire and burned down and all the pigs were roasted. And when the farmer saw all the burnt pigs, he tasted some and discovered that roast pork was very good. And so from then on whenever he wanted that Chinese delicacy, he would pen some pigs under a house and set it afire. But as time went on, he began to use fire for other things.

Q: *Now, you must be making that up. You don't expect us to believe that do you?*

A: Well, maybe not, since we are all college people and that story was a part of my mother's folk knowledge. Though to the best of my recollection, she really told it to me as if she believed it. But in any event, meat and other food does not have to be cooked to be edible. All the monkeys and apes got by very well with uncooked food, including meat. Of course, you may say that cooking kills germs and parasites and thus makes meat safe, which is true nowadays. But that is primarily because we live in such dense populations where contamination is everywhere. In the sparsely-populated campgrounds of the hunter-gatherer, person to person disease was not such a problem. And so to come back to the Peking person, fire was not nearly so vital for cooking as for heating. The Eskimo, those very heavy meat eaters, delighted in eating raw meat, and so far as I know, did not suffer from this custom. In fact the name Eskimo, given to them by the neighboring Algonkians, means "eaters of raw meat."

Q: *It seems that by the time of Peking person, that man was clearly into family. Big Mouth seems to have lived happily with Flower, Nosey and Jumper. Modern American politicos would have claimed in approval that they had strong family values.*

A: We don't really know when the universal institution of marriage was invented, but we do know that all the peoples of the world, when encountered by Euroman, had some kind of semi-permanent liaison between man and woman, usually socially sanctioned. So some time between the ape stage of existence and 1492, marriage and the nuclear family (husband, wife, and children) came into existence among all peoples. After all, we are now dealing with the genus *Homo*, if not yet the species *sapiens*. But remember that this is another bit of speculation, which is the mainstay of archeology.

Q: *And so I guess you would say the same about the new kind of communication, that it too is based on speculation?*

A: Yes, I'm afraid so, though that's alright with me, too. I think most students of early man feel that true speech emerged in the time of Neanderthal, the next stage of human evolution, and probably because he had a brain at least as big as that of modern man. The dramatization of *H. erectus* shows an intermediate stage. It endows him with a communication system that has arbitrary meaning, though it is quite a bit simpler than a true language.

Q: *What do you mean by arbitrary meaning?*

A: Well, as you may remember, *Australopithecus* had a system of sounds but these were more like that of the apes than like true language of mankind; that is, the sounds denoted messages that were quite general and they were probably inscribed in the genetic code.

That little tropical person didn't have a system based on arbitrary names. You probably remember that though there was a sound for danger, there was no specific word for the exact cause of danger, words like lion or leopard. Nor could our first upright person indicate actions or states of being, things we later came to call verbs. In other words, he didn't have the capacity to bestow arbitrary meaning on things and actions. but *erectus* comes to life for us as being able to give arbitrary meaning to sounds. He can say words like "come" and "go" and "water" and "men," or their equivalent. No one knows whether *erectus* could actually do this, much less what the exact words were, so we just gave the English equivalents. We could have made up sound combinations but it would be kind of hokey and purely the product of imagination.

Q: *So he had a simple language then?*

A: A pre-language, but much more extensive already than what the apes and *Australopithecus* had. He had the capacity to name things, to give arbitrary meaning to sound units which represented events and things. In linguistic science these things would be called morphemes, or the smallest units of meaning, made up of phonemes, the smallest units of sound. These are the basic building blocks of all languages though there is one more characteristic necessary for a fully-developed language, something called syntax, which is the set of rules for putting morphemes and words in order. Then the system is capable of producing statements, the most basic of which is what grammarians call sentences. With those three ingredients, basic sound systems, arbitrary units of meaning, and syntax, man could go wild naming things and that is what he did. He invented language after language so that now there are several thousand. But most important, he could describe his universe. And whether it was Neanderthal some 200,000 years ago or *erectus* more than a million years ago, culture became a system of names and man became the talking biped.

Q: *The new human is described as having a dark skin though perhaps not as dark as* Australopithecus *and there's no mention of body hair. Could you comment on the appearance of Peking person?*

A: Of course you know by now that the softer parts of the body didn't remain in the fossil record. The only direct evidence we have are of skulls, teeth, and a few long bones. But we do know that body hair diminished through time and a good guess is that clothing had something to do with it. When our ancestors started wearing clothing, they didn't need body hair so much. It could have lessened through time by simple mutation. According to the rules of natural selection, body hair would then have given no advantage. You have heard of the blind fish who live in caves. Their ancestors had eyesight but after many generations in total darkness, they lost their ability to see. They also became light colored because they lost their need for protective coloration. Mutation, or random changes, brought it about. So too, an animal which has its body covered by something else has less need for body hair.

Q: *But what about men's beards and hair in the genital area?*

A: I was afraid somebody would ask that. And the answer is, I don't know. And if there is an explanation, I haven't learned about it.

But of course that shouldn't be bothersome. Science does not pretend to give all the answers. It is a system of explanation that tries to give as many answers as it can, but always in readiness to give more, or to modify or drop some. It's an open system, which to me is what is so comfortable about it. And as you may realize, all explanations about origins are basically unprovable anyway. So, shall we go on?

Q: *I was particularly interested in the hunting methods. They were really based on cooperation, weren't they?*

A: Yes but this isn't really a human invention, though mankind undoubtedly was better at group effort than the other animals. The hunting apes, and particularly the chimpanzees, which are the best documented, usually do their hunting in groups. When they spot a colobus monkey, one of their favorite prey animals, they spread out and close in on the victim, some coming up the tree from the ground, the others closing in from the surrounding branches. So when one makes a dash for the monkey, that poor devil has to try to get past one of the others to escape. Other hunters, like wolves, lions, and wild dogs are also group hunters. Wild dogs are particularly impressive since the group brings down prey that the individual dog could not hope to handle. It is quite striking to see their hunts which have been recorded often on film or video. After deciding which animal, say a wildebeest, is to be the victim, the whole bunch zeros in on him and literally goes careening through the herd without paying any attention to the other animals. All members of the hunting group concentrate on the one animal which they literally wear out. Hunting in groups has some real advantages, so it should be no surprise that early man did it.

Q: *Man must have added some of his new abilities to the group hunt, though.*

A: Of course, we saw that the drive over the overhang, and even the attempted ambush of the mammoths were group efforts. Mainly these were techniques that enabled him to get large or fast creatures that he couldn't hope to get in a straight-out chase, even as a group, but particularly as a lone individual. The drive over the precipice was incidentally a technique which lasted all the way through the age of hunting and gathering. The Plains Indians of the American West were still using this technique to get buffalo.

His new naming language, no matter how simple, also helped the ancient hunter in his group effort. Though their group was not at all authoritarian, probably less than that of some of the four-footed hunters, individuals could give directions and information to one another. And the human hunters could spread out or come together or even manage a simple division of labor by means of their pre-language. You remember how the overhang hunters split up into drivers and butchers?

Q: *Yes it was quite impressive, and then being able to get some of the women to finish the butchering. I could see how cooperative effort worked for greater efficiency. But they really didn't have any clear-cut leadership, did they?*

A: No, societies with leaders and followers came much later. The hunting and gathering society was the true democracy, not ancient Greece where the majority were slaves, non-citizens, and women who had to take orders from the male citizens; or newly-independent America, where the majority were slaves, factory workers, Indians, and women who had to obey white males who owned property and controlled the police and military forces. In contrast, the true hunters of the world were so democratic that they had no real leaders. Whatever leadership there was came from being the best hunter. And even he could be disobeyed by anyone who did not wish to participate in any given venture. There was no police force or military.

Q: *Yes, I noticed that even Big Mouth, who was evidently the best hunter still felt reluctant to direct others. But what impressed me even more was the fact that no matter who did the hunting, everyone got a part. Was that true?*

A: Yes, it is called redistribution. One depended on keeping only part of the kill, and then when others were more successful, the original giver got a part of theirs. It was a system which worked when there was not a lot of surplus or methods or storing goods over long periods of time.

Q: *The women did dry the meat, though, didn't they?*

A: Yes, I am not saying there was no processing of food for the future, but it was simple. And for that matter there wasn't much of a surplus in the hunting and gathering way of life. It was a lot of work to collect stuff and then when there wasn't any way to keep it very long, why go to all that trouble? No, I'm afraid the human way of over-production and then squirelling the stuff away was a pattern not yet developed.

Of course, you have to remember that almost all the social procedures are extrapolations from the way of life of existing hunting and gathering societies after the Discovery and Conquest. We don't have any direct evidence of what Peking person did. But that is one of the primary techniques used by anthropologists to understand the evolution of culture, to rely on studies of existing simple societies as parallels of the ancient ones.

But to get back to Peking person, we think he became a group hunter, and cooperation was in, while individualism, at least in hunting, was out. Big Mouth was truly uncomfortable in trying to handle Pass Wind, the individualist.

To give a quick and dirty summary, the stage of human evolution represented by *Homo erectus* was primarily important because man learned to adapt to a cold environment through the use of clothing, fire, and shelter. With these, he escaped from the tropics and ultimately spread throughout the world. Also, he may have taken a first step toward his other main achievement in developing a pre-language, a system capable of naming things.

So now let us go to the last hunting and gathering stage when modern man, *Homo sapiens*, comes on the scene.

3

The Wise Man Cometh

Storm

Three men hunkered in front of a fire at the entrance to a cave. All wore skin clothing, the fur side in—shirts, loin cloths, leg wrappings, and robes which they had pulled tightly around them. Fur caps were pulled down over their ears, and all three had thick, dark, dirty-looking beards.

Stone-tipped weapons lay to one side—three spears and two heaving sticks, about three feet long, with a hand hold at one end and a carved hook on the other. They were used to propel the spears, the user sticking the spear in the hook and steadying the heaver with one hand, hurling the spear forward with the other. This gave the man greater throwing power than throwing the spear directly. The spears were tipped with symmetrical stone points.

The man called Storm got up for some sticks of wood to put on the fire. He was about five feet ten inches tall. He brought an armful of sticks back to the group, and stooping down, placed them on top of the remaining embers. Blue Nose poked with a stick to encourage the flames, saying "While you're over there, bring along the rosin bundle so I can be fixing torches while we're waiting."

Storm picked up the wrapped bundle and dropped it in front of Blue Nose. "Okay. By the way, what kind of tree did you get the stick from?"

"Oh, they came from a swamp pine. Blackduck brought them back when she came from getting nuts yesterday. She knew I was planning a trip to Bountiful Cave and that I would certainly need some torches."

Blackduck was the wife of Blue Nose, and she was now back at camp making rabbit stew.

The other man, who was younger and whose name was Runs Fast, spoke. "The fire is good, especially if the cave is cold and damp like most we go into. Too bad we can't do the paintings on an outside cliff wall, one that would be sheltered from the wind."

"You know how hard the work is and an outside drawing simply wouldn't last," Storm said. "The storms would just take them off in no time. Besides, we all know that the Game-master requires drawings to be in protected places where the spirits stay until the animals come out in the open. It's no accident that there are so many old drawings on the walls of Bountiful Cave. I mean, there are so many on the walls that it's hard to find a place not already covered, which is why, of course, we have to put new drawings on top of old ones. That's why Blue Nose put that drawing of a reindeer in the shoulder area of the drawing of a rhino last year in the third room of Deep Cave."

Blue Nose said, "And believe me, I looked hard for an empty place in each room before I went deeper. Of course if I had wanted to go into the fourth or fifth room, I might have found a bare wall. But most of these caves have few flat places. The rocks fall every time there is a rain or when the snows melt, leaving the surfaces jagged. And besides, we still don't know how deep the Game-master will go in."

Blue Nose busied himself fixing three torches by tying sticks together with cord made of plant fiber. The other two waited or tended the fire.

"Okay, let's go," Blue Nose said. He started to get up when Storm said, "May as well light them. We'll be in the dark quickly."

Blue Nose handed a torch-stick to each one and they lit them in the fire. Standing, the other two men were relatively tall also, certainly taller than the men of the Northeast, *Homo erectus*, or those out of Africa, *Australopithecus*. Runs Fast was younger than the other two. They got their weapons and bags of equipment and headed into the cave. The daylight faded rapidly, replaced by the flickering light of the torches. The passage lowered until Storm, who was in the lead, had to get onto his knees, one hand holding the torch up. The others followed. They tried to keep going fast at this point because the smoke of the torches got into their eyes. Having done this before, the older men knew when the cave would widen again. One after another, they stood up and looked around in the first gallery. On every partially flat surface there were line drawings of animals, some by themselves but many with one figure superimposed over another. All the large animals they hunted for food were represented: reindeer, swamp deer, elk, wild horses, hairy mammoths, and rhinos. There were no small mammals and few birds, even ones they did hunt. There were no drawings of predators, either, no wolves, bears, or big cats. After all, the drawings were put on to make the animals more plentiful, so it made sense to put down the ones that provided most food. And though the People would eat carnivores when they got a chance, these were not the main source of food. There simply were not enough carnivores to depend upon compared to the grass eaters. So magic was done to increase the numbers of the grass-eaters. And this was a bad year. The People had moved to this camp in the Valley of the Acorn River in fall after hunting out the area of the High Grassland. There had been enough animals there, though they were far from abundant. In the last few years there had seemed to be fewer animals moving each year, and it was getting warmer and rainier. Storm had noticed that the areas of trees seemed to be getting larger and the grazing animals generally preferred to be out on the grasslands. And he had noticed that some animals, like swamp deer and elk, were not staying in herds so much, but were beginning to move about individually. This made it harder to hunt, since they had to be chased and killed alone which required a lot more effort than a group of men surrounding or driving a herd to the kill. Even the wolves were breaking up into smaller groups, two or three chasing one animal rather than larger groups hanging on the edge of herds to pick out laggards.

Hunting had not been so good on the Grassland and the People had been happy to leave for the Valley of Acorns. At least there were plenty of nuts there for the women to gather and it wasn't far to a grassy area. But the rest of the fall had not been very good either. There had been game, but not much. It was almost as if other hunters had cleaned out the area not too long before. And since Storm didn't know of any other People in the area, he thought that perhaps a group of Bigheads had been there. Even the nut crop had been smaller than

expected and women had often come back to camp with only partially full bags.

The People had got through the winter, which had been less cold
and snowy than usual, but not with a great abundance of game. They
had depended on rabbits much more than they liked. At least there
had been plenty of them. And now it was early spring and most of the
snow had melted off and the People were hungry. So the group of three
had decided to make one last try at increasing the animals by coming
to the magic cave.

Storm was running his fingers over the lines of a mammoth. Blue
Nose came alongside. "Nice drawing, isn't it? The earlier people certainly were good at drawing mammoths."

"No doubt about it. As many as I've done, I've never done one this
well. My elks and reindeer are better, though, I think."

"Do you want to do your drawings in here?" Blue Nose asked.

"No, I think we should at least go to the next gallery. Although I've
done it, I don't really like to put one drawing on top of another. It
might not please the Game-master. And then what good would it be?"

"Okay, shall we go then? I think Runs Fast is waiting."

"Sure." Both men picked up their weapons and carrying bags, and
headed toward the flickering light of Runs Fast.

The next gallery was similar though there were a few bare places
on the walls and ceiling. Storm went around carefully inspecting while
the other two waited. He was the primary artist while Blue Nose would
do the dance. Blue Nose had done some paintings too, though he was
better known for his dance. They had brought Runs Fast along because
he was trying to learn the dance and he also wanted to leave his handprint in the cave. And another man could always be helpful, especially if the artist had to go very high.

Storm called from behind a projection, "Come over here, men of
the People, this looks like a good place."

The other two went to where he stood. "Up there," Storm pointed.

Although it wasn't perfectly smooth, there was enough flattening
to at least do a couple of animals. Blue Nose said, "It looks okay,
although it is fairly high. You will have to stand on one person's shoulders while the other man can hand you the things you will need. What
animals do you intend to make?"

"I think I'll do a reindeer and a rhino. We haven't seen many reindeer this winter, or rhinos either, for that matter. Both should be moving north soon. And with the Game-master's help, maybe we can

increase their numbers, particularly the reindeer. And the women could certainly use some fresh rhino hide for moccasins. Unless there is an enormous increase of animals, the camp will have to move in the next couple of months anyway, probably up to the Green River Camp when the salmon will be running."

"I'm ready," Blue Nose said. "How about you, Runs Fast?"

The younger man was generally quiet since he was learning most activities but he was pleased to have been asked. "Storm can stand on my shoulders."

Runs Fast was the sturdiest of the group, despite his relative youth, so the suggestion made sense. His only trouble was that one of his legs was shorter than the other. As a boy, he had fallen from a tree and the bone had not healed exactly true. But this was a minor physical problem for the People, many of whom had far worse ailments and still carried on.

The three got busy then, Runs Fast getting into position with his hands against the wall and his legs spread for stability, and Storm climbing up, holding onto Blue Nose. As soon as he was stable, Storm asked for a piece of charcoal and began the outline of the reindeer. The animal quickly took shape. He lavished particular attention on the antlers, which more than any other feature identified its species. With red ochre he drew the rhino which did not come out as clearly identifiable. He had a problem keeping the line true around a particularly difficult projection. Runs Fast remained immobile, feeling good that he was helping as much as he was. Storm said, "Shall I put a spear into the animal?"

Blue Nose answered, "I think so, at least one of them. It does make it clear what the drawing is about. I would think the Game-master would know but there's no reason to leave anything to chance. Besides, you generally do it, don't you?"

Runs Fast added, "I'd like to see a spear, Hunter."

Whenever younger men wanted to compliment a mature man, they added the title Hunter. Storm was one of the best hunters among the People, as well as being the chief line drawer and weapon maker.

"Which animal?" Storm asked.

"The reindeer. We could use the meat from dozens of animals. And they are more numerous. The Game-master wouldn't have to put so much effort into increasing the numbers of reindeer.

"Wait until I get my headdress on," Blue Nose said. "Then I can do the dance right away while the animals' spirit is still well captured in the drawing."

The People had the idea that though the spirit of an animal could be pinned down in a line drawing, it soon got restless and would drift away. Ritualizing it made the drawing more permanent and thus more effective over the long run.

Blue Nose was a person who could communicate with spirits. Just as Storm was known for his hunting and artistic abilities, Blue Nose was known for his ability to influence spirits. Thus, he was called upon for help with the main problem the People had to deal with, their health. So frequently when someone was depressed or wasting away, Blue Nose was called either to suck out the intrusive object that had been put into the ill person by an evil one, or to get the person's wandering soul back. In both cases, he would call upon his spirit guardian, Black Wolf, for help. The other main health problem the People often faced was getting enough food. The game animals frequently did not appear in sufficient numbers, or the seeds, nuts, or roots failed. Then Blue Nose would go into action, especially to call game animals, always with the help of Black Wolf. And that is why he had brought along his medicine bundle and wolfskin headdress.

Storm got down, and taking the torch from Runs Fast, stepped back to look at his work. It was a good job. Both animals were recognizable, though the rhino was less so because of the projection the artist had had to work around. The reindeer, with a spear in the heart region, was better.

"I'll bet the Game-master will send us thousands of reindeer after he sees that," Runs Fast said.

"I hope so, and perhaps it will be, especially after it has been well magicked by Blue Nose." Storm turned toward the other man who had by this time put on the headdress of Black Wolf and was holding a gourd rattle. "Are you ready, Blue Nose?"

"Yes, I'll do it on that smooth place just to one side. Runs Fast, would you hold the torch for me, and watch closely."

The younger man raised the torch, then handed Blue Nose his spear. The shaman positioned himself, and then holding the spear in one hand and the rattle in another, began a shuffling dance mostly in one place, weaving his wolf's head from side to side. Periodically he would mime sticking the reindeer or throwing his spear at it, all the time chanting:

See the reindeer,
See the fat reindeer,
She comes from the south,
She comes with the multitude,
She comes with the belly full,
She comes with the belly very full.
She comes to be caught,
She comes to be caught by the People.

Then jabbing his spear forward, Blue Nose would scream.

I spear you in the side, fat one,
I spear you in the side, fat one.

He continued for thirty to forty minutes, moving ever faster and jabbing ever more often, until screaming louder then ever he yelled, "Aaaagh!" and hurled his spear. It went straight to the mark and broke against the rock wall. Blue Nose crumpled and heaved, out of breath. Storm put his hand on the shaman's back as if to support him. Runs Fast picked up the broken spear point where it had fallen from the wall.

The two older men were preparing to leave when Runs Fast spoke, hesitantly, and without addressing one or the other. "Could I do something before we leave?"

"Sure, what?" Storm answered, adding, "If it doesn't take too long. I have to get back to the encampment."

"It will just take a moment. I was wondering if it would be all right to leave my handprint, the one of my good arm, maybe next to one of the animals you made. I have heard that hunters sometimes do that, that it gives them personal luck."

Blue Nose, the expert on supernatural influence, answered, "I don't know that it does but certainly some people do it. I've seen several in different caves."

Somewhat impatiently, Storm said, "Anyway, let's do it. Have you got some powdered charcoal?"

Runs Fast quickly pulled a small skin bag from his carrying bag. "Here it is. I made it last night."

"You know how to do it?"

"Sure, my friend, Beaver, and I practiced last night on a big flat rock."

"Okay, let's do it. Come over here." Storm stepped back to the wall where he had made the drawings and showed the younger man where to put his hand. "Just spread your fingers flat and blow the charcoal between."

Runs Fast did as he was told, blowing charcoal from the flat of his other hand. He still got a lot on his hand but managed to impress an outline so when he pulled his hand back, he had left an imprint that would last eighteen thousand years on the wall of Bountiful Cave, graffiti of the last ice age.

Long Cloud

Storm's wife was among the four women working at the edge of the swamp, prying roots out of the muck with digging sticks. The sticks, simple pieces of saplings or branches, didn't look like much, but it was almost impossible to get the roots out without them. Two of the women had brought babies along, and had left them in basketry containers under a tree by the bank, in the care of Long Cloud's teenage daughter and another girl they had brought along. The two girls were playing house with sticks.

The women had taken off their moccasins and leggings and were standing in shallow water, their dresses pulled up to their knees, above the water line. They were not as tall as the men, though still taller then the women of either the *Australopithecus* or *erectus* variety. Their skins were tan and their eyes brown. Their hair was brownish or black except for one who had yellowish hair.

Although the winter was well over, the day was cool. It was warm enough for the spring plants to have started growing, which was what had brought them here today. The People were still hungry, despite all the magic that had been done. The grazing animals simply had not come in their usual numbers. The men went out day after day hunting but if they brought in one reindeer, the group felt lucky. After dividing it up, there would be little enough for each person. And then there might be several days with no meat. Rabbits had become a mainstay. An so the women had come out to do this cold work very early in the season.

Long Cloud heaved and pried up a large root which had two prongs. She pulled it to her and cut off the trailing rootlets with a stone knife that she had kept tucked into her belt. Then she heaved it up on the bank. She spoke to Yellow Hair with whom she usually went out on food collecting trips and who she usually visited at night. "Whew, this is a lot of work, isn't it? And you know I never did like digging for marsh lily roots."

Yellow Hair answered, "I don't like any work with digging sticks but what else can we do when the men don't bring back meat."

Her yellow hair was rare among the People. The great majority in the group had brown or black hair. Every once in a while an infant was born with white hair and skin and pink eyes. But the People's custom was to leave such a child out on a cold night and in the morning it would be dead. They believed that the mother of such a child had violated some taboo or otherwise offended a spirit, provoking it to cause the colorless, pink-eyed child to be born. But even though it had been a custom of the People for as long as they could remember to abandon such babies, it was still hard sometimes to get a mother to agree to it. Long Cloud could even remember having seen a grown up boy whose mother had refused to abandon him. He was not well, his skin a patchwork of white and pink, and his eyes so sensitive he could go outside only on very cloudy days, and even then he had to squint all the time. She remembered the group among whom he lived, a neighboring band called the Hillmen, wanting to abandon him. She also remembered that at one band reunion everyone was talking about nothing but Pinko. They thought he would bring bad luck to the band. People were even nervous about getting spouses from the Hillmen, afraid that there might be more white, pink-eyed babies.

But Yellow Hair was not like Pinko, and she did not worry the People so much. She could go out as much as the others, and she did not even squint in the sunlight much more than the others, not that there was much sunlight in this region. And her skin, though lighter than the others', was certainly not pink, and as the days grew longer in the spring she would tan like the others. And some people even liked her yellow hair. She had no problem in getting a man when she became old enough to marry.

Long Cloud spoke again. "Do you have anything to eat at home now?"

Yellow Hair jammed her digging stick in the mud and stood up to face Long Cloud. "I've still got some bones I can crack, though I get tired of doing that. It's much better when there are real pieces of meat. I keep telling Squeaky to work harder at hunting. But he gets mad, telling me I don't know how difficult it is, especially when the animals are so scarce. He must think slopping around in the muck is a lot of fun. If the men would come along with us a few times, they would find out, right?" She went back to probing the mud again.

"Yes, but you know the men will never do that. Hunting is their job, they say, and gathering is ours. I wouldn't mind going hunting once in a while, how about you?"

"Squeaky says I can never do that. I must say men are really fixed in their ways."

They accumulated several roots each until Rounder called them from where she was working up near the point. "Looks like we're going to have visitors," She said. "A group of the People are coming down this way."

Long Cloud yelled back, "Okay, how many?"

"About six, I think, and no kids."

Yellow Hair said, "I'm sure there's nobody from our group that was planning to come here today. And I didn't know there were any other bands of People around. Who could they be?"

"If they are from another band, you'd think someone from our band would have found out about it. But that could explain why there's so little game around. They could have hunted them out."

"Let's go up on the bank," Yellow Hair suggested. "We've got enough roots for now. And besides, I don't want to be away from the baby if some strangers are coming."

They joined the two girls, who looked quizzical at their game being broken up. "What's happening?" said Stargazer, Rounder's daughter. "We thought you'd be gone longer. Are you finished?"

"Some strangers are coming. You go up to the point and find out from Rounder who they are. But be quiet and keep out of sight."

The girl said, "What's the matter? The People don't' generally bother one another, do they? At least that's what you told me."

Long Cloud picked up her baby to nurse while she had a chance, since she didn't know whether they would be returning to work or going back to the camp. The baby was a year and a half old and highly experienced by this time at finding the nipple and feeding. Its preliminary name was Pinchface and it wouldn't get its regular name for another two years. The People, knowing realistically that the first few years were the most likely period for loss through illness or accidents, gave their infants uncomplimentary names. That way, the spirits and sorcerers were less likely to become jealous and attack the infants. Then, after the most dangerous period was over, the individual would be given his more permanent name. But even that was subject to change if something of significance happened in the person's lifetime.

62

There were no last names, although sometimes when there was a possibility of confusion, say at a band reunion, the individual might be further identified by adding the band name to the given name. Thus a person could be Storm of the Acorns or Hawkeye of the Hillmen.

Yellow Hair gave the roots a final cleaning and put them into the carrying sack. The women used sacks made from plant fiber netting. After Stargazer was done, the other girl helped Yellow Hair. When they were ready to move, Yellow Hair sat down and, picking up one of the roots, began to cut it into pieces with a thin stone knife. She gave pieces to each of the others and put one in her own mouth. The sky was getting cloudy and the day was turning cool.

Stargazer was gone a long time, coming back by keeping close to the bushes so she wouldn't be seen. She was breathing heavily from running and hurried up to Long Cloud, saying excitedly, "Mama said she didn't know exactly who they were but that they looked kind of funny. She wasn't even sure they were People. She said she and Big Bird were coming right away. Big Bird wanted to get her baby."

It was no time at all before the other two women came around the bend, carrying their netting bags of roots. Big Bird rushed over and took her infant while Rounder came up to Long Cloud and Yellow Hair. She was a little excited, too.

"Who is it?" Long Cloud asked.

"It's nobody from our band," Rounder answered. "In fact, they look like they may not be People."

"You don't mean Bigheads?" Long Cloud asked.

"Well, they don't look right. Their clothing has the fur side out and they do not seem to be wearing leggings. I can't tell exactly because they are still too far away but I think they are not wearing moccasins."

"Can you tell if they are men or women?"

"It seems like the group is mixed, though most are women. I could see their bags. The men have spears, though I didn't see any throwers."

Yellow Hair said, "What will we do?"

"I say we go up the hill a way and hide and watch," Rounder suggested. "Then if we are sure they are Bigheads, we can sneak away to tell our men. If that's what they are, they are probably out hunting or gathering. The men might be along for protection."

She paused, then continued. "Though we all know that Bigheads never fight People if they can avoid it, I suppose they might try to protect their women if some People men attacked them. They probably know that although People men either kill or drive away Bighead men, they do keep some of their women."

"That's for sure," Yellow Hair said. "Every time I get into a fight with Squeaky, he tells me I can be replaced by a Bighead captive who would never argue with him."

Long Cloud said, "Let's go up the hill, where that thicket is. And let's get going or they'll be here before we are ready."

The group gathered their things and the mothers took their babies, the girls carrying the bags of roots. When they were almost at the thicket, they could hear the voices of the arriving group. "Stop," Long Cloud said in a low voice. "Listen."

The newcomers were talking to one another but though the sounds were still not clear, it was certain that they were not speaking the language of the People.

"They have to be Bigheads," Long Cloud said. "They are human since they talk, but I hear it is a very primitive language. After all, Bigheads are disappearing. They can't even defend their territory."

The People continued on quietly to the thicket where they could speak without being heard. They watched the newcomers come to the place they had just left and saw them move about looking at the disturbance and plant debris the People had left. One of the two men picked up a digging stick that Big Bird had left behind, then looked about worriedly. He and the other men went to the edge of the clearing and inspected the underbrush all around the clearing. Then they came back and, gesticulating animatedly, talked rapidly, pointing back to where they had come from and up the hill.

Rounder said, "The men are getting worried. I'll bet they are trying to get the women to go back. They are real cowards, all of them. No wonder they are losing all their territory. The women who get taken captives are lucky. All the others simply disappear but if one of our men gets to use a woman, at least she gets taught how to make skin clothing properly."

"And don't forget they get taught how to speak a good sounding language," Long Cloud added. "Although I hear that some can't learn our language very well."

By this time the Bighead women had pulled up their dresses and were in the water after the same roots the People had been after. Yellow Hair said, "I think we ought to just jump out and yell at the top of our voices. We'd scare them to death. This is our gathering place. Why should we let them get all the roots when we may still need them?

After all, they are probably the reason we are out here in the first place. Their men have probably hunted out the area and now they don't have enough either."

The women listened to Long Cloud more often than they did others, even though she wasn't the oldest. She said, "I don't think we should. We know they are all cowards when attacked by People, but let's remember they have two armed men and we don't have a single weapon. The men might do something foolish. I think we ought to sneak out of here and back to the encampment. We can tell our men. It's certain the Bigheads should be run out but let the men do it. After all, they are always bragging about how strong they are."

Storm

The hunter squatted at the base of the rock overhang where the camp was located. Beehive houses covered with skin extended along the rock base in both direction. Smoke rose from the roofs of some houses and also from fires outside where individuals were working. Hedgehog, another hunter, sat on one side of Storm and Runs Fast on the other.

"That mastodon was the first we've seen for several weeks," Hedgehog said. "If only we could have got it, it would have helped us enormously. What do you thing happened?"

Three days earlier, Storm and Hedgehog had found a mastodon at the edge of the swamp where the women had gone for roots. And though they followed it for a day, it still got away. "Well," Storm said, "you know it's not normal for a mastodon to be alone. But something was wrong with it. It limped, it may have been wounded."

"Yeah, I know. I thought we had a real chance to get it, it was moving so slowly. Maybe that's why it was alone. The rest of the herd had moved on and it couldn't keep up. But that sucker just kept going."

"The only other possibility is that some local spirits drove it off," Storm said. "And maybe they had injured it. Although after our magic in Bountiful Cave, I should think the Game-master would help us."

"I thought the cave magic would really change things," Runs Fast said.

"But let me tell you something, Runs Fast," answered Storm. "Magic is fine to use, but it has to be done right to work. Do one step wrong and the spirit is unaffected."

"Do you think it was because I put my hand on the wall?

"No," said Storm. "You can never tell what went wrong exactly. Anyway, we did what we could. And I think nothing is going to work here. This place has bad spirit power in effect and nothing is going to change that. We're going to have to move on, probably up to the Green River in time for the salmon run."

Runs Fast reached for a piece of spear wood and began shaving it with a sharp piece of flintstone. Storm picked up another long piece of stone that had been flaked off a core. Taking an antler tip, he began pressing down one side so that flake after slanting flake flew off. Then he turned it over and made similar parallel flakes on the other side. His dexterity was obvious.

"Here," he handed the piece to Runs Fast. "When you get that spear shaft straight and smooth you can put this point on it."

"Thank you, Hunter. I'm sure it will bring down some large animals."

"Well, it will help, though of course only if there are any animals."

The younger man was encouraged by the attention of the hunter and spoke out more openly than he usually would. "Some people say there must have been others in the area who hunted it out. What do you think about that, Hunter?"

The older man had taken another long piece of stone from his skin bag and was pressing off small, parallel flakes as he spoke. "I think so, or else someone has violated a taboo and the Game-master has locked the animals underground. Some people don't take that seriously enough but the Game-master can get very offended."

Hedgehog said, "I agree. Why I know men who are very lax about letting their women touch their weapons. And everyone knows that is a sure way of driving the animals away."

"Anyway, this place is not good anymore," Storm said. "I say we move, and the sooner the better. Though if we had the meat from one good kill, it would surely help."

Runs Fast had moved closer and was watching Storm closely. "Will you show me how to do it, Hunter?"

"Sure, because it won't be long before you will have to be a primary hunter. I'm getting along in years now, somewhere between 40 and 45 years." Storm neglected to mention that pain came often these days. It took longer each morning to get the kinks out of his bones.

"Oh, Hunter, you shouldn't say things like that. Anybody who can stay out for several days, and usually bring back game, must have many years to go."

"I'm not saying I have to quit the chase, but it won't get any easier." Storm could still lead the group, and by using his experience he could get into throwing range of hunt animals more frequently than most of the younger men, but he knew he wasn't as fast and that he tired more quickly. But he didn't like to dwell on this so he changed the subject. "By the way, Runs Fast, how old are you? Around seventeen or eighteen years, I would imagine, no?"

Runs Fast had finished smoothing the spear shaft and was tying the spear point to the split end, wrapping it with a moist tendon strip. When this dried, it would tighten, holding the point firmly in place. He was fantasizing about hurling the spear point into the shoulder of a rhino or mammoth. But still he answered Storm, "I'm nineteen."

"That's a good age. Your real hunting period is just beginning. I remember when I was that old I couldn't wait to take off with my buddies." Storm got right near the tip of the point he was making and, having difficulty getting right to the end, held it down on his legging-covered knee and pressed down particularly hard. The tip broke off. "Aw, shit," he said. "You'd think after all the points I've made, that I could keep that from happening."

Runs Fast bent over and looked at it. "It looks like it can be saved. Most of the point is still there. And it is mostly chipped already."

"I know, I know. But I was making it long for a big game spear. I can still trim it down for rabbits and birds." Then he added, "And I guess I shouldn't complain. Rabbits are mostly what we kill nowadays anyway."

With a sigh, Storm picked up the broken point and began rechipping it. He said to Runs Fast, "You are old enough to get married and start a family. You young fellows without a father don't try hard enough. Doesn't your mother want you to get married? Then she'd have someone to help make pounded meat and fix clothing."

Runs Fast's father had been mauled by a cave bear. One of the band shamans had done everything he could, believing the cause of the illness was the spirit of the bear which had invaded the injured man's body. So while he was growing up, Runs Fast had attached himself to one man after another. Storm had been the last. Runs Fast answered, "My mother doesn't mind fixing clothing and food for me. And she does have my sister to help. And besides I bring her some meat whenever I get any."

Hedgehog tipped his head to one side, listening.

"What do you hear?" Storm asked. He didn't hear as well as he had during his youth.

"Someone is coming," Hedgehog replied. He held up his hand to get the other two to be quiet. "It's women."

"Oh, that's probably the group coming back from gathering. You'll be seeing Long Cloud before long."

He was right. Very shortly Long Cloud appeared from down the hill, followed by the others. She saw the men almost as soon as they saw her. As soon as she picked Storm out she came up to him.

"Ay, husband, you will get the news first. We now know what happened to all the game." She paused to let it sink in.

He waited. When she didn't continue he said, "Well, what is it? The men and I have things to do."

"It is that we are not alone here in the Valley of the Acorn. Strangers are not far."

He started to get irritated. "Well, out with it. Who do we share the beautiful valley with?"

"I will say one thing. They are not People."

Almost in exasperation he said, "Spirit people, you saw spirit people?"

"No, Bigheads. A gathering party of Bigheads came to the Swamp of the Wild Lilies."

Suddenly everything fell into place for Storm—the scarcity of game, the footprints he had seen of bare feet, the broken stone points which were obviously of the Bighead type, not nearly as well made as the People type, even the limping mastodon. It had to be Bigheads. If it had been another band of People they would have visited. The Bigheads had been avoiding them. Long Cloud interrupted his thoughts.

"There were six women and two armed men."

What else was there to do, the country wasn't big enough for two races of people. And besides, the Bigheads weren't civilized.

He said tersely, "We'll organize a raiding party."

Long Cloud

She squatted in front of a stretched reindeer skin, one of the few that had been brought in during the last few weeks. With a well-retouched flint blade she scraped the hide to make it thinner. Next to her, Yellow Hair sewed the sections together to make a bag. Neither woman was concentrating on her work.

Finally Long Cloud spoke. "I know that the men have to go on raiding parties, but it still makes me nervous, even if it's just Bigheads."

"I know, I know. I worry about Squeaky too. He gets too excited sometimes and then does something rash. I can see him rushing the Bigheads in camp and one of them stabbing him with a spear. Even if the Bighead runs for it, he might stick Squeaky first and he might get an infection. And you know as well as I how dangerous infections are. Though I did hear about a new method of curing them. You know how the shamans generally try to get their spirit helper to assist in curing illnesses, or give the sick person some herbal tea. Now there's one at the other end of the encampment, a man called Slant Eye, who puts some mud on the wound." She paused. "Anyway, I'm glad he's with Storm. He always has a good influence on Squeaky. Squeaky trusts him."

"I know how you feel. Storm made me nervous the night before they left. In the first place, he was very careful that I wouldn't touch his weapons. He finally put his spears and spear thrower out in a tree for the night. As if he thought I didn't know enough to keep away from them. And then he wouldn't have sex with me that night."

Yellow Hair quickly replied, "Oh, haven't you heard? There's a new idea among the hunters that having sex before a raid or a major hunting trip is bad luck. It's the same idea as not letting a woman touch their weapons."

Sighing, Long Cloud responded, "I suppose the men are right about all that avoidance. But somehow it hardly seems right that they blame everything on women. And as if it wasn't enough pain to have the period." She undid the cord holding the skin on the frame and began to roll it up. "Anyway, I'll feel better when they come back."

Storm had organized a hunting party to raid the Bigheads the day after the report had come in and they had been gone for two days. It was late in the afternoon.

"I have an idea," said Long Cloud. "We're not doing much good at our work, so why don't we put it aside and go up to the lookout to wait for the men. They will surely be coming soon."

Yellow Hair wrapped her skin pieces up also. "It sounds good, though is your baby ok?"

"I think so. He usually sleeps during the afternoon. And Willow knows what to do to keep him happy for a while. We'll just go up there and wait a little while. I think it might help speed them back."

The two women had no difficulty clambering up the wall. There was a slanted crevice at one place where it was not hard to climb. They helped each other at the hard places. The place was used mostly for lookouts watching for game coming to drink at the river. The People had got discouraged lately and had stopped watching because there was so little game to report. So no one else was there. The two women settled down on the little ledge and chatted while watching the sun get lower. There was little to see. Once an eagle carrying a fish passed over- head. Some squirrels were chasing one another in a nearby tree. Then they heard the sound of voices, which grew louder as the group approached. They were men's voices, obviously not trying to be quiet, not a party going out on a raid. It wasn't long before people in the camp below heard the commotion also and started to come out to the edge of the overhang to see what was going on.

"I knew it," said Long Cloud. "I knew the men would come soon- er if we came up to watch. It must be them." She knocked some rocks loose and they went clattering down the wall face. Someone down below yelled, "Watch it! You'd better come down if you want to see what's going on."

The first men of the raiding party appeared coming up the hill. Two men of the People band came first, and then several strangers, their heads bent. A People hunter walked at each side of the group, fol- lowed by two more People raiders.

"Oh, they've caught some Bigheads," Yellow Hair exclaimed. "They have prisoners. And there's Squeaky walking behind them. Let's go down. I want to be there when they come into camp."

The two scrambled down from the lookout, causing a small avalanche. They hurried to the front of the camp where a group of People had assembled. The raiding party had got to the camp's edge by this time and came parading by. Storm and Runs Fast and the other People men were all there. Some still had on stripes of warpaint.

"Doesn't Storm look fierce?" Long Cloud said.

"Yes, though a little tired, too," responded Yellow Hair.

"I don't think any of our men are even injured," Long Cloud said. "But look at the Bighead women and children."

And then she saw the two men in the rear of the troop, their hands tied with rawhide strips, their heads bent. One of the People men jabbed one of the Bighead men in the thigh with his spear. "Come on, now, hurry along, you pile of crap. Step lively, you are now in the camp of civilized people. Show your respect."

The Bighead man shuffled a little faster. He had a big bruise over his left eye.

This was the first time Long Cloud had seen live Bigheads up close. These were probably not typical since they must have been roughed up. They were almost the same size as the People, but they had larger heads, even the girls and children. Long Cloud could see why they had got the name. But their heads were somewhat different in shape, with sloping foreheads and large ridges over the eyes. Also their eye orbits were quite large. Furthermore, they were almost chinless. And the back of their heads bulged out in a veritable bun. The men had much body hair and thick beards. All of them were without moccasins or leggings and their skin clothing was in different stages of disarray.

The group stopped in the middle of the camp, where they made the prisoners squat. Long Cloud went up to Storm. "Oh, we waited for you, Hunter. You must tell us about your mission."

Storm didn't even bother to keep his weapons away from her, but stopped her by holding his hand up. "Let Talker describe what happened."

Talker was called a Talking Chief, one whose specialty was just that—talking. He genuinely liked to tell stories. He stepped forward and, placing his spear against the back of one of the Bighead men's heads, said, "This is the day the Acorn Band of People brought back the Bighead prisoners, the game destroyers."

There was a chorus, "Tell us Talker, how the People hunters did it."

And though Talker put many flourishes on his description, the gist of the raid was that the party had travelled all day, locating the Bighead encampment also below a rock overhang just before dark and that night they slept in a thicket, wrapped tightly in their robes. They attacked at dawn just when the Bigheads were starting to move about. A few men tried to defend themselves but true to form, most ran for it out the other side of the camp. The People warriors had been able to kill several men, women, and children, but saved six to bring back. They had not run fast enough.

When Talker had finished, Yellow Hair said, "Do we women get to make the men to run the gauntlet?"

"Sure," said Storm. "That's what they were brought back for."

She knew from the stories that such prisoners were forced to run between two lines of women, armed with sticks and whips. Often they would be knocked down by the savagery of the blows. Yellow Hair said, "Oh, I've never done it before, but it sounds like such fun. And the

71

crappy Bigheads deserve everything they get. Hunting out all our game! I'll get a good stick."

Long Cloud and the other women joined in, "Me too, me too."

"And the Bighead children?"

"We'll keep them as slaves. They are young enough that they will forget their former people."

Yellow Hair said, "And I know what will happen to the girls. Though before it gets settled, I want Squeaky to know that there will be a lot of trouble if he keeps one."

Talker said, "Storm tells me that there are a couple of young men who are still not married, and some may not have had a woman. Runs Fast, come up here, one of these is yours."

Runs Fast stayed in the back. "Come on, we know it's sometimes hard for a young man but since you went along on the raiding party, and even helped chase the Bigheads, you get first choice. I know now why you got your name. But it's time. You don't have to keep her forever. Some day you will want a People wife. But this one is good for practice. Come on up here and choose.

Talker stepped forward and grabbed one of the Bighead girls by the hair, pulling her head back. Then with his other hand he tore open the front of her robe. He did the same with the other, but since her dress was already almost torn off, her breasts were already exposed. Talker said, "Come on, look young man, take one and try her. I can assure you that no matter what she looks like on top, she's the same at the bottom. And you'll never need to worry about her father or brother coming after you. That Bighead band is clear out of the territory by now."

~

Q: *The first question has to be about the title, and this one is really puzzling. Moreover, it is far from clear in the dramatization why these should be called "the wise men."*

A: Quite right, and as usual with me, the title has a sardonic significance. This particular form of humankind was called "man the wise," or "man the knower," in the Linnean classification *Homo sapiens*. This is the official name for our species.

Q: *I thought the previous sections were about humankind also, the animal who stood upright and evolved a system of survival depending on intensive learning.*

A: Certainly, in the broadest sense both *Australopithecus* and *H. erectus* were humanoids. They both stood upright and had simple forms of culture. But now we have the fully-human type. I used to try to give my students an image that would make this distinction meaningful—if a humanoid of the earlier type, say *Homo erectus*, were to be cleaned up and dressed properly and then put into a modern college class, he would look out of place. But if we were to do the same with Cro-magnon man, who is the type we are dealing with in this chapter, you wouldn't be able to distinguish him from the guy who sits across the aisle now.

Q: *Okay, so he looked like us but how is it that he got his name, man the wise, or man the knowing?*

A: Ah, yes. Well it's a complicated story as so many are, you know. He got it because the namer named himself. The system of classification for living things was devised by men, a particular one in fact named Carolus Linnaeus, and being a human in eighteenth-century Europe, he thought humans were the supreme achievement of the Almighty. Practically everyone thought so in those days. Even today the majority of human beings undoubtedly think they are superior to all other forms of life though there is a large minority, of which your professor is one, who view humanity as no more than one of the competing life forms which is temporarily dominant. There is no reason to believe that the human form will remain dominant anywhere near as long as the dinosaurs did, but that's a hard message to get across.

Q: *But what has dominance got to do with the name of modern man?*

A: Okay, let's try to nail that down. Simply put, the fellow who gave the modern type of humankind its name was working with a mind-set called "centrism." That means he started out convinced that his own type was superior. So instead of looking at the different qualities of animals, he simply decided that whatever humankind was best at must be the best quality. And so he settled on brain power. Humans were rational, thinking animals, so rational thinking must be the highest quality. And so he named the modern human, man the thinker, or knower.

Q: *And that's how you got "the wise man." But the name doesn't really say "man the wise," does it? It says "man the knower," right?*

A: Well, yes, but that is significant itself. No other species in this classification system is called "the knower." The other animal and plant types are supposed to operate mainly on the basis of programmed responses, generally called instincts.

Q: *Isn't it true, though? Doesn't man really operate on the basis of rational analysis?*

A: Yes, to some extent, at least more than the other animals—and plants. But that is still no proof that such an ability is superior overall for survival of the group. Frankly, the more I have thought about it, the more I have thought that a short life span and rapid reproduction give a species more superiority for survival than a rational intelligence does.

Q: *But how can you say that? You are not going to tell me that rabbits are superior to human beings, are you?*

A: No, not rabbits. But perhaps cockroaches and viruses and bacteria. But perhaps even rabbits. I suspect this variety has been on earth a lot longer than the piddling forty thousand years of modern man.

Q: *So here we are with modern man,* Homo sapiens, *and you praise cockroaches and viruses. I thought anthropology was the study of man and that anthropologists considered man's achievements the most impressive of any animal.*

A: It's true, I am an anthropologist and I am consequently dedicated to the study and teaching of the human way, but one of the things I learned in my study of humans is that they are as centric as any other type of life form. But since they developed the most complex brains, they got very good at rationalizing, which means that they can justify their own characteristics very well while disregarding unpleasant information to the contrary. They see themselves as the most accomplished animal by taking themselves as the standard. I suspect there are few humans who see the virtue of a high reproductive rate and a short life span for survival and competition. You can imagine that if a cockroach had been the classifier, it would have found that the superior characteristics were large numbers of young, a short life span, a flat body, and an ability to eat almost anything. But I'm still dedicated to studying the human way, which even if it is probably doomed to extinction in the not distant future, is still interesting. And so we ought to get back to Cro-magnon man, the first representative on earth of *H. sapiens.*

Q: *This of course brings up a lot of questions. Where did this "modern" man come from?*

A: Unfortunately, you ask the hard ones first. As with so many transitions in prehistory, we don't know for sure. He just appeared, mainly in Europe, during the last advance of the ice in the Glacial Period. There was a different type which existed just before him, Neanderthal Man, who lived from the middle of the Glacial Period to the last ice advance, until Cro-magnon appeared. In the dramatization, Neanderthal was Bighead.

Q: *Why do you call him Bighead?*

A: Neanderthal got a bad press for a long time. He was the hairy cave dweller with bent knees who walked around carrying a club in cartoons. Gary Larson loves him. Sometimes he was dragging a long-haired, scantily-clad lady. Also some cartoonists had him bashing dinosaurs, a total impossibility, since the last dinosaurs had been extinct for more than sixty million years. Cartoonists loved to do Neanderthal, and a whole slew of TV serials was based on the poor fellow. Of course, most such producers were treating the stereotype of Neanderthal, the Slob Man. Now we realize that this image was also a product of humankind's centrism. Until the nineteenth century, Europeans were so convinced that they were the epitome of creation that they rejected the idea of including any "lower" creatures as relatives. That was why they fought so strenuously against Darwinism, which claimed that all "higher" forms evolved from "lower" ones. And so when the skulls and other bony parts of Neanderthal began to appear, they bothered so many anatomists so much that they described him as being far more primitive than he actually was; moreover, the Euros, who were most affecting world opinion in those days, claimed that Neanderthal went extinct and could not have been an ancestor of *H. sapiens*.

Q: *If all that is true, why did you call him Bighead?*

A: One of the crucial characteristics of Neanderthal that the ethnocentric Europeans conveniently ignored or downplayed was that Neanderthal overall had a big brain, and some even claimed that on average it was larger than *H. sapiens*. The anatomists liked to emphasize how his forehead sloped back, how big his eyebrow ridges were, and how chinless he was. They deduced that because he didn't look like a modern Englishman in these respects, he couldn't have been an ancestor.

Q: *And so I take it that paleontologists have modified their ideas about Neanderthal.*

A: Yes, indeed. They have upgraded his classification and put him on the family tree. Now he is known as *H. sapiens neanderthalensis*, while our own type is called *H. sapiens sapiens*, which might be translated as "man the knowing knower." But so much for the cultural influences on science. And it is certainly true that because of the centrism and capability for rationalization, man will skew his data and theories frequently. The one good thing about scientific thinking is that it tends to correct itself more than do other methods of thinking.

Q: *Okay, I guess the image of "modern" man is a little clearer than before, but why do we give this honor to Cro-magnon man? Apart from the fact that he is fully evolved physically, he doesn't seem to have accomplished so much culturally. He was just a hunter and gatherer like everybody else, including Neanderthal, wasn't he?*

A: Yes, that's true, his way of life was not that different. True, he was probably the best hunter we have seen so far but still that's a far cry from more modern ways of life. I only decided to include Cro-magnon man in this series later and primarily for two reasons. First, he was truly modern physically and so presumably could learn anything any modern man could. We don't actually know that Neanderthal could not but at least in skull shape he was a little more primitive.

And as you may have noticed, I gave Cro-magnon credit for being a full-fledged talker, a humanoid type which communicated with the full four elements of modern language: sound bits, sound bytes, grammatical construction, and symbolic meaning. I had him really talking up a storm. And from here on all other humanoids will talk your ears off because that is what humans do. A good working definition of the human animal is "the talking biped."

Anyway, I deliberately chose to have Cro-magnon be a talker, to show that fully-developed language was certainly on the scene by this time.

Q: *But I thought you had Peking Man talking too, and even old* Australopithecus *using a sort of verbal communication. What about them, didn't they have language? And what about Bighead, even the People thought he had a language, though they thought it was inferior to theirs.*

A: Yes, for the most part, to both your questions. In the first place I didn't give *Australopithecus* credit for having a communication system much superior to that of the other primates. I did set up *erectus* as having a system with meaningful units, but without the capacity of recombining them by means of grammar. Also, his language was composed of arbitrary units of meaning, which in the jargon we call symbols. But with *sapiens* I add grammar and *voila* we have a full-blown language that you and I would have recognized as such.

About Neanderthal, I think most linguists believe he had language, too, though whether it was more primitive than modern languages is hard to say. I'm sure I told you earlier that this elaborate history of language is based more on speculation than or hard data. The first hard

76

evidence we have of the existence of language is when writing occurred and that brings us to about 5,000 years ago. Before that, languages were only spoken, and this includes all the types we have been discussing so far. The only hard information we have, then, is in the development of the skull. And before *sapiens*, and perhaps *neanderthalensis*, all skulls were more primitive. And then when Euros encountered native peoples all over the world after 1492, they found them all talking up a storm—linguists later considered these all fully-developed languages. So the general assumption is that all "modern" men, from Cro-magnon on, had fully-developed languages.

Q: *So you are saying that because Cro-magnon was fully developed physically, he must have had a fully-developed language and for those reasons ought to be included in the select roster of quantum cultural achievers?*

A: Yes. They were still hunter-gatherers, though evidently they were quite good at hunting, and they did make finer tools than previous people, thought these were still of chipped stone. They had developed pressure flaking which is what Storm was doing in his off time.

Q: *Wait, how can you say they were such good hunters? Throughout this whole piece, they were hungry, living mainly off rabbits.*

A: Yes, it is true they were having trouble in the narrative. But part of that is a consequence of fictional license. As you may know, good fiction is made up of life problems and their solutions, or perhaps more rarely their non-solutions. This particular band of People were stressed because someone else, presumably the Bigheads, had hunted out their territory. This was a fictional device to show the primary cause for strife among hunter-gatherers was territorial competition. We know from archeological sites that Cro-magnon layers were superimposed over those of Neanderthal, and after that there is very little further evidence of Neanderthal's existence. It has been widely believed that Cro-magnon man "offed" Neanderthal, a theory that is easy to accept. If there is any primary cause for conflict among all animals, it is territorial competition, and the reason is not hard to find. Territory means food, whether it is a lizard protecting its few feet for the insect population or Serbians trying to eliminate Bosnians so they can take over the farms and cities. This started with life and the need to get food and it still goes on among "civilized" people. Most modern nations, including America, got started by taking territory away from someone else.

But even apart from the competition of People with Bigheads, and even though these hunters were good at their trade during the last Ice

Age, the fact is that hunting has a big built-in risk, which is that the game animals do not always exist in sufficient numbers. Thus famines occur. And this is why humankind shifted to the next stage of achievement, keeping domestic plants and animals.

Q: *Okay, but why did you call Cro-magnon People?*

A: That's a good question, one that I was hoping for. I have already talked about the ethnocentrism of *sapiens*, who believed their language and physical appearance were superior. They even looked down on the Bigheads because they were not aggressive, as did Columbus with the Indians he encountered, and who proceeded to eliminate them as Cro-magnon was evidently doing to the Neanderthals. Ethno- and other forms of centrism have ruled the world until now. One way to justify eliminating or displacing others is to downplay them verbally while praising one's own. So the most common name tribal people have had in referring to themselves is "the people" or the "realpeople," while they would refer to others with a derogatory name like "dog eaters" or "stinkers" or "shitheads." In the modern world we have got away calling ourselves "the real people," though undoubtedly many cultures still teach their people that they are; but we still use epithets in common speech, terms like greaser, hun, frog, slant, or gook. It seemed most appropriate to have Cro-magnon look at himself as a very admirable fellow since he was in the business of eliminating the opposition, a characteristic of humanity ever since.

Q: *One thing about his achievements you haven't discussed are the cave paintings. This is one thing that is widely known though I'm sure many people who do know about them don't know what the particular culture was. Could you say something about that?*

A: Glad to, because I am aware too that the cave paintings of France and Spain are widely known. The most common theory as to why they were made is as a form of magic, to make the food animals more numerous. At least this is what most archeologists believe.

Q: *How can they tell that? Is there any hard evidence that they were painted for that reason?*

A: No, but as I think I said before, archeology, like most other studies of origins, depends primarily on inference. Certain probabilities are suggested. In this case, the paintings, with few exceptions, are all of the animals the people hunted. And in a few instances a spear was painted in a place that seemed as if it had been driven there, thus it could be interpreted to mean that the animal had been killed by a man. A couple of exceptions were portrayed in the dramatization, the man dancing with a wolfskin and the young fellow who painted his hand on the wall. In the cave paintings the actual animal seemed to have been a deer and painted hands were in several places. The animal head has been interpreted as a part of the magic ritual and why the hands were put there is anyone's guess. My own interpretation is that it is an early attempt to reach out to posterity, a form of paleolithic graffiti. The cave paintings are always treated as a kind of applied art. They did not continue into later periods but of course that makes sense since that way of life was coming to a close. The age of big game hunting on a grand scale ended with the last glacial period.

Q: *The People seemed to be heavily into magic, taboos, and other supernatural beliefs. Or was all that inference?*

A: Unfortunately, until we get to the age of writing, we don't have much evidence of supernaturalism or religion. So a lot of what was in the dramatization was inference. I have already discussed the inference as to how the cave paintings were done as a kind of magic. The fact that they had shamans is inferred only because it was a very widespread practice among hunting peoples when they were described by the first anthropologists. The shaman was the first religious practitioner, an individual in a tribal society who, through the use of a spirit helper, tried to cure illness and help solve other human problems such as obtaining food. In urban societies he was replaced by priests, who continued to try to solve such problems but who also got into the business of proclaiming and defining morality and explaining existence after death. And because of its widespread existence in tribal societies when anthropologists came on the scene, I am inferring that shamanism goes back at least to the time of Cro-magnon man when all societies were tribal.

Q: *Do you also consider such superstitions as hunters avoiding contact with women being a part of a people's supernaturalism?*

A: Yes, in a way. Generally we think of supernaturalism as any belief not validated by observation of natural occurrences. Thus although people may believe that their magic dance has brought game, the actual connection has not been proven. So also a hunter can believe that the reason he did not do well was because his wife touched his weapons without any clear proof. In the same sense it has not yet been proven that prayers to the Virgin Mary have contributed to cures for cancer or that the conjunctions of planets have contributed to relationships "made in heaven." Naturalistic, ultimately scientific beliefs exist because the same effect was caused by the same conditions through the observations of many people, believers and non-believers. Thus, it was observed year after year by multitudes of people that the Nile River rose at about the same time each year, long before anyone knew anything about the conditions at the water's source; and peasants all over the world observed over and over that penicillin cured infections even if they knew little or nothing about the bacteria causing the conditions. So such beliefs and actions as not sleeping with your wife before going off on a raid, and saying prayers to cure an illness, fall into the category of supernatural, while sleeping with your wife to make her pregnant, and consulting an internist to cure an illness, fall into the naturalistic, or scientific, category of explanation.

The Cro-magnons, like all other peoples, had complex mixtures of natural and supernatural beliefs. They had to depend primarily on naturalistic beliefs and actions to hunt game successfully, though if the animals did not come at the proper time in sufficient numbers, they would fall back on supernaturalism. We in the modern world may depend more on naturalistic beliefs, but when they don't work, as in treatment for cancer or AIDS, we may also fall back on supernaturalism and pray to our god.

Q: *Okay, there are just a few more items. One was the climatic period. I certainly got the feeling that it was cold or cool. But would you mind placing it more exactly in the geological framework?*

A: Our heros were living in the last glacial advance of the primary glacial period we know in geology as the Pleistocene. I hate to load you with fancy words, but a few of them are worth knowing. The Pleistocene seems to have been very significant for human development, mainly because it was made up of alternating warm and cold periods. Humankind, who had moved north, probably following the game animals, was faced with the necessity of changing to different climatic conditions several times, and though it doesn't look like so much from our vantage point now, they were in a continual process of change, which seemed to have promoted the development of the human way more rapidly.

And not only did the change take place in Eurasia and Africa during this period, but the mighty hunter also migrated to the remaining areas of the world, except Antarctica. In particular, human hunters migrated to Australia and the Americas in the latter part of the Pleistocene. This of course had great significance to the later history of *H. sapiens sapiens.*

But so far as conditions for Cro-magnon were concerned, it was indeed cold but, surprisingly, there were large numbers of game animals on the tundras of the north, including the hairy versions of the tropical elephants, rhinos, and some others. And at the end of this period, about ten thousand years ago, the climate changed again, to what it is today, and the great herds disappeared and the way of life rapidly changed again, at first to a poorer way of hunting and gathering, but soon to the settled way of life of the farmer. And that ultimately spelled doom for all hunting and gathering peoples.

Q: *An intriguing occurrence in your narrative which you didn't mention in your description of the physical appearance of Cro-magnon was blondism as it appeared on one of the women. I assume there is no direct evidence of hair or skin color for these people, right?*

A: Correct. As you must know by now, the only material of the human body which is hard enough to have lasted for several thousand years is bones and teeth. We don't have any solid evidence for skin or hair color until well after the beginning of writing, some five thousand years ago. The first direct evidence I know of blondism was a Roman description of its occurrence among the northern peoples, the Angles of Britain. But as the Roman Empire declined and the Germanic peoples took over, there was a constant increase in lightness of skin color, eyes, and hair. Blonds appeared ever more frequently in artistic paintings. One of the most striking kinds was that of a blond Jesus and Virgin Mary as Northern Europeans adopted the religion of the Semitics of the Middle East. And blondism was spread all over the world after 1492 as Europeans conquered all other peoples.

We don't know when lightness of skin and hair appeared, though there seems little doubt that the place was Northern Europe. The rest of mankind, and the primate ancestors for that matter, were all dark-skinned, from black to tan. And without going into the details, darkness of skin is adaptive in the tropics while lightness of skin is adaptive in the northern zones. So some time in the past, as genetic mutations for lightness took place, there was selective pressure in Northern European populations to continue this trait. And I simply took this lightness back to the Cro-magnons although we have no direct evidence of light skin, hair, and eyes then. But since they were modern physically and lived in Europe, I thought this little bit of speculation was legitimate.

Q: *One other item—the family, or family values which have been bandied around so much by American politicians in the late twentieth cen-*

tury. You had it existing as fully developed during the Cro-magnon stage. Is that also speculation?

A: Yes, and basically on the same grounds as blondism. You may be coming to believe now that so much that is advanced by historical anthropologists is no more than speculation. And I would be the last to deny this. But what else can we do? Humankind has this seemingly unquenchable thirst to know how things began, and since the possibility of proof is so unlikely for most conditions, we rely on speculation, either scientific or unscientific, from the origin of the universe to that of life, or man, and ultimately the family, etc. Some origin explanations may help in modern life, but most are of no value except to satisfy that unquenchable thirst.

And so with the origin of the family. All we really know is that the social unit of husband, wife, and children was well nigh universal when Euros first explored the world. Whether it will continue into the urban, industrial world of the twenty-first century is another matter, no matter how much the politicos hark back to traditional values.

Q: *And here is the last query, taken from the final event of the narrative. Explain a little more fully about the treatment of the Bigheads, particularly the captured ones.*

A: Alright, but please remember that this is a reconstruction of what we know from studies of existing tribal peoples after they were subjugated by Euros. We depend on this source of information a lot for describing the way of life of prehistoric peoples; and again it is because we have no direct evidence. And we American anthropologists depend mainly on studies of our own tribal people, the Indians. So I describe the raiding party and its aftermath as they were described for American Indians.

In the first place, raids were the primary means for displacing or eliminating other peoples. Most of the tribal Americans were involved in such, either aggressively or defensively. Although it is popular nowadays to criticize the Euros for their aggressive greed toward all Indians, the fact is that the different Indian groups did the same to one another. Raids served the function of territorial displacement.

Tribals didn't generally have enough surplus to make it worthwhile to loot them for goods. But some types of people were worth grabbing. One such was young children because they were not so fixed in their mind sets that they couldn't be molded into the ways of the conquering tribe. Another type was young women because they could be used sexually. One of the prices humanity had to pay for all the rules of the family system was sexual deprivation. Men, the usual sexual aggressors, just did not have free access to most women in their own societies, and they chafed. So when women of other societies were taken, they were frequently used sexually. Rape and long-term sexual use such as concubinage were the results. And so with the Bighead women. I might mention that nowhere on earth did physical difference prevent members of two cultures or races from getting together sexually.

Q: *And did they really torture the male prisoners?*

A: I'm afraid so, and according to the ethnographic reports the women were the worst torturers. I'm afraid humankind have not been very nice toward "others" and moreover the highly-touted female capacity for nurturance more often than not only applied to one's own. The tortures inflicted on male captives by the tribals of North America, particularly the women, were well-described by anthropologists. The gauntlet by beating was a real ordeal.

So shall we part with our People on that happy note, although I must emphasize that humankind hasn't done any worse than the other animals, though from an anthropological perspective, he hasn't done much better, either, no matter his ethical religions and pious platitudes. So let's go on to the next stage and learn how humankind learned to enslave animals and plants for his own benefit—the Era of Domestication.

4

Slaves

Saiba

An eagle flying over the village would see perhaps forty stone houses nestled on the side of a hill in country of mixed brush and trees. A stream flowed along the foot of the hill, past the cleared fields. Wisps of fog lay along the sides of the stream and up adjacent hollows. The sun was just beginning to come over the eastern hills of this region that would one day be southern Turkey. Signs of spring were evident in the new growth and the flowering trees.

The village lay quiet, with only an occasional cough breaking the silence. Tendrils of smoke began to rise from roof holes here and there. The skin door flap on one of the houses opened, and a figure emerged, the flap closing easily as the person moved silently away from the house.

On her head the woman put a woven basketry pad and a pottery vessel, and walked easily down the beaten paths of the village toward the stream, holding the jar on her head with one hand. As she walked, a dog came around the corner of a house, barking. Patches of its short yellow hair were missing, lost in fights or from mange. The woman stooped gracefully, picked up a rock and, without losing control of the jar, hurled it at the dog, yelling as she did, "Kut, kut."

The rock hit the bottom of a standing storage vessel and the dog turned silently away. Saiba, also known as the Grower, continued on her way, stepping effortlessly across shallow ditches of standing water, over slow running sewage and around small piles of discarded pottery shards, bones, and mollusk shells.

Her dress hung from one shoulder of her medium-built frame. Her legs were not covered, but she wore skin sandals. Her black hair hung in waves and stringlets almost to her shoulders, framing her light brown face and dark brown eyes, and her narrow nose that flared at the nares and turned down at the bridge in a shape that would eventually be known as a Jewish or Roman nose. She wore shell earrings and a necklace.

Saiba put her jar down at the river's edge and stepped behind a bush to urinate. Returning to the stream, she washed her bottom, then her face and hands, then took a drink from her cupped hands. She filled the jar, put it on her head, and turned to go back. Walking away, she had to be careful to step around some piles of feces.

People were stirring when she returned to camp. She went directly inside the hut—a large room with raised stick beds covered with dried grass and sheep skins. Clothing and other objects hung from hooks made of antlers or wood pegs on the walls of the hut. Piles of clothing lay on the floor or on wood platforms. Three bodies slept under skin covers while two other sleeping places were uncovered, hers and that of her daughter, Mishrai.

A groan came from one of the covered bodies. Saiba knew that Haras, her brother, ached from the wound he had got two days before when he had been caught with two wild piglets in his hand by their mother. Haras and Jorald, Saiba's husband, had gone out to dig out a pig's burrow. They knew it had six or seven piglets inside which were just the right size for taming. Even the little boars that they wanted to keep for eating could be cut easily, and the sowlets would be no problem.

Jorald and Haras had waited until the sow had gone into the marsh and then began to dig as fast as they could with fire-hardened sticks. They took turns climbing up on the nearby rock to keep an eye on the sow. The digging was harder than they expected. Quite a few good-sized boulders were mixed into the clayey soil, and just when they heard the piglets squealing, a particularly large rock stood in the way. Together they pried and heaved and it loosened. They both grabbed it and pulled hard. It moved, and in front of them were the piglets, cowering and squealing. Jorald grabbed two, followed by Haras who grabbed two more by the hind legs. Two others dashed past the men and scurried into the nearby brush. The caught piglets began squealing louder as the men hurried out of the excavated area. They knew the squeals could bring the mother if she heard them.

And unfortunately she did. She had disappeared from the sight of the watchguards, they thinking she had simply moved further into the marsh. She had gone in far enough to disappear, but then had moved parallel to the edge, diagonally back toward the burrow. And when the two men had dug out the piglets she was moving steadily up the slope. But when the piglets began to squeal loudly, she broke into a run, chomping her curved canines.

Jorald saw her first and knew he couldn't face her without his bow and arrows, which he had left back at the village. And when he had picked up the piglets he had dropped even his digging stick. He yelled at Haras, "Run for that tree to our right. I'll go for the one straight ahead."

Haras, who had no weapons either, did not answer, cursing their luck for not having brought along at least one armed hunter. Usually, when men from Broadbean Village went to capture animals, particularly dangerous ones like pigs or cattle, they took along at least one or two men armed with bows and arrows. That way there was always someone who could kill or turn back angry adult animals. The Broadbeaners always caught young animals because adults which had grown up in the wild were too dangerous.

Haras knew why he and Jorald had done it alone. They didn't want to share the piglets with others. Both men were intent on building up their herds, especially with females which would reproduce more. But all this went through his mind while they had been walking toward the burrow. At the moment, he was running desperately toward the oak Jorald had indicated, even while he heard the sow coming up fast, crashing through the brush and grunting. The tree was only about ten feet away when he decided he couldn't make it quickly enough. A branch was hanging low enough to swing on to, but he was still carrying two piglets, one in each hand. He dropped one of the animals, freeing one hand for climbing and at the same time diverting the sow. She slowed down momentarily, but the other piglet squealed louder than ever, bringing her attention back to it and Haras.

Just as Haras grasped the branch, he felt a searing pain in his right leg and he knew she had raked him with her tusk. He dropped the other piglet and pulled himself up. She ran around the tree a couple of times, grunting angrily.

Haras heard the other piglets still squealing, and though he could not see them, he felt sure Jorald had got up his tree. He could picture Jorald trussing up the piglets with fiber cord so if they were dropped, they couldn't run away. Looking down, he saw blood oozing through his legging where the sow had ripped him. He cut a strip from the hem of his knee-length cloak and wrapped the wound to stop the bleeding.

Saiba had learned all this after the men had come back and she was cleaning her brother's wound. Though she did as well at cleaning and binding it as anyone in the village could, the slash still became infected. Within three days Haras' body was hot and red streaks had appeared around the wound.

The two men had been lucky to have got away in a couple of hours. Angry pigs who had driven a person up a tree were sometimes known to wait for a whole day. Haras mused that it was strange that men had to domesticate such mean animals. At least it was lucky that someone had figured out the procedure for castrating the ones they didn't need for breeding. A pigpen or herd of non-castrated males would be impossible to handle. And in his pain-wracked thoughts, Haras relived the ending of their effort. Although he had got no piglets, Jorald did still have his two. For a while the sow had run back and forth from one tree to another, the two piglets that Haras had dropped trying to keep up. But then the sow evidently heard or thought of the other two that had escaped. She would run in that direction, grunting and snuffling, then turn back toward the tree. She did this over and over, going further away each time. Finally, she had gone over the top of the hill beyond the burrow and returned at a much longer interval. When the intervals became long enough, the men climbed down cautiously and headed back toward the village.

Saiba turned to the cooking area, anxious to get a pot of barley mush going. Everyone would be hungry soon and she especially wanted to fix a bowlful for her sick brother. He had quit eating since his temperature had gone up and she knew this wasn't good for him. She was pleased to see that Mishrai already had a fire going and was putting a pottery jar half full of water on the rocks that had been placed there for that purpose. Saiba set her full jar of water next to the other one, and said, "Have you pounded the barley yet?"

Without waiting for an answer, she bent over to peek into the wood mortar. Cracked barley flour was at the bottom. "Good girl. I must say, little daughter, that it was a lot harder before you grew up big enough to help. Some young man is going to be well taken care of when you get married."

Mishrai was about fourteen. Village people were generally not sure about anyone's exact age since there was no writing. The only way they had of keeping track of longer periods of time was by means of the best memories. And though some people were good at remembering the events of years before, few people pretended to know exactly how many years had passed since a person had been born. Most did know that Mishrai had been born in the year of the great earth rumble which most thought had been fourteen years before.

Saiba put the barley into a wooden dish and squatted down by the fire, waiting for the water to boil. "Did you put in any salt ash?" she asked.

"No, I didn't know there was any left."

Saiba reached for another pottery vessel and took a large pinch of the ash mixture to stir into the mush pot. The Broadbeaners got their salt from another tribe who would take trips to the seashore to get it. They burned seaweed and then used the salty ash for trade with inland tribes in exchange for local specialties. The Broadbeaners' specialty was pottery vessels.

"How about milk? Is there any left?" Saiba asked.

"I used what was left of the cow's milk yesterday to make cheese. You know Daddy has trouble digesting it if it's not made into cheese, and it's not easy for me either."

Jorald's problem was worse than Mishrai's. He would get gas on the stomach and discomfort and even a skin rash if he took cow's milk by mistake. Frequently he would even vomit. Sheep's and goat's milk weren't as bad and were the only kinds he would take willingly. Mishrai continued. "Luckily, there was some sheep's milk left."

Saiba stirred in the pounded barley, satisfied that at least it was a good food in itself. There was still some wild honey that she could mix in. Fortunately, she thought, Haras didn't have any trouble digesting milk, so she planned to fix him a good bowlful with both honey and milk. There might even be enough for him to drunk a cupful of milk.

The sun was well up by the time Saiba came over to visit Istafa, the old potter. Her husband had been dead for many years, so she lived with her grown daughter and family. Her daughter, Nouri, was a friend and work companion of Saiba.

The old lady had been well known for her pottery. She had been so good that she had taught several girls the skill, from kneading the clay mass and mixing in crumbled bits of old pottery, forming the vessels with a paddle, putting designs on them, and finally firing them. She used to have a group of apprentices working together around the outdoor ovens where she served as supervisor. The Istafan product had been the primary trade item for Broadbean Village.

When Saiba sat down next to Istafa, she was clearly aware of how hard it was for the old lady to work. She had got aches and pains a few years before and now her body was bent and her fingers twisted. She was going through a basket of rye grain, picking out tiny pebbles that had got mixed in when it had been harvested. She could just barely close her fingers while pushing the seeds into little piles. This was one of the few jobs she could still do, having long given up working on pottery. Saiba said, "Is Nouri about ready to go?"

"I think so," answered Istafa. "She just had to finish nursing the baby."

Though Saiba was looking forward to going out with Nouri to plant some of the new seeds, she couldn't take her mind off the old lady of so many misfortunes. First, she had lost two children, one, a girl, to stomach sickness, and the other, a boy, who had been carried off by wolves. He had been herding the sheep when the wolves had come in a pack. No one else had been there, though the men had gone later to study the tracks. They had found a torn piece of the boy's tunic. Though boys were always told not to fight wolves or other big predators to save their own animals, Istafa's boy had been very proud of his ability to handle the herds and always took a stone-pointed spear along. The men thought he had tried to fight the wolves off with the spear; but a ten year old boy had little chance against a really hungry wolf pack. And this was the time of the year when young animals were being fed and wolves would take more chances than at another time. The boys were supposed to scare wolves or other predators off simply by making a lot of noise and commotion. This usually worked, especially if a dog were along. But on this occasion there had been no dog.

Then Istafa's husband had been killed by a neighboring group in a village called Foggy Bottom. The borders between villages were frequently contested but especially when the adjacent soil was fertile; and the flat plain between Broadbean and Foggy Bottom Villages was one such area. Barley and wheat did particularly well there. Generally a village or village cluster would keep watch over the territory they claimed and if the neighboring village people got too close to the border, a guard would be stationed there during the day. Usually they built wood towers from which to watch. It was impossible to get anyone to stay during the night because of the fear of ghosts. If a group got too close to the border and especially if they crossed it, the guard would come back for help. This was particularly true if the guard saw cultivation groups made up of men with digging sticks and women with seed baskets. Such groups would frequently plant fields which went on both sides of the border and then claim that the edge of the field was the border. It was more risky the longer the plants were allowed to grow.

Istafa's husband, Poro, had been such a guard on the border and had been speared to death. Another guard had been across the valley, within long calling distance, but had heard nothing. The killing had provoked a revenge killing against Foggy Bottom, then another on the Broadbean side and then a real skirmish. In the end the Broadbeaners had lost two men, a woman, and a child while the Foggy Bottomers lost a man, two women, and a child. It was always less dangerous to ambush women and children because they wouldn't fight back. The Foggy Bottomers also lost two good fields. After the elaborate rituals to dispose of the dead and to settle things with their ghosts, village life settled down again for a few years.

Of course things were not the same for those who lost family members, and Istafa was the first of these. She gave up her house and moved in with one of her daughters. But then she had got the pain in her hands and had to quit making pottery.

Watching the old lady move so painfully, Saiba couldn't get her mind off the miseries of existence. Generally, however, it seemed that men took the most risks and had the most accidents. For women the worst thing was childbirth, but there were also the problems of old age for those that got that far, conditions like aches in the bones.

Saiba watched an emaciated dog snuffing in a ditch of slowly-moving water. It was a female, her teats greatly stretched from the tugging of her pups. The dog found a piece of bone, picked it up, and started to move away. But before she could get far, a group of boys came around the corner and one of them pegged a rock so accurately, it hit the dog right in the ribs. The dog simply shuffled a little faster without dropping the bone. Ah, Saiba thought, the dog is just like a human, managing to continue no matter the misfortunes. She looked back at Istafa but at that moment Nouri came out, carrying her hoe and seed basket. They were going out to plant a new kind of seed which they had obtained through trade with another village.

They started off, well laden with their baskets and hoes. Saiba spoke first. "Jorald asked me to go by the pen to see the new pigs. He castrated both this morning and wanted to be sure they're all right."

The new pigs he had escaped with were both males, and since Jorald already had a breeding boar, he had cut them. They would be raised to be eaten on a feast or other special day. The village people didn't eat pigs often in regular times, but they did use them for sacrifice, especially at funerals.

Saiba and Nouri came to the other end of the village where the animal pens were located. The pens were simply enclosures of wood fencing and were used mainly for young animals, or during the night when lions and other predators were on the prowl. During the day the adult animals were generally taken out for grazing, usually by the boys or young men. Some lambs and calves were in one fenced enclosure and near them an old man was chipping stone arrow points. Being hard of hearing, he didn't know the two women had approached.

"Greetings Balang, may the day be warm and moist," said Nouri.

This was the greeting favored by women in the village because they were so concerned with the growth of plants. The men favored the one most critical in their lives, "May the tamed beasts be numerous."

The old man did not look up, so she touched him on the shoulder and repeated the greeting. He jumped at her touch, but quickly settled back when he recognized her.

"Ay, Nouri the Seedster, so be it." He looked up at the sky and said, "It looks as if prayers about the weather may well be answered."

The sky was partially filled with stratus clouds, though to the north they were mostly solid. "We think it is going to rain so we've come to plant our seeds."

He leaned back and put the stone point which was about half chipped on a flat rock to one side. "And I bet you two have got something new to plant, no? At least that's what everyone says, that you women are always trying some new plant. What's the matter, isn't what we have enough? And besides, you know that the men never get enough meat."

Saiba spoke then. "It's true about the men, though we have meat usually once a week, apart from the ceremonial feasts. Anyway, that's why we stopped by. Jorald asked me to check up on the piglets."

The old man pointed with his face at two small piles of flesh in the shade of a tree, surrounded by a fence. "They're all right."

He laughed, "Of course, they don't feel so good, but what would you expect if you lost your balls."

Then he added, "Of course you ladies wouldn't know about that." As if he knew what it felt like to be castrated, Saiba thought.

She walked over to the fence. "They always mope and sleep like this after being castrated."

"It must hurt. But after all, they are only pigs, created for sacrifice and human food." The old man picked up his arrow point and bent down over it again. Little flakes began to fly off.

Saiba looked up at the sky. "We ought to be going too, otherwise we will get wet."

They picked up their things and began to walk away. Nouri said, "I was surprised that old Balang called the piglets' male organs balls. Generally that is a term the men use with one another. At least Fael always uses the words 'men's organs' around me and other women. I mean we do have different words for a lot of different activities and things, don't we? The women and men, that is."

"Sure we do. There's body waste and shit and piddle and piss and pump and fuck, and all the rest. Men use one kind when they are together and another when they are with women. Besides the tone of the voice, it's what makes men's talk different from women's."

Nouri said, "I wonder sometimes why we have this difference. Why isn't men's talk like women's? There doesn't seem to be much sense in saying the same thing two different ways."

Saiba answered, "That's true, though there are a lot of things about speaking that are difficult to understand; though of course one thing we do know is that the old men and even old women are allowed to do things that younger people don't do. I suppose it's because there aren't so many."

The two women crossed a creek and when they came up the bank on the other side, they could see several adjacent fields extending out to where the next hill began. Rocks were piled along the borders of most. In one of the last fields two figures could be seen working with digging sticks. "That's Jorald and Benji," Saiba said. "They're making the hillocks I asked for. It isn't a hard job, so Jorald decided Benji could help."

Benji was their boy, about twelve years old, usually out during the day with one of the herds. Jorald had asked him to come in to help dig the hillocks and to leave the sheep with his cousin, Balian. This had pleased Benji since he got tired staying out with the animals so much; and besides, this was men's work and he felt proud his father had asked him.

Saiba and Nouri were walking past a field of winter wheat which was flourishing, the plants were almost three feet tall and beginning to come out in heads. Nouri giggled.

"You know what I did in this field, older sister?" Saiba was not her real birth sister, but people frequently used the terms for other people with whom they had the same kind of relationship.

"No, should I?" They kept walking toward the two males.

"I should hurry and tell you before we get to them," Nouri pointed with her face. "It's not something they should hear, even though Jorald probably already knows about it."

"Oh, do," Saiba said.

"Well, it happened before we were good friends. Otherwise, you would know already." She was speaking fast now and in a conspiratorial tone.

Saiba loved this kind of woman talk, so she slowed down in order not to reach the males so fast. Nouri continued, "Well, you know how the men are always making offerings to the Great Tamer, every time they go out to get some more young animals or when they have to do something hard and dangerous, like notching the ears of cattle or trying to catch a breeding bull. Then they have to make a blood offering, usually of a lamb or small goat. Of course I know many of the things they do are dangerous or difficult. I certainly wouldn't want to have to try to handle a breeding bull, but then men are bigger and stronger. And besides a lot of the animal tending is their own choice. We could get along perfectly well without so much meat and milk."

The story was going on and on in the way Nouri's stories frequently did, and they were getting steadily closer to the men. Saiba interrupted, "Okay, but what has this got to do with what you did in the wheat field?"

"Well, you probably heard the story in camp before that Broadbeaners and other villagers used to do magic for the fields also. Oh, I'm not saying they sacrificed animals but it was thought that before the Great Tamer became paramount, when the Earth Mother was still the presiding deity, that ceremonies were done for crops also."

"Of course I've heard that. Probably everybody has, and certainly the girls. There was hardly ever a story telling session that some old woman didn't bring that out."

"Right, well that idea always intrigued me, and I never could figure out why such ceremonies were dropped. So one spring when the winter wheat had just come out and Balian was complaining about it so much because the new shoots looked so sickly, I told him laughingly one night that the trouble was that we Broadbeaners had dropped the Copulation Ceremony."

"You didn't?"

"Yes, I did, and I'm sure I partly believed it. After all, it was indicated that in the old days we must have done other things besides cutting lamb's throats for influencing the spirits. What about those pottery figurines that farmers would sometimes bring home, you know the ones with the big breasts and thighs and tiny heads and feet. They certainly seemed to represent a special kind of female figure. And what about the paired spherical designs on the seed pots. If those weren't modelled on female breasts, then you and I don't have any."

Saiba motioned toward a rock outcrop which was just below a hillock and out of sight from Jorald and Benji. "Come over here. This is one story I don't want to miss. They can wait a little longer." She looked up at the sky. "It looks like we still have a little time before it rains."

Nouri sat down. Saiba said, "My gosh, what did he say?"

"Well, he was interested. But you know him, if there's something kinky, old Balian is interested."

"But the Copulation Ceremony wasn't supposed to be kinky, was it? I thought it was serious business to make the plants grow."

"Sure, but a guy like Balian could see something kinky in all kinds of activities. I don't know if I should tell you, but I heard that he still does it with sheep sometimes. And you know as well as I that most men give that up when they get married."

"Yes I know what you have told me. And yes, the Ceremony was supposed to be serious. But anyway, what did you do?" she said with a slight tone of exasperation.

"Well, I told him to cut a little sheaf of wheat stems and put them in one corner of the field where it would be hard for anyone to see us. And then we waited until one night when there was a moon in a partially cloudy sky so we could move unnoticed during times when the moon was behind a cloud. Balian was pretty good because when the best night came, he waited for me patiently instead of trying to get me to go to bed with him in the house."

Saiba was soaking in all the lurid details like the first rains in dry earth after a drought. Nouri was the only women in the village with whom she could share such intimate details. "And then?"

"We went out to the field after it got quiet and I don't think anyone saw us. And when we got there, I saw that Balian had made a good laying place with extra stems and the sheaf was carefully placed to one side."

A few drops of rain fell from the approaching cloud mass. Saiba said, "Hurry, and tell it. We still have to plant the seeds and the men will be angry if they get wet."

"Okay, I had him take off his clothes and I did the same. And then I took part of the cut stems and began to brush him with them, saying at the same time that little prayer the old women used to tell us about. I couldn't remember all of it, but I did the best I could, thinking it went something like,

I brush your shoulders,
I brush your arms,
I brush your legs,
I brush all your body,
To give you strength,
To make growth,
To be fertile,
To bear seeds."

Nouri giggled as if to excuse herself. "I don't know if it was right, but that was the best I remembered." Then she spoke hurriedly, "And I had him do the same to me."

"You must have been getting cold by this time with nothing on."

"I was, but it was exciting."

"And then?"

"And then we got down on Balian's pallet and we pumped."

Jorald

He was known as the Domesticator because he had such success with animals. Jorald always seemed to know what to do, even when an animal got sick or had to be treated in some special way. So people would call on him frequently to help. If an animal became lame, Jorald might be called on to treat it. And if he said it couldn't be helped, his advice would usually be taken and the animal would be killed to be eaten. He was also often called on to castrate the little males people didn't want to keep for breeding. On some animals he would do this with his teeth, biting through the tube that went to the penis; on others he would use a chipped stone knife to cut the scrotum then yank out the little balls. The animals he cut rarely became infected, so people were willing to give him something, usually another baby animal. Not surprisingly, Jorald's herds were among the largest in the village. People were starting to come to him for different kinds of advice.

Jorald was polishing the piece of stone by rubbing it against a flat outcrop of a similar granular rock. A little pile of stone dust had accumulated on both sides. Beads of sweat stood out on his forehead. Pakot, his neighbor, was gently tapping a stone which he had just knocked loose. First he had to crudely shape it by tapping, then he would polish it. Jorald watched him concentrate on the tapping because he knew one hard blow at the wrong place would break it. Pakot became aware of being watched, perhaps because the sound of polishing had stopped. He looked up. "How do you think this piece is going to turn out?" He held up the piece he was shaping. He intended it to be an axe when it was finished.

Jorald grinned, "Oh, you know me, Pakot. I really don't care for stone work much, and the rough shaping for polished stone tools like you are doing is one of my least favorite."

Pakot, who was known as the Shaper, held the stone forward. "I know, you've told me many times and I have seen you. But just imagine how it would be if we didn't have any polished stone tools. How would we gird trees?"

"Of course we need them. And though my father was a good shaper, I just never developed any interest in it." He laughed. "I am here doing it, of course."

"As you know I don't mind," Pakot said. "In fact, I enjoy making a perfect stone tool, chipped or polished, as much as anything. I suppose it's like you with animals. Everyone admires your ability to take care of and tame animals, probably a lot more than my tool making. But what the hell, a guy has to do what he's good at. And frankly, I'm good at making tools." He paused for a moment, thinking, then said, "That may be the way to do it. You take care of the animals and I'll be the tool maker. And we can exchange the things we make or do. So I can keep you supplied with stone axes and grinding stones and knives, and you can give me one of your baby pigs or lambs from time to time."

Jorald chuckled. "Doesn't sound bad. Then we would really be doing what our names said. I would be the Domesticator and you the Shaper."

Pakot picked up his rock again and began tapping. Reluctantly, Jorald began polishing again. The one way he could keep going without becoming too bored was to imagine what the future would be like. And invariably his mind came back to the land and animals. Although no one among the Broadbeaners was encouraged to accumulate goods, there was no rule or taboo against it. And perhaps because they had been poor when he was a small boy, Jorald had become interested in the idea of accumulation. Land couldn't really be accumulated because it didn't belong to anyone. The fields were parcelled out to those who used them. If someone did not use a field for two or three years, it was given to someone else by the clan council. Also, there were frequent arguments about which parcels belonged to whom year by year. There was a current argument going on about how long a field could be left fallow before it had to be reassigned. Jorald spoke to Pakot. "You had some problems with the council last year about a field, didn't you?"

"Sure, but what made you think of that?"

"Well, I was thinking about this new idea of letting a field stand for two years before planting it again. That seems like a long time to me."

"I don't know. I know my neighbor, Misram, swears on two years. But he doesn't run animals on it so their droppings will fertilize the land. I don't even think he and his family make any special effort to relieve themselves there."

The general practice in Broadbean Village and most of the other villages in the area was to have family members relieve themselves in their fallow fields.

"Anyway, many on the council believed that one year fallow was enough. And that was why they didn't want to assign you that field of land up by Willow Creek, because you had left it fallow for two years? I missed a couple of meetings so I don't know the details."

"That's right, more or less," Pakot replied. "They did assign it to me anyway when I told them that I had been taking my sheep and goats up there so their droppings would fall on the ground. Though I have some second thoughts about how good that is, the way sheep, in particular, eat up everything."

"Yes, that's true. I would prefer to have cattle though they need a man's attention more than the smaller animals. Benji is always willing to take the cattle out but it's pretty tough for him. And I always worry that he might run into some lions."

"You're right. That Benji is a good kid. And I think he's too smart to fight it out with lions. I noticed you had him with you the other day when you were digging up mounds for Saiba and Nouri."

"Yes, he's getting to the age when he can really be useful. There's nothing like some stout young fellows to help in the farming. The girls are a big help, though only to their mothers. Anyway, we could use more children."

They worked quietly for a while until Jorald put down his tool with a sigh. "You about ready to quit? I think we ought to get going pretty soon or it will be dark before we get there. I don't think anyone is working in nearby fields anyway. I'd like to check on that jar also. I'm sure the rats are carrying a lot of grain away. And if there's really a good-sized hole, someone is going to have to go up there to fix it tomorrow."

Jorald had noticed a big crack in one of the grain jars with rat droppings around it. Pakot continued a little longer but then put down his stone piece also. It had come along nicely, and now clearly showed the shape of the axe it would become.

"Sure, I'm ready, and it would surely be better to get there too early rather than too late. Then if anyone was in sight, we could hide until they left."

They both got up and picked up their spears and leather carrying bags into which they put the stone pieces they had been working on and headed out of the village, quietly though not secretively enough to attract attention. Jorald let Pakot go first. He watched his friend and decided he had made the right choice. Pakot didn't mind helping, though all he would get out of it would be a young goat or sheep and perhaps a few portions of grain. But Pakot, like a lot of villagers, was not anxious to accumulate land or animals, especially if it involved extra work. He seemed to be satisfied making things.

Jorald's dog came running up behind him and Jorald turned around. He was pleased that the dog had made no sound, but he did not want it along. In a low voice he gave the command to go back. The dog stopped and stood there indecisively for a moment. Pakot reached over to pick up a stone.

"Don't throw it at him," Jorald stopped Pakot. "That's a dog I've been training to handle sheep and you have to get them to just take voice commands or gestures." In a low voice he said to the animal, "Back!"

The dog turned and went back, his tail down. The two men moved on. They passed a few people, though at enough distance that they didn't need to speak to them. It was getting darker faster than Jorald had expected. He went around Pakot so he could hurry. Pakot said, "I thought you said you wanted to check on the grain jar."

"I'll do it tomorrow. There's not enough time tonight. If we can get those two big rocks moved, I'll be satisfied. And if we come back too late, there will be a lot of questions. Saiba was already curious why I asked her to milk the cows."

They went along the hillside until they came out to where the grain fields lay, one next to another, some with crops, others fallow. There were no herds to be seen anywhere. All had been taken in for the night. Jorald looked out across the fields for some stray worker. None were in sight.

"I think we're in the clear," Jorald said. "Let's just go over there in the shade of that oak and wait until it gets darker."

The two men squatted. Pakot said, "You know the clan can be difficult if someone gets caught doing this. You may remember the last time when they caught Shednam, they not only took his fields away that year, but they gave him nothing but poor fields for another two years. And if the guy the field belongs to catches someone, he will surely beat him, usually with help from clan members or friends.

"Sure, I know that, but I don't think anything's going to happen. I don't think anyone is out here and I told you that Lefty had already changed the boundary. I know he did. He already moved the ones I want to move. And I'm sure the council is going to make this into one of the permanently-owned fields. Don't worry. You'll be home eating barley soup before you know it." Jorald got up, becoming a little nervous that Pakot might back out.

"Let's go," he said. "It's dark enough. And we can still see well enough to move the stones."

They went quietly across the darkening hillside, Jorald a little tense but with all his senses alert for any sound of another person. He heard a long halloo but too far to cause them any problem. It might even be Foggy Bottomers. The two men came to a field marked most of the way with field stones and mostly straight. However, in one corner of the field two large stones stood well inside while the rest of the field stones of that line, which were much smaller, were about ten feet further out.

Jorald had been here moving the smaller stones the last couple of nights. The two large stones were too big for him to move alone.

Pakot surveyed the scene as well as he could in the coming darkness. "I see what you mean. It would give you a larger field for sure. And that would certainly be worthwhile if it became permanently yours. Though I'm not sure it's worth the trouble."

"The soil is very good in this field." Jorald had not told Pakot that he had moved the markers on other fields and had not got caught. He said, "I've got a couple of stout poles over there in that brushy place just outside the field. Let's get them and get this done with."

The two men got the poles, pried the stones loose, and rolled them to the new boundary line.

∼

Q: *Certainly one of the first things about which we need clarification is the title. Why "Slaves?" There were none in the narrative.*

A: Ah, yes, I understand you are seeing the situation in a homocentric mode. You are thinking of slaves strictly as human beings. And though I will admit that mankind generally takes this restrictive point of view, if some being from another planet were to come to Earth, he might well see it more broadly, and see that slaves are many kinds of creatures. Animal life of course depends on the use of others, either of the same variety or of one another. Animals must eat plants or other animals. They either pick them (plants) or catch them (animals). Our own ancestors, as we have seen, being specialized animals (upright apes), did the same. In the four to five million years of most of man's history, he was a collector/hunter like all the others, only somewhat more efficient. But then he got the idea that if he could control the whole life cycle of the plants and animals he wanted to use, he would be even more efficient, which is precisely what slavers of human beings did. And thus the Age of Domestication began.

But before we give man too much credit, let it be remembered that a number of other animals also enslaved or domesticated other types, the social insects, for instance. I am particularly thinking of ants. Ask any gardener who has been fighting aphids. If he gets rid of the slavers, the ants, he gets rid of the plant suckers, the aphids. Or watch a line of leaf-cutters in the tropics as the workers meticulously carve up the leaves of a plant and march back to their burrow to feed the fungus they will later eat. Sounds like a human domesticator, doesn't it?

And it is true that man took to enslaving members of his own species also, but that comes later in our story, at least on a mass scale. And though in this chapter we are finding a human way more complex than the previous ones, it is still on the simple side, and whatever slavery of humans there was during the first stage of domestication had to have been on a small scale. But before man got around to enslaving his own kind on a mass scale, he worked out a means of enslaving other species. And that is what we are discussing here, the enslavement of plants and animals for human benefit. It is usually more politely referred to as the domestication of plants and animals. But it certainly was done for the benefit of the slaver, man, and it certainly was done by force against those creatures.

Q: *But plants and animals were put on earth for man's benefit, or at least that's what we were told by our parents and teachers in grade school.*

A: Yes you were, and so was I. And though you probably think of it as something taught in the Bible, I will inform you that from anthropological studies of other peoples, including tribal people, the idea is usually similar. That is, they have beliefs, usually based on myths, that the animals were there for human benefit, whether through hunting and gathering or through domestication. And though many, if not most, hunters ritualized their relationship with the other animals, the myths always made clear who was going to use (eat) whom. The North American Indian hunters frequently had a ritual in which some parts of an animals killed for food would be prayed over and then put back into its natural milieu so it could tell its relatives to come and be caught also. The Australian aboriginals and other tribals propitiated the spirits of animals they wanted to kill through dances so they would send more of their relatives. One of the last widespread rituals of the American Indians was one called the Ghost Dance. It was believed that after the proper dance, ghosts of the dead would come back to life and the buffalo would come back from under the ground, to be eaten by men, of course. The origin tales of most people taught them that plants and animals existed for human benefit, so it is hardly a surprise that the Bible did also.

It might be argued that the universality of this idea is a proof that the origin myths are true, that God or some other spirit being did create all these creatures for human benefit. But of course, we would then have to deal with the fact that the exploitation of one type by another is universal among animal forms and thus one could hardly accept the idea that there was anything special about humans which of course is contrary to the intention of all the origin myths I know.

Q: *And so you are saying that the idea of taming or controlling other life forms through domestication was simply a more efficient way of using them?*

A: That's the idea. It is sometimes called food production rather than food gathering, because it produces a lot more for a given amount of energy expended. Not that that made things easier for mankind in the long run, but that is another story which we will get to later. Now we merely need to recognize that it was more efficient. In fact, it was so important in the overall history of mankind that it was labelled a revolution, a quantum leap in knowledge. Even now in the age of gene splicing and extensive chemical use, we still have not found a better way of getting food and other commodities.

Q: *Though you told us where Saiba, Jorald and the others were living during this period, you did not indicate the exact time period, did you?*

A: Perhaps not, but you know that sometimes in trying to keep the narrative flowing, I don't get around to presenting all the facts. And let's face it, this was a more complex era. Anyway, that's what we are doing now, trying to fill in the story. In round numbers the Domestication Revolution began about ten thousand years ago. Our hominid friend began, as you will remember, in Africa some five million years ago as a hunter-gatherer. And he remained as such for 4,990,000 years, though admittedly getting better at his trade and evolving into modern man physically. Then after a long cold period it became warmer and the great herds of mammals he had preyed upon became fewer and fewer. That long early period when man was a hunter-gatherer is called in archeology the Paleolithic, which simply means the Old Stone Age. Technically it meant chipped stone which was the type being made by all those early hunters, by Squint in the beginning, then by Big Mouth, and then by Storm. Then a short intermediate period took place, called the Middle Stone Age, which was a period of change when pottery and polished stone were invented and the dog was domesticated. And after that, there emerged in the highlands of the Middle East of Eurasia the period of true domestication, which brings us to Saiba and Jorald.

Q: *You mentioned that they lived in what would eventually become the modern country of Turkey.*

A: Yes, it was the highlands of the Middle East, in what would become the modern states of Israel, Syria, Turkey, and Iran. This is a region of moderate climate with enough rainfall to cultivate crops without irrigation and where the wild versions of the original animals and plants were found. In other words, the men and women could find the creatures they needed to tame once the idea became established.

Q: *You've named some of the crops and animals, though when I think of all the things we humans grow today, there are quite a number missing.*

A: True, but remember I said the original domestication. The process has continued ever since and we are pretty sure it happened independently elsewhere, at least once. But some of the most important crops and most of the domestic animals of today come from the original place of domestication. The most important of these were wheat, oats, and barley, plus cattle, sheep, goats, and pigs. There were a lot of less important plants and a few other domestic animals as well.

Q: *So that's why you featured wheat in the ritual? But this list certainly doesn't include all the other important plants of the world and some other animals. Where did they come from?*

A: Well, once the idea of domestication got going in the Middle East, we think it spread and other peoples domesticated other plants. In South Asia, villagers domesticated such important plants as bananas, sugar cane, and various kinds of peas, as well as one of the three great super-grains, rice; and they tamed the water buffalo, chickens, and perhaps ducks. In all instances, hunters and gatherers settled down in permanent villages like the Broadbeaners.

Q: *But you still have not accounted for many other widely used plants. I am particularly thinking of corn, potatoes, beans, cotton, and tobacco.*

A: Okay, you hit the last one, the Americas. And that is a story in itself and dear to the hearts of anthropologists because specialists of this profession, archeologists, have ferreted out many details of the very important domestication of plants of the American Indians. When I started to write this chapter, I thought of doing two separate pieces, one for the domestication process in Eurasia, and one for the Americas. but I decided against it simply because the story would be too long. It would also be impossible to discuss the domestication of plants in the Americas without mentioning the American Indians. Although they weren't very interested in taming useful animals, they went crazy with plants; and the world is that much richer in foodstuffs. I won't go into all the details, but most believe they domesticated more than 100 useful plants, including those you mentioned. Of course, we are not convinced now that tobacco is so useful, but it certainly has been widely used. It has been referred to by some as "the red man's revenge," in that while the white man took his land, the red man inflicted the "weed" on the white man and others. The red man only tamed a few animals, none of which except the turkey and guinea pig (used for food by the South American Indians) became useful to others. But potatoes, tomatoes, corn, and beans have had an enormous influence on the rest of the world.

So the next time you chow down on a burger, french fries, tomato, and onion, remember that about forty per cent of that food came from plants domesticated by the Indians. If you have a shake or cola to wash it down, you have to give the credit to the Old Worlders.

Q: *Okay, and now that we seem to have the Domestication Revolution pretty well pinned down, I will continue, if I may. One thing I noticed in the narrative is that it was mostly a woman's story, in contrast to the previous ones of the hunters and gatherers.*

A: Yes, that's true. This was mainly Saiba's account. And not only that, it was the last great epoch of man's history during which woman's place was so high.

Q: *You mean woman's status was higher then than now? I thought we had just come into the era of women's liberation, at least in the advanced industrial nations.*

A: Okay, I'll modify my generalization to that effect. Women have obtained more rights recently, but this is only in contrast to the recent past which was primarily controlled by men. But in most of man's history, we think woman's status was relatively high and for the most usual reason—her contribution to daily existence was very important, probably just as important as that of men. And her productivity was tied directly to the most important half of the foodstuffs of mankind, plant products. Despite the great fondness of modern men for beef and other meat products, the bedrock of almost all cultures' cuisine has been plant products. Even the meat consumed has always been directly dependent on the plant products eaten by the animals.

Woman has been the plant master throughout most of human history, for the reason that due to her need to succor infants, she was less mobile than her mate. She was also not as big and strong. So in the long early period the old boy could more easily take off to hunt down wild animals or scrounge carrion of other predators while the woman was out picking berries and seeds or digging up roots while taking care of baby. In the few surviving hunting-gathering cultures of recent times this was the invariable division of labor.

So when the idea of domestication emerged, it was almost inevitable that the primary innovator with plants would be the women, while the men were busy taming the animals.

Q: *But then why is it that in the main agricultural cultures of recent times the status of males was so high. We even have called such societies patriarchal.*

A: That's a good question. And the best answer that I can come up with is the influence of what Professor Burke would have called a connection, or perhaps two such. There was a primary, very important invention which shifted influence and authority to the male—the use of animal power for pulling things, and particularly the plow. This had not yet happened in the era of Broadbean Village. You may have noticed that men used digging poles to break up the ground before planting, while it was mostly women who took care of the growing cycle. In other words they were equally important in producing plant food. The change that took place was men's preoccupation with animals and particularly the larger ones where the greater male muscularity was an advantage. But when somebody came up with the idea of harnessing the animals to the pole, and then added a handle and something to attach it to the animal (at first an ox), and made a few other little changes, you had a plow. And who would you suppose would take over to drive the animal? And then the woman's role in agriculture, and I suspect her general status as well, became much less important.

Q: *All right, but why is it then that we are now coming to an era of higher status for females in industrial times.*

A: I can answer that question by asking another. Do you see many men driving plows with animals on the farms of industrial societies?

Q: *Hmm, no. But the men handle the machines which have replaced the animals, don't they?*

A: Well, yes, grudgingly. But the real fact of the matter is that farming in itself has become a minority occupation. Status now derives from city mores and occupations in the industrial countries because that's where 95 per cent of the population lives and works. And even the machines, especially the advanced ones, that the farmers use can be handled by a female as well as by a male. She can push computer buttons or power controls as well as her mate.

Q: *And so you are saying that the physical difference of the male no longer gives him much advantage?*

A: That's correct, though I'm not saying that cultures react automatically to new developments. There is always some cultural lag. And males in general will not freely give up all the privileges of the patriarchal society. But the era of the female is coming back, along with her increasing importance in production.

Q: *So if I understand correctly, women's status was high during most of human history, but declined some time after the domestication of plants and animals when men took over farming, and is now rising again because farming has become a less significant occupation and women can handle machines anyway.*

A: That's it.

Q: *A few other questions about animals. First, what about castration, was it necessary?*

A: Well, although the male could rough up smaller animals, the big ones were pretty tough to "horse around." A big bull or later a male horse or even a big boar could be a pretty rough customer. So some animals tenders figured out that if the old boy was parted from his "family jewels" he would be easier to handle. Nobody knew anything about testosterone in those days, but it must have been pretty clear that when you saw a bull pawing the ground in the vicinity of a female in heat, his sexuality was stirring him up. So they realized that the answer was to get rid of the sexuality. And unfortunately for the male that was easy—the testicles were out in the open and easily removed when the animal was young. The first animal tenders had to learn that removal of the testicles eliminated further breeding, but they got more tractable work animals, or more tender animals to eat. This must have been one of the key discoveries of animal husbandry. You couldn't do a similar thing to the females, but then they were not so aggressive either. Apart from the physical modification of the males, taming in the early stages seemed to have been mostly a matter of penning animals in (at first only when not taking them to graze) and having them get used to being around people. It still must have taken a long time and as we know, many animals could go back to being wild again if let go. For instance, in Australia there are wild cattle, water buffalo, and camels, all originally brought there as domesticated animals. Wild horses, pigs, and donkeys thrive in many parts of the world.

Q: *The one domestic animal which seemed to have been apart from the others was the dog. And I remembered that Jorald was taming one to help herd the other animals.*

A: The dog was the earliest domesticate and by the time Europeans spread all over the world, the domestic dog was being kept by all people. Archeologists found evidence of the domestic dog in the encampments of the Mesolithic people, those who lived just before the plant domesticators. So in that sense the dog started the whole revolution. Men learned to use it in certain ways, initially as a helpmeet in hunting it is supposed. Then he started taming other animals. And eventually men learned to use the dog as a herder of sheep and goats. We don't really know exactly when that happened, but I took the literary license to start it with the Broadbeaners.

Q: *I guess that doesn't surprise me too much. I always think of dogs and people together. And there is such variety nowadays, I suppose it took a long time to breed them. One animal you did bring up did surprise me though— the cow. What was that business of people not being able to digest milk? I thought it was supposed to be the perfect food.*

A: That's a real complicated story and one which we in the West have only begun to learn recently. First some facts rather than more promotions for getting us to drink more milk. The majority of people in the world only drink their mother's milk when they are infants. Milk is baby food and varies according to the species. So it is difficult for a lot of adults to digest cow's milk—the statisticians tell us at least two thirds of the world's adult population. That was Jorald's problem, and undoubtedly that of many of his fellow villagers.

Q: *Well, why is it that we are all taught that a body needs milk so much and why do so many children drink it as if it were going out of style?*

A: When I said that two thirds of the world's population didn't drink milk, I didn't mean Europeans and Americans, nor for that matter, people from India. But I did mean Chinese, Japanese, almost all other East Asians, most Africans, and all the American Indians before they were taken over by Europeans. It seems clear now that the idea of taking the milk of the domestic cow was an idea that emerged in the Middle East and spread from there. It never got to the Far East or most of Africa, the Americas, or the islands of the Pacific. So those people did not develop the habit. And not only that, they did not get such a high incidence of the gene that permitted them to digest milk sugar. They lacked an enzyme called lactase and were thus intolerant of lactose. We think the emergence of the enzyme was a genetic mutation that occurred after the Middle Easterners started using cow's milk as food.

Q: *But if milk is hard to digest for so many people, why do we produce so much and advertise to get people to consume more?*

A: That has to be explained on the basis of economic advantage, not health concerns. Milk, like tobacco and alcohol, is deeply integrated into the culture of Europeans and Americans. These are also the cultures of advertisers, and the producers are more interested in making money from them than from making people healthier. I don't know what economists call it, but there has to be a principle that individual men, and other animals for that matter, naturally do what is most advantageous for them. In fact, it is undoubtedly the basis for the common human, and other animal, motivation of greed. Animals try to maximize their ability to get the necessary good things for life. Thus if there is any universal cause for aggressive behavior, it has to be control of territory. From the simplest creatures to mankind, animals act to claim a particular piece of real estate. The reason is simple, whoever can control a piece of territory can get food and procreate. But that is not all. Many other animals will grab more than they can use if they get the chance and it is not too difficult. Thus predators like coyotes will kill more sheep than they can eat when the rancher provides them. And we know what foxes and weasels do to chickens in the hen house. Also, chimpanzees tried to pack off far more bananas that they could eat when Jane Goodall provided them. In other words, greed is not a special human motivation. Mankind was probably the same during the hunting and gathering stage of existence but things changed considerably when domestication occurred. All of a sudden a person could produce more than he could use without too much trouble and then he could store it. And the natural animal tendency of greed took care of the rest. Thus we see the simple need for territorial control become a means of accumulation. Land becomes something you can get rich with. And animals can be accumulated. A person can build up his herds. It is storage on the hoof. Also of course, grain can be stored and accumulated. So the big three of wealth became land, animals, and grain. And we see this animal drive toward accumulation intensifying in society steadily until we come to an era in our day when there are many homeless people living in the same communities as people with very large mansions and a whole decade (the 1980s) becoming known primarily for its greed. Probably the only way humans could have kept greed in check would have been to keep life simple—in other words to have remained hunters and gatherers—but knowing the nature of culture, I doubt that would have been possible.

Q: *It's all a little depressing. Here we have been told that there has been steady progress in our way of life up to the present and now we are told that life might have been more just when it was simpler.*

A: Unfortunately, I suspect it was, but the fact that we have been taught that things have become steadily better is probably a consequence of ethnocentrism and the idea of progress. Generally, a culture teaches its children that they have the best way and then we in the West adopted wholeheartedly the idea that things were getting better and better for us through time. And since things were getting more complex, how could we advocate a simpler way of life? Anyway, since neither we nor anyone else is voluntarily going back to being hunter-gatherers, we will have to accept the fulfillment of greed as a part of our make-up, although surely we will try to contain it.

Q: *But to go to another kind of human problem, surely we have achieved progress in health, haven't we? Some of the problems the Broadbeaners had are easily taken care of now. I am particularly thinking of infections and diseases of old age.*

A: Well, yes if you concentrate on health rather than quality of life. Thus in childhood and early adulthood the two main causes for illness were accidents and infections, and the Broadbeaners didn't do so well with them. Another cause of illness had to have been the new sedentary style of living. You may remember that the foragers (hunter-gatherers) didn't stay long in one place because they cleaned its wild products out too fast. But once field cultivation, along with keeping animals, came, it paid to stay in one spot permanently, or at least until one's own people were driven out or eliminated. Men learned how to improve their fields which is what made them valuable. But for good health, the nomadic way was probably better because men left their wastes behind. The foragers did not need sewage or garbage collection systems. But by staying put, and producing more, more trash and waste accumulated. Probably the worst was human feces, but other stuff that decomposed could also contribute to the problem. Then too, rats and mice and other creatures found out about the stored food of cultivators. Among the peasant peoples of the world as in India the rat and mouse still consume enormous amounts of grain as well as any other edibles they can find, and spread diseases in the process. So in the sedentary villages of the world the infectious diseases come into their own and are with us still. A special kind of infectious disease is that carried by domestic animals. The "poxes," chicken pox, smallpox, and measles are all derivatives of animal-borne diseases, as well as quite a few less important ones. And it is only recently that the more favored cultures have learned how to prevent these without getting rid of the useful animals.

Men couldn't do much about the diseases of old age like arthritis, or loss of hearing, sight, teeth, or muscle fitness, but then old age was not a stage of life most people got to. So I would suppose they didn't worry about it very much. And the old people that did manage were kept within their societal units and contributed what they could. It's quite a contrast to the modern way when old age is normal, and considered a right by most, but when people are largely separated from their lifetime social units just when they need support most. The "good" of modern times is achieving old age, the "bad" is the non-social status of its members.

Q: *And since we are discussing social status, I noticed that children were incorporated into the way of life quite a lot also. Was that really true?*

A: I'm pretty sure it was, certainly based on the generalization of what modern peasants do. Children seem to have been desired and loved in forager society primarily because of the emotional attachment. But when the domestication revolution came about they could be useful as well. The one special job for older children was to watch over younger ones, but this was true of all other later societies also, at least until education came to be provided outside the home. The business of getting baby-sitters is primarily a recent development. Before the era of formal, universal education, the watcher of small children was either some older person in the home or an older child. But as long as education was a matter of what children learned from their parents, as was true among the Broadbeaners, children learned to help their respective parents, the girls in household tasks and in the fields and the boys with the animals. So we have seen that the little boy became the family herder. Children became quite valuable, a condition which ultimately created one of the major world problems. Peasants learned to have many children, and in the recent past when fewer small children died, peasants became the great populators, a situation mankind still has not learned to deal with.

Q: *The domesticators seemed mainly to eat vegetal products, right?*

A: Yes, and except for the cultures which survived in cold climates, this has been true throughout man's existence, as indeed it was with his ancestors, the monkeys and apes. Most of the apes liked to eat meat, even if only insects and small mammals and birds, but the plant food always was more plentiful and easier to gather. The hunters of the late Paleolithic and their recent counterparts, the Eskimos, were principally meat eaters, but that is because in their climate vegetal food was scarce. Oh yes, I should add the Indians of the Plains after they got the horse. Wild animals were so plentiful that they developed a diet primarily of meat. But when plants and animals were domesticated, there were considerably more plant products; and so except for special occasions, that was what peasants ate. You may remember that the one particular type of animal consumed by the Broadbeaners was the extra males. The animal tamers quickly recognized the fact that although males and females are born in approximately equal numbers, for breeding purposes only one male was needed for many females. So the peasant way was to castrate most of the male mammals and eat them. Male birds, which are more difficult to castrate, were eaten without being castrated. They were still doing that on my grandparents' farm in Indiana when I was a boy. Chickens were left out in open flocks in those days and when chicks grew up, the roosters were caught for Sunday dinner. Old, non-productive females also went into the pot.

Q: *But nowadays we eat meat every day. What about that?*

A: That is relatively recent. We Europeans and Americans live in a favored economy, at least by world standards, and we produce enough meat for ground beef or sausage to be considered very ordinary food. Most of the people of the world, and particularly the peasants, only eat meat on special occasions. We could produce much more food in vegetal form than as meat. Cattle in particular are poor converters of vegetal products, particularly grain, so grain fed beef can be produced only by rich, wasteful cultures.

Q: *But I suppose that is one of the reasons for the Middle Eastern villagers to have developed milk and milk products, no? At least that way one doesn't kill off the producers. And one does get some protein.*

A: Well, yes and no. First the no. It was certainly possible to have developed a diet without eating much beef or milk products. All the East Asians did, even though they had plenty of cows and water buffalo. And nowadays nutritionists consider the traditional diets of the Chinese and Japanese to be second to none and better than many. They consume much fish, pork, chicken, and duck, and many plant products, and especially the products of the soy bean. And the people of the Americas got along without milk products and beef also.

But then the yes. A herding technology which does depend primarily on milk and milk products, especially cheese, does get more protein without eliminating the producers. Also, of course, it causes people to eat more animal fat which nowadays we do not consider to be good. And then there is the lactose problem. So far as I can figure out, the development of milk products as food was a particular occurrence in the Middle East which spread to Europe, East Africa, Central Asia, and India. But when Europe sent its explorers and settlers to all parts of the world, they introduced milk consumption everywhere. The world could have got along fine without milk products if the Chinese had followed up on their fifteenth century explorer, Cheng Ho, in which case soy sauce, rice, and stir fried veggies would have become universal, with perhaps a little pork and fish thrown in.

Q: *I know we have already discussed the woman's role in cultivation, but there was one interesting event we did not review, the fertility ritual.*

A: Ah, you mean the copulation ritual. I understand it is difficult to call it what it is, even though that is already a kind of circumlocution. But just like those Broadbeaners, we have gender-linked vocabularies. As you well know, there is a four letter word for copulation in English, one not to be used in formal social situations where both women and men are present.

Q: *Right, even though we are now supposed to be in the era of the sexual revolution when people can call a spade a spade.*

A: Yes, though obviously there are still limits. The male vocabulary (the four letter words) is still regarded as obscene by guardians of morality. In any case I feel more comfortable using the word copulation in these circumstances and I suspect you do also. But what about the ritual, what do you want to discuss?

Q: *Well, according to the account, it seems that mankind functioned with superstitions regarding cultivation, and in this case particularly the women. Is that what the event meant?*

A: Yes, but with a few clarifications. In the fist place, we anthropologists are always reluctant to use the word superstition, since ordinarily it is merely some supernatural belief of another people with which we do not agree. To be perfectly honest, a person from another culture could easily interpret the ritual of taking a wafer and wine as the body and blood of Jesus as a superstition. But since Christians believe that particular tradition, they consider it a legitimate belief. We in anthropology have found it best to accept supernatural beliefs of all kinds of people as legitimate.

And yes, the women would have been involved more than the men, but simply because they were more concerned with cultivation. However, in this case they needed male participation.

Q: *But my question is, is there any evidence that people really did such a thing?*

A: Let me answer that indirectly, the usual tactic of an academic. First, supernaturalism has always been used for helping solve problems in this life. And the primary problem of all living things is to get food. You may remember that the shaman artist and dancer in the Wiseman narrative were putting the paintings on the wall in order to make the game animals more abundant. And between then and the time of the Broadbeaners there was other evidence of the use of supernaturalism to help get food. There were those Venus figures found in various places in Europe, female figurines with exaggerated female characteristics and tiny heads and no hands or feet. They were thought to represent the fertility principle as embodied in the female form. No one knows how they were used exactly, but it seems to be a reasonable supposition that they were used to promote growth. Then too, pottery sometimes had decorations which suggested fertility. And the act of copulation for this purpose was described among peasants at a later period of history in the famous collection of magic, *The Golden Bough*, by Sir James Frazer. This description fascinated me when I was a young man starting my anthropological studies. It was like other young men or boys studying the anatomy drawings of medical books to learn about sex. Anyway, since such a ritual had to take place in a society of cultivators and since no one really knows when it started, I took the liberty of starting it with the Broadbeaners.

Q: *Pretty wild stuff. But then anthropology does have quite a bit of such. But let me go on to another matter, fighting exemplified by the Broadbeaners against the Foggy Bottomers. Is this the beginning of warfare?*

A: I don't know that there was an absolute beginning. Animals have resorted to violence against one another almost from the beginning of life and the overall most important reason has been to control territory. And though one can go back much further, I will in this instance cite only the chimpanzees as reported by the queen mother of chimpanzee studies, Jane Goodall. And like other ethologists, observers who study creatures in their natural environment or society, she advocated the way of her "people" as ideal. She was particularly pleased that they did not seem to inflict violence on one another. But as her studies lengthened, she discovered that they did use violence, especially to control territory. One of the bands she was observing literally wiped out a neighboring band. To her great credit, she reported this occurrence and then, somewhat sadly it seemed to me, she accepted the fact that the chimpanzees were just like us.

When anthropologists described the tribal cultures of the world, they had to include the fact that, except for a very few exceptions, most peoples use violence either to take someone else's territory or to keep others from taking theirs. And history certainly tells us that civilized people were no different except that they did it on a larger scale. The Greeks, the founders of civilization for the Europeans, were up to their eyeballs in bashing and killing until they were conquered by the Romans. The primary ethic which controlled Roman culture was warfare and of course their inheritors, the Europeans, carried it on with a vengeance. Probably the most massive use of force the world had seen was the Euro-conquest of most of the rest of the world after 1492. The scale seems to have become larger until the Euros evolved massive conflicts known as world wars, and this despite the fact that they always advocated peace and claimed one of their deities was "the prince of peace." So to answer your question, no, the territorial conflict of the Broadbeaners could not have been the beginning of warfare but it probably was a broadening, primarily because of the change from foraging to cultivation. It had become more worthwhile to defend or take over land. But as we will see in future chapters, the scale and intensity keeps increasing.

Q: *A couple of final questions. There seemed to be an increase in trade too, right?*

A: Yes, people were developing specialties which they traded with one another on a barter basis. Real money had not yet been invented. Real trade begins in the cultivation era because people were producing a surplus. And as time went on, the surplus continued to increase, along with trade, until we come to our day when the whole world is one giant market.

Q: *And the language, I presume, was well developed even though they had no writing system.*

A: Well, we don't' know what it was because there was no writing, though we assume it was fully developed. As I'm sure I mentioned before, after the Euros spread throughout the world, linguists discovered that all peoples, no matter how primitive their technology, had perfectly functioning spoken languages.

Q: *With regard to their technology you say they were still using stone tools, although now both polished and chipped.*

A: This period is called the Neolithic, which means the New Stone Age. People continued to chip stone as the earlier hunters had but now they had learned to rub certain kinds of stones against one another and make from these anything from an ax to a grinding stone for making flour. Their tools were technically quite a bit better but they still had to wait a few thousand years for the age of metals.

Q: *And last, their housing. The houses seemed to be more substantial than those of the foragers, but I suppose that is reasonable since they stayed in them much longer, right?*

A: Correct. Houses were made of stone or clay or some version of adobe, and though the houses of the ordinary men were not so spacious, this was the construction basis of the monumental architecture to come.

And so I suggest that we go on to the next chapter when the basic cultivators came down to the valleys and built the first cities—to the Urban Revolution.

5

The City

Ammul

In the land between the rivers, called Ir, a scribe worked in close quarters. Stucco covered the walls of the room, except in one corner where it had flaked off, exposing the bricks underneath. An opening in the top of the room and two uncovered windows on the sides brought in air and light. The single wood doorway stood partly closed. Through the windows on both sides, one could see neighboring buildings a few feet distant.

The scribe squatted in front of a clay tablet, punching in the wood stylus periodically, until the clay where he was working became too dry; then he would swirl the reed brush around in the water pot, dab it in the little mound of fresh clay, and brush it on the line which had not been marked. He was copying another tablet which had come in a couple of days before from North County where they were still using some of the old-fashioned characters. It was a tally of the barley and wheat stored and the number of animals being kept, sent to him by the tax collector. The chief priest was anxious to get the tally from all the counties up to date since there was an expeditionary force in preparation and the troops were always sent off with some provisions, to keep them going until they could loot a foreign place.

The scribe was a man of middle years, dressed in a loincloth and knee-length skirt made of linen. Over one shoulder he wore a blue cloth strip which was tucked in at his waist. He wore sandals, a copper necklace with a silver nugget, and a lapis lazuli earring. He had a full beard of curly black hair.

The apprentice boy, Maddas, came into the room carrying a fresh jar of water which he put down next to the older one. The boy was about thirteen, and wore a knee-length skirt, but no jewelry or sandals.

"Come here," Ammul said, pointing to the place beside him. "I want you to see what the old characters were like and I also want to have you practice some of the new ones."

The boy squatted next to the master. "Now look at that character," Ammul said. "It looks like the head of an ox with the horns, doesn't it?"

In a low, careful voice, the boy answered, "It does."

"Well in the old days, most of the characters looked like something that really was. But they changed and after a while you couldn't recognize the thing. But you knew which combination of marks represented which thing, say an ox, a sheep, or goat, like the things that are counted on the tallies from the outer counties. That's what real punching is. And that's what you will learn before you are finished here. And then you can be a scribe too."

The boy made no move until Ammul told him, "Now get yourself a tablet and a stylus and you can practice doing what I am doing."

Maddas silently did as he was told and settled down next to the scribe. The tablet was made of baked clay. The boy got another brush and dipped it into the water, then swabbed his tablet to put a thin layer of liquid clay on it.

"All right," Ammul said. "You can start here by punching in the character for oxen. Just the modern one, not the country one."

The boy laboriously pressed his stylus into the wet clay, character after character. He was slow but had practiced enough to make some headway. Ammul continued his work as he kept a monologue going. "You will undoubtedly note that what we are doing is keeping track of the amount of food available in the provinces. That's why we keep listing the numbers of sheep, goats, cattle, and the amounts of grain. Do you know why we do that?"

The boy kept his eyes glued on his work, punching the marks in steadily. "I guess to know how much we have."

"Yes, that's true, but why do we want to know? You know this tablet is from North County, don't you?"

"No master, I didn't know exactly. But now I do."

"Well take it from me it is. And those other tablets are from other places." Ammul waved his arm to indicate the rows of tablets with writing on them. "And the reason we keep track is because the supreme Priest-King needs to know so he can get the provisions when he needs them. That's why he keeps hundreds of scribes working. All the numbers on these tablets will be added up and the master tablets will be taken to the palace for His Royal Holiness. Just remember that there wouldn't be much use for a scribe if good tallies weren't made."

The boy copied the character for cattle and then the number, 1,080. Ammul stopped him. "There's another thing—look at that number. Do you think that's correct? Do you think they have that many cattle in North County?"

"I guess so. It says so, doesn't it?"

"Ha!" The scribe laughed. "That's another thing you had better learn, and early. Otherwise people will think you are a peasant. Writing doesn't prove anything except that it's something the writer wants you to believe. The people who don't know how to make and read writing think it's almost magic. Why I heard there is a district on the other side of the Euphrates, one which was settled by the father of His Royal Holiness, Mishaq, where, when someone got very sick, they would use for medicine the essence of a writing tablet. They would take a part of the clay tablet that had been written on and break it up, then grind it into a powder and mix it with boiling water. The drink would then be given to the sick person. Now do you believe that makes any sense?"

The boy wondered but day after day he was told so many strange and wondrous things, and the scribe would not tolerate signs of disbelief, so he always agreed. He said, "It must be so."

But Ammul was far from finished. He was intent on getting his message across. After all, that was the reason scribes and men of other privileged occupations used apprentices, to give them the same beliefs they had. He said, "Well, I can tell you that drinking powdered clay in hot water is not going to cure anyone's leprosy or fever. Writing is not magic or supernatural in any way. It is something that some privileged men do and which is very useful for controlling the workers, particularly the farmers, but that is all. It's not that I'm against the idea that the peasants and other workers think writing is magic. In fact, it may be a good idea. But we city people of the upper classes have to know what it is. And that number of cattle, 1,080, may be correct or it may not. I always suspect that the numbers of goods from the provinces is generally low. The peasants know that the levy is based on the numbers they report. So it is natural for them to under-report. Of course, the local scribe who knows that Central is always looking for high numbers may over-report, but even so I think the under-report of the peasants is generally more than the over-report of the local scribes. And besides it is easier to get in trouble with the minister of His Royal Holiness by over-reporting than by under-reporting. The ministers think they've gained something when there is more than reported."

In shifting his weight, Maddas bumped into another tablet which had been propped up to dry and which fell, breaking off a corner. The master was on him in a flash, cuffing him on the side of the head.

"Now look what you did. I spend all this time translating bumpkin writing and teaching a stupid boy at the same time, and he breaks my work as fast as I make it."

The boy cowered, rubbing his head where the blow had landed. He reached over and picked up the broken piece. The master stood up.

"Well, I just can't stay here all day, watching my work going to pieces. I'm going out to the plaza. Maybe there will be someone there who needs some writing. In the meantime just for your clumsiness, you can copy that tablet you broke. Think you can do that without making a mess?"

Without looking up, the boy answered, "Yes, master."

Ammul got three small blank tablets, a stylus, and a potful of paste, wiped his sweating forehead with a piece of cloth he had tucked into his skirt, and went out through the doorway. The heat poured over him like liquid. It was the middle of the hot, dry season. He came out of his alleyway onto a larger street where people and animals moved among the carts. Donkey and oxcarts carried grain and other food supplies and goods. Some carts were loaded with bricks, others with pottery and basketry, others with grain or animals. Pedestrians moved alongside them and in between. Ammul walked around a cart which was full of pigs going to the slaughterhouse.

People of the lower class, workers and farmers, saluted him and stepped out of his way. From time to time he raised his hand slightly, but most often he ignored them. He was of the privileged class and this was his due. It wasn't like the deference the priests and royalty received, but still a scribe was an important person.

Ammul greeted most of the shop-owners along the way. After all, he had lived in this neighborhood all his life. He stopped at a jeweler's shop and workplace, and watched the jeweler hammer a piece of gold, spreading it by making it thinner. The jeweler looked up from his work and Ammul spoke, "May his Royal Holiness look down on you with beneficence."

"And on you also, estimable scribe. And what may this lowly one do for you?"

Though considered of lower status, the jeweler was still an artisan of some merit and much of the deference in his speech forms was flourish. In a society where people were very precisely graded by status, many practiced the custom of speaking up to others, often even more than was required. It was a little insurance for not alienating the more powerful, even those only a grade higher.

The scribe was pleased that the jeweler did not launch into a long preliminary discussion because he had other things to do. He said, "I was wondering what I would have to pay for a decent pair of earrings, say of turquoise or some other precious stone."

"For a man or a woman?"

"A woman." There was no need for Ammul to tell the jeweler that the earrings were not for his wife but rather for a young woman who worked in the priest-king's palace. Ammul had met her once when he had gone to the palace to deliver some accounting tablets and he had been visiting her in her quarters about once a week since. He would be seeing her again the next day.

The jeweler rummaged around in a basket, saying, "There was a decent pair that a military officer brought in the other day, a turquoise pair, one which he had brought back from his last expedition."

The military, and particularly the officers, were usually well stocked with jewelry and other precious goods they could trade when they came back from expeditions. Everyone knew that one of the first things they did when they conquered a new town was to loot it for tradables, often even before they performed the executions. They would trade them for different things they needed to support their lifestyle. Ultimately most such goods came into the hands of the local jewelers who would refashion them or simply trade them at a profit to citizens of the middle class.

"Ah, here they are," the jeweler held up the earrings. "Nice pieces in the style of the western tribes, though you might like to have them reset. The setting now is just plain copper. If it isn't cleaned often, it will become green."

Ammul took the earrings, momentarily wondering what kind of barbarian woman's ear they had been stuck in and how they had been removed. Sometimes the advance troops, in their anxiety to get as much as possible before the rear troops arrived, tore valuables from the conquered without bothering to kill them first. But Ammul did not dwell much on the idea of bloody earlobes since the conquered people were not civilized anyway, better than animals, perhaps, but only just. Most of them didn't even have writing systems.

He fingered the earrings a bit and said, "And what is the price?"

The jeweler said, "I think it would probably come to ten sacks of barley."

"No, I would pay in coins." Ammul had almost given up paying in barley or other grain. He did accept it sometimes since many people who wanted letters written had little else to pay with. But it was a pain to keep in storage since the rats were invariably attracted. And then it had to be transported for payment. Coins were a real improvement, as long as Central kept up with demand and had enough made.

"That's better for me also," the jeweler agreed. "But I have another idea. I need a couple of letter tablets made, lists of my services, of the kind of jewelry I can make, to send off to other towns for more business. And though I can use the stylus, my style isn't as good as that of a fully-experienced scribe. Maybe we can make a deal. I'll fix the earrings and you can make the tablets. How does that sound, well-born sir?"

When men wished to use a little flattery for others of middle rank, they often used the term well-born, frequently when they had little knowledge of its truth. Generally speaking, those of privileged occupations did come from privileged families, and they were almost always natives of the realm. Moreover, it never hurt to use a little oil to make a bargain. Since Ammul was on the lookout for some work himself, this would kill a couple of birds.

"It sounds good."

Ammul felt pleased when he stepped out on the street again, since he had made what seemed to be a decent deal. He felt so good in fact that he didn't even get angry when he stepped into the edge of a pile of manure. He just scraped it off and washed away the stain at a ditch that ran alongside the road. Then he continued on, humming a little tune, and thinking about the pleasure he would have with

Pomegranate the next time. After he had presented the earrings to her, she would be willing to do anything. And she would have a very cold jar of barley beer and many sesame crackers of the kind the palace baker made so well.

Ammul was so preoccupied with his fantasy that he did not even notice that his friend Latu had just caught up with him. Latu was also a scribe. In fact they had been apprentices to the same master and often told stories about him. The old master had been particularly gaseous, cutting farts frequently, no matter what the occasion. It seemed that whenever he squatted, he couldn't help himself. Latu put his hand on Ammul's shoulder, making the other scribe jump. Latu laughed, "Ay, old crock, are you nervous? Did you think the police of His Royal Holiness were after you? You must feel guilty."

Ammul's face mellowed when he turned and saw who it was. This was the man he had shared many an experience with, the man from whom he did not have to hide secrets. He said, "Ah, my friend, it is good to see you. And you can hardly imagine what I was thinking of."

"I had noticed you were humming a little tune, so it must have been good thoughts."

"Yes, it was. I was thinking of drinking barley beer and eating sesame crackers with my little Pomegranate before fucking her. Oh, yes, this was just after I had given her a present of turquoise earrings."

Latu put his arm across Ammul's back in camaraderie. "I could have guessed that my lecherous friend would be thinking about women. Is this a new one? I don't think you told me about her before."

A crowd was gathering at the next corner, obviously to see what was crossing the street. Already the sound of soldiers' voices could be heard yelling. The two men were heading that way, so they hurried. Ammul spoke quickly.

"Let's see what's going on. I'll tell you about Pomegranate afterwards."

Though some people got out of their way, the crowd was dense enough that the two had to push and elbow through many to get to the front. A line of prisoners, their hands tied behind their backs, their necks attached to a line from each to the next, was being marched up the street as far as could be seen, the crowd pressing in on both sides. Soldiers with shields and spears were marching at intervals on both sides of the line. In the front there were men, mostly in their early and middle years, wearing nothing but bedraggled and torn loincloths. They were dusty and sweating, covered with dried mud. Many had wounds, and all had deadened eyes. Whenever one stumbled, a soldier would yell at him, but if that didn't produce results, the soldier would prick him with a spear. The prisoners all had dark copper skins, thoroughly sunburned and peeling in places. Their hair was dark black and curly, like that of the natives. In fact, they did not look much different, except that they had obviously been badly treated. Not that this bothered the two men since they knew the bound men were just slaves.

Ammul spoke first. "You know who these people are, don't you?"

"Well, they look like westerners, I suppose from the desert tribes."

"You mean nomads, wanderers?"

"Sure, they look pretty dirty and thoroughly burned by the sun. The army probably caught them out herding sheep and goats somewhere."

"Well, that's not very likely. Although I'm sure the army would grab bedouins if they came across them, the fact is that those people are always wandering. They are not easy to catch. And besides there aren't that many. No, it pays to head for fixed settlements, even if the people are not that much more civilized than the bedouins. At least there are more of them and since they stay in one place, they are easier to capture. And these, my friend, are people called Hinaanites. They live over between the great lakes, Sweetwater and Salt. They're only a little more highly developed than bedouins but they do live in small towns."

Latu said, "I think I've heard of them. Though it is impossible to be sure since there are so many barbarian tribes around, in all directions. But it doesn't matter much, as long as they can be made to work and don't create too much trouble trying to escape. Why, do you know something about them?"

One of the men was in particularly bad condition, and was continually falling. The man behind him would help him up and he would struggle several steps farther, then fall again. A guard kept close by, yelling at the man whenever he fell and jabbing him with a spear. The guard suddenly stepped forward and cut the rope with his bronze knife. When the man fell again, the guard reached down and with two slashes cut the man's tendons at the ankle. The man groaned but made no attempt to move. The guard pulled him quickly to one side and left him lying there, knowing he couldn't walk any further. One of the execution detail that followed at the end of the procession would kill him later.

"There's one who won't do any work," Ammul said. "Sometimes one wonders if it is worth all that work to bring in barbarian prisoners. Might be better off to get the local peasants to do the work, even if one had to pay them a smidgeon. But that is the custom of the great cities—to capture barbarians to work on civil projects.

"Anyway, what I was going to tell you about these people, the Hinaanites, is that they claim they are something special. They even claim they are the perpetual owners of their territory, which they call "the promised land." Can you believe that, a tribe of crude barbarians, slightly better than bedouin wanderers, think they are something exceptional? Why I don't believe they even have a writing system."

Latu laughed, "It's amazing the conceits some peoples can develop, even barbarians. At least this is some fresh muscle to work on local projects. You know that slaves die so fast.

"There are some men who are satisfied with slave girls. But as for me, I need something with a little more spirit, not someone who cowers every time you come into the room. But by the size of her breasts, that woman would make a good wet-nurse."

To get the milk to flow, wet nurses had to have babies of their own, and the practice in Ir was to dispose of the natural babies of slaves so the milk could be used for babies of rich women who either did not have enough milk or did not want to nurse. Some of the very kind-hearted would let the wet nurse keep her own baby and nurse it along with a baby of the privileged. But that required a woman who had a very large amount of milk. Also it was understood that her child would be a slave when it grew up.

Latu said, "My friend, the sight of these hot and weary slaves and the heat of the day itself has made for me a thirst you wouldn't believe. I suggest we wet the whistle with a fermented drink. And then we can both be off to our own affairs. I am sure you have important plans. It's not far to Otul's drink shop. How about it?"

Ammul was still intent to get another client or two for a letter tablet and the plaza was yet another thirty minutes' walk. He said, "I don't know old buddy, I'm on my way to pick up a letter or two and I can't be gone too long. My little apprentice is such a klutz, he might break many tablets. And if a client came to the workroom, he would probably scare him away."

Latu squeezed his friend across the shoulders.

"Come on now, old buddy, I know what a workaholic you are, intent on building up a family fortune. But you can't turn your old friends down. Come on down to Otul's and quaff a couple. He's got something new, not the same old barley beer but now the fermented juice of the grape."

Mattuz

The field was near enough to the great river that you could get a good view of it from any slight rise in the terrain even though the countryside was mostly flat. You could see boats with oars and sails on the river until they faded in the haze of distance. You could make out a ziggurat-temple to the south right on the river. This was one of the temples that had been built by the priest-kings during the current dynasty. His Royal Holiness boasted that there was no place in the king's land from which a temple could not be seen. They were circular brick structures three to four stories high, built in levels which became smaller as one ascended the winding stairway to the top. They were the only structures which stood above the flatness.

A road ran parallel to the river, on which pedestrians, oxcarts, and driven animals passed. Peasant women carried jars of water exquisitely balanced on their heads. Cart drivers tried to get their oxen to move faster, jabbing the animals in the anus with a stick. It was hard to tell which were more tired, the oxen or the men. Most of the full carts were heading toward the city.

Beginning at the river's edge, the land was divided into sections, most of them green with crops; it was the height of the growing season. Canals ran between fields. In some of the fields farmers worked, weeding, spreading water, or plowing. Wheat would be planted late in the fall, to germinate and grow slowly during the winter rainy season and to complete its growth with the setting of grain in the spring. Mattuz was plowing a dry field in which to plant wheat. His plow was made from a sapling that had been seasoned and pointed and which had a crossbar onto which the ox was attached with a simple leather harness. Saplings had to be imported to the village from the hills beyond since no trees except palms grew on the river plain. The cut trees and other lumber were brought to the carter, who, in addition to making oxcarts, made the farming tools. Mattuz had to pay for his tools with barley or wheat.

He walked tiredly behind the ox, exerting the minimum force on the handle of the plow to keep it in place and lightly churning the dry surface soil. One couldn't bear down too hard because if the point went to deep, the ox couldn't pull it. A little cloud of dust followed the plow. Mattuz' bare feet were covered with dust, almost up to his knees. He wore only a tattered loincloth and a dirty cloth hanging loosely around his neck, with which he would periodically wipe the sweat from his face. He was burned by the sun as dark as the slaves the scribes had seen.

The river silt made good soil, and with a proper amount of water and good seeds, it would produce a good crop, not that it made that much difference since the part he could keep for the family was so small. There were so many levies, each time the district officers figured out something new. There was one part for His Royal Holiness, then one part for the priests of the local ziggurat, then one part for a new road, then another part for the army. It made Mattuz' head swim and since he didn't read, he always felt that the district scribes were always cheating him.

When he turned to go back he saw Rinani coming, carrying the lunch basket on her head. She did not have the child with her, so he knew she had left it with her sister. They exchanged watching children, or sometimes Rinani's ten year old daughter would take over. Mattuz used his waning energy to move a little faster toward the palm tree at the end of the field where he would sit in the shade. Even the ox moved faster, knowing it would at least get water and a little rest, though it would have to wait for food until evening. They headed straight toward the single tree that bordered the field.

Rinani was already squatting when he got there, the basket set in the shady spot which, though it wasn't large, it was enough for two people to get out of the sun. She had brought along a pottery cup which she had already filled with water from the canal alongside. She handed it to him and he drank fully, then reached into the basket for wheat bread. Because it had more gluten in it, it stuck together better and was preferable to barley bread. It was thick-flat, the way he liked it. She put a bowl of cooked root vegetables on the cloth she had spread and alongside it a mound of roasted locusts. He reached immediately for the crisp baked insects and quickly popped one in his mouth. The locusts, with their roasted crunchiness, were among his favorite foods. After eating several he took a big pinch of salt and mixed it into the vegetable stew, then took pinches of the mixture, wrapped in torn pieces of the flat bread. After coming back to the locusts and eating several more, the plowman said with satisfaction, "Ay, for the gifts of Earth Mother. How could she make the great destroyer of the seed crops into such a delicious morsel?"

Every few years, the locusts would come out of the soil in incredible numbers and although everyone worked to their utmost to stop the ravenous horde, there were still invariably great losses and frequently famines. There were such numbers of the indefatigably chewing insects that the farmers quit eating them. But afterwards, when the last of the sky-darkening creatures disappeared and the people of the village got another crop or two, they returned to the feast. Perhaps he liked beef or pork better, but they were too expensive. Peasants like him could afford to eat those only on special ritual or social occasions. He sold almost all he raised. But he could eat locusts any time of the year if there were enough to gather. He finished the dried locusts, savoring each crispy bite. Then he stretched out in the shade. savoring what little breeze there was. She munched on some of the bread that he had left. She was used to eating after the men.

"Don't eat all of that," he said. "I will eat it in mid-afternoon when I get tired." She was just putting a piece in her mouth, but stopped and put it back in the basket.

"I didn't mean what you had already started on. You might as well eat that since you started, just save me the rest." He put his head down for a moment, then raised it in renewed irritation.

"By the Spirit of the Great River, woman, I'd think you would have figured out something by now. A man needs some little sustenance to keep going all day. Plowing up this dry ground is hard work."

"I'm sorry, master," Rinani said. "It was a long walk out here and I was a little hungry. I thought you wouldn't mind if I took a little."

Mattuz tried to parody her tone of voice, though making it into more of a whine than it was. "You thought, you thought. That'll be the day when a woman starts thinking. You just keep to your work and forget about thinking. I'll do that for the family. Thinking is the responsibility of men, not women. And you just don't forget that."

Though Rinani was as good as most farmers' wives, lately Mattuz could get very irritated with her. Her brideprice hadn't been very high, but now she had produced two girls and no boys. And girls always went away to their husband's families and were lost as workers. He already had to pay a neighboring boy for taking the animals out to pasture.

She bowed her head while continuing to wrap the lunch leavings. "Yes, master."

He was stirred up by this time and this irritated him more since he had counted on a little nap.

"Did the district officer come this morning?"

"Yes, master, he came with a scribe who was carrying a tablet." She quickly added, "They came in a donkey cart."

"Ha! I can see them, the cheating dogs. The district officer walking ahead officiously, rapping on things with his cane or twirling around his badge of office as if he owned everything. And he goes snooping into everything, but especially the grain bins and the animal stockades. It's a good thing I had the boy take out the goats and sheep today."

She whimpered, "He asked me so many questions. And whenever I would tell him anything, he would turn and ask the scribe, who would inspect his tablet. Oh, it was so frightening. I don't know why you didn't stay at home, master. You could answer the questions so much better than I."

He raised up to a full sitting position.

"I hope you didn't tell him anything important. You didn't tell him how many goats and sheep we had, did you?"

"I couldn't help it, master," she whined. "They had the tablet and whenever I would tell them anything, the district officer would say to the scribe, 'And what does it say?'"

He struck her on the cheek.

"Oh, woman, I told you not to tell them."

"I had to, they had the tablet and it had the numbers on it," she wailed. "Oh, master, you should have stayed and done it."

He raised his hand again but then reconsidered and lowered it. What was the use, a man couldn't expect any more than that from a woman. He put his head on his hand.

"Oh, it will cost us. I know they will raise the amount of barley and wheat I'll have to pay. They might even take a field away."

"Oh, woe is me," she wailed. "I knew you should have stayed at home master."

The fields all belongs to His Royal Holiness in principle, though they were allotted to the farmers on a rental basis for indeterminate periods. As long as each farmer turned in the prescribed amount, he got to keep his fields, but if the allotment for Central was not met, fields could be taken away. Theoretically, a man could end up with nothing, though this rarely actually happened. He could be cut down, though, until the family was barely managing. This caused the farmers to work as hard as possible.

Mattuz growled, "Well, what is done is done. Nothing to do about that now. We can only hope the district officer won't believe you knew, or that you weren't telling the truth. To change the subject, how's the supply of beer? You remember that Aksaan and some others are coming over tonight, don't you? And I'm sure they will be thirsty. And believe me, woman, it is a poor beginning for wedding arrangements not to have enough beer."

"Yes, master, I used the last of last year's harvest to make a new jar with. It is well fermented now. You and the other gentlemen should be pleased."

"Well, we'll see about that. Just so long as you have done your job properly."

Making beer was one of the important responsibilities of the country wife, a skill which was taught to the girls early. Rinani had a good reputation for that and other wifely skills when their marriage had been arranged. Mattuz said, "I pray, man's support, that you have well started the daughter in the skill—because I feel sure that Aksaan or one of his people will ask about it."

"Oh, yes, master, older daughter, Seenaran, could do up a batch by herself now. She is indeed a smart girl and will make a good wife someday."

"Let us hope so, since with all our other problems, having two daughters to marry off could send all of us into bondage.

Rinani

The farmer's wife hurried toward the main road which was marked by a little cloud of dust from the feet of passers-by. She had little enough time to accomplish both the tasks she had set for herself and get back in time to oversee the making of the evening's gruel. Once she was on the road she still had two hours' walk to the temple. A group of soldiers on leave passed, and one called to her, "Hey good looking, what's in the basket?"

She was still carrying the basket she had brought the food in. She pulled the head cloth around to cover her face and walked faster. Men came by driving cattle, and boys herding goats or sheep. This made her feel worse because it made her think of her fault in telling the district officer the number of animals they had. She had heard so often how careful peasants had to be never to tell the truth to the authorities and then Mattuz had been so explicit in explaining what to say before he left. She knew they would expect nothing from her, that they would think a mere woman wouldn't be worth the effort, or that she would not even talk to them. But what could she have done, they had to know they could get some information from her. And that writing was so frightening. To know that they had a record already fixed. She worried that they would come back now when Mattuz was there and insist on taking some of the animals or inflict some other kind of punishment. Her thoughts became more gloomy all the time. So she was happy when she caught up to a group of women. One of them, a woman in her middle years, spoke first.

"Ay, sister, have you come a long way?"

"I'm from Riverbend Village and I'm on my way to Greatrock Temple. Do you know how far it is?"

"It's only about an hour and a half. You can go with us, we are going there, too."

Another woman spoke. "I suppose you have something special to petition for." She made a sound that was half sigh, half groan. "God knows there have been enough things for which a woman needs help. Have you been there before?"

Rinani felt better. The talk would make the time pass faster, and she might even find out something.

"No, of course I've heard of it, but I've never come before. We have a temple of our own in Riverbend, but most people go there just for ordinary needs. Everybody has heard about Greatrock Temple and how close the Spirits are to it and how often the petitions are granted."

"Ha," the first woman said. "I should hope so, but so far it hasn't done me any good."

The second woman spoke then. "I don't know why you are going again then. If it didn't work before, how is it going to work now?"

A loud yell came from an oxcart driver.

"Ay, you cackling females, move out of the middle of the road. How do you think a man will get his work done?"

The group moved to one side without pausing in their conversation. Rinani said to the first woman, "And what, neighbor, was the petition?"

"Ay, misery, it was the child, the only boy, who was born without sight. And now that he gets older and should have arrangements made, how can it be done? Who will take a blind man into the family?" She sighed again. "To tell the truth, it's a miracle the boy is still alive. My husband thought we shouldn't keep him when it was clear that he would never see. But I insisted and I've taken care of him these last ten years. And for what? He'll probably end up being a beggar in front of the temples."

Another woman spoke. "Ay, it's sad. We work so hard to bear children and keep our families going and what good does it do? First the birth is so hard, and many women don't live through it. And when the child comes out, one can never know if it will be whole or not. And then the mother has to worry if there is enough to feed the infant. And even if there is, it might be another girl which will provoke endless quarrels with the husband. And then the child may never live through the first few years. And after that is the expense of the wedding. One wonders sometimes why the gods have created such conditions. Ay, such misery!"

Although Rinani knew there was truth to most of the things the woman said, she thought she was particularly gloomy. Rinani couldn't believe life was as hard as that, even though she herself was on her way to try to solve a family problem. The first woman interrupted her thoughts.

"Why neighbor, I would wager that you are in the same boat as the rest of us with family problems of your own."

"Well, yes," Rinani admitted. "But I thought that was the main reason women went to Greatrock Temple, that the priests there were particularly good at helping in family matters. I thought that was why women would walk there from distant villages."

"Yes, so they say," another woman said. "That it would only be true. And I must admit that I don't have that much faith in all this temple business. It seems to me that it may be just another way for the priests to get rich."

"Then why did you come?" the first woman asked.

"What else can a body do, just let nature take its course?"

A trading caravan materialized, a group of men cracking whips over heavily loaded donkeys.

"Where do you think they're going?" the second woman asked.

"Probably over to Lashag," replied the first. "There are almost always caravans going that way. They say business is very good there. They say the brother of His Royal Holiness takes much less in taxes, particularly from businessmen."

Lashag was a city on the other side of the Euphrates which had got a reputation for the leniency of the ministry of taxation. The city had been conquered by the army of His Royal Holiness, who had installed his brother as the ruler. It turned out, however, that the brother levied much lower tariffs, which was attracting goods from other cities.

The second woman said, "My husband says that if things don't improve, that if His Royal Holiness doesn't cut back on the taxes, we may all go there. He says they need farmers there also, but the farmers get to keep more of what they produce."

One of the donkeys was so heavily loaded that it staggered just to stay on its feet. Suddenly it stopped. The driver turned around and, walking behind the animal, struck it several times with his whip. The animal dropped and was almost immediately pinned down by the load. The driver beat the donkey even more, but the animal had plainly given up, and simply bowed its head farther and farther down. The man finally tired of beating the animal and began to untie the straps. Three other drivers helped to load the bags from the downed donkey to one of the others.

The group of women stood to one side, watching the event. When the remaining donkeys were again loaded, one of the drivers looked at them and said, "Hey mothers, why don't you go with us? Where could you be going that's so interesting? If you went with us, you could see and do many things." He winked and looked down. "You know what I mean."

A couple of the women giggled, but the others started to move away.

"Don't go, mothers. Come see new sights and have some fun." He paused, and then added, "And find out how donkey drivers do it."

"Come on, let's go," the second woman urged. "Who wants to stand here and listen to the dumb remarks of donkey drivers."

The group reassembled and began their trip down the road again. Rinani found herself next to the second woman, who asked, "And what, dear, are you asking for?"

"My problem is that I have two children and they are both girls. I know that is the reason my husband is angry all the time. You know a farmer's wife has to have boys or the husbands will not be happy. How else can the land rights be passed on?"

"I know, I know. It's a real problem. Sometimes it's hard to treat boys and girls equally. After all, the girls always go away when they get married. And without a son in the house in old age, who is there to take care of you? I'm lucky in that my first birth was a boy. A woman can relax for a little while when that happens. But of course one isn't enough. One never knows when a young one will get sick and die. There are so many afflictions for the young."

"Anyway," Rinani continued, "I was told by so many that Greatrock Shrine was the best place to go for boy babies. Isn't that true?"

"That is commonly believed, no doubt about that. And we will see soon."

They could see Greatrock Temple from a distance down the road. It was one of the only things that stuck up from the plain other than the ziggurats. Unlike the villages they passed, the rock and temple stood by themselves on the dusty plain. From a distance it looked like a column rounded on top, perhaps half the height of a ziggurat. Alongside was a temple building. It was unique in that rocks were practically non-existent on the river plain. The silt covered the plain in years of flood, burying whatever rocks might have once been.

"It looks so strange," Rinani said, "so different from all the other land around it, almost as if it had been brought there. Do you know anything about the history of the rock?"

"Ay, there are many stories," the second woman said. "I have heard that the column was created by the Great Earth Goddess in honor of her son, to perpetuate the race. Others say it was put there by her in honor of her husband. Still others say it was brought to the place by the founder of the earliest dynasty, floated to the spot from the mountains and then dragged into place by slaves. The priests say that it came floating down from the sky, a gift of the spirit founder of the dynasty, Life-Giver."

"So that's why it looks like a great rock penis."

"I suppose so, since the priests and most everyone else thinks that human life is directly caused by the male drive and enhanced by continuous successive thrusts in the months after the baby is started. It seems to me that the female must have more to do with it than is generally believed, but it must be admitted that women and animals who don't have sex with males don't have babies."

"But of course there has to be something more to it than just the act of intercourse," the first woman said. "After all, plenty of women have sex but don't get pregnant. There are two of our group who have no children, even though they have been married for several years. In fact, the temple must depend primarily on childless wives. Oh, there are other reasons for coming, but I would guess the primary one is to have a child."

They were approaching the structure and could now see several other women headed in the same direction. Rinani said, "Anyway, it's good we have a place like this to go, and for many kinds of pregnancies, including boy babies. Life for many wives without boys is made into a living hell, both by the husband and the mother-in-law."

"I know, I know," the second woman said. "I shall make part of my offering to your cause too."

As they approached the building next to the column, Rinani noticed that there were no men to be seen. She said, "Don't men ever come here?"

"They say very rarely," the second woman answered. "After all, the temple is primarily dedicated to the female need for pregnancy. The men of course believe they have done their duty simply by having sex with the women; and if she doesn't get pregnant, she has to do something about it." Then she added, "Oh, yes, I hear there are the men-men who come sometimes, certainly not for pregnancy, but for sex with one another. They seem to be more concerned about sex than husbands are with wives."

By this time they were in front of the temple where vendors squatted behind their wares, offering them with raucous cries to the approaching women. Some had bunches of flowers, others fruit, still others chickens, and one man had a small group of tethered goats. Rinani whispered to her new-found friend, "What are we supposed to do, get something for the ritual?"

"Well, you can do as you like, but the priests are not happy if you don't bring anything in. They say all these vendors are working for the temple priests. So the priests get a double benefit—most of what is given to the vendors, and then the sacrifices themselves. That's why they prefer animals, since they get to eat them. You will notice when you get inside that the priests look quite well fed. Did you bring anything along to buy something with? I have some barley."

Rinani answered, "I had to take my husband his lunch and I had quite a bit to carry, and I didn't want him to know where I was going. Luckily I had two coins that I had saved for quite a while. I got them by working in the weaving factory down the street from where I live. They hire village women and pay them with coins to make carpets. It's hard work and they don't pay much, but at least I have something I don't have to explain to my husband."

Rinani stopped in front of the chickens. "Why do they use these here?"

"Well, you know, any time the priests perform a ritual, the first thing they think of is an animal sacrifice, no matter what they intend to get from it. They say that animal flesh is what the gods like to eat and if you are going to ask them for anything, you better give them what they want. You've heard that, haven't you?"

"I guess, but it doesn't seem so right for having a pregnancy. Anyway, I think I'll get some fruit and flowers. That seems better to me for this purpose." She added, "Maybe I'll get some eggs also. Since they turn into chickens, they seem right for a pregnancy, and the priests can still eat them while acting like they are gifts for the gods."

Rinani's friend got a chicken and some flowers and the two moved into the temple. The floor inside was polished from multitudes of passing feet and it was also wet from the water that had been sloshed around. Although there were windows on the sides, it was generally dark. Women's bodies were indistinctly visible as they moved toward the center where a large flat stone was placed on a hummock of earth. To one side of it a writing tablet was propped upright. Rinani stared at it, wondering what it said. Writing truly amazed her and deep inside she wished that somehow she could learn to read. But she had never seen a female scribe and assumed this was another task that women were incapable of mastering.

A priest squatted next to the tablet, waving flies away from his face while mumbling a prayer. A boy was picking up some of the fruit which had been placed on the stone as offerings and putting them in a basket. Rinani watched others to see how it was done. Two women came up to the shrine on their knees and put their offerings on the rock. Without stopping his mumbling, the priest pushed the fruit and flowers to the back of the rock with a crooked stick. The women each moved forward and kissed the rock. Rinani whispered, "Do you have to do that?"

"No, but they say it makes the priest feel better toward you, and particularly if you are going to ask for an amulet."

"I don't want to kiss that rock after everybody else, but I do need an amulet." She mumbled softly to herself, "I have come all this way."

"It's all right," the other woman said. "Just put your lips close. You don't even have to touch it."

The other two women went up to the priest in turn and bent down to touch his feet with their hands. They spoke so low, Rinani couldn't hear their exact words, but whatever they said was enough to get him to reach over for a little carved piece of stone and hand it to the supplicants. One pushed a small piece of turquoise toward the priest and the other couple of coins. The priest continued to mumble while he stowed the donations into a sack tied around his waist. The two women got up and backed away. Rinani and her friend took their place. Rinani still could not understand the mumbling. She supposed it was an ancient language or one used only with the gods. When she touched the priest's feet, she noticed how dirty they were. He put his hands on the top of her head and she said quickly and almost incomprehensibly, "Oh, speaker for the Column Spirit, I have two daughters and no sons and I beseech you for help to get a boy baby."

Almost automatically the priest replied, "That is no problem, daughter. The great Column Spirit is magnanimous and it will be done. Just address the great spirit often and think male all the time."

He handed her a little elongated stone. She presumed it was supposed to be a replica of the column outside. She put it in the carrying basket. Later at home she would put it in a tiny sack with a cord attached on two sides so she could tie it around her waist. She was thinking about telling Mattuz since he would inevitably see it and he was always scoffing about her reliance on the spirits.

As they walked away she said to her new friend, "I wanted to ask the priest many things but I was too scared." She had particularly wanted to ask if she had to wear the amulet when she was having sex. It seemed logical to do so, but it might create a problem with Mattuz.

The other woman replied, "Well, you are allowed to, you know. Though the priests get sharp if one woman stays too long. They accumulate more if they can do a lot of people, you know."

As they walked away, Rinani asked, "Where do you take the chicken?" It was hanging limply, its legs tied together as it tried to hold its head up.

"Through that door," she pointed. "They have a place down at the end of the building where they do it. It's too messy with feathers and blood if they do it inside. Also they have a special priest to make the blood sacrifices." She added, "He gets all messed up with blood and feathers too."

Rinani had seen enough blood sacrifices to be able to picture it. And though she knew that sacrifices were done in almost all important rituals, she was glad she had chosen flowers and fruit only. She said, "I'll wait for you over by the column, alright?"

"Sure, I won't be long. The killing priest is really fast." And she walked in that direction, swinging the chicken by the legs.

Rinani walked toward the column. When she got closer she could see that it was a little rougher than it looked from a distance. It almost looked like a tree trunk, though made of stone. Around the base, as far as up hands could reach, it was shiny smooth. Several women were walking around it, passing their hands over the stone. In one particular shiny place, a woman was standing still rubbing the forefingers of both hands back and forth. Rinani could see then how those places had got so shiny. One woman was also putting her lips to the stone at a polished place. Rinani decided then that though she would walk around and caress the stone, she wouldn't kiss it.

Very shortly her companion returned and the two went to the stone together.

Meshaq-Bis-Imrabi

It was a large room with a high ceiling and windows near the top to carry off the heat. The brick walls were covered with stucco, and decorated with colored geometric designs. His Royal Holiness sat cross-legged on a raised platform of polished wood in front of a low table, also highly polished and decorated with precious stones. Behind him was a woven fiber screen and behind that could be heard the sounds of whispers and bodies moving. Standing slightly behind and to one side a tall, light-skinned man with blue eyes and light hair waved a long fan over the ruler. He was a slave from one of the northern tribes. On the other side another man sat on a lower platform behind a row of tablets. He was the Minister of Information, and the tablets were reference works with data about goods available in the kingdom. He wore a red peaked hat and a medal of his office on a chain around his neck.

The potentate was a middle-aged man with thin legs and a slight paunch. His linen skirt was colored blue, and he wore a crown ornamented with precious stones. At his side lay an ornamented scepter.

There was a commotion in a far corner of the room and the door opened. A tall man holding a spear entered and said, "Your Royal Holiness, the Minister of Offense and the military delegation are here."

Meshaq, waving his hand, said, "Let them enter."

The delegation moved slowly to the front, bowed at the waist, and when they were about twenty feet from the ruler, got down on their hands and knees and crawled the remaining distance, the Minister of Offense first, distinguished by a peaked round hat. The military officers carried no arms, though they wore woven fiber armor and fiber helmets, and the insignias of their ranks. All the men moved up to the edge of the carpet and touched it, then moved backward a few steps. Meshaq, waving his hand again, said, "Arise, be without fear."

A unit of royal bodyguards remained just outside the audience room whenever the king was presiding, on instantaneous call. The assembled men stood and the minister asked, "This humble person requests permission to have a bearer bring a writing tablet."

This was the standard procedure because it was too difficult for a high-ranking person to crawl while dragging or carrying something.

In a bored tone the king replied, "Let it be."

The minister waved to someone at the rear of the room and in the doorway another slave materialized, carrying the pottery slab. He walked bent at the waist to a position in front of the Minister of Offense and stood up, holding the tablet to face the minister. The king spoke.

"Subjects state your business."

"Your Royal Holiness," began the Minister of Offense, "we have assembled today to consider the proposed war against the barbarians of the northwest, the people known as the Druks. As you may remember, Your Royal Eminence, we discussed this last week and it was decided that we would get an accounting of the goods available in the kingdom to support the army until it could capture some loot. And so we have done and it is our honor to pronounce that conditions are highly favorable. As you may know, Your Eminence, the Druks are not a people with great rich cities, but they have two products that are worth fighting for—large caches of turquoise and herds of animals."

"Are they nomads or townspeople?"

"Ah, Your Eminence, they are not nomads exactly. They do live in towns, but of course these are nothing in comparison with the glories of great cities like Ir—and even the other cities in the basin. But we have calculated that their sheep and cattle alone are worth a raid." He added, "And then, of course, there would also be some slaves."

"I was told that a great number of slaves were captured in the raid against the Hinaanites recently. Why is it necessary to get more so soon?"

"Ay, Your Eminence," the minister said, "there is so much to do. As you know, we are in the process of building two new ziggurats. And the canals always require repair." He sighed. "And the truth is that slaves die so easily. We have already lost half a dozen of the Hinaanites. You would think they would be grateful to be brought to a place of high civilization where they get to see great ziggurat-temples and palaces and wondrous gardens, but all they can do is complain about all the work they have to do and whine all the time about what a marvelous people they are, chosen by some ridiculous deity made in the image of themselves. As if the Supreme Eminence would be honored to be like them."

"These Hinaanites seem to be on your mind much, minister subject, which surprises me, since they are only slaves. Do all slaves bother you that much? How about these Druks, will they be as troubling to you?"

"Oh, no, I don't think so, Your Eminence. The Druks are more straightforward. Oh, I suppose they think they are special people, too. But all the barbarians think their society and way of life are best, no matter how miserable it is. But as for the Druks, I suggest we don't count too much on getting slaves. We can take enough strong young men to replace our recent losses among the Hinaanites and others, and of course we will bring back any beautiful young women for your seraglio and to sell as concubines to the upper class. But I recommend that we emphasize getting their animals and turquoise and perchance other loot that we don't yet know about." He added, "However, I think our spies have given us good information. We also have a couple of Druk renegades who have come to Ir and who have told us much. Then we can burn down their miserable towns and disperse them."

Meshaq scratched his thick black beard, considering, then said, "How many troops will we lose?"

The minister answered, "Perhaps we should let General Ramram give us that information, Your Eminence. He has worked out the details of the campaign with the chief military scribe."

The king spoke impatiently, "All right, but have him get to it. I have many other things to do. This meeting will have to be finished in one half hour because that is when my royal audience will begin. And I have no intention of being late for that." The ruler, as well as most of the high-ranking officials, was convinced that the royal audience served a vital function in keeping the commoners pacified and cooperative. He spoke again, "All right, but before he begins, have him tell me the kind of troops he will be using. I think it makes a difference in loyalty."

By this time the general had got in position, his accountant-scribe at his side, a slave holding a tablet facing them. General Ramram, a sturdy man with a long scar across his cheek from an old battle wound, rested his hand on his knife from long habit rather than aggressive intent.

"Ah, yes, Your Royal Eminence, it is indeed so," he said. "And if warfare were the only consideration for the kingdom, we would always choose our own commoners for troops. But we must always consider other needs, and probably the most important is that we have enough grain and other food for the troops, at least to begin with. As the campaign progresses, they can count on eating captured supplies. And in this case, they should get much meat from the captured animals. Ay Your Eminence, the troops are already looking forward to that."

Meshaq's impatience was growing. "Get to the point, General Ramram, answer my question."

"Oh, yes, Your Eminence." He whispered to the accountant, then turned back to the king. "It seems, Your Eminence, that about half will be citizens of the realm, almost all young men from the villages; and the other half will be mercenaries. Many of them are hill people who will know how to deal with the Druks. Although our own people have the greatest loyalty, most of them have never been to the hills before."

"That is about the proportion you usually have, isn't it? I wonder sometimes why we don't get more of our own people in the army. Seems like they would be more trustworthy."

"It might be so, Your Eminence," General Ramram replied. "But the fact is that we have to be careful not to deplete the villages. Otherwise, the supply of grain would diminish." Then to cover himself, the general added, "But of course, Your Eminence, if that is your wish, we could increase the numbers of citizen soldiers." He paused. "Though it would probably be necessary to postpone the campaign several days so we could make another sweep of the villages."

He did not mention that when they made the recruitment sweeps villages were surprisingly empty of young men of military age. Somehow the word always went ahead of them when an army sweep was coming, and the young fellows made themselves scarce. But there were always plenty of mercenaries available, and particularly for raids where the plunder and women would be plentiful.

Meshaq thought of asking again how many men the general thought they would lose, but did not. Though the ordinary soldiers were better than slaves, they were still commoners and rustics, and they could be easily replaced. But he would still feel better if there were more men from Ir and fewer mercenaries.

"All right," he said, let's make another sweep, and if we have to postpone the campaign a few days, let it be."

The king remained in the royal audience hall after the military delegation left and a palace girl brought him a decorated pottery mug of barley beer and a tray of seeds and nuts which he promptly began to break apart and chew. Another girl stayed by his side and whenever a few beads of sweat appeared on his forehead, wiped them off gently. At his side sat the Minister of Works. The Minister of Information was still in his place, and a working scribe had joined him.

Meshaq spit some pistachio shells to one side, just beyond the carpet, and spoke. "Let the first petitioner enter."

The door opened and behind the guard stood a man dressed in a farmer's loincloth, though he wore sandals and had a cloth hanging diagonally from one shoulder. His clothes were worn but clean. Behind him guards held back a small group of others who were also waiting for an audience. A couple of men tried to move forward to join the first one, but a guard pushed them back roughly.

"The king sees only one man at a time," the guard said, and tapped one of the men on the leg with his spear.

The entrance guard lowered his spear, using it as a barrier for the petitioner to stay behind and said, "Bow and step forward toward the king, staying behind the spear."

The man did as he was told, watching the spear carefully and looking thoroughly frightened. When they were a few yards from the king, the guard said, "Now down on your hands and knees and crawl toward His Eminence." For added effect, the guard tapped the farmer on the back with his spear. The farmer got down and crawled to the edge of the carpet. The guard said, "Now very carefully touch the edge of the carpet, but no further."

Again the man obeyed. The king tapped his staff and said, "Farmer subject, you may raise yourself to a squatting position and tell me your complaint."

At first the man could not speak, though he kept waving his hands around in small, nervous gestures. The king said, "Cease for a moment and rest, subject. No harm will come to you. This is the Royal Audience and your Highborn King is here to help." Whenever the king spoke to commoners, he used the objective case to refer to himself. He thought that made him sound higher and mightier, more like a permanent fixture in the universe than a mere mortal.

144

Meshaq had had petitioners before who became so unnerved by the procedure that they never could come out with their story. There was little doubt that the procedure was potentially unnerving since none of these people would have had the opportunity to talk to the king otherwise. The king cajoled patiently for a few minutes and was about to call the next petitioner when a sound came from the man's mouth, something like "Arrr."

The king said, "Good, subject worker, I was about to call the next person, but it seems you will be able to speak yet. Now just take your time and tell me your problem. Speak slowly and clearly but loudly enough that the scribe can hear. But first tell us your name so the scribe can put it down in the record."

The man was twisting the end of his loincloth as he spoke slowly and carefully. "Ay, Your Most Exalted Highness, Ruler of the Universe, Grantor of All Good Things of Existence, Great Priest of High Ziggurats—"

"Just let that be enough titles, subject worker," the king interrupted, knowing this could go on endlessly. Though he believed it was useful to have common subjects in awe of him, still he had too much to do to listen to such endless superlatives. "But first, your name."

The farmer paused, disconcerted, seemingly having thought such flowery addresses would help his cause. But he was learning how to conduct himself, so recovered quickly, saying, "My name, Your Eminence, is Bedulan, and I am a farmer in the village of Thirty-nine Palms. I have been accompanied here by three other men from the village, Muqtan, Khiroj, and Hammur. The village is three hours' walk south of Ir and a half mile to the West of the River. We grow barley and wheat and—"

All right, all right," the king interrupted again with some asperity. "You can give all those details to the scribe afterwards. Now get to the heart of the matter. What is your complaint?"

Typical of farmers and other commoners, the man tried to embellish his tale with other asides, but finally got down to the real reason for his coming. It seemed he and his companions were from a good farming district which depended on the primary irrigation canal, and which produced good crops of wheat and barley, and more recently grapes, when the government opened new farmland farther west and extended the canal to carry water to the new district. According to the plaintiff, a new district officer was appointed who spent all his efforts on the new district. Consequently, irrigation water was drastically reduced in the old district, on the farms of Thirty-nine Palms.

"Ay, Your Eminence, we have gladly provided our quota for Central's granaries before because then we were bringing in good crops. But since the lowering of our water quota, this has not been possible."

"It seems to me that this is a matter to be settled by the district officer and the Department of Irrigation." He turned to the Minister of Work.

"Minister subject, do you know anything about this matter?"

"No, Your Eminence. We are expanding in that region, along with several others. And there is a new district officer. But there is nothing unusual about either of those occurrences. We are usually expanding farmland and district officers are replaced frequently."

Meshaq turned to the farmer.

"Have you taken this up with the district officer or any other officials?"

"I have tried, Your Eminence, but he refuses to see me or the other farmers involved." The man added, "It is said, Your Holyship, that the district officer has installed his relatives on the new land and so favors them with water allotments."

Meshaq always wondered during these complaint sessions how much of what he was told was true. It was generally agreed that commoners, and particularly peasant farmers, told only as much as would help their cases, and if it would help, were deceptive. He sighed inwardly, telling himself that the purpose of these audiences was not so much getting at the truth as convincing the people that they were listened to. He knew that such meetings could hardly settle the many problems, but they could serve as a means of keeping the people in line. And getting in the harvest each year was of prime importance, so some willingness on the part of the peasants was needed. He said, "Very well, subject worker, the Minister of Work will look into this matter and you will be notified of the decision. May the Son of the Great Mother Goddess bless your efforts and may your harvests be plentiful."

The plaintiff looked up and the guard said, "You may get on your hands and knees and back away from His Royal Holiness, worker. I will let you know when you can raise yourself and walk away—backward."

The king listened to cases for three hours. Most were about land or other economic matters, disputes about boundaries, quarrels about water usage, complaints about excess taxes, loss of a son needed for agricultural labor to an army sweep, too much corvee labor, the police taking daughters for days at a time without recompense to the father, and failure to pay for other goods and services. By the time it was over the king was weary and ready to head back to his seraglio where he would first get an oil massage from his favorite concubine, to be followed by a royal feast of roast bird or antelope, thin wheatcakes, and steamed barley, and wine. For dessert he would have milk custard with honey and a glass of cow's milk. It was at times like that when he appreciated being a king, not the tiresome duties such as listening to the complaints of whining peasants and tradesmen. Who cared, he thought, about whether the police were keeping some ill-kempt peasant's daughter for a few days without paying the man. What avaricious characters the peasants were.

Meshaq rode on a cart, covered by a shade cloth hung from posts. The king was warm, though an intermittent breeze cooled him. He wiped his forehead with a soft cloth from time to time while watching the beads of sweat accumulate on the slaves' backs. There were four pulling the wheeled vehicle. Two were enough, but it was a smoother ride when four did the work. Some of the royal party were riding in oxen- or donkey carts, as the ministers usually did. But Meshaq felt it was more imposing and impressive to the populace to be pulled by men. The usual royal retinue extended before and after the mancart, the royal bodyguards just adjacent to the cart, an army contingent next to them, various members of the court in a group, the minister of religion, and the minister of royal buildings, and in front of it all a contingent blowing rams' horns and beating drums to notify the populace that the royal procession was coming by. Along the sides locals gathered to watch and cheer, orchestrated by local officials but kept back by the guards and army units.

Meshaq had the royal astrologer in the cart with him, sitting on a stool consulting his tablet. He was an older man who wore a high conical hat decorated with dots. He wore a long wraparound skirt and the medal of his office. His beard was long and scraggly. Meshaq had arranged for the astrologer to come along to save time. He would settle the military business before they got to the ziggurat.

"Now there is no problem as to whether we will make the campaign against the Druks," the king said. "That is already settled. But what we need to decide is when exactly the army will set out. The military need a few more days to get more troops but any time after six or seven days will be alright. And though I do not think this will be a particularly difficult campaign, it is normal procedure to get a reading, which is why I asked you to figure it out and come along with me this morning. What did you find out from the stars, subject astrologer?"

The astrologer consulted his tablet, running his fingers across the punched signs, nodding his head and mumbling. When he did not answer immediately, the king said, "I thought I told you to work it out last night. Don't you have the answer yet?"

"Oh, yes, Your Eminence, it has been done as you requested. I am only checking back to be sure. If Your Royal Holiness will wait just a tenth of an hour, I will give him the date, and the prognosis."

"Oh, alright, although I can't understand why you astrologers make such a mumbo-jumbo of everything. After all, it is only an alignment of the heavenly bodies with the sign of a person. And since you know my exact time of birth and thus my sign, I should think you could figure that out in a hurry."

"Well Your Eminence," The astrologer replied, "it always pays to be careful, so I don't think checking back is a waste of time. After all, the King has been generally fortunate in his campaigns and I think that has been to no small extent the consequence of careful soothsaying."

"Oh, alright, I didn't expect I would get a little lecture about soothsaying this morning, but finish it up as soon as you can."

There was periodic cheering from the people along the road, but it was kept to a reasonable level. The king always ordered the guards to keep public acclaim within reasonable limits. The populace at each location might think their shouts of acclaim were moderate but that was because they did not hear it all the way along the route. After a while the steady hubbub got on a person's nerves. The king added, "I think we will be there in a little bit. After all, it is only at the edge of the city."

They were heading toward a ziggurat which had just been completed the last week. There would be an opening ritual and a blessing by the king, the chief high priest of the priesthood. After a little more mumbling and tracing with his fingers, the astrologer said, "Since Your Holy Eminence is in the sign of Capricorn, and the time of your birth was between midnight and dawn on the thirtieth day of December, the best day for initiating the campaign would be Thursday. Sunday and Monday would end in disasters and the other days would be only slightly better."

The king tried to think if there was anything else important going on that day and suddenly remembered that he was having a state meeting with the king of Dukmar, a meeting which would require much preparation and would go on a large part of the day. Furthermore, it was an important meeting since he was counting on an alliance with Dukmar against the new eastern coalition. Of course, it wasn't imperative that he be there when the troops departed, but he felt it was a good idea, that a royal send-off was also important for a successful campaign.

"Of all days, on that one it is important that I be in and around the palace most of the day. A procession to the cantonment area to address the troops would be very difficult, if not impossible. Wouldn't one of the other days, say Wednesday or Friday, serve in a pinch? We do not consider the campaign will be very difficult." He tapped the conical hat of the astrologer. "And I know you fellows can fudge some. The signs can always be read a little differently."

Meshaq had dabbled in astrology himself in his early days, as in other forms of priestcraft. After all, he was the Supreme Holiness and he needed to know a little about most kinds of supernaturalism.

The astrologer began running his fingers over the signs again, seemingly in deep concentration.

"I will see what I can do, Your Royal Holiness."

When they arrived at the base of the ziggurat, a large crowd was already gathered and the people cheered loudly as the king in the long robe of official gatherings stepped out of the cart. A carpet was already in place. The king adjusted his crown and clasping his public staff, headed toward the place where the government officials were gathered. A boy stayed behind and helped in holding the trailing end of the robe, turning it when needed and otherwise holding it just a little off the carpet. The king walked slowly and imperiously to the royal seat, which had been brought in advance. The officials stayed back and on their knees. Farther out, the guards had induced the populace to their knees also. The king sat down and said, "Arise, subjects and proceed."

There was a moderate amount of pageantry, a couple of musical pieces by the horn and drum corps, some short speeches by officials, and finally the procession with the sacrificial ox. It was a pure white one, a color favored for sacrifices at important rituals, and it was bedecked with garlands of flowers and wearing a cloth caparison with colored stones dangling at the lower border. The animal walked docilely though its eyes darted back and forth in fright. It was surrounded by too many noisome beings. The animal was already well dampened by the priest walking at its side, and when it had reached a point in front of the king, the priest sprinkled more water on it. This was water from the Tigris, which was almost always used for religious ritual. It was taken from the main river flow in jars and carried to sacred places for blessings. The people believed that the Tigris-Euphrates were spirit-induced rivers which ennobled anything they touched. While sprinkling the water, the priest intoned, "To His Royal Eminence, builder of great ziggurats, conqueror of barbarians, and sustainer of life for all his people, we dedicate this consecrated beast, and may its blood sustain for all eternity this noble temple, to be committed this day in the exalted city of Ir, forevermore." Whereupon he took a cup of water to the king who, holding it in both hands, bent over it and mumbled the prayer of sacrifice.

The procession moved on to the killing place where the ox was pulled over by several men and its legs tied together so it couldn't get up when its throat was cut. Then the killing priest joined the water priest and they jointly sprinkled water again while reciting the sacrifice prayer. Then the killing priest cut the animal's throat.

The one other event of significance for the blessing was the speech by the king and the climbing of the stairway where he would stake his claim over all that was visible. When it was time, Meshaq stood up and orated in the time-honored fashion if Irian kings.

"Let it be known to all and sundry that on this date, in the year 486 after the year of the founder, Bintan, in the exalted dynasty of the Imrabis, from hereon to eternity, Your Noble Protector, He Who Smites Barbarians, the Upholder of Morality and Justice, the Maintainer of Fertility and the Waters of the Tigris-Euphrates, the Great Master of the Universe, hereby dedicates this ziggurat, etc., etc., etc."

Meshaq was indeed grateful for the boy to help him with the robe as he ascended the winding staircase to the top of the ziggurat.

~

Q: *This chapter, unlike the earlier ones, has a title which makes sense as soon as you start reading the narrative. So this is the beginning of city life? Did it really start here in the valley of the Tigris-Euphrates, in what is now the nation of Iraq?*

A: Yes, all archeologists and historians agree on that point. The time was between five and six thousand years ago, say for a round figure, 5,500. Of course, because the calendar most of us are familiar with starts at the supposed time of the birth of Jesus Christ, some of us refer to it as 3500 B.C.

Archeologists prefer B.P. which stands for "before the present." That way you get the little bit of ethnocentric taint out of the figure since all the major religions developed calendars based on the supposed birthday of their prophet.

Q: *And how does this period fit into the traditional time schedule you mentioned before, the Paleolithic and Neolithic?*

A: As I said before, those were periods named according to how tools were made. Paleolithic means old stone age because the tools were made of chipped stone, while Neolithic refers to polished stone tools, remember? But you will also recall, I am sure, that now we think the real significance of the Neolithic was the change from food gathering to food producing, the consequence of the domestication of plants and animals. Since the remains of tools is what archeologists find most of, they name their periods after the materials. The period we are now describing is what was earlier called the Chalcolithic, the Copper Age, but which later came to be known as the Bronze Age. And what it signifies is that men had learned how to smelt metal for tools, a considerably different procedure from either chipping or polishing stone.

Q: *And so bronze was the new material used for tools. But it did not figure very much in the narrative and I didn't think bronze was so wonderful for that purpose, was it?*

A: Actually, bronze never did become a widely-used metal and men switched to iron as soon as they learned how to smelt it. Bronze simply indicates that men had come to the metal age, one which has lasted right up to the present. The age of metallurgy was born. Men had learned how to subject certain rocks (ores) to heat and when they became malleable, they could be shaped with exactitude. Actually, the first metals were copper, gold, and silver, but all of these were soft and unfit to be used as tools. But if tin were added to copper, the resulting product was harder and a tool or weapon was possible. And so that is how it came to be known as the Bronze Age.

Q: *You mean the guards and soldiers of the narrative were carrying spearpoints of bronze?*

A: Probably most of them weren't. You see, neither copper nor tin is a widely-found mineral. So bronze remained a fairly exclusive metal. It wasn't until iron, which is found in large amounts, that everybody got to use metal. Someone referred to iron as the democratic metal. And it is certain that a lot more people got skewered with iron spearpoints than with bronze ones.

Q: *And you tell us that metallurgy is no longer used as the defining factor of the era, correct?*

A: Yes, we now think it was mainly the bringing together of large numbers of people in a small area and all the consequences thereof, an era now known as the Urban Revolution.

Q: *I thought a revolution was an overthrow of a government or other large social unit, like the American, French, and Communist Revolutions?*

A: Actually, all the word revolution means is a sudden but momentous change from within. So all the above fit that definition and the rise of a city also does—except it does not seem to have been so momentous. All we really know is that about ten thousand years ago there were some village-size communities and that about four thousand years later there were some much larger, more complex communities along certain great rivers, also farming but with irrigation and with many social changes. If one wants to consider four thousand years sudden, one can, and certainly compared with other changes in the universe, it is, though of course compared with traditional historical events it is not. But the city evolved in this era and it has remained the main production and administrative unit of mankind ever since.

Q: *There are two or three other changes you mentioned for which I should like some clarification. For instance, what about complexity?*

A: Well, when we talk about the evolution of mankind, the only things we are sure about are that he became steadily more able to learn, thus to create greater complexity, to exploit his environment more, and to become more numerous. We can see the changes in complexity going on even in the Paleolithic and Neolithic periods but when it gets to the Urban Revolution, it becomes a landslide. I could cite all type of endeavors, but I think one will be sufficient—the division of labor. The prehuman primates had no division of labor except in child rearing and that was biologically controlled. Then the man creatures during the entire foraging stage of existence had the simplest division, men doing the hunting while women did the gathering. A slight shift took place when the Domestication Revolution came along, with men taking over most of the animals while women did some cultivation and food processing. Now in the Urban Revolution, in addition to the simple division of labor by sex of the earlier period, we have all kinds of new specialties that people learn, everything from kings and priests to jewelers and scribes. For the first time in human history, you could not assume you knew what kind of work another person did. By the way, the oldest profession or specialized occupation, prostitution, probably began in this period because for the first time in the history of mankind, a means of quick payment was available.

Q: *So society became more complex as people became more numerous. And another thing you mentioned but which could use some more elaboration was irrigation. Didn't men do that before?*

A: So far as we learn from archeology, farming in the Neolithic Period was done with natural rainfall, up in the hills; but in this period, men moved down to the river bottoms where the soil was rich but since the cultivation was being done in dry environments, water had to be brought to the fields. Then the yield was much greater, although of course so was the work required. And a large population of non-producers could be supported. This happened first in the valley of the Tigris-Euphrates but not too long after also in the Nile Valley and a little later on the Indus River of India-Pakistan and the Huang-Ho of China. In fact, an explanation for the rise of the first cities was called the Hydraulic Theory, the idea that the necessity for controlling the great rivers with drainage and irrigation canals led to the development of bureaucracies, class systems and all the complexities of cities. Later cities did not need to be based exclusively on water control but then bureaucracy, taxation, inequality, and all the rest of urban civilization were with us forever after.

Q: *Civilization is a term that keeps cropping up from now on also. Did that begin here too? Were these people with their warfare for loot, slavery, exploitation of the working class, and poor treatment of women civilized?*

A: I'm afraid so. Prior to this era, mankind had a fairly simple way of life. But from here on the complexity increases more rapidly, and civilization is defined as "An advanced stage of development in the arts and sciences, accompanied by corresponding social, political, and cultural complexity." As you will note, nothing is said in this definition about democracy, egalitarianism, or quality of life. Actually, the broad scale savageries indulged in by mankind have been most characteristic of "civilized nations." But men have told themselves since the beginning of history that atrocities were committed by barbarians, which is why they have no problem explaining how European nations have been so bloodthirsty in wars of Protestants against Catholics, in wiping out tribe after tribe in the conquest of the New World and the rest of the tribal areas, in the wars of Christians against Muslims, in the elimination of the upper class in the French Terror and the Russian Revolution, and the elimination of ethnic minorities by fully-civilized peoples like the Germans and the Yugoslavs. No, though I have no reason to believe the tribals of the world were gentler people, they simply did not have the resources to conduct major savagery. But since the histories of the world were always written by the conquerors, they downplayed their own barbarities and laid guilt on the tribals. There is little evidence that gentleness grew with the development of the city.

Q: *So what is the defining characteristic of civilization?*

A: Well, the generally-accepted custom is writing. Erudite men have decided that the ability to put down language in a permanent form is the dividing line between barbarism and civilization. The study of history is the past of mankind after writing became a reality. Although we in anthropology consider man-ness to have gone on for about five million years, historians normally begin with the era of writing, that is 5,500 years ago or less, depending on when a particular people began writing. Oh, the historians usually give an abbreviated chapter on the much longer earlier period, but then quickly get to the Sumerians or Egyptians or Shang Chinese. European historians frequently begin with the Ancient Greeks, about 2,500 years ago, generally downplaying all that the Greeks had got from the earlier city people who had been in business as "civilized peoples" by then for 3,000 years.

Q: *So the beginning of writing is considered to be the watershed by historians. Does that make sense to an anthropologist?*

A: It's okay, though we generally think of writing as a consequence rather than a cause. That is, the major change was the creation of the city itself which brought about writing as well as many other inventions. But of course once writing was in existence, it couldn't help but cause other changes such as building up the bureaucracy and exploiting the workers more efficiently, both slaves and commoners. And as you must realize, writing has continued to have these functions throughout history. Imagine how a complex system of exploitation like taxation or the maintenance of complex power control systems of government, like socialism or democracy, or world wars depending on draft armies could take place without writing. And with the advent of writing, people could keep a record of historical events. So writing is not bad to mark the beginning of complex systems, or civilization.

Q: *One thing I wonder about is what happened in the New World. Didn't they have an urban revolution?*

A: Yes, they did, at least in two centers, Mexico and Peru. In both instances, they followed the same pattern in developing sound agricultural bases, then the typical development of classes, a high degree of inequality, warfare, and exploitation of the workers. They seemed to have invented metallurgy independently, with abundant supplies of gold and silver. Though the Mexicans and Mayans invented writing, it never became so important for building up the bureaucracy and exploiting the masses, and the Peruvians never got writing at all. Both civilizations developed great cities, which impressed the Spaniards mightily even though as soon as they had conquered the natives, they set about to make the cities over to be like Spanish ones. But there is nothing unusual about that; conquerors have always set about to remake whatever they found in the form of their own civilizations.

Q: *What about the rest of the world, didn't those peoples go through an urban revolution?*

A: Not really, though in sub-Saharan Africa the people were on the verge of doing so by the time Europeans got there; but of course the European conquest halted all of that.

Q: *You have mentioned several times that there were many inventions in the early city-states. How did that come about?*

A: Well, when you get a lot of different kinds of people living together, there is something like cross-fertilization that goes on. People stimulate each other. And we think that happened in the early city-states for the first time. For instance, someone might have learned how to smelt gold or silver and then this stimulated him or someone else to try some other metals. And so copper came to be used. And then someone who learned the technique mixed it accidentally with tin, and bronze was invented. Then someone down the line experimented with a new ore, iron, etc. We think this kind of exposure to other ideas explains how inventions occur better than does the idea of the lone inventor hiding out and experimenting exclusively on his own. Of course he might go off on his own for a while to figure out how to get the ultimate solution, but this is after he has been stimulated by some other new information. So we think the city is a prime breeding ground for new ideas. And so in the early city-states we find for the first time writing, complex numeral systems, a calendar, irrigation systems, the plow, the wheel, glass, bricks, metals, weaving, and many social and economic innovations such as social classes, a priesthood, taxes, coins, and many other basics which we still rely upon.

Q: *I noticed that education was a kind of apprenticeship as practiced by the scribe and his assistant. Was that the only kind?*

A: Probably. Apprenticeship is just a system of passing on specialized knowledge from one generation to another outside the family. The most basic learning method known and practiced by people in simple societies is on-the-job learning within the family. The boy learns how to hunt or to take care of animals from his father while the girl learns how to gather plant foods and process food from her mother. So an apprenticeship system is merely one stage beyond that when the young person learns from a specialist outside the family, and usually in a more prescribed fashion. This has lasted up to the present, even though we now learn through more formal classroom procedures also. But a doctor still learns through a kind of apprenticeship when he does his internship. Also, what we call on-the-job-training is a kind of apprenticeship. I am assuming that true apprenticeship learning began with the specialization of labor of the city, though there is no direct evidence of that. Again literary license.

Q: *You showed writing as primarily a means of exploitation. Nowadays we think of reading and writing more for education and information. The most commonly-read items nowadays are probably newspapers, magazines, and books. Did the function of writing change so much?*

A: One basic change that took place much later was the democratization of writing, a consequence primarily of the printing press in the 1450s. It made writing widely available and it became worthwhile to learn to read. Then making education universal in the nineteenth century, when most people in the well-to-do countries learned how to read, made it worthwhile to publish for profit. Of course, the exploitation and control used with writing continued also. The tax agent and the conscript official are still with us, and rely on writing more than ever.

Q: *I was interested in how the scribe and the king also did not trust the truthfulness of the peasants. I assume there is no direct evidence for that also?*

Q: Yes, I took a general characteristic of the powerless and the poor and this certainly includes peasants, and attributed it to the characters in the narrative. You see when you get big disparities in power, the people at the lower end really have no other recourse. The information seekers use what they learn against the powerless and poor, whether they are peasants or poor blacks in an American ghetto. The law enforcement officials may say they are doing it to maintain law and order, but the social control system of a group is designed by the rich and powerful and naturally they use these forces for their own benefit. So if the poor tell the truth and it is damaging, they will suffer. They learn to "know nothing."

Q: *One interesting change that seems to have taken place is in clothing. People are no longer wearing skin garments. I can see that this is a consequence of the domestication of plants, no?*

A: Yes. Although skin clothing, leather, has continued to be used until the present, fiber has gradually replaced it throughout the world, and beginning some time between the Domestication and Urban revolutions. People learned how to use fiber for clothing when they learned how to domesticate food plants. The earliest cloth was linen made from the fiber of flax, followed later by cotton, and much later by synthetics. Men also learned later how to use two other animal products for clothing, wool from sheep and goats, and silk from worms. One other invention from this period which was critical for cloth-making was the loom for weaving. It enabled the user to make cloth which was both more flexible and stronger by weight than leather.

Q: *The type of garment worn in this narrative didn't seem so extraordinary, actually not so different from the earlier skin garments.*

A: That is true. The one great innovation in clothing styles which occurred throughout history was tailoring, or making garments to correspond to the human figure. Prior to that, everybody wore some variation of wraparound garments. In historical times the Roman toga was no more than a long, fancy, untailored wraparound and right up to the present the woman's dress is mostly untailored. The one great change of worldwide significance was the consequence of fitting garments to split for the human legs, the invention of pants. Of course, there were other minor changes, such as fitting garments to cover the arms separately and cinching in garments at the waist. But splitting the pants was the most revolutionary change and it is hypothesized that this innovation came about when man learned to ride astride a horse, probably in Central Asia and obviously after the horse was domesticated some time after the Urban Revolution began, about three to four thousand years ago. The semi-nomadic Germanic barbarians probably got tailored pants from the Central Asians in a process we call diffusion, and brought them into Europe, where they rapidly replaced the wraparound of the Romans for men. It is interesting to note that the European woman, who stuck to the untailored skirt, first learned to ride side-saddle. And it is not until modern times when the unisex blue jean has become the most popular garment in the world that women have begun to ride horses astride.

Q: *I saw some Eskimos on TV the other day and they were wearing pants. Surely they didn't get the idea from the ancient Germanic peoples, did they?*

A: No, and that's a good observation. The Eskimos did have tailored clothing and the North American Indians had a kind of halfway garment, tailored leggings. The well-stitched pants and parka were vital parts of the Eskimo defense against the bitter cold. The leggings of the Indians were separate tailored pieces for each leg, held in place by a thong belt, and were useful both as protection from the cold and for horseback riding. The North American garment was either an independent invention or had been diffused across the Bering Straits and southward from Central Asia.

Q: *I see money became a reality in this era. somehow I had thought that barter had lasted much longer. Could you elaborate on that?*

A: Sure. This is when money started to "make the world go around," as the popular song put it. It marks the beginning of a significant surplus of production as well as a much greater variety of goods, the consequence of specialization of labor. You noted, I am sure, the problem of exchange between the jeweler and the scribe and also that between the fertility priest and the farmer's wife.

Q: *You mean that standardized money didn't exist among the cultivating or foraging peoples?*

A: Well, it depends on how you define money. Trade seems to have occurred quite a way back, from what we can make out about what the surviving tribals were doing when Europeans began describing them. Probably one of the earliest items of trade was salt, though almost anything would do if one people had it and another did not. For instance, cultivators would frequently trade agricultural products to hunters or nomads for animal products. And they had to either trade directly, say animal hides for wheat, or have some common medium of exchange. This had to be something rare enough to be valuable. A very common kind of early trade medium was special seashells and in particular one called a cowry shell. One people, called Trobriand Islanders, became famous in anthropological accounts because of their "trade circles," one kind of shell going in one direction, another in the opposite. Some tribal peoples got quite imaginative with their invention of trade mediums. The people of the island of Yap in the Central Pacific made as a medium or exchange a great doughnut-shaped circle of stone with a pole through the center that had to be carried by two men. Then metallurgy came along, and two kinds of material that were to last for almost the rest of history became a reality, that is, gold and silver.

Q: *That's because they are so valuable, right?*

A: Actually, gold and silver are not so useful, but they are relatively scarce and they can be made to be bright and shiny. The very early metallurgists learned that they were of little value for making tools. But gold and silver served well for ornamentation and they were scarce, so from the time of the earliest cities, they were treasured. Gold rushes in all parts of the world were fuelled by the universal craze for this practically useless metal and many native peoples got destroyed by being on land that prospectors wanted. And the gold wedding band is still loaded with more emotional weight than any other metal or jewel by the ladies of Western society. Furthermore, those in the third world who get a surplus frequently prefer to keep it in gold rather than in the paper money of their countries.

Q: *But in any event the peoples of the early cities were using gold and silver as money, right?*

A: I am sure they were, at first by the simplest method, which is to weigh them, though the new medium, money, came in not too long after. This is the validation of a piece of material by some kind of imprint. The value comes from the imprint more than from the fundamental value of the metal. The imprint has usually been a notable person, a king or president, or some thing or event the authorities want to commemorate, like the Indian and the buffalo on the American nickel. There is some difference of opinion as to when coins actually appeared, but it was either at the time of the earliest city-states or among a people in Asia Minor called the Lydians some two thousand years later. It really doesn't matter for our story and so we will attribute the first money to the earliest city peoples. And from that time on, money remained the lubrication of market trade and the mainstay of commercialism. Two later innovations were paper money which seems to have been invented in China, and in our own day "plastic money."

Q: *I was interested in the relations of the Irians with the people outside their political system, the barbarians. Were they so much less civilized?*

A: Well, you have to remember that the word civilized means to have a more complex technology and social system, no matter that nowadays we imply that to be civilized means to have a higher morality; or, as it was put by one of our recent presidents, to be kinder and gentler. Ironically, he got most of his fame by having the modern descendants of the founders of civilization in Iraq well bombed. Unfortunately, having a more complex technology and social system enable a people to wreak more havoc on others, not less, no matter what religious creed is espoused. So the civilized Irians with their greater numbers and improved technology were capable of treating people in the outlying areas roughly, whether through warfare, looting, raping, pillaging, or the general mayhem that armies have typically wreaked on weaker others during the past. And the less numerous, less urban, less technologically sophisticated were the victims. This has been so at least through the nineteenth century when colonialism was in vogue and probably since. The most recent victims of military mayhem by America, which is generally considered the number one superpower, have all been third world nations, notably little Grenada, Panama, and Iraq.

Q: *It sounds terrible, not at all the picture of being civilized that we got in our earlier classes.*

A: Well, the primary reason for the different pictures is that in early schooling we are given the mythological version of history and only later do some of us get a more realistic account. For instance, we were almost all taught that the first Thanksgiving was a happy feast between the Puritans and Indians. But in how many classes were we told that the head of Metacom, or King Philip, the Indian leader in one of the earliest acts of resistance to land takeover, was displayed at Plymouth Fort after he was killed. And how many of us were taught that scalping an enemy, no matter in which tribe the practice originated, was spread primarily by white men to one tribe after another. But since history is almost always written by the conquerors, their most unsavory practices are usually left out of the mythological versions.

Q: *Well, it is a relief to go on to something more positive, I mean some of the fun parts in the human way. I was interested to note that both beer and wine got started at this time.*

A: Yes, all the specialists agree that the fermented juice of both the grape and barley began with the early city-states, both along the Tigris-Euphrates and the Nile. Actually, the idea of fermentation, of letting bacteria convert carbohydrates and sugars into alcohol, probably began earlier among the original cultivators. It is not difficult to imagine how it began. Cultivating peoples let some grapes or grain soaked in water stand too long and bacteria went to work, resulting in the brew. And when they drank some, it made them feel better; and they learned how to make it happen by putting a little of the fermented mix into the new supply or by chewing some barley or corn and spitting it into the container. The saliva made the juice ferment. This was a particular technique used to make corn beer, a specialty of the New World.

Q: *Didn't the earlier peoples, the foragers, make brew?*

A: I never heard of one who did. Fermentation seems to have originated along with cultivation, presumably because at this juncture, men had more than enough carbohydrates and sugars to be able to afford to play around. The roots, nuts, and berries of the foragers were presumably too hard to come by.

Q: *One item you mentioned but did not explain in detail was wet nursing. Though I have heard of it, I'm not sure what it is. Could you explain that?*

A: Sure. The term is a little out of date because the practice is, in the well-to-do countries anyway. It means nursing someone else's baby at the breast. I have no idea how long it has been practiced. But it has served to keep babies alive who would otherwise have been deprived, often to the point of death. To the best of my knowledge, the non-human primate female does not take over other animals' babies, no matter what happens. Humans do, presumably because they have the idea of kinship and are more cooperative. Some of the tribals even extended their care to other animals. The women of many tribes in New Guinea, who were simple cultivators, used to nurse baby pigs at the breast if a pig mother couldn't do it. This of course shocked Westerners who believe that humans and animals are thoroughly different creatures and cross nursing is disgusting if not blasphemous, as true believers believe cross-sex is also. The practice was followed most often with human babies when a mother did not have milk or had been taken away. Presumably in the early, egalitarian days such wet nursing was done as a favor or to accrue informal exchange rights from neighbors or relatives. But when the city evolved, wet nursing became a matter of the uppers getting the services from the lowers, paid for or exacted, depending on the degree of control by the uppers. And it remained with us for the rest of history until formula feeding became possible in the nineteenth century.

Q: *Although you have talked about cultivation already, there are some points which might deserve amplification. I get the idea that the farming in the city-states was done in rich soil using the water of the big rivers. Is that right?*

A: Yes, it is. Almost all the rivers of the world have high and low levels, depending on the different amounts of rainfall throughout the year. And the high waters of the rainy season bring down rich silt from the hills. The geographers call such a place an alluvial plain. If it can be planted when the waters recede and kept moist enough with irrigation, rich crops can be harvested.

Q: *I noted also that oxen were being used for agricultural work. This was new, wasn't it?*

A: Yes, it was another of the new inventions, or rather the use for a different purpose of something which already existed. You probably remember that the animals of the village cultivators, those which were being tended by Jorald and Benji, were used primarily for food, either directly as meat or indirectly by means of milk products. They also used the hides and wool and perhaps made some tools of their bones. You may remember that in the Bible one of the Israelites struck down an enemy with the jawbone of an ass. It didn't take long, relatively speaking, before someone got the idea of putting the beasts in harness. Who knows what use was first made of this idea, though we think the first wheeled vehicles were pulled by domestic animals and certainly later ones were. At about the same time, the beasts were hitched to the plow. This required the new implement which wasn't all that difficult to create—a shortened digging stick with a crossbar to hitch to the ox. And *voila* a plow, a tool that, with a number of refinements, has lasted to the present day. My uncles were still plowing with horses in Indiana in the 1930s, and most of the farmers of the agrarian nations still plow this way.

The evolutionists consider the amount of energy available in a culture an index of its technological advancement. Thus, for most of history humans relied on human power; then with the agricultural revolution they advanced to animal power; and with the internal combustion engine they got to mechanical power. In the 1930s my uncles switched from horses to tractors.

In the early cities work was being done by animal power plus the human power of peasants and slaves. Later, of course, mechanical power got so cheap, it wasn't worthwhile to use peasants or slaves for the hardest, most monotonous jobs. It is no accident that slavery for agriculture faded out all over the world at the same time the industrial revolution was taking place, irrespective of any change in public morality. It is likely that slavery would have faded out in the American South if there had never been a civil war. Human labor still has to be used to pick strawberries, avocados, and a few other crops, but that is because no one has invented a machine that will pick them. But it is no problem to harvest corn, potatoes, wheat, and barley with machines.

Q: *Life must have been much easier then, though it doesn't really seem so, at least not for the workers and slaves.*

A: Well, that's an interesting problem. In popular culture we are taught that the more labor-saving devices and inventions there are, the easier life will be. But we in anthropology now believe that the era of true leisure was that of the foragers, the hunters and gatherers of the world. It has only been in my lifetime that anthropologists have done time and motion studies of the work done by hunter-gatherers and they have found that these simple people only spend three to four days a week working and during the remainder of time they rest and visit and indulge in that omni-present activity of the talking biped, gossiping. And it must be remembered that in the foraging period of history those great time extenders, books and electricity, were not available. Almost everybody went to sleep when it got dark and arose with the dawn's earliest. Cracking the books or working all night were not possible because the light bulb had not been invented.

Q: *Wow, that sounds like a real contradiction. As more and more inventions are made, there is less and less leisure. How could this be?*

A: Simple, man has persistently eliminated his labor saving advantage by taking on more tasks. While the forager got where he was going by walking, the modern has to have a car, with all the costs involved. And while the forager got his entertainment by gossip and folklore, the modern has to have radio, TV, videos, and movies, with all the costs they require. As more and more things were invented, man's expectations rose.

Q: *And you say this was happening to the common men in the early cities also? They didn't seem to have so many labor saving devices.*

A: Well, they didn't have as many as we are accustomed to, but an animal-drawn plow and cart are more efficient devices for cultivation and transportation. And the loom for weaving and the pottery wheel are also labor-saving devices. Remember, the forager got by with skin or fiber clothing and containers. But there is another cause for the increased amount of work for the peasant and other workers. This was the period when the economics of class began. Before this, everyone consumed about the same things. Some might have had a little more than others, but there are limits to how much one person can eat. There were not any real luxury items during the foraging era. But by the time of the cities, alongside the simple mud huts of peasants, there were the great palaces of the royalty. Even in food there are differences. While the royalty can feast on wild game (reserves to provide game for the upper class were established early in human history in several parts of the world), peasants usually lived on vegetal food. And of course there is a world of difference in such luxuries as jewelry and clothing.

Q: *So I assume you are saying that extra production goes into the support of the rich, correct?*

A: Yes. The peasant lived in a dual economy, one part in which he provided for himself, which is called subsistence, and another part in which he produced for the well-to-do and specialist producers. That is the surplus part of the economy. You could see how the royalty and administrators got theirs, though taxation, and the specialist producers like the goldsmith and cart manufacturer got theirs through trade for some of the grain of the peasants. This was the period when that brilliant idea for the exploitation of commoners, taxation, was invented.

It is popular these days for politicians to imply, if not to claim outright, that taxation is designed to help all citizens. But of course it helps some more than others. The politicians and other administrators are maintained in a better state than those they tax without having to produce anything other than methods of controlling those they tax.

Q: *It seems that the woman defers to men much more than the women or earlier eras. Is that true?*

A: Yes, no doubt about it. I'm sure I told you that there was a major shift when cultivation became a reality, that the men became the primary producers and asserted their power over the other members of the family accordingly. This was the era when the wife became the helpmeet rather than a direct producer on her own. Also, children continued to be important, but particularly male children for two reasons. The boys learned the cultivation tasks of their fathers which they would take over when the head of the household got too old. And the boy would be expected to take care of his parents in their old age. Also, with agriculture land became a valuable commodity which was worth keeping in the family; thus, inheritance.

Q: *I thought that in the narrative it was claimed that all the land belonged to the king and that he rented it to farmers.*

A: Although we do not know what the exact pattern of ownership of those people were, the nominal claim of ownership was common by hereditary royal groups for most of the next five thousand years, up through the medieval period in Europe. But usually the workers had some kind of claim or rights of use also, except for slaves. And it was important to pass those rights on to someone else in the family, if for no other reason than to have support in one's old age. So having a boy or boys was important.

Q: *So that is why the women went to such lengths, from having blood sacrifices done to wearing amulets, to get the gods to intercede?*

A: I am sure they did everything they could. That has been typical of agrarian people everywhere, up to the present. That business of the giant phallic stone I lifted from my knowledge of village India, also a thoroughly masculine-oriented culture. The main manifestation of one of their prime deities, Shiva, is the *lingam* stone which is an erect penis in stone and found in temples all over the country. Though Indians worship the Shiva *lingam* for other purposes, the Indian ladies pour water and put flowers on the stone to get pregnant.

Q: *And girls were not wanted as much. It doesn't seem fair.*

A: One of the problems we have in understanding various cultural ways is our own cultural biases. And we in a bilateral society, where women have more rights, tend to judge patrilateral societies by our standards. But fairness is relative. There is no doubt that girls are desired much less in patrilateral societies. In fact, the one occurrence that improves a woman's status is having a boy baby, which is why they go to such great lengths to make that happen. Another reason boys were preferred is that they normally stayed home when they married while the girls went to the homes of their new husbands. You couldn't count on girls in your old age.

Q: *Now I begin to see how the various parts fit together. That was also why parents arranged marriages, wasn't it?*

A: Yes, marriage was too important to parents to leave in the hands of the children. Among other things, there were serious financial arrangements. Romance had to be a secondary consideration. We who live in bilateral societies are the true believers in romance because we have abandoned most of the other considerations for marriage.

Q: *Then there was the priesthood. The priests seem to have had close ties to the administrators, right?*

A: Yes, in most of the early city-states the two worked together, if not being the same person. Religion became one of the institutions for control. We know that very early, supernaturalism functioned to take some of the terror and unpredictability out of life, but this function was placed in the hands of the individualistic curer-magician, a person we generally know of as the shaman. But with city life and larger groups of people living under the control of all-powerful rulers, the organized priesthood began, and that has been a part of civilized life ever since. One of the sources of power of the early priests was their perceived ability to foretell the future and give people hope, whether in predicting the best time to plant the crops or helping a woman have a male baby. They learned the rituals and other priestly knowledge like other specialists and the rewards were great.

Q: *Government was certainly no democracy, even to the limited degree that the Athenians had it. How could men have changed so much from the systems of individual rights of the foragers and even the early cultivators?*

A: Well, the big change seems to have occurred when men developed the capacity for accumulating surpluses. The foragers just did not have that capacity and even the early farmers were limited. But with better cultivation techniques, transportation, and storage facilities, it became possible to keep large supplies on hand. This brought all kinds of changes, many of which I have already discussed. Another new social innovation was large scale war for loot. Presumably men have always fought each other for territory and on occasion for women. But that was penny ante stuff. From now on, in civilized societies, it pays to devastate other peoples. In addition to animals, stores of grain, and valuables, it becomes worthwhile to grab people to use as slaves. One ruling group organizes its peasantry to devastate other peoples' peasantry after which they collect the bodies and loot.

Q: *I noticed that the style of warfare had changed. Instead of localized raids, the military organized everything, from getting soldiers to planning a strategy in advance. could you comment on that?*

A: Sure. It went along with the change in the way of life generally. During the city period, mankind began organizing. Before that, people did things more informally and spontaneously, like their non-human forebears. But with civilization this informal way of doing things was no longer feasible. There was an elaborate social organization based on inequality and rules, a supreme leader, and a bureaucracy, and these people tried to manage everything as political leaders have tried to do ever since. Getting wealth was one of the chief functions of the system; and an important way of getting wealth was through warfare. But like everything else, it had to be organized. This was when true organization got started.

Q: *Perhaps the last thing I would like to ask about is astrology. Is that literary license or did the early Middle Easterners really invent it.*

A: In this case there is evidence. Although prophesying must have been going on for a long time, we give the Sumerians credit for the system of predicting the future by reading the celestial signs as they are related to one's personal horoscope, depending on one's time, date, and place of birth. As you know, most newspapers of our "advanced" society contain an astrological forecast on one of the back pages. One of our recent presidents is reported to have made important decisions on the basis of astrological predictions. This is one of our many continuing ties with the past of the great cities.

Q: *We seem to have spent a lot of time on this phase of history, so I suppose it is time to move on.*

A: Yes. Though I find the early city builders an interesting crowd, it is time to go on. And I suggest that we now look down well down the ages of city builders at the most significant conquest the world ever suffered through.

6

The Conquest

They had been heading south for six weeks, at first over the central mesa where they had threaded their way through the high volcanos, and later through villages surrounded by corn fields. Juan Fierro still kept a sharp eye on the villagers, even though there had been few uprisings lately. It was only four years since the conquest, but there was no indication that the Mexicans would ever rise again. For those who had not seen it before the final battle in 1521, it was hard to imagine what Tenochtitlan had looked like. The Aztec pyramids and temples were all gone and the canals were being filled rapidly. Churches and Spanish-style houses were being built everywhere, with locals doing the labor. Spanish-led expeditions were going out in all directions, under orders to watch for any signs of revolt. The orders were to attack immediately unless the native forces were enormous, in which case runners were to be sent to the capital for reinforcements. So far, nothing had occurred to make Colonel Juan Fierro take such a step. Guatemala City was quiet. They had rested and replenished their provisions there for a few days and then continued southward for another four weeks. Now they were camped by a river in the jungle, ready for the final march up the central mesa.

Juan relaxed, sitting on the folding chair facing the fire. Around him were the officers of his command, their clothes loosened and shirts opened. Here in the forest it almost never cooled. Juan surveyed his men and tried to remember how it had been when he had been a corporal in Cortes' command on the march to Tenochtitlan. That had only been six years before when he had been 25. The immensity of events since he had left the dusty village near Sevilla and his job on a horse breeder's farm seemed almost dreamlike. During his boyhood he had heard stories about the marvelous riches in what had been thought to be the Indies. Since the news that Balboa had sighted the Pacific, though, it was generally assumed this wasn't the Orient at all but a separate continent. Juan had been almost penniless when he had volunteered to join a group on its way to Cuba. But he had followed orders without complaint and had managed to get promoted to the rank of corporal. And like others in the Spanish settlement, he had heard the constant flow of rumors about the riches to the west. They were almost always about gold, though less often there were rumors about treasures of silver. He and the other troops were in ferment night after night, discussing the expeditions that were setting out or being planned. It was almost as if the whole world to the west was covered with gold and that the peoples there would give you great quantities of the precious stuff for a pittance or nothing at all. But Juan had wait-ed until an expedition came along that had tremendous promise, in no small part because of the reputation of the commander, Hernan Cortes. And then there were the tumultuous years of conquest, the march up onto the plateau to Tenochtitlan, the formal acceptance by Moctezuma, the steady loss of trust between him and Cortes, the terri-ble night of tears when the Spaniards had to fight their way out of the city across the causeway, each man carrying as much gold as he could.... Juan still remembered the bag full of Aztec gold ornaments he had tried to get out. There hadn't been enough time to melt them down and he had lost all in the escape.

Juan's dreams were interrupted by his orderly. Young Matteo was actually one of the troops, a corporal in fact, but Juan used his services when he needed them, especially when they camped at night. Matteo proffered a box of cigars which he had carried from Cuba. Many sol-diers had taken to smoking the long black tubes which they found the Taino and Caribs smoking on the islands. *Tambacu*, the Indians called it, and both sexes and almost all ages were found smoking it. The men had already taken some back to the Spanish court and in New Spain it was becoming common among the troops.

They had found the Aztecs smoking smaller tubes with wrappers of corn husks, also filled with tobacco. A few Spaniards had started smoking these "little cigars" but generally they felt the long black ones of the islands were more manly.

"Colonel Fierro, try one of the Cuban cheroots. It will settle the digestion."

It was four years since Juan had been made a colonel. Cortes had promoted the original troops rapidly once the Spanish were established as masters of the empire. They didn't know if the new ranks would be accepted in Spain and so Juan, like many others, had decided to stay in the new land. He took one of the cigars and licked its sides as smokers had learned to do. Matteo offered a burning ember to light it. Juan drew in the acrid smoke and savored its bite.

"Gracias young man. It has been a while since I've had a good Cuban."

"I thought so, sir. I've seen you smoking the Aztec cigarettes during the day, but I said to myself, 'I would wager that the commandante would really appreciate a good cigar.'"

"Yes," Juan answered. "There's some satisfaction from the little maize-wrapped smoke, but there's nothing like a Cuban, especially after a good meal."

The officers had been served tapir steak along with boiled corn and tortillas. Back in Mexico City they were getting more Spanish food. They had even had a little wheat flour the last couple of years, though generally one still managed with tortillas made of maize. Juan thought longingly of having a slice of bread. It wasn't that he didn't like tortillas, but some Spanish bread once in a while would keep them from forgetting what life had been like in the old country. The tapir steak, though, had been very tasty, probably a young animal. Their hunters had brought it back along with a couple of deer. They always took hunters along on outlying expeditions. They had some beef jerky also, though that was meat of last resort, since, coming from Cuba, it was costly.

Juan leaned back in comfort, smoking the big cigar and watching Matteo polish his helmet. All the Spanish troops wore these, having brought them along from Cuba, though some new ones had come on the last shipload into Vera Cruz. They tried to keep them shined. Apart from the value of the helmets to deflect arrows or spears, the men had learned that lines of soldiers on horseback with glinting casques seen from a distance inspired fear in the native communities.

"Sir," Matteo said, "would you like a cup of *chocolatl*? The cook's woman has fixed a pot."

Juan insisted on having a Spaniard as head cook, although he did not object to the man having a female Indian assistant. He knew that many of the men had Indian mistresses anyway, but he felt that they should do something more than just sleep with the men. He noticed that Matteo still used the Aztec word, *chocolatl*, though most Spaniards were already using the Spanish pronunciation, *chocolate*.

"Sounds like a good idea," he said. "But I don't want just a frothed up drink with nothing in it but cacao bean paste and water."

That was the way the Aztecs had been using it when the Spaniards first came, a whipped-up frothy drink which they had been so crazy about that they wouldn't let the commoners have any. They acted like it was food for the gods. The Spaniards tried it when it was first offered them and many got used to it the Aztec way. But many did not find it very good, and so they tried it with honey. There was no sugar yet, but they had learned that the Aztecs had a little stingless bee which they kept for honey.

"We don't have any honey in camp, do we?" Juan asked. "If I could put a spoonful in the chocolate, I would like a cup."

"I don't know, colonel," Matteo answered. "But I'll go ask." The young man put down the casque and hurried toward the cooking shelter.

Good young man, Juan thought, the kind of fellow you need on these arduous expeditions. No question that he was bucking for promotion, but that was all right, too. There was still plenty of territory to explore and put under the Spanish crown, though Juan didn't think about this very much. Although Cortes had done it in the name of the Spanish crown, he pretty much ran things his own way. Anyway, Juan thought, the conquerors still had a long way to go in the Americas and there was plenty of room for young Spanish soldiers to get high rank.

Matteo returned with a steaming cup of sweetened chocolate.

"They found the honey in the last village we went through," he said. "You know, the one where there were only a couple of girls left. The troops scouted everywhere but could find nothing except a couple of dogs and the girls. So they brought them along. They are down in the enlisted men's section now."

Yes, Juan knew. That was what happened to young girls when invading troops passed by. And these two weren't even that special, but there was always somebody who was willing to have a go at a "liberated" female.

"Did the interpreters find out anything from them?" Juan asked. "I mean, what happened to the rest of the village?"

"They said that many had died from the pox disease and the rest were greatly weakened. They did everything they could to drive off the evil spirits, but nothing worked, so they fled into the mountains, abandoning their fields and villages."

It was an old story, repeated time after time, since the first days of the conquest. The Spaniards got smallpox and other illnesses also, but most got better after a few blood-lettings. But the Indians almost never recovered. He thought they were a weak people besides being pagans. No wonder they lost all their battles.

"But those two girls did not look sick or pocked."

"No, sir, but they say they had come from another place. The village people had already left when they came."

Juan thought that it was impossible to sort out all these stories. One thing was certain, though: the whole country was in turmoil; and another certainty was that the people lied.

"The faster we get the padres down here, the better, " Juan said. "Most of these people are going to die and they had better be baptized or the other world is going to be filled with the damned."

He sipped his chocolate and found it pleasing. The number of new foods he had experienced since he had come to the New World was considerable. He still looked back nostalgically at the Spanish food of his youth, but he had to admit that many of the Indian dishes were tasty.

"So what about the honey," he asked. "The troops found that in the village?"

"Yes, the girls showed them where there were several hives. We think they were too bulky for the villagers to carry away, at least in a hurry."

It still amazed Juan that the only way these people could move something was by foot. Everything had to be carried, mostly with a tump line across the forehead, though the royalty in Mexico had been carried about on litters and the reports were that the rulers of Tierra Calma were also carried about in that fashion. Well, they would soon see. Juan puffed his cigar between swallows of the chocolate.

"Did you ever eat the spicy chocolate sauce they cook their turkey in?"

The Aztecs' favorite way to prepare it was in mole, a sauce made of ground chocolate, jalapeno chiles, and various other spices, served with tortillas to pick up the pieces of meat and to sop up the sauce. Juan's woman, Axolotl, prepared a delicious mole.

"No, colonel sir," Matteo said. "I have not yet had the pleasure, but when I get back to the capital, I will surely try to find it, perhaps at the market."

The one place the Spaniards had left almost untouched was the central market. And though the market had changed much, villagers still carried their products in to sell for *pesos*. Among themselves they still sometimes exchanged cacao beans as money. When Juan had finished his cigar he said, "Bring the Terreno here, Matteo. I need to plan the final approach to the city."

They had brought one man from Tierra Calma along, a man they had found during one of the expeditions out of Guatemala. Reports had been coming in for two to three years about the people to the south, the place of platform temples where high chiefs ruled, wearing extravagant headdresses of bird feathers and wielding large symbolic stone scepters. None of the reports described the place as anything so elaborate as Mexico, though the population was supposed to be sizable, and the largest town, Volcan, to have a population in the thousands. There were reported to be even more volcanos than in Mexico, and one to the east of the town was active. It was said that to get to Volcan one needed only to follow the great plume of smoke that extended to the west farther than the eye could see. But the thing that most attracted Juan was that the place was reported to be full of gold ornaments. According to reports, the royalty were bedecked with them, others wore fewer, but great numbers were buried with the dead. Juan thought that somehow he might make up the great loss from the sad and violent night when he dropped his sack of Aztec treasures into the lake.

The orderly returned with the Terreno man, who walked with his eyes downcast, and an interpreter. The Terreno, dressed in a breechclout, kneeled before Juan, and the interpreter squatted next to the Terreno. The interpreter wore a pair of knee-length pantalons and a cotton shirt, the costume of Mexicans who were trying to merge into the new regime. Both he and the Terreno wore sandals. The Terreno had an extended lobe, evidence that he had once worn something heavy in his ear.

The recent commandantes were of two types, those who believed that most information could be obtained by frightening informants and those who believed that some kindness, even if it was only tactical, worked better. Juan was of the latter, so he indicated to the man to squat.

"Ask him what the name of his chief is," Juan said to the interpreter, who then spoke the name in Nahuatl, the language of the Aztecs. When he was satisfied with the answer, he responded to Juan in Spanish.

"He says it is something like Zipotelec, but that it means Temple Hill, Senor Temple Hill in Nahuatl." Juan was impressed with the man's ability to pronounce Castilian.

He had learned by this time that everyone's name in most local languages was taken from some object or process in the local environment, and that the interpreters always translated them from Nahuatl to Spanish. Usually the Spaniards gave the people they worked with Spanish names but they used the names of others as given, at least until they were brought under Spanish control. The interpreter, who was baptized, was called Pedro. "And ask him how many warriors the chief has under his command," Juan continued.

Pedro and the Terreno spoke back and forth two or three times, then Pedro turned to Juan.

"He said at first that there were many thousands and all of them well armed and that they were great warriors who had helped Zipotelec conquer many cities until he had become supreme ruler of Tierra Calma. But when I tried to get him to be exact, it seems he wasn't sure."

"Do you think he is telling us the truth?"

"Senor, one can never be sure with these men who are telling on their own people, but I think he may be doing as well as he can. He knows that we will march on the city and he will be with us; and if he has lied, he would know that the commandante would have him executed. He could have escaped on the way from Tenochtitlan, commandante. So the very fact that he is here is an indication that he is on our side."

"So how many warriors did you finally arrive at?"

"I would estimate, noble commandante, that there are between one and two thousand."

"And how well armed?"

There was another interchange between Pedro and the Terreno.

"He seems to believe that most have either swords or atl-atls, though there are some with bows and arrows also."

Juan figured that the swords were wood clubs with inset blades and the atl-atls were throwing sticks, both of which they had faced against the Aztecs. The bows and arrows were probably long ones, the kind favored by hunters in lowland forests.

"Any guns?" He knew from experience that firearms were moving rapidly into the hands of tribals, as fast as they could get them.

"He says he doesn't think so. There hasn't been much trade so far."

Good, Juan thought, it was best to subdue all these tribes before they got too much modern equipment.

"How about horses? Have they seen horses?"

Again, the exchange between Pedro and the Terreno.

"No, he says he is sure they haven't seen them. They have heard about them, though they still think like the Aztecs did at first that horse and man made a single animal. But the Terreno says he never saw a horse before he came north."

Juan leaned back. "It sounds like it will be a piece of cake," he said, though he had never thought this would be an arduous campaign. After the conquest of Mexico, everything had been easy. The only really difficult parts were the marches, to the north through the arid regions where the main problem was just getting enough water, or into the jungles of the south with their heat and fevers. And this was one of the last. From Tierra Calma to the south was Panama where a sizeable Spanish settlement already existed. Juan brought out his pouch and pulled out a couple of gold objects. One was in the shape of a frog about one inch square and the other a bat about twice as large. He laid these on the log table in front of him.

"Ask him if there are many like these in Tierra Calma."

Without touching them the Terreno spoke to Pedro. When he stopped, Pedro explained to Juan.

"He says that there are. Volcan, which is the name of the central town, is a place which specializes in their manufacture, though they make them in many other places as well. They are symbols of a person's clan totem. A person who wears earrings or a pendant of a bat belongs to the bat clan, while one with a frog piece is a member of the frog clan. That is also why people are buried with them."

Juan picked up the frog and turned it over in his hand, studying it more carefully. These had got to Tenochtitlan through trade and the man who had them could tell the Spaniard in the market only that they came from Tierra Calma. Juan spoke to himself, though his words were audible.

"The bugger is certainly well made; too bad so many will be melted down into ingots."

He had seen it happen in town after town. Whenever a tribe or village area was taken over, the first thing the commandante did was to order all the weaponry and gold and silver ornaments brought in. The swords and atl-atls would be destroyed on the spot since these were the weapons of warfare and had of course been used for defense against the Spanish. The ornaments would be put into bags for transport after a short speech about how they were symbolic of Satan and superstitious beliefs and would be destroyed. And if there was a padre along, he would be brought up, and after more speeches, there would usually be a mass baptism. Afterwards, the ornaments would be melted down into ingots, some kept by the conquistadors, but most being sent off to the Spanish court. Anyway, Juan thought, it was certainly proper to melt them down since they represented tribal superstition, if not Satan himself.

Zipotelec

The procession moved down the main street of Volcan in the coolness of early morning. The mountains around the mesa were bright green with forest growth. Here and there on the sides were cleared spaces, farmers' fields. From the east there was a continuous trail of smoke drifting from an erupting volcano, twenty miles away. Townspeople, clad in breechclouts, skirts, or tubular dresses stood along the way, in front of the houses and other buildings, most of adobe, though a few of fieldstone. All were covered with thatch roofs.

First in the procession were warriors, armed and bedecked. Most wore slatted armor and feathers or other ornamentation. Some wore ocelot or other animal skins over their shoulders. The officers had jaguar skins and necklaces of animal teeth and carried stone war clubs. After the warriors came a line of men tied to one another by rope, their hands fastened behind them. These were the captives from the recent expedition to Turtle Bay, the large town on the west ocean. Behind them four drummers beat out a rhythm as they walked. After the drummers, a group of young women, wearing bright cotton skirts and decorated with face paint and feathers on head bands, danced from side to side. Several clowns followed, gesticulating and miming toward the onlookers. The children watching became particularly agitated as the clowns passed. Finally came three litters with tent roofs, carried by four men each. The first held a man sitting cross-legged, more elaborately bedecked than any before with feathers and jewelry and elaborate face painting. He wore a large gold pendant on a chain. He was the war chief and of the butterfly clan. Lately he had insisted that no official procession could proceed without his presence. And since he was leading most of the raids against other tribes, he could not be denied.

Behind him was the litter of Zipotelec, who was dressed in the same fashion, though with a pendant of an eagle. He also held a polished ceremonial ax. His headdress was made from the feathers of the *quetzal*, which was only permitted for the cacique and others of the ruling family. He periodically waved his ceremonial ax toward the viewers.

He was preoccupied this morning, not knowing what the day would bring. He hadn't slept well the night before, feeling so gloomy that he did not even visit one of his concubines. He had dreamt that a great snake larger than any ever seen had slithered up to the mesa and no matter what they did to stop it, nothing helped. It kept moving closer and closer to Volcan, eating people as it went. Apart from its enormous size, the snake was different in several ways. As in the way of dreams, many of the details were not clear. Though it seemed more like one of the great swallowing snakes, it sometimes appeared to have feet which it used to help climb up the mountainsides, like a monstrous centipede. And certain parts of its skin glittered. At that moment he took his pendant in his hand, pleased at least that he belonged to the great eagle clan, the bird that killed snakes.

He was also worried about his war leader, Huantzin, who was continually pushing for more control. Ever since his success in conquering neighboring villages and even tribes, Huantzin acted and talked more and more as if he was the controlling authority. Zipotelec pushed from his mind the fact that he had achieved his position in the same way, ultimately fighting his way in to Volcan. And that, once well established, he had given over the military responsibilities to his young lieutenant to savor life as supreme cacique in the capital. He couldn't deny that Huantzin was good at his task, but it seemed very clear that he was not satisfied with the limited position of war chief. He kept assuming prerogatives of the cacique, insisting that he and his had the right to use the quetzal feathers as well as to be carried on a litter, even though he knew that was the prerogative of the chief and his family. Zipotelec sighed and readjusted his position.

And finally there were the rumors of the approaching *kabajo* killers. For the past several years they had heard the stories about the new creatures, going from village to village and town to town, great tall beasts with shiny sides and heads, carrying hollow metal sticks from which smoke belched while hurling forward an invisible object which killed whatever it struck. There were all kinds of additional details about the *kabajo*. Some were reported to have escorts of giant wolf-dogs which breathed fire and tore apart anything that got in front of them. Some *kabajo-men* were reported to carry lances of unbeliev- able length with which they could skewer many warriors at a time. At first the stories had been hard to believe and Zipotelec thought they must be fantasies. Then he thought the *kabajo-men* might be supernat- ural creatures which would remain far away. They were reported to be in the north and then the south and also on great boats off the east coast. And just five days earlier, a line of creatures had been reported in the jungles to the northeast. It was for this that they had decided to do the sacrifice. No one knew what god to propitiate, but they finally decided it was serious enough to make offerings to the Creator and the Continuator.

After an hour's march through the streets and the edge of town, they came to Lake Tlantla, which meant the lake with no bottom. Everyone knew there was a bottom, but it was very far down. Evidently the ancient peoples had given it that name before they had been able to measure the depth. But it was deep enough to serve well as a place for offerings to the spirits. A platform had been built at a cleared place and extended out over the lake where objects and bodies could be hurled directly into the water and which also served as a viewing stand.

The three litters were set down and the two chiefs got out, sur- rounded by warriors and priests. The prisoners were forced to squat in a group to one side. All were quiet except one of the girls who was weeping. No one paid any attention to her. Most of those in atten- dance had seen sacrifices before and it did happen that some of the prisoners wept or protested, even though it was believed that sacrificial victims went directly to the spirit world.

As soon as everyone was settled, the priests took over. One of them told the gathered audience to keep quiet during the ritual so all messages would be carried without noise to the spirits. They beckoned to the warriors to truss up the prisoners. Several came forward with cotton rope and began to methodically tie the men's arms and legs to their bodies so they would be completely immobile. This was to be a live sacrifice, which was believed to be more effective than those in which the victim was first stunned or killed by an ax blow. The drummers kept a slow chant going, along with a continuous beat. When the prisoners were all trussed, the priests drew designs on their heads, backs, and arms. Then one lit a cheroot and blew smoke over the victims, afterwards blowing it in the cardinal directions, reciting, "Great spirits of the people of the mesa, and particularly the Creator and the Continuator, founder and maintainer of the land of rich forests and cultivated fields, we pray to thee. We thank thee who has seen fit to create this paradise on earth where food crops grow in abundance and wild animals—the deer, javelina, tapir, the succulent agouti, iguana, and the howler monkey—are ours for the taking. And we thank thee for the many skills you have taught us—how to make cloth from cotton, and pottery from clay, to cook our food and to use throughout our lives, for storage or ritual, especially the multi-colored tripod vessels, obsidian to make sharp blades for weapons, and granular stone to be made into metates and manos to grind our corn, and especially for the large ones in the shape of a jaguar used in rituals or burials. We thank thee for these and also for the *tambacu* to make offerings with.

"We thank thee, also, oh great spirits, for the minerals of the land, the bright shining silver and the incorruptible gold to make all the many brilliant objects and jewels for the living and the dead.

"And we thank thee, sublime ones, and the multitudes of spirit forces you have created for the heavens and earth, as well as the spirits which have founded the clans of our people.

"And last we thank thee for the successes you have given to our warriors and leaders in the conquest of other tribes and villages and all the booty and captives that have resulted.

"Indeed the life you have bestowed on us, great spirit beings, could hardly be improved upon. Except that now we have concern for the events that have come to pass in recent weeks. There have been unexpected occurrences in the sky, once when the sun was eaten by a great round sky spirit, once when the shaking spirit shook the earth with particular ferocity, and then the intermittent belching of the Razu spirit."

Many of the participants at the ritual looked up at the sky at this moment to see if the stream of volcanic smoke was continuing or had been interrupted. The stream of smoke was steady.

The priest continued. "And in the last few weeks there has been the continuous stream of reports about the approach of the *kabajo-men*. We know not what these creatures are, whether man or beast, but whenever we hear of them they are described as particularly ferocious. We have mighty warriors who stand prepared to defend our towns and villages, but they can succeed only against real men.

"We feel it would be best if such creatures never came, but if they do, we believe we will need all the help we can get. And so we have come today to seek your help, either to keep them far away or, if they come, to give us strength to resist, because from the reports we hear there is no possibility of making any peaceful arrangements with them.

"So we bring these goods and these captives as offerings to show our earnestness and to seek thy blessing."

The other priest came forward and began directing the taking of things from out of the third litter—several multi-colored pottery vessels, about half of them tripods, two large jaguar metates, and three ceremonial axes. Beside these, the priests placed a basket containing many ornaments, most of them gold.

The first priest gestured and an assistant brought forward a container of maize beer from which the priest began with a gourd dipper to sprinkle on the objects, reciting, "Oh spirit rulers, all we have is hereby consecrated by the drink of the gods, the sacred beer of the noble plant." Then he turned to the captives and sprinkled beer on their heads, reciting, "That their journey into the sacred way will be smooth and untroubled."

He finished by offering a cup of the sacred drink to Zipotelec and Huantzin. Then he gave a cup to the other priests and quaffed one himself.

They moved the litter of offerings to the edge of the reviewing stand and the priests stood on either side and began, in turn, blowing puffs of smoke on the objects and reciting, "With this smoke of the sacred weed, we the people of the clans, and especially those of the eagle and the butterfly—"

Zipotelec got a jolt when he heard the clan totem of Huantzin included. He was sure the war chief had spoken to the priests before the ritual, since this was not at all usual and he had certainly not been consulted.

The priest continued, "We hereby offer the finest products of our people." While he was talking, the other priests picked up one of the tripod vessels and hurled it out over the water. It floated momentarily but since it had a small hole chipped out of the bottom, it soon began to sink. Whereupon the first priest did the same with another, and one item after another disappeared into the lake.

The first priest motioned to the troops and two of them brought one of the bound captives forward. The priest inspected the cord to see if the man was tied completely. Satisfied, he motioned to a man in a dugout canoe to get in position. The man in the canoe was usually not needed since a tightly-bound captive had little chance to do anything after he was hurled into the lake, but it had happened before that a prisoner got his cord loose and managed to get back to the surface. It was then that the priests had designated a boatman to be on hand so he could crush the man's skull with a war ax. The sides of the lake were so steep that anything thrown in went almost straight down.

The second priest took the first prisoner by his hair and pulled his head up.

"Creator and Continuator, and all the lesser spirit beings, we hereby offer the most sublime thing that can be consecrated to those beyond and we beseech that you continue to listen to our pleas, particularly now in the frightening times of the *kabajo-men*, that life on our beloved mesa be continued through time beyond imagining. Thus, we offer you this noble captive warrior."

The priest stepped back and motioned to the two assigned men who picked up the bound captive, one on each side, and with a heave threw him out from the edge of the platform. Like the material objects, he quickly disappeared from the surface, leaving large concentric rings to spread from the point of disappearance.

They did the same with the other captives, including the weeping woman.

Matteo

The combined Spanish and Indian forces marched toward the town of Volcan. Now and then they saw in the distance local farmers or other natives. Juan Fierro rode a horse at the front of the company with Matteo on a mule just to his right and a little behind, though close enough for the two men to talk. Behind them rode several horsemen and in their midst, walking, was Huantzin, the war chief, who had appeared in camp two nights before. One horseman had a pair of mastiffs on leashes. More horsemen followed, then a priest on a mule, and finally the Indian troops, all on foot, armed with spear throwers or bows and arrows.

Matteo was thinking of the impression he would make when he came back to Dos Fuentes, his village in southern Spain, particularly if they were successful in their mission and got a lot of gold. Then they would listen to him, even the girls, even Blanquita, who had laughed at him and his work. Matteo had heard that she had asked of him, "What does he do, spread horse manure?"

Certainly working on a horse farm was not such a high-class job, but what else could the third son expect in a family that had barely five hectares? There was little doubt that the property would be inherited by Pablo, the firstborn; and Henrique, the second, had early decided that he would become a monk. And there were always those stories about the Indies. Matteo had suspected that things were not always wonderful in the new territories. Most men never came back. But those who did had the most fantastic stories, and it was because of them that he had taken the job with horses, in the hope that he could end up like them. And perhaps this expedition would be the answer to his dreams.

His mule slowed down, and in some irritation, Matteo whipped it across the ears, thinking that if all went well, the first thing he would get when he got back to Mexico was a horse.

Juan turned and waved him forward.

"How are you feeling, young fellow? A little excitement at the prospect of your first fight?"

"A little, senor," Matteo answered. "Though this is what I prepared for and it doesn't seem too daunting."

"It isn't, really," Juan said. "Compared with the conquest of Tenochtitlan, this is small turnips." He paused. "Though the payoff might be a good one. That is, if all the reports we have got so far about the gold are true." He patted his tunic where the two pieces he had carried from Mexico City were located.

"Yes," Matteo said. "I've heard the stories about the terrible fight against the eagle and jaguar warriors, particularly on *La Noche Triste*, the sad night. They say that many Spaniards were lost, but those who escaped were reunited under the mighty commandante, Cortes, and came back to conquer the center city. I'm sure the organizers of that rebellion—those who survived—had second thoughts about what they had done."

"Yes, it was indeed a turbulent time, but as you know, with God on our side, the non-believers have no chance against the arms of the Spaniard. And you will see it for yourself soon—even though the people we conquer are a far cry from the Aztecs. And we have also learned a lot about how to conquer barbarians."

At this moment a snarling fight broke out between the mastiffs behind them. Juan pulled his horse around and hurried back to the scene. One of the dogs had got his rope loose and had turned on the other. A soldier was cracking him across the head with the handle of a whip, while the man who had lost the hold was pulling back on the leash which he had just retrieved. Other soldiers had moved back to form a loose circle about the scene. Juan pushed his way in.

"Pull those dogs apart!" he commanded. "Immediately!"

The soldier with the whip dealt a blow that almost stunned the dog, the leash holder gave a yank and the aggressor dog was pulled back.

"You men may think these dogs are for our entertainment," Juan said. "But they have been brought along as a part of this fighting machine. I know you think that taking the temple mound tribes is easy after the great conquests to the north, but I can assure you that it is not over until the barbarians kneel before us and the padre pours baptismal water over them. And that will come only after they are defeated, which means the use of everything we have brought along—our weapons, armor, horses, and dogs. Until you have seen the terror those dogs can put into a force of barbarians, you can have no idea of how valuable they are. And that means they do not use up their ferocity against each other. They use it against barbarians whom they will automatically attack."

He pulled his horse around and waved his arm. "Now forward march!"

Matteo found his commandante imposing at that moment. He hoped that he, too, would be able to live up to the reputation of the Spanish soldiers. As soon as he could, he maneuvered his mule into position behind the commandante again.

"Sir, do you think there will be a pitched battle? We have seen no troops so far."

Juan chuckled. "Well, young fellow, I'll tell you, since if all goes well you will become a commander on your own some day. Do not worry, just be prepared for the worst. Sometimes the barbarians resist in force, but more often they do not. You see, we have learned a lot since those early days when we marched in from Vera Cruz. We now know that the barbarians are a fearful, omen-reading people, who can be brought to their knees by playing on their minds. Even the big one, the conquest of Tenochtitlan, might have been managed without any out-and-out battle. But we didn't know so much in those days. We thought we would have to fight those troops as we would in Europe."

"I suppose the difference is that God is always on our side," Matteo said, "while in Europe all men are Christians—at least now that our noble monarchs have been able to drive the infidels out of Spain."

"I wouldn't refuse God's help," Juan answered. "But you will learn that we soldiers have to make our own choices too. Oh, yes, we can say prayers before a battle, but from then on it is up to us and our arms—and our minds. We try to confuse the other side."

In the distance they could see Lake Tlantla where a group of men were assembled. Juan said to Matteo, "They are too far away for us to know if they are armed. But they hardly seem prepared to attack. A paltry force of barbarians like that would be no match for our forces. With a Spaniard in command, our barbarian allies could probably take them."

Ever since the successful use of allies in the taking of Tenochtitlan, the Spaniards had made a regular practice of using native troops. Juan had brought the troops on this expedition from the Cholla Tribe, which had served many expeditions. Besides having become Christians, most of the young men had learned quite a few Spanish tactics as well as enough of the Spanish language for military needs.

"But the best way for a fast conquest is to first create doubt in their minds and then to strike terror in their hearts," Juan continued. "That legend that Cortes was the returning white god certainly never hurt. And the belief that a mounted horseman was an invincible man-beast also helped. And by now our reputation has spread throughout the countryside, so we no longer need to worry about the fear in their minds. So frequently all that is necessary to conquer a new tribe is a clear-cut act of terror."

Juan put up his hand for the rest of the troops and halted.

"Now I want to show you, young fellow. There are many ways to make an act of terror, but one of the best that we have learned to use has been to take hostages. One never knows exactly how to use them, but when opportunities arise, one takes advantage of them. So, would you go back and get Captain Sangre, as well as the Terreno war chief and the interpreter. I am going to show you, young fellow, how a true commander operates."

Matteo turned his mount back and got the mounted Spaniard and the two Indians who were on foot. Mounted troops marched on each side of Huantzin, though he was not tied. Matteo wondered how trustworthy he was. He had appeared in camp two nights before with a story about how despicable the peace chief was and that he, Huantzin, was the true reason why the Terrenos had prospered. He claimed that he should be the cacique and that if the Spaniards would help him, he would help them. He had said there were plenty of gold pieces available and that he would help them get all they wanted. It all sounded too easy, but the commandante had assured Matteo that there were always some discontented individuals in every group and that if they had important followings, it was worthwhile to use them. One had to watch such turncoats, but it was worth the risk.

Juan pointed toward the distant figures and said to the interpreter, "Ask the war chief who those men are over near the lake."

The interpreter spoke and the man responded.

"He says they are probably a burial party. There is a large burial mound over there and people who can afford it like to bury their dead there. He says it looks like they are finished and they are on their way back to Volcan."

Matteo thought that at least some people were going on with their usual activities, that they were not on a war footing.

"I assume they are not armed?" Juan asked.

"That is right, senor, they have just finished carrying the corpse out on a litter and performing the ritual, and now they are on their way back."

"It seems to me that there must be about twelve, right?"

"Yes, senor, he thinks that is about right."

Juan turned to Captain Sangre. "Take a dozen mounted troops and bring those men here. We will use them as hostages. Just herd them over here and we will tie them in a line for the rest of the march."

He turned to Matteo. "You can go along with them, young fellow. There will be no fighting and you can learn another of the operations that you may someday be carrying out. You might, for that matter, carry the interpreter along. I'm sure your mule will have no trouble carrying the two of you. We will continue slowly until you and the prisoners catch up."

Matteo got the interpreter on the mule behind him and took his place behind the troops of Captain Sangre, who headed to intercept the party of natives. They moved at a fast walk at first, but when they got closer it became clear that the native party had changed direction and was moving away at a faster rate. The captain had the troops increase their speed to a slow gallop. The distance between the troops and the natives shrank rapidly and the horsemen split to encircle the victims. By the time the troops met to close the circle, the Terrenos were in panic-shock, crouching as if to receive their death blows.

Captain Sangre called to the interpreter, "Tell them to stop and give up and no harm will come to them. We will take them to Volcan."

All the men except one continued their huddle. The one jumped up and ran through an opening, racing toward the woods. Captain Sangre turned his horse and galloped toward the man. Upon reaching the victim and without pause he cut him down with his blade of Toledo. The man's body collapsed, blood spurting from the neck, the head rolling to one side.

Matteo had heard many stories about the blood letting during the battles of conquest, but it was different to see the raw violence directly. Yet he was fascinated as he watched Captain Sangre turn and leisurely trot his horse back to the group. The man showed no emotion of any kind as he put the blade back into its scabbard. Matteo looked at the group of crouching men and could see immediately that they were under complete control. And when the translator repeated in their language the command to march, they did immediately. That was evidently what the commandante meant when he said that terror had to be instilled.

The commandante turned to Matteo when the younger man had caught up with him.

"And now young fellow, you have seen how it is done. Sangre is also a veteran of the battle for Tenochtitlan. Like all the old-timers, he knows well that a Spanish soldier is without mercy when he is facing the enemy."

Matteo still had trouble understanding how these people had become enemies. One could hardly blame them for resisting or fleeing, but these had not fought against the Spaniards. Anyway, he thought, since they were pagan barbarians they had to be subjugated. Otherwise, how would they ever become civilized?

The prisoners were quickly tied together in a line and the column continued. They were coming into the outskirts of Volcan where the adobe houses were more frequent. They saw a few people running from house to house. Then over to one side a group emerged, everyone on foot except one litter being carried by four men. They were armed with war-clubs and bows and arrows, and wearing slatted armor.

"The official greeting party!" Juan said as he halted the column.

Matteo crowded up as close as he could to the commandante. He wanted to hear everything that was said. He noticed the interpreter just next to him, and behind the interpreter, Huantzin.

"Young fellow, watch all this closely." Juan said to Matteo. "What happens in the next few minutes is critical. If it were a question of a major battle, I would order you back and get the troops in an attack formation. But as you know by now, these are not the battle-tested troops we faced up north. These people are barely beyond being savages and are easily defeated by experienced Spanish soldiers. Still there is no need to lose a single man. So we will go ahead as if it might turn into a real battle." He called back, "Captain Sangre, are you ready?"

"Si, senor, at your command."

By this time the native party was getting closer and the details of their arms and clothing were becoming apparent. Huantzin began speaking to the interpreter in a controlled, tense voice. The interpreter turned to Juan.

"He says it is the peace chief, Zipotelec, and his best warriors."

Juan laughed. "Those are his best warriors? If that's the best he can do, we shall be melting gold by nightfall. Tell him we come in peace, in the name of the great king and queen of Spain and of the mighty commandante of the empire of Mexico, Hernan Cortes. Tell him that we come to offer him the friendship of the Spaniards and the religion of Jesus Christ."

The interpreter relayed this, and Zipotelec waved his battle ax and answered in an excited voice.

"He says he appreciates all the noble commandante offers and he realizes his great strength and that of the other *kabajo-men*—"

Juan couldn't help interrupting. "What did he call us?"

There was another interchange between the interpreter and Zipotelec, then the interpreter said, "He says *kabajo-men*, the creature that is man on top and horse on the bottom."

Juan turned to Matteo and his own men. "That is amazing, don't you hear what they are calling us? It is a distortion of the Spanish word for horse, *caballo*. They don't have a word for the animal in their own language so they have taken the Spanish word and changed it for their own barbarian language." He laughed, but only for a moment and then said, "So then what does he say, does he accept our generous offer immediately? Because if he does not, tell him we will have to use our troops." Juan gave his horse a light dig with the spurs and the animal jumped forward, only to be held back by the bridle, upon which it danced in short steps. The troops facing them jumped in response, even the litter bearers. Juan knew his horse well and knew such a quick surge of movement could put an Indian group on edge.

When both sides had settled back, Zipotelec spoke. After he was finished, the interpreter said, "He wants to know why Huantzin is with you. He says Huantzin should be with him. He says he wants you to send Huantzin to him immediately."

"Tell him that the war chief chooses to be where he is and that no Indian tells a Spanish commandante what to do. Also tell him that we are prepared to give the Terrenos protection from all their enemies but that it will be under the Spanish crown."

Zipotelec leaned over to discuss the situation with a warrior who was bedecked with feathers, second in decoration only to the cacique. Huantzin whispered to the interpreter who spoke to the commandante.

"He says the fellow next to the cacique is acting as war chief now, that he used to be next to Huantzin."

The cacique spoke to Juan, and the interpreter responded, "He says that he needs to consider this further and he will return tomorrow. And he asks the commandante not to go any further into the town but to return to the open place on the other side of Lake Tlantla, and that he will send some food and women there."

Juan responded quickly, "Tell him that the Spaniards came here in peace and have offered the opportunity for the Terrenos to become part of the mighty empire of New Spain, with a perpetual reign of prosperity and happiness. But tell him also that the Spanish do not have a limitless amount of time and that the decision will have to be made immediately, and that in the meantime the troops will march to the temple mound in the center of the town and put a Spanish flag on top."

There was more agitated consultation between Zipotelec and his new war chief and finally the interpreter's reply. "He says it is impossible to decide so quickly, but that he will be here tomorrow morning. In the meantime he says he sends a greeting of friendship."

The commandante ordered, "Banners and weapons at the ready, forward march!"

The column, already at alert, began their forward movement. They marched directly toward Zipotelec and his men. The native unit gave way as the Spanish approached and soon a space between the two developed. Then the two moved in parallel lines, Zipotelec obviously keeping watch on the intruders. They came near the center of town where the buildings were larger, some of them two stories. Soon there were armed men on top of some of the buildings, scuttling from one to another. Then one shot an arrow, followed by several others. Most of the arrows fell out of range, though a few reached the column. It was easy to deflect most of those which did reach the troops, but one hit a horse in its flank. The horse jumped, and the trooper pulled the bridle hard to prevent the animal from bolting. The armed men had already turned in the direction of the shooting, their guns at ready.

Juan ordered, "Dismount and make ready to fire!"

The men got off their horses and trained their guns on the natives who were continuing to fire sporadically, most of the arrows falling short.

"Fire!" Juan ordered.

The volley went off, a spurt of smoke rising from each gun. Two men were hit, but how badly one couldn't tell, since they dropped or were dragged from sight immediately, and the rest of the archers disappeared also. The first line of gunmen fell back to reload, while the second line replaced them. Silence overwhelmed.

There was a brief hesitation as the men awaited Juan's new command.

"Captain Sangre," Juan said, "cut loose two of the prisoners and drive them away from the unit. As soon as they are clear, set the dogs free."

The second in command ordered one of his men to cut the rope on the two front men in the prisoner line-up. And when they cowed in fright and incomprehension, the Captain grabbed a whip from another trooper and cracked it across the backs of the men. They jumped up and ran toward Zipotelec's unit. Just as they cleared the Spanish column, the mastiffs were unleashed. They had already seen the moving men and leapt toward them. In several bounds they had closed the distance and, as they had been trained, each leapt on one of the men. The weight of the dogs bowled the men over and the dogs were on top of them. One man tried to protect his head with his arms and the dog immediately began ripping his abdomen. The other man seemed to be in too much shock to make any defensive movement and the dog began to savage his neck and head. The jaws and necks of the dogs soon became bloody.

Matteo

The two young troopers squatted in a courtyard keeping the fire going and feeding ornamental gold pieces into a crucible they had brought along from Tenochtitlan. Matteo had been put with Hector who had some knowledge of smelting from his days as an apprentice with a goldsmith in Spain. He had quit his apprenticeship and joined the Spanish force when he heard of all the gold and silver they had found in the New World and had eventually made his way to Mexico City where he was selected for the expedition to Tierra Calma.

He was making molds for ingots in the sand while Matteo fed gold pieces into the crucible and supervised the two Terrenos who kept the fire hot. One man pumped the bellows which they had also brought from Mexico City while the other put charcoal into the fire.

Matteo held up a large piece in the shape of a crocodile. "It might be good to save this one. Though most are pretty well-made, this one is especially fancy."

When Juan had assigned them to this job he had told Matteo to keep a few of the best ones to take back to Mexico from where most would be sent on to the Spanish court so they could see the workmanship.

They had been melting down gold pieces for three days and the pile of gold was building up in its storage place in the house where Juan was staying.

"Yes, they are good at this," Hector said. "Though spending all that wealth by making weird creatures is beyond me. They use the lost wax method, making the figure in wax, covering it with clay, melting the wax to leave the impression in the clay, pouring the molten gold into the clay mold, and after it has cooled, breaking off the clay and taking out the finished piece. It is a good method for making figures. But don't forget that this is all heathen stuff and this will be the last of it. It's certain that after the men are baptized they will not be allowed to make any more of these."

"Have you seen any of their goldsmiths?" Matteo asked.

"Not working. I was taken to one of their smelters but no one was there. They said the goldsmiths had run away."

Matteo held the crocodile up. "So what do you think? Should we save it?"

"Might as well. We only have a couple so far today."

The two men lapsed into silence, doing their respective jobs. Matteo was reconstructing in his memory the events of the last week. He broke the silence.

"Did you think they would give up so easily?"

"I was a little surprised," Hector answered. "I know the Indians are cowards, but they had only lost a few men."

When Juan's unit had marched on Zipotelec a few native warriors had shot from a distance, but there was never any organized resistance.

"Commandante Fierro was exactly right," Matteo said. "He told me before that the idea was to create confusion and then terror, and that is exactly what he did. Attacking and surrounding them with the horses was the best thing to do. Like most Indians who haven't seen horses, they were frightened by them."

"And guns, too," Hector said. "They just do not know the range of guns, so picking off some of their bowmen worked wonders."

Zipoletec had been captured and put into one of the houses under guard and Juan used Huantzin as the Terreno representative from then on. And though a few arrows had been shot at the troops, this had only lasted a couple of days while the Spanish and Cholla went from house to house and on orders shot someone anytime an arrow was shot at them. All those who stayed soon surrendered, assuming the position they quickly learned from one another—kneeling and laying their arms on the ground.

"One thing bothers me, though," Matteo said. "The commandante never seems to worry about punishing innocent people. For instance, those Indians who were killed by the dogs had never done anything. They weren't even armed. And shooting someone every time someone else shoots an arrow, even those who never had any weapons, that doesn't seem right."

Hector laughed harshly. "Well you ought to know. You're the one who said the commandante was intent on creating terror among the population. That's the best way to do it, to punish in the most harsh manner possible, whether those you punish are guilty or not. After all, they are all just Indians. And what rights do they have?"

Two native men came into the courtyard with baskets on their backs, held by tump lines across their foreheads. A Spanish trooper was guarding them. He directed the men to go to Matteo. "Here's another load, *amigo*. Where do you want it?"

"Just have them put it on the ones we have."

Under the direction of their guard, the native men poured the gold pieces on top of the other ones on a cotton blanket.

"Where did these come from?" Matteo asked.

"The digging parties found two more tombs loaded with gold pieces."

One of the first orders of business after it was clear that there would be no more fighting had been to search the houses for gold or anything else of value. Huantzin had been most useful in leading search parties. But even before they were finished, he had told the interpreter that there were many gold and silver pieces out in the tombs around the town. And from that time on, there were new parties out digging up the tombs.

Matteo picked up a large piece that looked like no creature on earth, but which was exquisitely made.

"Somehow it seems sacrilegious to dig up their dead for the gold ornaments.

"Aw, just remember, it is all heathen stuff."

~

Q: *The title certainly fits the narrative in this instance, though it is not what we have always learned about this period. Most of us were taught that this was a discovery, begun after Columbus reached the New World. Was this not primarily a period of discovery?*

A: Yes, sort of, since the people who did it initially were ignorant of what was out there. The Europeans did discover the Americas and after that the islands of the Pacific Ocean and most places in Asia, about which they had little good information, and Africa. But of course they weren't the initial discoverers. All the land areas of the world had already been discovered and occupied by humans for any-where from twenty thousand years (the Americas) to five million years (Africa). But of course the entire period of the "discovery" was domi-nated by ethnocentrism as pronounced as any we have ever known, and the Euros did not really think that non-Euros counted, or at least that they counted as no more than workers or customers. As a matter of fact, the Euros were so little interested in how the others got to these lands that they made practically no effort to find out where they came from until the nineteenth century when the science of archeology came into being. Even in our own day we hear of someone who climbed a mountain or got somewhere else remote claiming that he was the first white man to get there. And by now, of course, everyone knows that some non-Euro has already been in every place in the world, no matter how remote.

Q: *That's not exactly true though, is it? I don't think there were any people in Antarctica before the Euros arrived, and perhaps some very high mountaintops and small islands.*

A: Okay, I did exaggerate slightly, a problem with us inveterate storytellers. Antarctica is the only big place that had not been reached by non-Euros. And people did not settle on high mountain peaks or on very small islands since these places would not support human life over long periods. There were mighty few places available for Robinson Crusoes.

Q: *But the Euros, beginning with Columbus and da Gama, did really discover new lands, even if they weren't the first, didn't they?*

A: Yes, though no one knows how many times a given piece of real estate was "discovered" by one group of people after another. We know from archeology that places like Mexico and Peru were "discovered" and inhabited by dozens of cultures. This of course is no different from other places in the world. Europe had been occupied by many peoples with different cultures. When we talk about Europeans now, we are merely talking about the people who took over and evolved after the Roman Empire crumbled, say for the last 1500 years.

Q: *So you seem to be saying that the discovery was not very important, is that right?*

A: I guess I am saying that. Beginning with Columbus, the discovery of the later Euros wasn't nearly so important as what they did after they discovered the places. There is now little doubt that the Vikings, who I will hereby designate as early Euros, also "discovered" the Americas, but all they did was to wipe out a few savages (they called them *skraelings*), after which they went back home. But the other Euros from Columbus on raised holy hell and did not go home. They indulged in a massive hunt for treasure (gold and silver) and territory, taking in souls as they went. And they did this primarily by conquest, since the natives they encountered did not willingly give up their land, treasures, or souls. So to be honest we should call this the age of conquest rather than the age of discovery.

Q: *It sounds better to call it the age of discovery, don't you think?*

A: Yes, and that points out a problem that Euroman has had to deal with both before and after Columbus. You see, he was taught that his way of life was moralistic, that there were noble sentiments which controlled his actions. This is generally thought to be a product of his Judeo-Christian heritage. So far as we can tell, the ancient Mesopotamians, Greeks, Romans, and Aztecs never worried about morality when they were taking over other people's territory. Moreover, the reality is that morals have always been put aside by Euros when there was a question of getting goods, territory, or other kinds of wealth. But the Euros have even claimed that the administration of power should be controlled by moralistic concerns. We had one historian in the European tradition who said otherwise—Machiavelli— but he was rejected by most. Others who claim that greed has been the prime motivation for international affairs are called cynics. I think of them as realists as I think Machiavelli was, but I would be considered a cynic by most Westerners, as Machiavelli is. In my realistic mode I would argue that the occurrence of greatest significance to mankind generally after 1492 was not that the rest of the world was discovered, but that it was conquered by the Euros. If they had just discovered all these places and documented them, that would be one thing. But the fact is that they raised holy hell in one place after another for almost four hundred years and left the world permanently changed. It began with Columbus who in his greedy search for gold decimated the native population of Hispaniola (Santo Domingo and Haiti) in sixty years; it continued with Vasco da Gama who in his greedy effort to get spices and other treasure, among other acts of Euro-barbarism, siezed a number of innocent traders and fishermen off the coast of India, hanging them, cutting their bodies into pieces, and sending the hands, feet, and other pieces in a boat to shore, informing the king that he could make curry out of them.

Q: *It sounds much like the incident in the narrative where Juan Fierro had the captured men torn apart by the dogs. Was that the idea you were trying to get across?*

A: Sure. The taking of hostages and creating an incident or terror have been military tactics at least as long as the existence of standing armies, say for five thousand years, and the Latin Euros certainly used them. But having been well brainwashed in Euro morality, I find such incidents very unpleasant. But they went on extensively among the Euros as they were subduing the savages, and I felt that I should have at least one such incident in my narrative.

Q: *To get back to the idea of conquest, I can see that the Euros did take over the territory of the Indians, but what about the places where civilizations have long been in place, like in Asia?*

A: That's a good question. It is true that not all places were formally taken over. It was only in the Americas and on the islands of the Pacific that the Euros set up their own governments, but elsewhere they also conquered the people and set up systems of control, either as colonies or in forced trading setups. We could take a journey from Europe westward and you could see how all places were conquered. First are the Americas, which were conquered from top to bottom. Then the small islands of the Pacific, all of which were taken over by Euros and Americans, which I consider to be from the same mold. A few were left in what were called protectorates and one such, Western New Guinea, ultimately got its independence as Papua, the only instance worldwide of tribal people who got their own nation. China and Japan were forced into trade "openings." All the countries of southeast Asia were colonized, with one exception, Thailand. I think all countries from India west to the Atlantic were colonized. Afghanistan, Saudi Arabia, and Iran remained as protectorates, but they all felt the heavy hand of the Euros.

Q: *There's one other large area that you left out, Russian Asia and Siberia. They weren't taken over by the Western Euros, were they?*

A: No, the eastern Euros, the Russians, did that. They learned a lesson from big brother, western Euroman, technologically speaking. When they became organized and well armed with guns, they went on a conquering binge east and south, not even stopping at the Pacific. They had settlements almost to San Francisco. Of course, we bought them out of North America. But that is how Kazakhstan, Uzbekistan, Turkistan, and some other non-Russian areas became socialistic republics. Siberia was generally inhabited by tribal peoples who were assimilated or submerged as our Indians were when we expanded westward.

Q: *Did all the western Euros indulge in this conquest, which in many ways seems like the feeding frenzies of sharks?*

A: Well, some countries did more than others, mainly depending on how strong they were and how fast they developed their navies, because travel to all the conquered lands was done by sea. The initial seafarers were the Portuguese, who carved out the territory of Brazil as well as setting up conquest trading posts in South Asia. The Spanish gobbled up most of the New World, of course, as well as the colony of the Philippines. The next and probably biggest grabber was England, who, after defeating the Spanish at sea proceeded to set up many colonies in North America, the Caribbean islands, Africa, India, Australia, and Southeast Asia, along with an enforced trading relationship with China. And then there were the Dutch who, besides some island colonies here and there, grabbed their big one in Indonesia. Since the United States only got decolonized itself after the big boys had pie all over their faces, it didn't really get well into the grab-fest, ending up with only the Hawaiian Islands, the Philippines, and Puerto Rico. Also, Germany didn't get its act in order for grabbing until well into the nineteenth century, so it only got some second-rate territories in Africa and the Pacific islands. Japan of course was the only non-European country who got into the land-grab game, but that was late, since Japan didn't have a Euro-type navy or army until well into the nineteenth century. In the twentieth century they did carve out their East Asian Co-Prosperity Sphere, which, fortunately for them, they lost in World War II.

Q: *Why do you say that it was fortunate for the Japanese to have lost their conquered territory?*

A: Most of the assumptions the men in control (administrators, politicians) have made in the past about cultures have been wrong; and the idea of grabbing other people's territory and making it into colonies to produce wealth is one such idea. Grabbing other people's territory and eliminating or absorbing the population, as we did in North America and as the English did in Australia, can pay off in dollars and cents, but leaving the population in place and trying to administer it with your own rules has turned out to be economically disastrous. It's all right at first when you can loot the existing wealth, but once this is gone, the cost of administration soon eats up whatever profit you will make. And if you merely want customers, you don't have to control the population, all you need to do is to make a better product more cheaply than anyone else. Both of the losers in the last big one, World War II, were forced to learn that lesson. Both had tried to take over much of other people's territory, but after they lost the war and were forced to give up their conquests, they began producing excellent goods and selling them to the winners of the war and to anyone else who wanted them. And lo and behold, the economic miracles happened while the supreme colonizer who hung on to its colonies as long as possible, England, went down the tubes, economically speaking. Even Spain prospered only as long as there was loot to be taken from the conquered New World empires, after which it went into an economic tailspin which lasted three hundred and fifty years. During this time it tried unsuccessfully to keep its colonies. And it has just recently rebounded when it came into the European economic brotherhood with no overseas territory to drag it down.

Q: *What about France, wasn't it a colonial power?*

A: I'm sorry, I forgot. Yes, France and even little Belgium got a good piece of pie. France came up second in the colonial sweepstakes, grabbing territories on all continents, and even fighting it out with Britain for primacy in both India and North America. Its last major holdings were Vietnam and Algeria. After it lost them, the French nation did much better. And Belgium only got one piece of pie but that was a big one, the Belgian Congo; after its loss, the Belgians also did better.

Q: *One thing which interests me is why you say that most assumptions made by the leaders about how to run their societies have been wrong. Why is that?*

A: I can think of two main reasons. One is that a society is a very complex combination of customs and the simplistic idea that you can change a limited part of it doesn't seem to work. Because all the customs are interrelated, what you do to one causes changes in others, a great part of which are unexpected. And soon you find that the change you brought about was nullified by the other consequences. A society is not a simple mechanism. Second, the great majority of our leaders have not really been trained to understand social systems. We have not really taken society or culture seriously. We frequently use military specialists as national leaders, people whose training has been how to defeat and destroy, not how to build. Or we use lawyers for this purpose, people whose training teaches them to try to defeat an opponent without regard to guilt or innocence. One of our most popular recent leaders was a second-rate movie actor. With leadership like this, we can hardly expect high-quality direction of the socio-cultural body.

Q: *I can see that you consider this a particularly significant happening in the history of mankind, but it certainly has not been stressed as important in the more standard histories. How does it compare for instance with the industrial and scientific revolutions in its effect on mankind?*

A: Although we now talk about one world as if this idea were an invention of the late twentieth century, in fact one-worldism began in 1492. Before that we had various centers of civilization, some of which had a little long-distance trade with others, along with vast regions populated by tribal groups. As a consequence of the "discovery" and conquest, we have ended up with a world in which all parts trade with one another and in which people flow back and forth as if the world were a giant mixing bowl. For instance, "white men" were only found in Europe before 1492 and now they are all over the world in large numbers; "black" people were found only in Africa and now they are found in large numbers all over the New World and in lesser numbers elsewhere.

And not only have people moved around, so have the products of the scientific and industrial revolutions. All peoples, or at least the elites of their cultures, now rely to a considerable extent on the germ theory of disease and believe that the earth revolves around the sun and the moon revolves around the earth, while military forces everywhere rely on firearms and use uniforms of factory-made cloth. What I am saying is that because of the "discovery" and conquest, anything of significance that happens anywhere in the world today is rapidly diffused to all other places, and has been for the last five hundred years. Euros were using tobacco and potatoes very soon after they were encountered in the New World, and the Indians were using oxen and plows just as quickly. We in anthropology have renamed Western medicine as "cosmopolitan medicine" because it is now practiced all over the world. But there are all kinds of other "cosmopolitan" practices now: the calendrical system, the system of time, clothing styles, national armies, music, and foods. Different places, of course, have their national cuisines, but in what cities of the world can one not find Coca-cola, chocolate bars, chewing gum, pizza, hamburgers, or French fries?

So in significance I would rate the conquest second only to the domestication of plants and animals. If there had only been a discovery, many changes might still have taken place, but certainly not as fast and certainly not as thoroughly. The Aztecs might well still be sacrificing humans to their gods, even though they would be driving cars; and the Japanese might be way down in the mercantile rank order, using electronic equipment made by western nations; because both Mexico and Japan were opened as part of the conquest.

Q: *All right, whether it was that important or not, it certainly has affected the world enormously. And though you have perhaps mentioned it elsewhere, could you specify in one place what the motivation for this tremendous effort was?*

A: It was the same as the motivation for many other human adventures—greed. A distinguished historian, Daniel Boorstin, includes the whole outward push of Euroman as inspired by man's perpetual search for something new. And I will agree that that was a portion of the motivation, but if that were all it was, Euroman would have stopped when he found these places. The initial motivation was almost completely a matter of finding wealth. Both the Portuguese and Spaniards funded their expeditions primarily to find gold and silver. But they very soon decided that the newly-found territory was worth grabbing also. The British and later grabbers were mostly after territory, places to settle or colonize. Then too, the earliest people were after souls; they wanted to convert heathens to their own religion. This was a form of greed that still continues, a special characteristic of Christians and Muslims.

Some may say that I am distorting the facts, that Christians were not so much greedy for other people's souls as giving them something special—the true religion. I will admit that you can't use someone else's soul (which empirically is nothing but a figment of man's imagination anyway) the way you can gold or territory, but I will still maintain that the insatiable lust for converts by Christians is like greed for other things.

And last came knowledge—were the Euros lusting for knowledge about the places they were discovering? I will claim that throughout most of the period, conquest was the primary goal and knowledge was only taken when it promised to help fulfill one of the basic greeds. That is, the conquerors may have had some interest in geography or geology, but only because it would help them find more gold. They were almost never interested in the peoples or cultures they discovered, except insofar as this would help them get more wealth or land or souls. For this reason, except for a very few padres, the Euros learned practically nothing about local cultures, and where there were records, as among the Aztecs, these were destroyed on a grand scale.

Q: *But I thought that the Euros sent out expeditions to learn about new territories. Isn't that true?*

A: Many later ones, like the Lewis and Clark expedition across the American West, were funded primarily to learn more about the new territory, in that case that of the Louisiana Purchase, in order to settle it; that is, take over the territory. However, in the nineteenth century, when most of the territory in the world had been conquered, there was some effort to get knowledge of the world apart from taking over more territory. I think of the voyage of the Beagle, which carried Charles Darwin, as one. Though it, too, was primarily funded for politico-economic motives (to get information to help the British dominate the seas more efficiently), it did carry a ship's scientist, Darwin. And the side product, the Theory of Natural Selection, ended up as far more important than British domination of the seas.

Q: *One other question comes up continually, which is, on what grounds did the Euros claim all this new territory, either for settlement or colonization? Is this a normal way of behavior for humans?*

A: I would say yes, even though now, in the days of high moral rights, we claim that a given people, an ethnic group, has a basic right to independence. If you look through history, you will see that independence has always been a matter of strength. Tribes and nations took what they could get, desisting only when the price was higher than the gain. There have been multitudinous justifications for takeovers and the last has been that it would bring civilization or justice. But of course the Aztecs, Incas, Greeks, and Romans all thought that any peoples they took over would benefit as a consequence. The Euros had a double whammy in their justification for the takeovers. In addition to the normal greed for wealth and territory, they honestly thought theirs was an era of progress. The French called it "la mision civilizatrice" or the civilizing mission, and most truly believed that it was a moral duty for them to take over others. And if the others resisted, the French were perfectly prepared to defeat them on the battlefield to enforce the takeover. Official Americans thought much the same when the Filipinos were beaten into submission and made into a colony.

Q: *The way you describe it, the Euros were not so moral as they claimed to be. What about that?*

A: My opinion is that the kind of morality we espouse nowadays became popular only after the conquest. When the native peoples are no longer contesting the takeover, one can afford to be generous. As long as the Indian wars were going on, we Americans hardly worried about the rights of natives. It has only been since the Indians have been divested of more than ninety per cent of their land and have been rendered powerless that we have become concerned with their rights. But this of course does not include giving them back much of their land.

Q: *Although you have claimed that the conquest by Euroman was highly significant, you have not yet described the ways, except that loot and territory were taken away.*

A: That is true. And the best way to explain it is to introduce the ideas of diffusion and acculturation. Diffusion is the spread of particular customs from individual to individual or group to group. Whenever a more efficient way to solve life's problems is discovered or invented, it spreads from the point of origin. Thus, when the iron ax was invented, it spread to one people after another because it was much better for cutting down trees than the stone ax. And when corn was domesticated by the American Indians, it spread to one Indian group after another; and when the Euros found out about it, they carried the seeds and knowledge of how to grow the plant to many parts of the world. That was because corn was better than other crops in those places. And in a nutshell, that is diffusion.

Q: *And what is acculturation?*

A: This is the spread of whole complexes of new ways of doing things, and from one group to another. Whenever two groups come into contact, they borrow new ways from one another. Thus the Greeks borrowed the alphabet from the Phoenicians, while the Japanese borrowed the ideographic writing system from the Chinese.

Most borrowing goes from the dominant to the dominated group, but it can go both ways, depending on the importance of the thing or idea. Even opposing peoples borrow from one another. The Crusaders who were trying to drive the Infidels from the Holy Land borrowed Arabic mathematics and Greek translations from them, and these were supposed to have contributed significantly to the Enlightenment which followed in Europe. And the Spanish borrowed an enormous number of useful plants from the people that they conquered in the New World—potatoes, corn, chocolate, rubber, tobacco, and many more. But most acculturation is from those in power to those who have been conquered. Almost all the Indians speak the language of their conquerors, while the conquerors rarely know the Indians' languages. And finally, while the focus of change in diffusion is the thing and the idea behind it, the focus of acculturation is the whole culture.

Q: *One thing that you do not bring up is invention. Isn't it necessary to have an invention before change can take place?*

A: Sure, but the social reality is the diffusion and acculturation. Discoveries and inventions are done by individuals, but until the new ideas spread within a social group, they are not significant to anyone but the inventor. And we in the social sciences are concerned primarily with groups.

Q: *And so what are some of these new ideas that spread throughout the world as a consequence of the conquest?*

A: I'll get rid of the first one quickly because it is the only one which is not a new idea. It is genetic and was spread throughout the world because of biology, not learning. It is what I call the Eurogene. When the Euro-conquerors reached new lands, they invariably got together sexually, usually Euromen with native women. And as a consequence, there was a massive process of miscegenation that went into effect.

Q: *Wait, that's a peculiar word. It sounds like doing some improper thing, you know mis—. What does the word mean?*

A: Actually it just means "to mix races (physical types)," even though I agree that it does sound funny. But for better or worse, we got stuck with it. The great majority of people the conquerors met had darker skins, hair, and eyes. And while none of these is important in function, they were enough to distinguish people—darker skins, hair, and eyes meant conquered, while lightness meant conquerors, and this set up the criteria for racism, which of course we still live with.

Q: *But how did the genes for these characteristics get spread around so much since I presume there were relatively few conquerors and a lot of conquered?*

A: True, but remember that it doesn't take many males to impregnate a lot of females. And the conquerors had access to plenty. Another factor which helped cause the spread of the Eurogene, especially in the Americas and on the Pacific Islands, is that when the cultures went into decline, the natives lost much interest in reproducing themselves. For instance, in North America at the same time that the Indians were being replaced, the White pioneers were having very large families. The upshot today is that while in the seventeenth century there were several million Indians and less than a million white men, in the twentieth century there are less than a million Indians, most of whom are mixed, and two hundred and fifty million whites.

The civilized nations, particularly in Asia, had populations too high to be inundated by the white gene, and moreover, they were not taken over so totally and had resistance to Euro epidemic diseases. But blue eyes and blond hair were spread all over the world, despite being genetic recessives.

Q: *What about the customs of Euroman, which ones were spread most?*

A: First and most important was the technology, the tools of Euroman. The first ones were the devices which got him to the new places—the ships. Euroman evolved the most efficient ships of the time, which is of course what enabled him to cross the oceans. And of second importance were his weapons and one other mode of transportation, the horse. Most important, he had iron tools and firearms, and against native bows and arrows these gave him a clear superiority on the battlefields of the world. And though the gun was of a primitive sort, it gave Euroman a psychological advantage in encounters with natives, and as the device improved through time, the advantage increased exponentially. And though the horse has been demeaned by many (John Wayne, the actor who got rich by riding horses, disliked them intensely, claiming they were the dumbest animal that ever lived), without it the great conquests by the Arabs, Mongols, and Euroman might not have taken place. But John Wayne was hardly a historian.

Q: *That explains the high points of the technology of the conquest. But there was much else to Euroman's technology, wasn't there?*

A: Yes, as soon as he took control, he began using and introducing to the natives most of the things which he brought from Europe, a process which continued as new things were developed. At first it was iron, the wheel, firearms, and the animals and plants he was using, primarily oxen, sheep, pigs, goats, and chickens, as well as wheat, oats, barley, grapes, and a few other plants.

Q: *You have already mentioned that Euroman got many plants from the Indians. How about animals?*

A: For unexplained reasons, the people of the Americas were very good at domesticating plants but not so with animals. So while there were dozens of new plants for Euroman to borrow, there were only a few animals. The only ones that became really significant were the turkey and the guinea pig, both of which the rest of the world could have done without, but both of which did serve some function.

Q: *But was that all that Euroman got from the conquered?*

A: No, there were many minor items which anthropologists like to count, like snowshoes and toboggans and Eskimo garment styles. But there was not much of the technology of the New Worlders or other tribals that became a part of world culture. The world did get quite a lot of foods from the Asian countries. The most important were probably sugar, rice, and soy beans. Ultimately, Euroman took these over for himself, as well as spreading them to other parts of the world.

Q: *And what about all the mechanical devices that the world uses today, they all came from Euroman, didn't they?*

A: Yes, most in the beginning. After the conquest, Europe went through the scientific and industrial revolutions and all the devices from these were diffused all over. You will read about them in later chapters.

Q: *And what happened next as a consequence of the conquest?*

A: Well, not long after Euroman had established himself in an unknown country by means of his technology, he was visited by the natives. And he learned very quickly that all peoples had languages. At first, he used interpreters, shipwrecked sailors or captives from previous expeditions or someone from a neighboring tribe who had learned both languages. But as the conquest proceeded, more and more learned the language of the other, usually the conquered learning the language of the conquerors. And when Euroman was fully established, his language began replacing that of the others, almost completely with tribals, to a slight extent in the colonies and trade-dominated nations of the world. And as a consequence, the languages that became dominant in the world are those of the primary conquerors: English, Spanish, French, and Russian. The tribal languages have become fewer every year.

Q: *What else then? I bet I know, it's religion, right?*

A: Correct. The first thing the conquerors did was to establish themselves by arms and fortifications while trying to communicate with the natives. But they also very quickly tried to get the souls of the new people. This was especially true of the Spanish and Portuguese, the first conquerors. This is because Christianity had been from the beginning, or at least since Saint Paul, a converting religion. And this has continued up to the present day. You will read some of the details in the chapter called "The Word." Here it is enough to mention that as English and Spanish became the primary world languages, Christianity became the primary world religion.

Q: *So the world got permanently changed by the conquest in technology, language, and religion. That leaves one other major element of culture, the social institutions.*

A: Correct, that is the one other biggie in cultural systems. In fact, some anthropologists and most sociologists spend almost all their effort in describing a people's social institutions. And they are important, no doubt about it. Moreover, Euroman's impact certainly made a difference. Probably the most important during the conquest was that

Euroman, like all other conquerors, set himself up as top dog. And through time this distinction between him and the locals evolved into a class or caste system. Where there was complete conquest, as in all of the Americas and most of the Pacific islands including Australia and New Zealand, the whole European system was introduced with Euroman as administrator, landholder, merchant, lawgiver, etc., while the natives were eliminated or reduced to being workers. Euroman decimated so many natives in the Americas that he set up a system for additional workers from Africa, slavery, and later when slavery was abolished, a system of indentured laborers. In all cases the workers were darker. In the Spanish and Portuguese countries, there was so much mixing (Euro-father, native mother) that a whole new type emerged, the *mestizo*. There were mixed types elsewhere but not enough to form a whole separate class/caste. The English-speaking people did not go in for breeding with natives much, though in the Asian colonies a mixed caste of Eurasians was produced through mixed matings.

In the colonies there were proportionally far fewer Euromen, though they of course set themselves up as the privileged also. And in the trade-dominated places such as China there were very few Euromen in proportion to those very large populations. In those countries the Euros exacted privileges but they were kept an arm's reach away.

The legacy in classes is most noticeable now in the places where there were many natives but which were completely conquered, the most apparent ones in Latin America.

Q: *And other forms of social organization?*

A: As would be expected, the Euros introduced their own kinds of government, mostly in places where they were in complete control. Thus, the other places of the world—with one exception, the Islamic countries—got heavy doses of the new kinds of governments that were evolving in Europe. So at first it was monarchies, but when the royalty was thrown out in European countries, the taken-over lands got all the forms of parliamentary and democratic systems, though of course without independence. That had to wait until the twentieth century when Euroman was losing his worldwide power. And when independence did come, the former colonies set themselves up on the European model. The one aspect of Euro-government the native peoples failed to incorporate well was the control of the military by the civilians, so military takeovers became common. But they did generally get European-type armies, navies, legislatures, elections, and systems of taxation.

Q: *What about that last? I assume that the Euro type of economic system was introduced, right?*

A: Yes. All those who were taken over by Western European countries inherited the system of greed which started the takeover and that which evolved from it, capitalism, where greediness is politely called the profit motive. But of course the system of sharing the wealth, called socialism, was carried to quite a few non-Western countries, and still survives in several, even though a very imperfect version failed in Russia. All the non-Western countries got one Euro-system or another, though of course their practice of these was rarely according to the book.

Q: *And last in social institutions, what about the family system of others. Was it influenced much by the conquest?*

A: Probably less than the system of government or economics for the reason that family relations are more private. But yes, the Euro also stuck his long fingers into that pie when he found out what was going on, depending on how much control he had. Euroman very early began working against polygamy in the places he administered, usually making it against the law. And the practice has practically disappeared except in the Islamic countries, where it survives because it became justified by the religion. Euroman came down hard on some customs he deemed barbaric. For instance he outlawed the Indian practice of wife-burning, which as far as historians know, was not practiced often. And he did this at the same time as he was setting up intolerable conditions for working class women and children in his new industrial cities. But as I have mentioned before, the whole takeover syndrome was based on ethnocentrism in which one sees other people's customs at fault, but not one's own.

Q: *So is that it?*

A: I think we have covered the major changes to the cultures of others. There are a few interesting though less important ones. One is sports. There were several that were passed from Euroman to the others and a few went the opposite direction. Thus we got lacrosse from the North American Indians, a game which continues to be played to a limited extent in North America. Then there was polo, developed by Indian and Afghan horsemen. It, too, has had a limited spread, primarily becoming a game for the wealthy. But the various ball games of Euroman—soccer, cricket, basketball, and baseball—have been spread widely. An interesting side note is that all these were only possible after Euroman got rubber from the American Indian. The Indians had their own ball games, but Euroman did not take them over.

Q: *Another of the pleasure-giving activities that seems to have been dominated by Euroman has been music, which seems now to have been spread to other countries. Is that not so?*

A: Yes, though music was universal among all peoples, the effect of Euro-dominance is that Euroman's own kinds of music spread to most places, in at least three forms. Classical music developed in Europe from the time the northern barbarians took over settled life, and has continued to the present there; but it has since been taken over by many non-European countries, alongside what is left of their own music styles. Another type is jazz, the music which began among the descendants of slaves, and which is now played in cities all over the world. And the final one is rock, the popular musical style which developed in the West since World War II, and which is now enjoyed by young people all over the world, who often do not know the traditional music of their ancestors.

Q: *And so is that all the world got as a consequence of the conquest?*

A: No, there are many less important customs. You see, the acculturation of the rest of the world by Euroman has been extraordinarily pervasive and intensive, and lasted about four hundred and fifty years, really coming to a close just after World War II, after which the other cultures of the world began to reassert themselves.

Q: *So what about some of the others which are interesting?*

A: One which has been big is the consumption of drugs, and particularly tobacco. You see, this was another of the plants (and the method of consuming them) that Euroman got from the American Indian. You probably heard of it in your American history class as beginning with Sir Walter Raleigh, who was supposed to have had water thrown on him in the belief that he was on fire. Actually, the use of tobacco probably began with the Portuguese and Spanish who encountered it among the Indians of the Caribbean and in Mexico in the form of cigarettes and cigars. It was quickly taken to Europe and the rest of the world by the circumnavigating Euroman, and became the drug of choice for the next four centuries. As you know, it has come into difficulties among Euromen because of its link to cancer, but it continues to be smoked prodigiously in the rest of the world. I have often thought of it as "the Redman's revenge," in that while Euroman took away the land of the Indian, the Indian gave to Euroman his worst carcinogen.

Q: *Interesting. Actually, tobacco cannot be considered such an unimportant custom if it causes that much havoc. But what else can you list in the Euro-acculturation of the world?*

A: Here's one that is interesting and pervasive throughout the world, but not with such serious consequences—clothing types. When Euroman encountered the natives, he frequently disapproved of the local costume. He especially did not care for degrees of undress—by his standards, of course. So he methodically engaged in a massive effort to clothe the body parts of the natives while at the same time the natives in their desperate attempt to mollify the ethnocentric takeover specialist, tried to look like him in the clothes they wore. Like so many kinds of acculturation it was a push-pull affair. Euroman, and especially his clerics, found exposed breasts on women undesirable, so a massive coverup campaign was initiated and was successful enough that one has to really look hard to find any exposed breasts nowadays—at least in public. On the male side, trousers and shirts were early introduced and have succeeded to the extent that two Western costumes, the business suit and blue jeans, have been adopted all over the world.

Q: *Wow, it goes on and on, doesn't it?*

A: Yes, I'm afraid so, though I suppose we ought to call a halt to this listing and get on to the next chapter. I might mention just a few other items, but without explaining them in detail. One is the handshake as a form of greeting. This is a gesture of friendliness which evolved in Medieval Europe to signify that the person offering his hand did not have a sword in it. Another is time. The clock with sixty seconds, sixty minutes, and twenty-four hours was invented by Euroman, though the idea of counting by sixties came from ancient Mesopotamia. Also, the week and year are Euro-derived, though the day and month, as natural units of time, are omnipresent. But the calendar beginning at the supposed time of the birth of Jesus Christ is Euro-evolved.

And with those last items, I think we should go on. Let us look at the great missionary force of Europe, Christianity.

7

The Word

Matthew

Matthew Haraldsen wrestled the steering wheel of the Land Rover over the dirt road, leaving a cloud of dust behind. He was a wiry man, having grown up on a farm in Missouri where he had handled his share of machinery and animals. In his late thirties, he was clad in khakis and a short-sleeved cotton shirt, both faded. Elvira, his wife, sat beside him in a flowered dress which was also faded. She had to wash all the family clothes since there was no washing machine at the house, and she used bleach heavily. Elvira wore a head scarf to keep some of the dust off. She periodically waved a fan before her face, both for the coolness and to keep some of the flies away.

The vehicle went past a group of scattered houses built on stilts. Some women stood at the side of the road, behind a lattice-work table piled with ears of corn. They wore dark blue woven cotton wrap-arounds, hung from the waist. Women still wove cloth from their own cotton in the villages of Laos. The corn vendors also wore cotton bras. They wore no shoes and their jet black hair was coiled on top of their heads. Matthew waved to them and called out in their language, "Greetings, may God be with you."

"Those must be Arakan, no?" Elvira said.

These were the people who were mostly Christian and whose language Matthew already knew. If he had not been comfortable in their language, he would have spoken in Lao. Most of the women understood Lao even if they were frequently too shy to speak it.

"Yes, those are ones who have begun to stand near the road during the last couple of years. They try to sell anything they can. The men are trying to get shotguns for hunting and the women always want jewelry."

"What about the Pathet Lao, aren't they concerned if the village people get guns?"

"They must be, since they are certainly arming themselves. But maybe they don't care as much if it's only shotguns. Their range isn't much, you know."

The Rover approached a cluster of houses where some men were gathered. They stood next to a horizontal pole from which various animal skins hung. The men were clad in loincloths of the same material the skirts were made of. Their black hair was loose, with bangs in front. Most were smoking crude stone pipes. Some of the men had pipes with wood stems, others sucked the smoke directly from a hole at the base of the bowl. A couple of the men had extended earlobes, one with a carved ivory plug in the stretch of skin, the other with several hand-wrapped cigarettes.

"Where do they get the tobacco?" Elvira asked. "Do they grow it?"

"Oh, sure, they plant it in the same fields where everything else is planted. They couldn't afford it if they had to buy it."

Elvira was always impressed at how much Matthew knew about the villagers. Of course, he was off in their compounds for days at a time, though he always saw to it that someone was at the church on weekends, either him or Bert. Matthew and Bert Funello were stationed at Lanchan with their families to cover the southern provinces for the Fundamental Christian Mission. The parishioners were mainly mountain people with whom the missionaries did much better than with Buddhists.

Matthew drove up to the group and got out of the car. He switched to Lao since many of the men would answer in the language of the dominants anyway. They wanted to appear advanced and, moreover, they knew that government officials wanted them to speak in the language of the rulers all the time.

"May Jesus bless you," Matthew said almost automatically.

An overall mumble came from the men and from one the words were comprehensible—"Praise the Lord."

Matthew turned his attention to the skins. There were three—a jungle cat, a sun bear, and a tiger. Matthew looked at the tiger. He had requests from several men in parishes back in the States for skins, particularly tiger. And since those were the people he and the other missionaries depended on for finances, he had found it a good practice to take back souvenirs when he returned on home leave every three or four years. This particular skin was in pretty good condition, scraped and dried well enough to last a few months in this heat. There were only a few holes in it, presumably where buckshot penetrated. Most of the cats were shot with buckshot by these people. He could take it to the Chinese tanner in town if it started to get mouldy.

"How much for the tiger?"

One of the men, presumably the hunter, stepped over and began running his hand over the skin.

"Monsieur Pastor, it is a big skin, a beautiful skin. A male in the prime of life. They say it has eaten a small boy. And we know it was killing our young buffalo."

The Arakan were known for their buffalo which they bred and raised on the grasses of the plateau. The fully-grown animals had little to fear from tigers, particularly if there were several together. But the tigers would pick off the young if they became separated from their mothers. The Arakan traded their buffalo to other tribes who used them for sacrifice, or to the Lao for meat.

Matthew belittled the item as the procedure demanded.

"The skin is not bad, but look at the big holes." He stuck his finger though one. "And besides, there's still a lot of meat on it. It hasn't been scraped very well. Probably it will start to rot before the cool season comes. But anyway, what is the price?"

The man's voice started to take on a whine. "Monsieur the Pastor, this Arakan you see standing before you is a poor man. He has little enough to make any money. Even when the crops are good, the price is so low, it is hardly worth the trouble to carry the corn out."

Matthew knew that was true. These people carried the corn and squash and whatever other vegetables they had out in baskets on their backs, the weight held by a tump line across the forehead. And in mid-season they were lucky if they could sell several ears of corn for the equivalent of one cent. But what could he do about that? His job was to save souls, not to bring these sinners into the capitalist world. And besides, these people were not used to having so many things, they couldn't miss them so much.

"All right, all that is true," he agreed. "But now you have this skin and you will make some money from it, so you must ask a price. And I can assure you it will go to another Christian. You will be doing Jesus' work."

The Arakan turned and talked in a low voice to a younger man standing behind him. Then he turned back.

"This is Ngam. He is my brother. The skin belongs to him. He killed the tiger. He wanted me to talk to you, Sir Pastor, because he is a little shy. He has never been to the church." Then he quickly added, "Though he is ready to become a Christian, and take a Christian name."

Matthew had been out here long enough to take these long-winded conversations in stride. Whatever impatience he had, he never showed any.

"Okay, the price then?"

"He says he doesn't want money, he wants a gun. He asks me if you can get him a shotgun." Then he quickly added, "Just a single barrel gun—and a box of shells."

This wasn't the first time Matthew had been approached for a gun. It made some sense because the tribespeople had no access to gun dealers who were all in town and were watched closely by the officials. After all, there was no doubt that the Pathet Lao were arming themselves all over the country. And though it was probable that the man wanted the gun for hunting, in these days one never knew who were members of the opposition. But the fact was that he and the other missionaries were not welcome by the Lao officials. Their visas could be cancelled at any time. And the American embassy would not stick its neck out very far to save some missionaries. Matthew decided to keep it straight.

"I don't have an extra gun. So I'll have to pay for the skin if I take it. Tell your brother that."

They whispered together again for what seemed to be an interminable length of time, so much that Matthew finally said, "Just tell him to think about it and I'll be coming back tomorrow and he can tell me then."

Matthew was looking forward to getting to the paved part of the road after five hours of jolting, even though the pavement would make it hot again. They had climbed up from Lanchan to the high country of the Bolovens Plateau and after stopping to see Verdoux, they would shortly reach the paved road. They would then drive to meet the mid-morning flight at Sepak to pick up Pastor Grant of central headquarters in Boone City.

He turned the Rover off the main road and lurched down the side road toward the cluster of houses and sheds where Verdoux lived. On both sides the fields were cultivated in rows, European style, rather than the mixed assemblages of the tribals which grew in the ashes of burned trees and between fallen logs, the slash and burn technique. There were carrots, radishes, lettuce, peppers, tomatoes, and strawberries, crops that could be grown in the cool highlands, crops that were grown from European seed. Matthew knew that Verdoux was a graduate of an agricultural college in France. His father, a Frenchman, had sent him there instead of to a Vietnamese college. His mother had been Vietnamese.

"We must take some strawberries back with us," Elvira said. "I haven't had any for almost a year, and I used to look forward to the season so much when I lived at home."

"We can pick them up on the way back. I'm sure the Funellos would like some too."

A dog tied to a post at the end of the road snarled savagely as the vehicle passed, tightening its chain by forward lunges. In the distance they could see another chained dog snarling.

"I hope he has good chains on those dogs," Elvira said. "They look like they could be nasty."

Madame Verdoux came out of the house, wiping her hands on a towel. She was a Vietnamese woman in her forties, not tall, slightly plump, with long plaited black hair, wearing slacks and a blouse, Viet style. She smiled with the great pleasure of isolated people when they get visitors. She shook hands with Matthew and Elvira in the French fashion, speaking in Lao. She had learned the language primarily to handle the servants, but since the Haraldsens spoke no French, she couldn't use that language, and she had no confidence in her English.

"The pastor and his good wife. What a pleasure. We knew you were coming one of these days, but not exactly when. Marcel and Jon are down in the shed by the river, but they will be here soon. I know they heard you coming. Come in, come in, and tell us all about Lanchan."

"We're on our way to Sepak and we have to meet the plane, so we don't have much time," Elvira said. "But we did want to say hello. We'll be coming back tomorrow. We're picking up the administrator of our division." She turned to her husband. "Why don't you tell the rest, Matthew."

In missionary families, the spokesman was usually the man. Matthew said, "We'll be coming back tomorrow. Just passing through, but I'm sure Pastor Grant would like to meet you people and see the farm."

Marcel and his son Jon appeared. Marcel was a *metis*, half French, half Viet, of medium height and sturdy, in his forties. He was dressed like a European farmer in pants and shirt, a leather jacket over his shirt. His son was a good-looking young fellow with light brown skin like his father. He was in his late teens and well muscled, wearing jeans and a shirt and carrying a rifle. Marcel spoke to the Haraldsens in good English, though with an accent. He had learned the language in college, but in the last few years had improved it greatly by talking to Americans. The Verdoux had come to Laos to get some of the cheap land and to get away from the troubles in Vietnam. But since then the troubles had spread to Laos and the Americans had come to replace the French in influence and numbers. Military officers and other American officials had been coming to the farm, ostensibly to go hunting. Verdoux obliged by helping them get their tiger or other big game animal. This was one of the few places left where tigers could be hunted.

"Greetings, pastor," Verdoux said. "Come in and have a cold drink. What brings you to the plateau? Getting too hot in Lanchan?"

The town where the missionaries lived, like the others in Laos, had been settled by the Lao who had gone up all the big river valleys looking for new rice land. Then later when the French had taken over, they had set up their administrative centers in the same places. Lanchan was lowland suitable for rice paddies, and so it was hot. The plateau where Verdoux lived was much cooler.

"It is hot, though we are all used to it," Matthew answered. "And also the mission house was already there and we have to go where our parish is." Actually, the main reason they lived in Lanchan was that the mission owned the house and there were as many amenities as you could expect in such isolated places. They did have their own well and a generator for a few hours of electricity each night, if the supply of fuel didn't run out. The parishioners were mostly from the mountain tribes who generally lived in higher country. But the valley there was quite narrow and the Lao were not spread very widely. The church was up the road toward the villages of the hill tribes and walking was no problem for the villagers. And if it was necessary, either Matthew or Bert would use the Land Rover for hauling people to church.

"Everything quiet in Lanchan?" Verdoux asked.

"No problems in town, though there are reports of bands of guerrillas going from village to village. Most people think they are collecting guns." Matthew couldn't keep his eyes off the rifle the young man was carrying. "How's it been here? You always carry a rifle when you go about the farm?"

Madame Verdoux called a servant and ordered some soft drinks. Marcel answered, "We haven't had any problems, although we don't take chances. I don't carry a gun around, but Jon feels more secure that way." Verdoux smiled as he said proudly, "You know, that boy is a crack shot. Any guerilla who comes after him better be good."

"We noticed the dogs when we came in," Matthew said. "I suppose they are out there to give warning."

"Yes, though they would attack if I turned them loose. This place may not look like a fortress, but if you knew how many guns and how much ammunition we have stashed away, you would be surprised."

Matthew had heard that Verdoux had been well equipped by the Americans, but that didn't seem like such a great idea to him. If the Pathet Lao decided to attack, they certainly wouldn't do it with a lightly-armed group. And the more arms they could get, the more tempting it would be. Matthew did not carry a gun, though he kept one in the house. What else could one do? What police there were spent most of their time checking on foreigners and skimming off foreign aid. He took the cola the servant offered and sipped it out of the bottle. Verdoux, said, "When are you coming for a hunt? We have several elephants available and we have seen a couple of good herds of wild cattle lately."

The Laven Tribe nearby captured wild elephants and tamed them to sell. Lumber companies used the animals for moving logs and the Lao liked them for parades. The local tribesmen would rent out an elephant with a driver for the equivalent of fifty cents per day. Hunters could shoot from the platform.

"I'd sure like to come," Matthew said. "But we've been pretty busy lately, building the new church. Of course the villagers do most of the work, but someone's always got to be there to supervise. And Bert has been having fevers lately."

"We know how hard you people work," Verdoux said. "Harder than the Catholics, I think. I know that Father Nouveau doesn't push himself that hard. And he certainly puts away as much wine as any French farmer."

Father Nouveau was a Catholic priest who worked with the lepers and tribals. The priests were leftovers from the French colonial days. The American missionaries had been coming in to replace them since the end of French influence in Indo-China. There was little mixing between Catholics and Protestants, even though both groups were intent on the same goal—to convert anybody they could to their belief system. The priests had early zeroed in on the lepers, who had been abandoned by the government authorities. Lepers were so grateful for anything done for them that becoming a Christian was little enough in exchange. Father Nouveau operated a basketry cooperative for his lepers, hauling in material for manufacture as well as medicine whenever he could get it, and hauling out finished baskets, in his diminutive Deux Cheveux. The American missionaries had never got a foothold among the lepers, though a Swiss pastor had managed to siphon off a few from Father Nouveau's village.

Father Nouveau doted on his *vin ordinaire*, which he got through the French military in Sepak. And since Matthew and the other American missionaries were teetotallers, and did not speak French, they did not mix much.

"So the big supervisor is due in town," Verdoux said. "You will certainly have to bring him by when you come back. Maybe he would like to take a day off to go hunting. If he had enough time, we could set bait for a tiger."

Verdoux would tie a young buffalo out in a tiger area and when the predator had killed the animal and had come back to feed off the carcass, the planter would arrange for a shoot from a platform.

Matthew had finished his cola and got up. "I don't know, since he'll be busy, seeing all the places. We're going to dedicate the church and he's only got a week here."

For a moment Matthew thought of inviting the planter down for the blessing of the church, but quickly abandoned the idea. It was better, he thought, to keep the Catholics and Protestants separate—not that Verdoux was much of a church-goer. So he said, "We've got to be going. The plane is due in a little more than an hour. And we wouldn't want to miss it."

They reached the shack late, but since there were several cars there, Matthew knew the plane hadn't arrived yet. The waiting room was little more than a sun and rain shelter, though it did have a rustic bar at one end and four or five tables and chairs scattered across the rough board floor. The sides were woven fiber hangings, constantly moving in the afternoon wind. The roof was covered by corrugated iron sheeting. Several small groups sat drinking beer or soft drinks served by the old crone who ran the place. She was a French derelict who had been there for as long as Matthew knew. Apart from taking orders for drinks, she never spoke and no one knew anything about her.

Several people spoke to Matthew when he came in, either in English or Lao. Even the old crone knew enough Lao to take his order, two soft drinks. Matthew spoke to the AID rep who was in charge of the three southern provinces and who had visited him in Lanchan several times. And since there was no consulate anywhere but in the capital, he was the senior American official in the southern region. So far as Matthew could tell, the man was genuinely interested in the villagers, including the mountain tribes, but he certainly was not sympathetic to the missionaries. He was sitting with several of the newly-arrived Green Berets and the United States Information Office rep, all drinking beer. Quite a few empty bottles already sat on the table. The voice of Saunders, the AID rep, was loud. "What's to worry? If the pregnant whale doesn't make it, we'll send you out by road. And if you don't make it, it will be a great story for your grandkids."

The U.S. Information rep, who was heavy in his cups, said, "But I don't have any children. I'm not even married. What's the use of worrying about grandchildren?"

One of the Green Berets, a man who looked like he had fought his way through a large number of bars throughout the world, laughed and said loudly, "Ri-ight, no use worrying about grandkids, need to worry about the 'towhaans.'"

This was what they had learned in six weeks of language training—the American military pronunciation for the Lao soldiers they were supposed to be advising to stop the Communist takeover of the old Indo-China. The soldier of fortune was not far behind the U.S. Information rep in drinking. It bothered Matthew to watch the group. They represented America to the locals, and some of them might even be Christians. The Green Beret, Rocky Holsum, continued, "Yes, indeed, what they need to worry about is that 'pregnant whale.'"

Bedecka, the U.S. Information rep, almost cried, "And here I am, ready to go on home leave, and they have to schedule me on Air Lousy. And it's two hours late."

Matthew spoke to Saunders. "Is there something wrong with the plane? We're waiting for an important person from the mission who is supposed to be on it."

Saunders turned toward Matthew. "No one knows what's wrong. It's just late."

There was no tower at the airfield. The only information came by way of the one agent who handled baggage and tickets and who had a radio in his office in town, and he had announced nothing.

Bedecka wailed, "Oh woe is me. Here I am giving my all for the flag and what do I get in return—a booking on a pregnant whale, and it doesn't even arrive."

"Aw, shut up, Bedecka, and have another beer," Rocky growled. He snapped his fingers. "Hey, garcon."

"Rocky, you don't say 'garcon' to a woman," Saunders said. "You say 'madame.' 'Garcon' means 'boy.'"

"Oh, all right. Hey, madame."

There was a flurry of movement outside. Then Matthew heard the drone of the plane.

"Let's go outside," he said to Elvira. They joined the others. Everyone stared intensely into the haze to the north where the plane would be coming from. It was a dot at first, gradually taking form over the rice fields of the Mekong. Since there were no other planes or directions from a tower, it came straight in. It was clear why they called it a pregnant whale. The four-engine plane was short and rounded, as if it did carry an embryo in its fat belly. It was the first model of four-engine propeller ships made by Boeing, these last survivors being cheap enough for the Lao to buy and make them the backbone of their fleet. Boeing made its successive models sleeker.

The plane came straight in to the paved runway in the brilliant heat, but when it landed, it began to zigzag, at first almost to the edges of the runway on both sides. A cry went up from the onlookers. It appeared that the machine might go out of control and flip over.

"My god," Saunders said.

But the plane slowed down without mishap, the zigzags getting shorter, until it was finally rolling straight on. Matthew had not noticed before that this model had a tail wheel, one of the last of the big planes to have one. All the rest had switched to nosewheels. He could imagine how disturbed Pastor Grant would be and made a silent prayer that all inside the plane were safe. The plane taxied to a spot in front of the waiting room and the agent pushed the stairway up to the open door. The passengers began to stream out and after them the crew. Matthew waved to Grant, who, like most of the other passengers, was pale and nervous. They exchanged greetings and then went inside. Out of the corner of his eye Matthew saw Saunders head toward one of the crew who was walking back to the tail wheel, a hammer in hand. After a brief inspection, the crew member whacked the axle of the wheel several times. Matthew saw Saunders speaking to the man. He knew that Saunders could speak French.

While the passengers were waiting for their baggage, Saunders returned and was quickly surrounded by the group he had been drinking with, plus some others. Matthew moved over as far as he could to listen without being obvious.

"What did he say, what did he say?" someone asked Saunders.

"Oh, nothing much except that whenever the plane did that, it was because the axle had slipped. But then when they tapped it with the hammer, that put it back in the right place."

Someone said, "Oh, my god, no wonder they call it Air Lousy."

Saunders added, "The guy said the pilots knew about it so when they landed, they were always ready. They had it under control, he said."

Another said, "And they say that the crews are all washed out guys from Air Chance."

That was the slang name for Air France, which, according to the wisdom of the local expatriates, had the best drunken pilots in the world.

"Sorry about that landing," Matthew said to Pastor Grant, who sat in the front seat as they drove away, "But their accident record really isn't so bad. But perhaps when you leave, we could book you on Air Vietnam. How are you feeling?"

The newcomer was wiping his forehead and neck.

"It's all right, Matthew, I've had some risky flights before. As you know, a man can't do god's work and have all the safety and comforts of home."

Bert

He was a tall, thin man with red hair, dressed in much the same nondescript fashion as Matthew. He felt a little better since taking the new medication that Pastor Grant had brought, so he had decided to get going this week or he would never master Lao and be able to start on one of the tribal languages. He and Matthew had decided that each would try to learn at least one tribal language besides Lao. Bert Funello was planning to get started on Khor as soon as he was comfortable with Lao. He had studied Lao at the Oklahoma Language Institute for about a year and had been working on it for another year since he had been in Lanchan. His current procedure was to lecture to groups of Buddhist monks as Matthew had done when he got started six years before.

Bert was standing at the front of a large room that the monks used for meditation and prayer in the building of the main Lanchan temple compound. The Lanchan wat grounds had only one temple since the believers in this area were not numerous. Lanchan was the largest town on the thin ribbon of Buddhist Lao on the Khong River. Beyond the flood plains were the slash-and-burn tribals all the way to Vietnam, which of course is why the missionary outpost existed.

Bert's assistant, Boune Louan, sat cross-legged on the floor, and behind him sat two or three dozen monks, their heads shaven, dressed in the orange robe of the order. Boune Louan was one of the few Buddhists who had converted to Christianity. He was very useful to the two missionaries because he was a Lao and an ex-Buddhist. The monks had finished their morning procession to receive food from the faithful, had eaten their sticky rice and vegetables, had then said prayers and had settled down to listen to Bert Funello.

Speaking in Lao, Bert finished his speech.

"And so, my brothers, in the search for everlasting salvation, though it is clear to us that you have journeyed some distance on the road to knowledge, we know that to go the whole distance, you will have to get on the road to Jesus."

He had a Bible in his hand and at this point he put the flat of his other hand on it.

"It's all here, my brothers, in the Holy Book." And so he finished as he and Matthew had decided to finish such talks, "And may Jesus be with you."

The room remained as quiet as it had been throughout, the monks remaining in their cross-legged position. The distant sound of a crow seemed unusually loud to Bert. He began to wonder if they had understood his Lao, although it seemed impossible that they hadn't. He was speaking it every day to people in the town, in the church, everywhere except with the other Americans. Still, the tenseness became almost palpable.

Finally, he made an effort to break the impasse, saying, "Are there any questions my brothers would like to ask, about Jesus or any of the beliefs?"

This caused a little stir and for a moment he had the crazy idea that they were going to clap their hands. But the group simply settled back into their position of rest. In desperation he said, "Well, do some of you agree? You know that when we give ser—talks in the village, there are frequently some people who want to become Christians." He refrained from actually suggesting the possibility with this group. He stood a little longer and was just about ready to get his things together and leave when the chief abbot stood up and spoke in the softest voice imaginable for a male.

"Sir Pastor, we monks of the Buddhist faith are so appreciative of the effort to bring us these ideas about Jesus and the Christian faith, because we want to know all things about life everlasting and how other people try to achieve it."

The abbot continued to fan himself with a small folding fan as he spoke.

"We are happy to know these things and to know that the *farangs* have sent some of their fine people here to learn our language and to teach us about their beliefs. And we want them to know that they are welcome to our temples at any time and we hope to know more about the noble Jesus." Whereupon the abbot folded his fan and turned to leave the room. The other monks began to get up in preparation to leave also.

As he was getting into the Land Rover, Bert's mind was in a dither. Although Matthew had told him before that he couldn't expect any converts or any indication that he had changed anyone's opinion, this lack of reaction really got to him. Didn't they realize that he was challenging their whole belief system? Couldn't they at least argue with him on some little point? He desperately needed someone to talk to about the affair. After he got the car going, he turned to Boune Louan.

"So how did you think the talk went?"

"Oh, I thought it went fine. The monks were very quiet and they listened very well."

He usually gave the key to Boune Louan to drive since the Lao man had been hired as a mechanic/driver. But the missionary felt so perturbed at this point that he felt the necessity of doing something, so he drove.

"I know they have the habit of not showing their feelings," he said. "But it would be easier if they responded in some way, even it if were negative."

Bert knew he was getting too philosophical for Boune Louan but he didn't know how to stop.

"For instance, do you think any of them know why we are really here? Do you think they know why any missionaries go out among non-believers?"

"Oh, sure," Boune Louan replied. "They know that you want to give the true word of God to everyone."

Oh, yes, Bert thought, that was the true line. And maybe the convert beside him believed it, but even if he didn't, there was no reason he would say so. Since it didn't seem the talk was going anywhere useful, Bert changed the tack.

"By the way, Boune Louan, why did you become a Christian?"

"Oh, sir, because I saw the light. I never realized before that if I did not change my beliefs, I would never go to heaven."

Bert knew that in Therevada Buddhist beliefs there was no heaven to go to, that one did not pray or worship to any god, because there wasn't any that anyone knew anything about. And life everlasting was an extinction of the individual, not a place of everlasting joy. A place for good people to go to in the afterlife, a heaven, was very much a Christian idea, one which the missionaries had a lot of difficulty explaining. It was hard for Bert to believe that his convert was doing anything more than reciting what he had only recently been told. He said, "Do you think the abbot was really serious about us coming back any time?"

"Oh, sure, they like to hear talks about other people's ideas of the afterlife, especially those of *farangs*."

"Well, what about any of them becoming Christians? You know that's why we give these talks."

Boune Louan said in a very matter of fact way, "Oh, I don't think so. I think they are very satisfied with their own faith."

Bert dodged some chickens on the road, and understood more clearly than ever why the missionaries concentrated almost all their efforts on converting the tribals.

Elvira

It was getting late in the afternoon and Matthew would be back soon, bringing Pastor Grant with him. The two men had gone to the site of the new church to check on the final preparations for the opening on Sunday. The supervisor was leaving Lanchan and Laos on Monday. Bert and Dottie would probably be coming to the house to talk after supper. Elvira knew she would be busy even though she had Haw in the kitchen helping prepare the food. Haw was a Black Thai who had worked for the French in Vietnam before coming to Laos. He was quite good at fixing meals in the way he had been taught, but he didn't know anything about American cooking. He had no idea how to make fruit pies, and Matthew was so fond of them. So she had to do it.

Elvira passed the field that was used as an open air toilet and the stench was overpowering. She saw a woman leaving at the other end and under some bushes in the center she could see someone else squatting. Matthew had spoken to the authorities several times about this field because when the wind was right, the foul odor came straight toward the house. But Matthew had been told that the local people had nowhere else to go and nothing could be done. He had insisted that there were plenty of empty fields outside town, but people would have to walk a little farther. Elvira knew that the ordinary people had no indoor toilets, but that didn't excuse them for going right in the center of town. An emaciated dog came wandering by and, keeping an eye on Elvira, hurried into the grass of the field also. She knew what it was going to do—search for a fresh human pile. And though she had got used to much since being in Laos, she shuddered at the thought of the dog eating it. She hurried on.

She didn't like Peter to wander this far away, especially over near the water hole. He had learned to take care of himself pretty well, but he was only eight, and though he already knew how to swim, he could still drown. And although she had never heard of any buffalo turning vicious, she still didn't feel comfortable about the boys playing with them. What if Peter fell and a buffalo rolled on top of him?

She heard the boys' voices before she got there. Climbing up the slight rise, she looked down and saw several buffalo standing or lying in the water or mud with the boys on top of them or flopping around in the water. Two other boys stood beside Peter. One was Bye, the Vietnamese boy he had met in school, the other she had seen around but didn't know. All the boys wore shorts. Peter stood out only because of his lighter skin and blond hair. His behavior was no different from the others, flopping around, splashing water on the other boys and the buffalo. They all were calling out and speaking loudly in Lao.

Elvira called, "Peter, come on out now. It's time to come home. You know that you should have been home already."

He had permission to go play after school, but only with the understanding that he would be back in time to do his homework. His daily schedule was full, but no worse than that of Helen, his older sister. They both went to Lao school until one o'clock, and then did correspondence studies in the afternoon. In the evening, they studied the Bible. They attended the Lao school in order to learn the language, and did the correspondence studies for their regular education, so they would keep up with the children in the States. The religious studies were given because they were the children of missionaries.

"Can I just stay a little longer? I'll be home in a few minutes."

"No, you come on. You have to finish your math and history before supper. Come on, now, we're having a surprise for supper."

His friend, Bye, grabbed one buffalo by the tail and vaulted to the animals's back. Astride the animal, he spread his arms wide and yelled in Lao, "Bye is the king of beasts, look at the king of beasts."

"Aw, I can do that," Peter called back. "That's not hard." And he made a move toward another buffalo.

But Elvira called, "No, I said come on. Helen is already doing her studies. You come on right this minute."

As they walked back, Elvira said, "Aren't you ever afraid of the buffalo? They're so big."

"No. I was at first, but Bye showed me that you don't have to be afraid."

Elvira knew that Bye had been a big help to Peter. When he had first gone to the school, the other children had teased him unmercifully. Some even threw rocks at him on his way home. Then when he started to learn a little Lao, Bye had befriended him and things improved.

"I'm glad you have such a good friend," Elvira said. Maybe some time you might bring him along to church. Do you think he would like that? Anyway, it's good that you have learned the language. Some day you might be a missionary like your father. Would you like that?"

"Oh, yes, mother, that's the Lord's work."

"Anyway, you'll like supper tonight. We're going to have banana cream pie."

Elvira put the pie on a window sill where there was a strong breeze. It was the coolest place she had until the electricity went on and she could use a fan. She was still amazed that she could manage to make such things with the equipment on hand. They used a movable oven which was put over a charcoal brazier for baking and, surprisingly enough, most things turned out all right. She knew that Matthew liked fruit pies best, though there were none of the home fruits available here. She sighed and went over to check on Haw. He was fixing his usual, a kind of Mulligan stew with buffalo meat to be served with rice. She would love to have some potatoes, but they were only available from the plateau, and Verdoux didn't have any now.

She went into Helen's room where both Helen and Peter were doing their studies at a table in the middle of the room. Ten year old Helen hunched over her workbook.

"Oh, mama, would you read me this list of words so I can write them for the test? I would ask Peter but he doesn't pronounce many words right. And if I don't get eighty per cent or more right, I have to go back to the early part of the lesson and do another group."

"Sure," Elvira said. "But after that I want you to take a break and come out to help me set the table."

Elvira believed that children should begin taking responsibility as soon as they could. And setting the table wasn't hard work.

The dinner had gone very well and Elvira was pleased as she settled down to listen to the men talk. Matthew sat in the wicker chair, while Pastor Grant and Bert Funello sat on the sofa, and Bert's wife, Dorothy, sat on a chair she had brought from the dining area. Elvira sat on their single rattan rocker. They had eaten at the table on one end of the living room where Haw had brought the food from the kitchen. Pastor Grant had praised Haw's buffalo stew with rice. The cook had made it fancy for the guests, with rice pilaf instead of ordinary steamed rice. And everyone had loved Elvira's banana cream pie. The children had behaved so well that Elvira had decided to let them come in and sit with the adults while Pastor Grant gave his thank-you blessing. She would let them listen to that in place of doing their Bible studies. She might even let them have some tea when she brought it out before the general discussion.

Pastor Grant spoke, "And so, Your Lord, it is an honor for me to preside at this little gathering, in the home of this dedicated couple, Matthew and Elvira Haraldsen, and their God-fearing children, along with their colleague, Bert Funello, and his good wife, Dottie. These are truly worshipful people, consecrating their lives to the noblest work there is on this earth, *the spread of the word of Jesus. They are* unremitting in their efforts to fulfill this noble task and, like the men of the past, missionaries for two thousand years, they will succeed in their task."

Elvira watched the pastor with unblinking gaze, impressed at the man's ability to give what amounted to a sermon with no preparation at all. Perhaps someday Matthew would be that good, but now he still had to make some notes for himself before giving the sermon on Sunday.

Pastor Grant continued, "Already there is a sizeable number of believers, coming to hear the word of the Lord on his day and carrying the principal morals from his teaching into their daily lives. And despite the difficulties and uncertainties, I am certain that the number will grow."

The pastor had a book of prayer in his hands, as did the others. They would close the formal part of the meeting by reading a section. Elvira hoped they would ask Helen to read it. "And Dear Lord," the pastor continued, "although I am aware that in your all-knowingness you are fully cognizant of the labors of these people, I would like to mention a few things they do to accomplish this end. First, as you know, they study long and hard to learn the scriptures and all that the church teaches before coming out. Then they dedicate themselves to long hours in the study of the languages of their parishioners-to-be, and with great effect, as you have noticed. And in visit after endless visit to the villages, they bring the word to the pagans until the true beliefs of God begin to replace the superstitions of the tribes. Moreover, all this is done in an environment of great insecurity, one created by the other unbelievers, the atheistic Communists."

Elvira wondered how much of this was getting through to the children and if some of it wasn't too much for them to assimilate. She was sure they already knew about the guerilla movement and it could be a little frightening. After all, Helen was having many bad dreams lately. But someone had to do the mission work; and no one had ever said that it was going to be easy or completely safe.

"And Lord, the workers of the field bring their good families to these pagan lands and these true believers make do with hardship and difficulties to support their men in this noble task."

Pastor Grant grinned slightly. "And Lord, I must say that the achievements of the helpmates are sometimes remarkable. I have never tasted a better banana cream pie. Why, it wouldn't surprise me if several extra new converts will be made as a result of the menfolk eating that delicious pie and working that much harder.

"So last, Jesus, let me say something about their new church which was just dedicated. It may not look so fancy as those built in the United States and elsewhere where more resources are available, but it is truly a work of faith and love, built by those very people who have accepted the word of God, using materials available in the local economy and as close to the local style as possible."

The men had decided to have the church built of local bricks, in the general style of a Buddhist pagoda, though with a cross on top. Since almost all the parishioners were tribals who had no religious structures resembling churches, the missionaries had decided that the Buddhist model would have to do. It might even help them get a few Buddhist converts. They had dedicated the church two days before, on Sunday. And since the pastor had scheduled his visit so he could participate in the dedication, he was leaving in two more days.

"And so that we can go on with the rest of this little meeting in a more relaxed fashion, I suggest that we have a reading of Prayer Number 16, 'The Word of Jesus,' and that we have it read by the fine young girl, Helen Haraldsen."

Helen looked flustered, then blushed, but began paging through her prayer book for the selection. The others remained quiet.

After Helen finished the reading, Elvira rose and went to the kitchen for tea, and Helen followed.

"I suppose I might as well begin," said Matthew, "though it will be a little difficult after that fine presentation by Pastor Grant. We are all pleased with the outcome of the new church as expressed so well already by Pastor Grant. There are still a few odds and ends to tie up, but I think they will be taken care of. And with a little well-directed prayer, the outcome should be sped up. I am particularly speaking of the roof. The thatch roof will do for three or four more months until the rainy season begins, but by then I think we will need the permanent roof on."

"I agree with Matthew," Bert said, "that the thatch needs to be replaced. It may be what the people are accustomed to, but the stuff gets infested with lizards, insects, rats, and even snakes in no time at all. I know from my visits to Pakmong's house to study the language. He and the rest of his family seem not to be bothered, but I can tell you that it is disconcerting to be in the middle of an analysis of some verbal form and have a lizard or rat drop on you. I can imagine this happening during a Sunday sermon."

The missionaries studied the tribal languages by using the method of linguistic analysis that had been developed in anthropology at the turn of the century, a method necessary for describing non-European languages. They had learned this method at the Oklahoma Language Institute, and had become quite proficient.

"So what alternatives are there?" Pastor Grant asked. "Tile? Shingles?"

Matthew answered, "Tile is all right, though it is expensive. The good pagodas have tile roofs but the Buddhists have more money than we do. You probably know that they believe they gain merit for their reincarnations by building or helping maintain the pagodas?"

"Of course that's true of our faith also," Grant said, "supporting a church to help one to heaven. It's only too bad that the money devoted to Buddha is not allotted to the cause of Jesus. So then shingles?"

At this point Elvira came in with a tray of teacups, steam from hot tea rising from each. Helen followed with a tray holding a container of sugar and one of sweetened condensed milk, the only kind of milk available. The local people did not milk their cows or buffalo, and the only tinned milk carried by the Chinese grocers was sweetened condensed. Elvira set a cup and saucer down for each person except Matthew, who had been raised as a Mormon and still refused to drink coffee or tea. She put a glass of water at his place. Helen went to each in turn to offer them sugar and condensed milk. Then she took the two trays to the kitchen and went to her room to put on her night-dress as her mother had told her. Elvira returned to her rocker with a cup of tea to listen to the rest of the discussion.

"Sorry, no shingles here," Matthew said, continuing the conversation. "They haven't got around to making any in this country, at least that I've heard of. No, the only manufactured product for roofs is what they call 'tole ondulee' or ridged galvanized iron sheets. They are imported, but they're still about the cheapest way to go. We don't have enough to buy them, but maybe we can get the donors to come through with the amount."

Each mission station had a parish group in the States where the missionaries went every three or four years to raise money. Matthew had been back twice, traveling from one church to another to give talks about the mission effort and to describe something about the country and the living conditions. He had been well received and had already tapped donors there for a few items. Bert was scheduled to leave the next year.

Grant asked, "How much do you think the cost would be?"

Matthew had already figured it out, hoping that something like this might happen. He knew Pastor Grant was in control of a general fund that could be used for special purposes.

"If the prices don't go up, we should be able to get it for three hundred and fifty to four hundred dollars. The parish circle should be able to come up with that, though unfortunately, we also need new tires for the Land Rover."

Pastor Grant doodled a bit on a piece of paper he had tucked in his prayer book, then said, "Well now look, Matthew, you people are doing a good job out here, and under difficult circumstances, and I think it is certainly justified for us to help fund something on the new church. When I get back I will be active for some time, reporting on my trip, and you can be assured that slides of the new church will be in the forefront. I am sure many parishioners will be impressed by the style and workmanship—and I have no doubt that some of them will want to contribute to the ongoing costs."

Elvira was particularly pleased by this development since she knew that Matthew had been worrying about costs lately. She wanted to thank the Pastor but felt it would be unbecoming. it was man's work.

Both Matthew and Bert thanked the visitor.

"And now that that matter is settled," Pastor Grant said, "shall we go on to the other problems that we have been talking about already?"

"Sure," Matthew said. "Which shall we discuss first?"

"I suggest the problem of the graveyard since that doesn't seem insuperable. I guess we've already decided that it should be Christianized, right?"

"There is no doubt about that," Bert answered. "As long as the villagers continue burying the dead in the traditional fashion, they will keep some of the beliefs. So it seems to me that we ought to decide if we want to have them change the style of burial as well as whether they should go to a new place. And as you know, I favor doing both."

The new converts were from one of the many tribes who buried their dead on top of the ground, covered by small replicas of traditional houses. They also put objects in with the dead, frequently bows and arrows for men, and pottery vessels for women. The spirit essences of these objects were believed to be of use in the afterworld. Later, after the bodies had decomposed, the bones would be taken out, rewrapped, and buried in an annual ceremony.

"I know it would be preferable if there was a bona fide Christian cemetery on hallowed ground for burial," Matthew said, "but I am of the opinion that we ought to go slowly on changing them in some respects. After all, our converts could still leave the church and there is no doubt that they could go to the Buddhist wats. So I suggest that we continue to preach against the traditional way of burial, but let them keep the grave houses they have. I suggest that we work in favor of regular Christian burial at first, and especially try to get them to give up their annual reburial ceremony. And then later on we can try to set up a new cemetery which will be consecrated and where final burials will be done for all the dead, and officiated by one of us."

"That makes sense to me," Grant said. "As you men know, we would all like to replace the pagan beliefs and practices completely as soon as possible. But natives are sometimes stubborn, and to accomplish the Lord's work we must have some patience. After all, we have been in this business for two thousand years and nothing was ever accomplished by driving the potential converts away. It seems to me that you men have a very good start here and as you master more and more of the native languages, the job will get constantly easier."

"Well," Bert said, "I'm in favor of at least setting up another cemetery, consecrating it, and perhaps letting them keep their old one for the existing burials. But I must defer to the experience of you older men. However, I do think we should keep this for further consideration."

Elvira was pleased with this decision. She knew that Bert was a little impatient, but that was because this was his first tour. With Matthew's guidance, he would learn.

And her ears perked up even more when Pastor Grant spoke again.

"Good, good. And now let us get on with the problem of the women covering their breasts."

~

Q: *It is apparent that this chapter is about the spread of Christianity. But I thought we had already done that in the last chapter. It isn't that I did not like to read about modern American missionaries, but there did seem to be something of a repeat.*

A: Okay, you got me. After it was completed I felt a little of the same, but I do think that the expansion of Euroman throughout the world from the sixteenth to the nineteenth centuries and the expansion of Christianity during the last two thousand years were generally different processes. I think that overall the expansion of European culture, the aftermath of Columbus, was much more significant than the spread of the religion of Jesus. Because the spread of Western culture affected all peoples very significantly, even those who never succumbed to the influence of the missionary movement. In fact, there were three great converting religions, Christianity, Buddhism, and Islam, and these last two maintained considerable strength well through the twentieth century, while the material and economic aspects of Western culture were taken over everywhere.

Q: *So if there were three converting religions, why did you describe Christianity twice and neither of the others?*

A: Although like most anthropologists, I have tried to remain as non-ethnocentric as possible, I may still have fallen into the trap. It just seems that I have seen the effects of Christianity everywhere while the effects of the other converting religions seem to have been less obvious. And in any event, I have no doubt that the most aggressive converting religion throughout history has been Christianity. Only Islam comes close, but the roots of that faith are parallel to those of Christianity, both going back to Judaism.

Q: *You keep stressing that Christianity was a converting religion. Is this something new in history? Weren't there others before?*

A: Well, anthropology has found that all people in the world, even those with the simplest technological cultures, had religious faiths and practices. But practically all the small societies in the world treated their supernatural systems like their languages, that is, they used them for their own purposes, but they felt no need to get others to follow the same practices. Only when societies became more complex, usually after the urban revolution, and began large-scale takeover warfare, did they begin trying to make over the people they conquered, which meant getting them to speak their language and follow their religious practices.

Q: *I see what you are saying, that the large-scale conquerors imposed their systems on others. People like the Aztecs and Inca and Babylonians and Romans.*

A: Yes, and Europeans, those who carried Christianity to all parts of the world. The Romans are a somewhat mixed example because, though they imposed Latin and much of their culture on the people they conquered, they were simultaneously being undermined by the Christians.

Q: *But what about the Jews, they weren't a converting religion, were they?*

A: No, and they are an interesting example in that they became fully urbanized but still maintained the self-satisfied attitude of the tribals. They never got around to trying to convert others, though of course the derivative religions of Christianity and Islam more than made up for it.

Q: *But there are other great religions that did not try to convert, aren't there? I remember the list of modern world religions usually includes Buddhism, Hinduism, Shintoism, and Taoism. Some even include Confucianism, though as I understand it, this last is more a code for social conduct than a true religion based on supernatural concepts. Isn't that true, and don't any of those others seek converts?*

A: Your understanding of Confucianism is correct, and so far as the others are concerned, except for Buddhism, they do not seek converts. Hinduism, Shintoism, and Taoism are all systems which minister to their own people. They don't mind if a foreigner wants to worship in one of their temples so long as he follows the local rules, but they couldn't care less if that same foreigner gets to be one of them. They are miles away from the Christian who is out to baptize everyone he can and get them to use the sacred book.

Q: *But what about all the Hindu swamis we have here, and in India, surely they seek converts?*

A: *There are a few cults which are basically Hindu which operate that way. But this is a minor part of true Hinduism and some believe that it has evolved at least partly in imitation of Western conversion practices, and primarily for foreigners. The usual Brahmin priest is not really interested in getting converts.*

Q: In that case, where did all the Hindus come from?

A: There have been some prophets and missionary types in India during the past. Buddha was one, in many respects having the same role in Hinduism as Jesus had in Judaism. But overwhelmingly the increase in numbers of Hindus has come from physical reproduction; they had lots of babies. And as you know, parents normally try to pass on the religion that was passed on to them. As a matter of fact, that is the primary way of maintaining all the non-converting religions, including Judaism. If populations grow, so do their religions, unless there is great loss of belief.

Q: *Are you saying that only Christianity evolved a special type of religious person whose sole responsibility was to get converts—a missionary?*

A: Yes. It all began with Paul in the first century, to whom many writers give credit as the person most responsible for getting Christianity established and getting it on a conversion roll. As you already know, on the heels of Columbus and the conquistadors there was almost always a missionary priest intent on converting the natives. And, so far as I know, no other religion ever produced a type like this, not even the Muslims who were effective in spreading Islam through other methods.

Q: *I take it then that this was the final blow to the tribal religions throughout the world, the assault of the missionary.*

A: Yes. Everywhere, the tribal group with its nature or ancestor worship came under attack. The missionaries tried to get converts anywhere they could but they quickly learned that the followers of large national religions, whether converting or non-converting, were the least susceptible. It was much harder to get a Muslim, Hindu, Buddhist, or Shintoist to convert than an Australian aboriginal or a mountain tribe in Vietnam or even a large tribe in Africa. Sometimes the missionaries would concentrate their efforts on groups or types of lower status in national cultures where the majorities were largely impervious to conversion. In India the missionaries had more success with the lower castes, and in China with the poorest peasants and abandoned girl babies. In many places people with serious diseases like leprosy were cared for and converted by Western missionaries.

Q: *You named the chapter "The Word" and throughout you keep emphasizing language as connected to the religion and to the missionary effort. Is that deliberate?*

A: It certainly is. As you have noticed in earlier chapters, language is a vital part of learning culture, especially for its role in teaching people how to make and use things. We in anthropology cannot visualize culture without language. But a funny thing seemed to have happened when language came along. Language functions through symbolic meaning and people can name anything they do or use. But they can do even more, they can name things that are not even visible and things that do not even exist so far as direct evidence is concerned. And most religious entities cannot be verified by direct evidence. There is nothing to verify that heaven or hell exist or that there is a life after death, much less that Jesus raised someone from the dead or ascended directly into heaven after being killed. The direct evidence for the existence of dinosaurs and the size and distance of the stars is overwhelming by comparison, all those fossil bones in earth strata dated by measuring its radioactivity and all the photos and measurements of stars. So how do we know that all the great prophets of the past existed? We know because of "the word." Someone wrote down what they did and put it into a book. That is why the Bible, Koran, Talmud, Book of Mormon and other holy books are held in such high esteem. Without them there would be no evidence at all. It's not like the case of the dinosaurs. If everything that has been written about them were eliminated, there would still be the fossil bones. So language is the very heart of religious systems.

Q: *And is that why the missionaries work so hard at learning the native languages?*

A: Yes, partly. When a missionary goes forth, that is primarily what he has to disseminate, a bunch of words. You remember from the last chapter that when the Euros appeared all over the world they had many things with them, new animals, plants, tools, weapons, as well as ideologies, one of which was Christianity. Well, most of these other things sold themselves. They had what we call high demonstration effect. Take the horse for instance. When people in the New World saw it and what it could do, they wanted some for themselves, which is why the Indians of the plains in both North and South America developed horse cultures from animals which escaped or were captured from the Spaniards. No one had to deliver any sermons to the Sioux or Comanche to convince them to begin hunting buffalo on horseback. The horses demonstrated their own capability. On the other hand, how was it demonstrated to the same Sioux or Comanche that a belief in three gods in one and virgin birth was any better than a belief in local nature spirits? There was no demonstration effect at all, which of course is why the missionary stepped in and delivered a sermon.

Q: *Does that process still continue?*

A: Sure. You probably remember that the tribals in Laos were trying to trade their tiger skin for a shotgun. Guns in general, and shotguns in particular, have a high demonstration effect. Try defending yourself with a small crossbow, still used in Laos, against a tiger, or knock a howler monkey out of a tree with a blowgun, as used by the South American tribals, and then do the same thing with a shotgun, and you will know which is most efficient. You don't need a sermon to be convinced to try to get a shotgun. But if someone tries to get you to give up your traditional burial ritual or to get your wife to wear a bra in church, you do need a sermon. Thus, the great importance of words for missionaries.

Q: *And that is why they got so good at learning languages and had very good methods for doing so?*

A: Right. Their institute in Oklahoma is one of the best. They have had top instructors of descriptive linguistics, the branch that is used to analyze and learn non-European languages. In my first linguistics class the book I used was written by a pair of missionary teaching linguists, Pike and Nida. It was top of the line then, in the late 1940s. As a matter of fact, quite a few missionary linguists became good enough to devise writing systems for tribal peoples who had never had an alphabet before. The primary goal of the missionaries was to be able to write prayer books in the tribal languages, the better to make good Christians of their converts. And like so much else that the missionaries do, this also has been going on since the beginning of the faith. The original writing system of the Germanic peoples was for a language called Gothic, and the writing system was devised by a missionary from south Europe called Ulfilas. And most of the alphabets of the other languages of Europe were devised by Christians intent on introducing the Bible or prayer books.

Q: *It seems then that the missionaries were pretty thorough students of the culture of the local peoples, right?*

A: My observations have been that they become quite knowledgeable in most aspects of culture. The one part of the local belief system that they do not learn much about is the local religion. And it is not hard to understand that deficiency. Their religious training teaches them to think of the local religious ideas as superstitions, and they are constantly trying to replace them. Thus the local people tend to clam up or to give the missionaries explanations they want to hear. I would ask missionaries about most aspects of tribal people's lives, but not religion.

Q: *Which leads to the next question. I am sure you know that students are usually curious about how their professors got their knowledge, and especially if it involved field research or some unusual experiences. I assume you had some field experience in the areas you were describing. Would you mind telling us what you were doing?*

A: No, I consider your request perfectly reasonable. I was acting in a role of what we call applied anthropology, working for the U.S. government in village development, trying to improve life for villagers, both Lao and tribal. But as an anthropologist I couldn't help asking questions and observing what I could about the local culture and the people there.

Q: *So I gather that these characters are based on actual people?*

A: Yes, most of them, though these accounts are fictional, and I moved people and places around.

Q: *That's interesting. I take it then that you know what happened to many of them, right?*

A: Yes, most. Is there anyone in particular that you are interested in?

Q: *Well, what happened to the missionaries?*

A: Oh, they must have gone on to other pastures. You see, the guerilla movement turned into a real war, with the United States on one side and the Communists on the other. It was a spin-off from the Vietnamese war. And when the Communists won, all Americans had to leave the country. This included the missionaries, soldiers, and all American officials. I would guess that the missionaries went off to some other part of the world to continue their efforts at conversion. That is what usually happened with missionaries.

Q: *So you had to leave also. Were you one of the American officials at the airport?*

A: More or less. The official called Saunders was primarily modelled on me, and for your information this was the first and last tour I did for the U.S. government. I refused to go out again and went into college teaching instead, a choice which I never regretted.

Q: *What happened to the Verdoux family?*

A: Ah, yes, the *metis* family living up on the plateau, growing strawberries and helping Americans get their tiger skins. They would certainly have won no medals as conservationists, but the Americans were no different in that regard. And this was one of the last places in the world where a hunter could still shoot tigers. But in those days ecology was still a word being used only in wacko organizations of animal lovers and as an oddball specialty of biology. Anyway, their fate was sealed by what was being related in the bamboo telegraph—that they were cooperating with the CIA or the State Department or U.S. Army, presumably gathering information about guerilla movements. If so, that is where all the guns and ammunition came from. But unfortunately they were so far out in the boondocks that they were vulnerable. And the Communists had an intelligence service themselves. At dusk one night a party of guerrillas opened fire on the little enclave of the Verdoux, killing the boy, Jon, and driving out the father and mother. They escaped with their lives and fled to Thailand. That's the last I heard of them.

Q: *Well, there was really a lot of insecurity in the country. One has to admire the missionaries for working in such places.*

A: That is true, and probably has been from the beginning, from the day Paul made his travels to undermine the Romans to when Bishop Ulfilas went north to tame the Goths and Patrick the Irish Celts, to the days of the Spanish invasion of the American empires. It is no wonder there were so many saints and martyrs. The missionaries were in the most impossible places, intent on converting the heathens. Who could blame the natives for eating or burning a few?

Q: *But evidently the great mission of conversion did not get the Christians to work together. Also, there seemed to be differences of nationality.*

A: It is true that apart from accepting Jesus as the central figure in their belief system, Christians have always had significant differences in their sects. Naturally, the missionaries carried these feelings into the field where their labors took them. And so French Catholics did not get along with American Protestants all the time.

Q: *And the other religion of significance in the region, Buddhism. I found the incident with the Buddhist group most interesting. If Buddhism was a converting religion also, how could they be so tolerant of the Christian missionary?*

A: Well, remember that of the three main converting religions, Christianity continues to be the most aggressive and Buddhism the least. It is certainly true that from the beginning Buddhists did seek converts. Gautama himself is depicted in many places as the preacher of the new word. And Buddhism was carried to most of South and East Asia even while it was dying out in India, the land of Buddha's birth. But Buddhism lacked one characteristic of Christianity and its two related faiths, Judaism and Islam: it did not demand exclusivity. If new converts had some other kind of faith and spirits, the Buddhists would simply accept those and incorporate them into the new form of Buddhism. So when the Buddhists encountered the new faiths of the West, they simply decided the more the better. Why insist that theirs was the only way? And if the brash Westerners wanted to preach about their beliefs, why not let them do it in the temple among those who devoted their lives to the study of supernaturalism, their monks? And so we have the sight of a Christian missionary intent on replacing someone else's faith with his own, and a group of listeners who have no trouble considering many ways of accomplishing the same goal.

Q: *Of course, the intolerance of Christianity is probably why it spread so much more efficiently, right?*

A: Yes, that and the self-righteousness of its practitioners. A true Christian believer had been taught that his own way is absolutely the best.

Q: *So to change the subject somewhat, may I take the woman's viewpoint?*

A: Sure, why not? That is very fashionable nowadays.

Q: *The missionary wife certainly put up with a lot of primitive and even frightening conditions, didn't she?*

A: Yes, and I suspect this was true of missionaries throughout the last two thousand years. After all, since they were working with "heathens," the conditions couldn't have been as comfortable as in civilized life.

Q: *There must have been a lot of contagious diseases.*

A: Sure. Remember there were still lepers there, and remember that open field used as a toilet. People got sick from fly-borne diseases. And although we didn't see it in the narrative, people had to sleep under mosquito nets in this place. Malaria was still a real illness. And since you know that I was there too, I can tell you that my wife got leprosy, probably from her stay there, when she accompanied me.

Q: *And all the other adjustments that the women had to make. I can visualize the fear of the mother, Elvira, seeing her blond son play with the water buffalo, along with his local buddies.*

A: It took a lot of stamina—and faith. And of course the missionary wives had plenty of that, normally. But even other women could live with such difficulties, even without the faith. The incident of the boy playing with the buffalo was based on the experience of my son. And my wife, who was a non-believer, stood up to that without any great stress.

Q: *Elvira's effort to hang on to something that was familiar by making the banana cream pie was touching.*

A: That is normal for all kind of folks. When thrown into different and difficult conditions, there is usually a strong drive to find or make something familiar. And however steadfast the missionaries were in their dedication to spreading the word of Jesus, I am sure they suffered from "culture shock" also. Moreover, the fruit pie is frequently seen as most American. The way we usually hear it is "as American as apple pie," but there were no apples available to Elvira so she made do with second best, but still American, banana cream pie.

Q: *The building of the church by the villagers sounded like an interesting idea, particularly in making it look like a local temple. Was that something new in that area?*

A: Perhaps by making it in a local style. But you did notice that they had them make it like a Buddhist wat even though the converts were not former Buddhists. The use of "volunteer" labor was an idea that missionaries all over the world have been doing for centuries. The first thing was practically always to get the locals committed which was signified by having them baptized. The next job was to get them to jettison their idols and other religious paraphernalia, then to build a real religious structure, a church. And since missionaries were not usually loaded, they invariably thought of using the labor of the new converts. The Spanish friars built one mission after another in this fashion. In the state of California about the only structural evidence still remaining of the Spanish period are these missions up and down the coast. You may remember I mentioned that I was supposed to be working in village development. Well, the kind I was actually assigned to do was called "community development" and consisted of buildings constructed through volunteer labor in the villages. These were secular projects; the church projects were of the same order, but of religious structures.

Q: *The missionaries in the narrative were very intent upon changing the people's customs. Was that typical?*

A: Sure, and though nowadays we are supposed to be more tolerant of other people's customs, the fact is that throughout history, groups who came into control or exerted strong influence on others almost invariably tried to change those they controlled to their own way of doing things. It stems from the omnipresent attitude called ethnocentrism, the feeling that one's own way is the best.

Q: *But you just got finished telling us that the Buddhists were willing to consider other people's beliefs and customs.*

A: That's true, but the Buddhists were not in control in this situation, and though they were willing to consider other people's ways, I feel sure that practically all of them thought their way was best. They were simply not so intolerant as the Christians. It's more a matter of degree than an absolute difference. For instance, they had certain customs which they would insist others should follow. Buddhists made a big thing about people taking off their shoes when they entered the temple. And in a sense this is not much different from the Christians' insistence that women coming into church have their breasts covered.

Q: *Are you saying that although all cultures are ethnocentric, some are more so than others? And that Western culture is very much so?*

A: Yes, which comes from their having been dominant for quite a while. And of all aspects of Western culture, it is probably in Christianity that they are most ethnocentric. After all, that is what gave Christianity its strength. Its adherents were taught for two thousand years that their way was the only way. And so whenever they came into control of any other group, and converted them, they immediately set out to change their undesirable customs. The first thing the Spaniards did when they conquered the great Aztec city, Tenochtitlan, was to force the natives to tear down the pyramids and other structures, and to have them build churches on the same sites. The same thing happened in Inca-land. When I was in West Africa, the last hold-outs were turning in their ancestor figures to the missionaries to be burned, eradicating the last vestiges of paganism.

So it shouldn't be any surprise that the missionaries in Laos were engaged in the process of getting the tribals to abandon their native graveyards, along with the reburial ceremony, one practiced very widely among tribals throughout the world, but of course not among Christians.

Q: *So the last question is, what is the business about the breasts? How did the missionaries get involved in that?*

A: Well, you know the primary job of the missionaries was to get people to accept Jesus as the savior, not a mean task in itself. After all, they had to get tribal peoples who were dedicated to belief systems concerning nature spirits, ancestor worship, and shamans to believe in an omnipotent, anthropomorphic god who had been born of a virgin, and after being executed for being a trouble-maker, had ascended directly into heaven after three days. In trying to spread a story like that, the missionaries have to be given credit for great courage or pure foolhardiness. But whether the locals were convinced at first, they did submit to baptism in no small numbers. There are very few tribals left in the world who still practice their native religions.

But to make the job even more difficult, the missionaries invariably carried a lot of accretions when they went to convert the heathens. And one of these was their code of proper behavior, and especially their style of dress. Many peoples of the warm countries covered their bodies only as much as necessary. If they wore anything at all, they usually covered the genital area, both men and women. But the body above the waist was frequently left uncovered. However, the Euros and, so far as I know, the Judaic peoples, covered the top also. So Christians got the idea that the proper body was one covered from at least mid-calf to the neck. And later, when Islam came on the scene, its adherents, especially the females, covered even more of the body.

The male in Christian-dominated countries was allowed to leave his chest bared but the uncovered breasts of the female came under taboo. And progressively, the message was delivered that the woman's breasts had to be covered. In culture after culture, then, the people were influenced or coerced to get their women to cover up. It was in fact called "the great cover-up." And it will come as no surprise that the missionaries were in the forefront of this campaign.

Laos was one of the last countries where women could still go about with their breasts uncovered. Even there the town women had knuckled under, but in the villages there were plenty who still went about unencumbered on top. A half-way measure evolved which was to use plain cotton bras as exterior garments. That is, instead of a blouse on top and a bra underneath, a woman trying to be modern would simply buy a cheap bra and wear it as the sole garment.

And this created a problem which the missionary trio was trying to solve at the end of our narrative—whether to permit the new female converts to come to church with nothing on top or with a bra only, or to require a bra and an outer garment.

There were surely some good sermons on the subject.

8

The Way of Science

Henry

The thirteen-year-old boy was only dimly aware of his mother and sister as he bent over his book. Mostly he passed his eyes across the line unaided, but periodically he would trace a passage with his finger. He was hunched over so far that he couldn't breathe easily. When enough air had been stored up, he would release it with a grunt.

His mother, Bertha, a plump woman in a flowered dress, concentrated on her work at a treadle sewing machine. She worked quickly, moving the cloth rapidly under the jabbing needle in syncopation with the rocking of the treadle. She was patching clothes, a task she took on most evenings after the family had eaten supper. She had had the sewing machine six years and was quite proficient in its use, making dresses or other women's clothes when she wasn't patching torn or worn garments.

Fourteen-year-old Matilda stood in a corner of the room ironing her school uniform, wearing a house dress her mother had made. She sprinkled drops of water on sections she had smoothed with her hand, then quickly passed over it with the iron which she kept on an insulated plate at one end of the ironing board. Periodically she held the iron up with one hand and quickly touched the flat of it with her moistened fingers when it would hiss. When it became too cool, she went to the kitchen and exchanged it for another iron which was heating on the burner. They had not yet got one of the new electric irons, though they had talked about it. There were so many new things to buy. And before anything else, everyone wanted one of the new Model T's. All were also anxious to get a radio.

The other two girls had gone to a neighbor's house for the night. In the living room Wilhelm could be heard folding and unfolding the paper, which he read every night, the sports section in particular.

"I knew he'd do it," Wilhelm shouted. "And it says so right here. Jack Dempsey knocks out George Carpenter in the fourth round. I knew old Jack would do it."

No one responded. They were used to Wilhelm's enthusiasms, particularly about baseball and boxing.

That afternoon, before it was time to deliver the papers, Henry had taken his bicycle to the branch library, a one-story brick building in Harrison Park. It was summer and there was no school. He had brought back five books strapped to the carrier—reading to last most of the week. He had started a special project—methodically going through all the library shelves, section by section, reading each title and author, and opening those books which seemed interesting. This time he had been in the section on biology and had taken out a copy of *The Origin of the Species* by Charles Darwin, which he had read about in other books. It was difficult to read with its example after example of details about animals and plants, and its dry style, very different from the story books he was used to reading.

The particular section he was reading in the living room was about selection through body decoration, particularly in birds. It was about sex, but the description lacked the excitement he thought such a subject would contain. His mother's voice entered his consciousness.

"Henry, sit up straight. You're not breathing right."

He sat in a corner chair, a standing lamp for light, his eyes on the book. Bertha's voice was louder.

"Henry, did you hear me? If you don't sit up straight, you'll end up having a humped back. Just the other day I noticed you didn't stand up straight."

She turned toward her daughter.

"Why I bet Matilda has noticed it too. Haven't you, Matilda?"

"Yes, mom. He ought to sit up straight."

Henry raised his head and straightened a little. His mother spoke.

"Now, that's better, but you have to remember it, especially since you read so much." She had stopped sewing and was looking more intently at the boy. "By the way, what is that book that's so interesting?"

"Oh, it's nothing, just a book about animals."

Though she tried, she couldn't read the title on the book. "What is it, a story book?"

He was usually reading something about animals. The latest stories he had read were by Jack London and Ernest Thompson Seton. Those were story books, even if the main characters were animals. This one was certainly different.

"Not exactly a story," he responded. "it's about animals, though."

Somehow he thought that might satisfy her. But she did not quit.

"What's the name of it?"

He had a feeling that the conversation was taking a wrong turn. He spoke in an almost inaudible voice.

"The Origin of the Species."

Bertha came to attention. "That's a book about that evolution, isn't it? What is the name of the author?"

Henry responded, his voice still barely audible. "Darwin."

"Oh, Mom," Matilda said, "that's the book about how apes turned into men. Sister Mary Joseph in my religion class was telling us about it, and that we weren't supposed to read it. It's on the League of Decency list in the church."

Bertha had dropped the piece of cloth she had been sewing.

"Now Henry, is that true? Are you reading that book about monkeys?"

"No, mom, I'm reading about birds, about how their colors help them to get together to have families, to raise babies of their own—" he was going to say "species," but decided it was a risky word, so he said "kind" instead.

"Well, I don't know," Bertha said. "You bring the strangest books into the house. But I do know that evolution is not a good religious subject. Why, the very idea of monkeys changing into people. We all know that monkeys were created by God just like everything else. Things didn't change from one thing to another. The church teaches us that." She paused, and then said, "And if it's on the forbidden list, we certainly don't want you to read it."

Henry had closed the book and put it down, trying to decide whether to gather all his books and go into his room or to try to read another—perhaps the story book by Seton about the red fox.

"I heard the other kids talking about Darwin," Matilda said. "They said he was an atheist."

Despite the fact that the light was very weak in his bedroom, Henry decided to take his books there. He could see that his mother was not going to let this matter drop. He put them in a pile and began to get up.

"Henry," his mother said, "leave the book about evolution here. I want to look at it and if it isn't good for you, I don't want you to read it."

"Aw, mom, I've already started it. And they say it's scientific. Can't I, please?"

"No. I want to look at it first and I'll let you know later. That's what we're supposed to do, protect the morals of our children."

Henry heard his father get up in the other room and knew he would be coming in to talk to Bertha soon. He decided to take the books he could and go to his room, since it was certain his mother would tell his father about it. He put the Darwin book on the edge of the table and, gathering the others, began to leave.

"The light in your room isn't very good," his mother said, "So you can't read too long. I want you to be in bed by nine at the latest. You're going out with your father tomorrow, aren't you?"

"Yes, mom." And he hurried away, wanting to say something nasty to Matilda but refraining just so the matter would die down. But before he got out of earshot, his mother's voice reached him.

"And before you go to bed, be sure to say your prayers."

After he was in bed, Henry heard his father come up the stairs and go to the bathroom. His father did not close the door tightly and Henry could hear the heavy pouring of urine. Then he heard his father's footsteps to his parents' bedroom, and his moving about as he undressed. Finally he heard his father's voice at the top of the stairs entreating, "Bertha, come on to bed, it's time to go to bed."

Henry couldn't understand the words coming from downstairs, though he heard his mother's voice. He had heard this exchange often enough, though, that he could pretty well guess what she was saying: "Not now, Will. I still have some work to finish."

He heard his father's tired footsteps return to the bedroom, then the sound of the springs of the bed creaking as he settled in, and Henry, too, drifted off to sleep.

He enjoyed the summer days when he went with his father on the milk route, especially being out in the early morning when everyone was asleep. It felt like he owned the world. However different it was from the activities of the school year, he had done it enough that it was almost a routine. And the fact that he only did it in the summer also made it seem special. There were no problems with the nuns or the other kids.

When the alarm rang, Henry was already awake, and by the time he went into the kitchen, his father would have the pan heating at full boil. Bertha had put the right amount of water in it the night before, and had measured out the oatmeal. Even so, Wilhelm would invariably forget to watch it, and it would burn. Wilhelm would rush back to the kitchen to take the oatmeal off the burner and then scrape the unburned part into two bowls, one for each of them. In addition to their oatmeal, Bertha would have left whatever medicines or special health items they needed. She usually left cod liver oil for Henry and a laxative for his father. Henry hated the cod liver oil, but his mother had been told that it contained a vitamin necessary for growing children. All the Baumann kids and many others took it daily.

After they had eaten and put the dirty dishes into the sink, they walked together in the sleeping night through the park to the milk company. Wilhelm let Henry carry the metal lunch pail with a rectangular section for the sandwiches and a tubular section for the thermos, the kind that all workmen carried. Sometimes they walked without talking but usually Wilhelm would talk to Henry. Tonight he talked about mathematics, urging Henry to study as much of it as he could so he would get a good job. Wilhelm said that Henry might even get to be an engineer if he learned enough math, and then he could build bridges and high buildings.

When they got to the milk company there was already a bustle of activity. Wilhelm took Henry along to the office, where he made out his order for the day, and introduced him to the drivers. "This is my son, Henry," he said proudly and Henry shrank in embarrassment.

As soon as he turned in his milk order, Wilhelm went down to harness the horses. As usual, he took one called Duke who knew the route so well he could go without being guided. Henry went from stall to stall petting the horses, looking for Billy, the goat who had free run and who Wilhelm said they kept because horses like to have a goat with them. Henry couldn't understand why this was so, but he accepted it as true since Wilhelm had grown up on a farm. Henry knew that his father had come to the city of Wewauken after returning from army service in World War I because jobs in the city paid more money than he could earn as a farm hand. There he had met Bertha, who also had come from the country and was working as a housemaid.

Henry kept a sharp watch when he was in the barn—Billy had a way of sneaking up on you and butting you from behind. But he did not see the goat. He joined his father who had finished harnessing the horses and moving the delivery van to the loading dock. The van was specially built for delivery, having storage sections in the front and back and a section in the middle tall enough for a man to stand up in. As the cases of milk were slid out to Wilhelm, he stored them in a special arrangement so he could get to the kinds of milk he needed for each customer.

The man helping to slide the milk cases out screwed his mouth up in a grimace and seemed to try to talk, but all that came out were sounds like the gasp-groans of a donkey.

"What's wrong with him?" Henry asked in a low voice so the man wouldn't hear him.

"Oh, Charley? We don't know. He just showed up and he helps wherever he can and everybody gives him a quarter or so."

"Can't he talk?"

"Well, he tries, as you can see. But you can't understand him."

"Does he live off that money?"

"I guess so. Some of the drivers bring him food from home, too, when their wives bake or have something left over."

Wilhelm finished loading his truck and started his horse up to get out of the line.

"Where does he live?" Henry was too interested in the defective man to drop the subject.

"Oh, they let him stay in the hay loft in the horse barn. I think he has some blankets there."

"What's wrong with him?"

"I don't know for certain, some disease that he had when he was a child or a birth defect or something. There's quite a few people like that but you usually don't see them. Families keep them at home, in a back room."

Henry liked the part when they delivered the milk because Wilhelm would bring two metal carriers for the milk bottles, and let Henry deliver on one side of the street while he took care of the other, as the horse kept moving on its own. Most people just took plain milk, others wanted a bottle of cream, buttermilk, or chocolate milk, or a pound of butter also. Wilhelm knew all of the combinations and he would tell Henry which ones took something special. Then Henry would run out on one side while Wilhelm delivered his at a fast walk on the other, both meeting up the street where Duke would have moved the van and be waiting for them to return with the carriers of empty bottles.

"Horses are so smart," Henry said. "I guess they'll never be replaced by trucks, will they? No truck could do what a horse could. I bet old Duke could do the milk route without any person along, couldn't he?"

"Maybe he could," Wilhelm replied. "Horses can learn a lot of things, We had a horse down on the farm who was blind but she could work along with another horse, just so long as she was in harness. Old blind Pet got hit by lightning but we couldn't afford another horse, so we just got her used to staying with the other horse in the harness. She did fine. But the trucks are coming. They're already delivering a lot of things and the milk company owners are already talking about getting some trucks for downtown routes. It's getting dangerous to go through downtown with a horse."

"Well, I hope they don't get rid of all the horses. What would the horses do if they didn't work in delivery?"

"Oh, they still use them out on the farm, though even there it's changing. When I was working up in Benton County, some of the big farmers were already switching to tractors."

Henry knew his father had worked as a farm hand in the prairie country up north before he had gone into the service. It was very different from the hill country of the southern part of the state where his grandparents' farm was.

After they had delivered all the milk, Wilhelm had Duke take the van to a place under some trees where they ate lunch. Wilhelm always offered Henry a full bottle of anything he wanted with his sandwich and cookies, and Henry usually took chocolate milk. He drank it out of the bottle because that's what Wilhelm and the other workmen did.

"Now you have to leave some in the bottle and don't put the cap back on," Wilhelm told him. "That way I can turn it in as spoiled and

I won't have to pay for it. That's because good milk is pasteurized, and good for you. You know what that is, don't you?"

Henry had heard often enough about pasteurization but he still wasn't quite sure. He thought it was heating the milk but not boiling it.

"Sure, mom told me about it. She said it was a way to sterilize the milk without spoiling it. Some famous scientist in Europe invented it."

"His name was Pasteur, and he was French, like your grandma."

They always talked about the Herbert side of the family as being French because their ancestors came from Alsace. All the rest of the relatives had German ancestors.

"But what about before they had pasteurization?" Henry asked. "Did milk make people sick then? And what about down on the farm, didn't you drink milk when you were little? Did that make you sick?"

"No, it doesn't always. People out in the country don't drink milk much anyway, but even when they do, they don't always get sick. But they found out that there were germs in the milk and sometimes you could get sick from it. So when they started putting milk in bottles, they started this pasteurization. It's just heating the milk below the boiling point."

Wilhelm finished eating and took out his pipe. As he pressed the tobacco down, he said, "Anyway, I told you that after I am finished collections today, I would take you to see Doc Grund, the scientist for the milk company. He can answer any of your questions, that's his business. He knows everything about milk and pasteurization and biology. And I'm sure he will let you look into his microscope."

Wilhelm had been promising to bring Henry to see the biologist for several weeks and the boy was looking forward to it mainly because he knew the man kept small animals. But before he did that, Wilhelm would have to collect money from the customers on his route whose day it was to pay. Henry had brought a book along.

"You want any more?" Wilhelm asked, crinkling his eyes. "There's another bottle of chocolate."

Henry knew his father was kidding, although he dearly loved chocolate milk, and though he momentarily considered having another, he just couldn't.

"No, pop, I've had enough."

Wilhelm took the empty bottle and put it in the case while Henry put the leftovers in the empty lunch pail. Willhelm got his account book to look up his customers, and Henry got his book and slid over in the corner of a small loading area and began to read.

"That's not that book on evolution, is it?" Wilhelm said. "Your mother told me about that and you were supposed to leave it with her."

Henry knew she would have told Wilhelm about it and it bothered him, but he didn't want to get it stirred up again.

"No," he said. "It's a story about a fox."

"I know your mother can get on your nerves sometimes, but she is really doing the best for you. And she's just trying to protect your faith." Whereupon he opened his account book and began marking with his pencil.

It was about three o'clock when Duke pulled the milk wagon up in front of the biologist's house and the two of them walked around to the back where the laboratory was located.

"He keeps a lot of animals here," Wilhelm said. "As much as you like animals, you'll find that interesting. He's a doctor, he had to go to college to learn all about biology and chemistry. Not a medical doctor, a scientific doctor. They're different. Scientific doctors do experiments, medical doctors cure you."

Doc Grund, wearing a white coat, answered the door and led them into a small office. A girl sat at a typewriter in the corner.

"Ah, Mr. Baumann," the doctor shook Wilhelm's hand. "And here is the young Master Baumann. Out helping his dad, I see. That's good. Maybe some day young Master Baumann will be working for the milk company too. Always glad to see the younger generation."

He went back to his desk and picked up a sheaf of papers.

"Just a minute and I'll show you around, just have to finish this report."

He turned to the girl, handing her the papers. "Could you type this report, Miss Green. I need to get it out today."

He turned back to the visitors. "It's a laboratory test for the milk company, to show how good the milk is after pasteurization."

Wilhelm looked at Henry. "See, Henry, it's like I told you. They are checking the milk all the time."

Grund chuckled. "Yes, well, you know we have to be down to a certain level of bacterial content or the milk company loses its license. But come on into the lab and I'll show you around"

The milk company had arranged for all the delivery men to visit the lab so they could impress upon their customers how sanitary the milk was.

"You can ask Doc anything you want about pasteurization now, Henry," Wilhelm told him.

Henry felt embarrassed as he always did when his father pushed him forward. "That's okay, Dad. I'll just look."

He could see the rows of cages in the back with white mice and guinea pigs. The biologist first took them to the table with the microscope. "We can let the young man look here. He can see some of the bugs himself."

Grund uncorked a vial and put a long tube into the water. Then withdrawing it, he put a drop on a slide and covered it with another piece of glass.

"This is ordinary pond water. I keep some just for demonstrations. It looks pure but it is filled with bugs."

The water on the slide did look perfectly clear as the biologist turned on the light and adjusted the eyepiece.

"Just full of everything they show the kids in class—" Grund continued. "Amoeba, paramecium, volvox, and all the rest. Why, that water would kill an athlete. Here young man, you take a look."

Henry climbed on the stool the biologist had pulled over, and bent over the eyepiece. It was all blurry at first, but when the man showed him how to adjust the focus, all the little animals came into view. "Are those germs?" he asked.

"Well, some are. The amoeba is related to one which causes dysentery. The others are just microscopic life forms. But you can be sure that pond water has germs in it. I'm just using the pond water because it has very distinct creatures in it."

He offered the microscope to Wilhelm who also took a look, then he took them around the lab, showing them the various pieces of equipment. He finished near the animal cages. Most of the animals were in separate cages and sniffed up against the wire when the group came close. Henry put his finger up to one guinea pig and the animal sniffed him with its blunt nose.

"He has pet rabbits at home," Wilhelm told Dr. Grund.

"Well, these are different. They are used to test our medicines."

The biologist worked for several companies on contracts. He said to Henry, "Well, young man, how would you like to work in a laboratory, where you would have so many animals around all the time."

"I guess it would be alright." Henry wanted to ask about how they tested the medicines, but he had to work up his courage. He already suspected he knew, but he blurted out, "What do you do to the guinea pigs to test the medicines?"

"Well you have to watch them along with the control group— those are the ones who don't get the medicine—and see if they don't get the disease."

"Where does the disease come from?"

"Well, you have to infect them."

Henry wished he hadn't started on this line of questioning, but at the same time he thought he needed to know. How else would he ever learn?

"As interested as he is in animals," Wilhelm said, "I would think he might like to follow this line of work."

"How do you infect them?" Henry asked Grund.

"Usually you do that with a hypodermic needle. You have to make a culture of the bacteria and then inoculate all the animals with it." He picked up a needle to show the boy.

Henry wanted to get finished with the discussion, but he still pressed on. "So then how do you know if the medicine is working or not?"

"The animals which don't get the medicine show symptoms of the condition. They lose their appetite or they just mope in a corner. But to be sure, you have to dissect them." He showed Henry a board on which he stretched the animals and some heavy pins he used to hold their bodies down. Henry couldn't help shivering. He hoped the man didn't notice.

"Usually the animal is dead," Grund said. "But even when it isn't, we give it anesthesia before cutting it open. It's easier to cut open an animal that isn't struggling."

Henry didn't really want to hear any more and he quickly pulled his finger back from one of the cages where an animal was sniffing it. The biologist said, "He just wants some pellets."

But Henry just couldn't help asking one last question.

"And do you kill them with a hypodermic needle also?"

"No, we just knock them on the head, like this." He demonstrated with his fingers, striking them on the edge of the work table.

Bertha/Adolph

She tried to keep busy throughout the morning to keep her mind off her tooth. It was the fourth she was to lose, which wasn't too bad since she had had four children and was forty-one years old. Many mothers had done much worse. But she had tried to do everything she could to save her teeth, including drinking all the milk she could. The doctors said you had to take in as much calcium as possible when you had babies. She would drink more if she could, but it gave her an upset stomach.

Periodically she took the bag of ice from the ice box and put it on her jaw to ease the pain.

"Does it hurt much, mom?" Matilda asked.

"Oh, it's all right. It's what happens when you get older. You'll have tooth problems too after you get married and have your family. You know your father lost several teeth also. One just puts up with it. Everything in life isn't wonderful. A little suffering is good for a person."

"I'm sorry, mom. If there's anything I can do, let me know."

"You just take care of your sisters and brother and watch the house until I get back and I'll be grateful." She opened the ice box door. "Now here's a bowl of potato salad and you children can make bologna sandwiches. You can have cookies afterwards. And be sure to drink a lot of milk. The calcium is supposed to be good for growing children, especially girls."

"I will, mom. I'll do everything you said."

"You keep your eye on your sisters, too. Remember, you're the oldest and I'm depending on you."

Bertha dressed and walked to Garfield Street to wait for the tram. She kept her head turned or put her hand on her cheek if someone was near, so no one would see the swollen part of her jaw. Fortunately, only two other people came, a young woman and an older man. Both were preoccupied and paid her little attention. The tram came in a few minutes and there was plenty of room for her to have a seat to herself. The tram was one of the things about the city that she particularly appreciated. When you considered that out in the country you had to walk everywhere or go about in a buggy or wagon, it made you believe that progress was very real. Of course, she knew that the priests did not deny progress in everyday life, only in peoples' morality. And it was certain that in that respect things had gone downhill ever since the

256

Garden of Eden. One of the few consolations was the Catholic faith by which they could struggle as families and individuals against the constant moral degeneration.

Her thoughts kept her mind off her tooth. She didn't have far to go; if she had been in the country she would have walked, but for a nickel she could easily afford to ride the streetcar. She began to read the ads in the row along the top where the straps hung. The clicking rhythm of the wheels on the track soothed her until her eyes settled on an ad which advertised literacy. A man, woman, and child looked confidently at a horizon of skyscrapers and a message proclaimed, "Be a part of this world of the future, learn to read and write. The Institute of Total Literacy will make you into a person of the future." The address was downtown and the cost was reasonable. She was continually amazed at all the things that were going on in the city, and wondered how she had ever managed when she lived down in Terre Bois. She was pleased that she and Wilhelm could already read and write, even though both had only gone to the seventh grade. After that, being the oldest of the children, both had had to stay at home to help their parents. There hadn't been a law yet to enforce school attendance to age sixteen.

By the time she reached her stop, her tooth was throbbing again, but she didn't hurry to get to the dentist's office. Though she had done it before, the idea of taking ether bothered her. She didn't like not knowing what was going on, but what else was there to do?

Dr. Adolph Seebach was a little older than Wilhelm, with black hair like her husband but with a thin moustache. He wore glasses and a white coat. He had her sit in the dental chair and began examining the tooth.

"Yes, it definitely has to be removed," he said. "But it will be no problem; you have had ether before. Later, after it has healed, we can put a bridge there."

"I don't really like to take ether, Dr. Seebach. Isn't there anything else?"

"Well, they are working on new methods. But ether is still the best. You know, for a long time they took ether just for the fun of it. Called them ether frolics. Why, Mrs. Baumann, you won't even know what happened when you come out of it, and that bothersome tooth will be gone."

He called his assistant and reached over for the nose piece. Placing the device over her nose, he said, "Now take a deep breath, Mrs. Baumann."

When her breath became regular and her eyes closed, he had the assistant hold the nose piece in place while he reached for his dental tools and began working. He had some trouble pulling the tooth, and had to cut around the root. Bertha stirred slightly and he said to the assistant, "Hold the nose piece on tightly and turn up the gas a little."

As soon as Bertha had settled down again, he rapidly pulled and twisted the tooth out. He pushed a folded piece of bandage material into the hole, then relaxed, taking over the nose piece from his assistant. He had decided to keep Bertha on the gas for a few minutes longer.

As he waited, he thought about the incredible saga of how ether had first been produced. Wells and Morton, the discoverers, had had to fight it out trick by trick. What a story of almosts and barelys compared to what the dental schools taught about how scientific discoveries were made. There was nothing neat about it as the textbooks presented the case.

Seebach could picture the carnies playing their game a little less than a hundred years before. There must still have been some Indians around. But there the dentists were, calling the hayseeds to come in and take a whiff of the great new discovery—ether, or laughing gas—and to take a trip into fantasy land. Then the decoy would come up out of the crowd, plunk his silver pieces down, and take a whiff. And the next thing you knew, he was making an ass out of himself.

In Seebach's mental reconstruction the guy fell off the stage. He would be helped up by the carny and coddled until he started to gain consciousness, a silly grin on his face. And there was Wells or Morton standing in the crowd watching in amazement. The guy was unconscious! Saliva was dripping from his mouth. And though he started to come out of it within five or ten minutes, the carny tried to speed it up by shaking him.

"See folks, he is totally off in fantasy land. Try to imagine, folks—you too could go on a trip like this for the simple sum of fifty cents, two quarters, one half of a dollar."

And within five or ten minutes the guy who had been gassed would be coming back. Wells in particular was thunderstruck. He was already thinking about the possibilities in dentistry. You could pull several teeth and the patient wouldn't even know it, he thought.

258

Wells would be having visions of his own, rows and rows of gums with no teeth and in their place would be the fine dentures he and Morton had developed. That was the problem he carried around with him all the time, the problem of getting people to let them pull out their bad teeth in order to put in the dentures. There were thousands out there who could use the fine dentures these men had developed, but the agony of having their teeth pulled without anesthesia was more than most people would put up with until the agony of the rotten teeth became worse than the expectation of the agony of having them pulled. They had to find something that would suppress the pain. And maybe this was it.

By this time the gassed person would be coming back to consciousness, first opening his eyes, then shaking his head. Wells would be excited, having noticed a bruise on the man's arm, evidently from his fall. "Look, look, he doesn't even know he has it."

And he would speak excitedly to the carny. "Look at his bruise, he doesn't even notice it."

And the carny, evidently concerned that he would be blamed for hurting the man, would say, "It doesn't matter, mister. He bruises easily."

"No, no," Wells would say. "This is not to blame, this is just to show that he was truly unconscious."

The carny would be getting irritated by this time since he had a regular routine and this was the stage when he expected to get customers to pay for a whiff.

But Wells would be so excited by this time that he would say to Morton, "One of us has got to do that and I think I want it to be me. Why, Mr. Morton, this may be just exactly what we are looking for." And he would turn to the carny and, proffering his fifty cents, would say, "Mr. ether-man, here is your first customer."

And that was how it all began, though the process of convincing others to use either it or nitrous oxide, which was being used in the same way, to make money out of it, was still a long way off.

Bertha moved slightly and Seebach automatically held the nose piece on a little more tightly. He was still caught up in the saga of Wells and Morton. A vivid scene came to his mind, as he saw the jubilation they experienced when they did their first dental work with the new gas, in this case Morton being the main actor. He would come excitedly into his partner's office, puffing hard on a newly-lit cigar, overflowing with excitement. "Mr. Wells, it's a breakthrough. I did five patients this morning under gas and there was hardly a hitch. Three of them were tooth extractions. I am sure there will be no problem at all in fitting each with a set of dentures. You know, if this keeps up, we'll not be able to keep up with the demand."

He would sit down and put his leg over the side of the chair. "And then there's the gas itself. Nobody else is using it. The idea is worth money. Mr. Wells, I think we need to patent our new idea. And just imagine what will happen in surgery when they start using gas. That famous surgeon that everybody joked about in dental school will be out of business. You know what I mean, the guy who was so fast that in one minute he amputated a guy at the hip, cut off two fingers of his assistant, and castrated an onlooker. I mean with ether or nitrous oxide he would have at least fifteen or twenty minutes to amputate the guy's leg."

But it hadn't worked out so easily, particularly for Wells. As well as Seebach remembered, his hero had never been able to convince any surgeons to use the new gases, despite the demonstrations he did. And he was never able to make any money on their discovery. He finally killed himself with a drug overdose. Morton had done better, convincing some VIP from Harvard to use the stuff, and perhaps making some money in the process, despite the fact that by that time quite a number of other people were claiming they had been the first to use gas. But that was the beginning of the age of anesthesia.

"Dr. Seebach, Dr. Seebach," an excited whisper entered his consciousness. "The patient is gaining consciousness."

He looked down and saw Bertha moving, her eyes open. The ether nose piece was awry. He heard the whisper again. "Don't you want to take the nose piece off, Dr. Seebach?" It was his assistant.

He quickly straightened up and lifted the nose piece. Bertha straightened up also, then moved her jaw back and forth, and put her hand to the swollen place.

"Is it gone?"

"Yes, Mrs. Baumann. How are you feeling?"

She looked at him directly. "Oh, I feel fine."

"Do you have a headache?"

"No, is that usual?"

"Some people get headaches, but they go away rapidly."

Mrs. Seebach brought two cups of tea on a tray to where Adolph was working. He sat next to his workbench, trying to put the new focal adjustment on his telescope.

"This hot drink will keep my favorite astronomer warm while he is looking at the distant places in the vast universe," she said.

The dentist put his screwdriver down. "Oh, thank you, my dear, it will indeed hit the spot, and especially when I get outside. It will be a fine night for viewing because of the high that came though this afternoon. Nothing better than a good fall high for viewing the skies. I might even see the great northern lights."

She sat on the other stool and picked up one of the cups. "Here, yours is ready, with sugar in it."

He picked up his cup and sipped the steaming liquid to test its temperature. He imagined the pleasure he would get from sweeping across the multitudes of those pinpoints of light. And he was satisfied to be with Amy. She had been one of the best additions to his life.

"How long have you been interested in astronomy, Adolph? You put so much into it now."

That was true, he knew. He spent all his spare time reading about the subject, or at the astronomy society, or at his telescope.

"Ever since college. In my pre-dental years I had to take two or three science courses and I chose astronomy. It was fascinating. In fact, I think I could have been happy as an astronomer." He didn't mention the fact that he had thought seriously of the possibility but his father was so intent on his being a doctor or dentist that he gave up the idea.

Well, anyway," she said, "you can spend all the night time you want on viewing now, and perhaps some day you might even find something new."

"I suspect that all the important discoveries have already been made. Anyway, the telescopes in observatories are so much bigger that the professional astronomers discover everything important. But who knows, we keep looking."

"Is there anything special you are looking for tonight?"

"There's supposed to be a meteor shower at about eleven o'clock, somewhere in the vicinity of Pisces."

The fishes, Adolph thought. He could never avoid thinking of the ancients when the constellations came to mind, those long-gone Babylonian shepherds who saw every kind of creature in the shapes of the stars and eventually decided that their own lives were controlled by the position of the stars.

"Will you call me to look when you find them?"

"Yes, if you haven't gone to bed already."

"I'll wait." It gave Amy a comfortable feeling to have Adolph searching the skies from the back yard while she was in the house comfortably reading. "I'll bring you a thermos of tea after you get located."

When she went back into the living room, Adolph quickly finished tightening the focus adjustment, put on his sheepskin coat, and took his telescope outside. He set it up in the usual place, put the chair in position, and began sweeping the skies—Capricornus, Aquarius, Pisces.

～

Q: *This time the title reflects the topic well. So I'll begin by asking if there haven't been other systems of learning that could be called scientific. For instance, what about the ancient Greeks, did they not begin the scientific way since it is claimed they started so many other things?*

A: I will try to answer the first part of your question, but only after I tell you what I think the scientific way really is, to wit, a way of knowing which is based primarily on observation, which produces generalizations, and which is totally open. In other words, observations themselves can vary by individual or by how or when they were made, and theories or generalizations are only as good as the theorizer and the quality of the observations. So they change. We try to eliminate the individual variation in observations by requiring multiple observations by different observers, and especially by those who are not yet convinced of their validity. The best thing about science is not the efforts to prove the validity of observations but the efforts to disprove them. Human thinking is littered with valiant efforts to prove hypotheses which turned out to be false.

And the theories, too, are just that. The great thing about science is that one theory after another has been abandoned or modified as better ones came along. The beginning of the scientific revolution was the substitution of new theories for those in force since the time of the Greeks, and in the five hundred years since, many, if not most, new theories have been modified.

Q: *But what about the Greeks, didn't they do the same thing?*

A: The Greeks were certainly great thinkers, but they just did not concentrate on observation, with some exceptions, such as Herodotus and Aristotle. But those who concentrated so intensely on observations, like the astronomer Tycho Brahe or the biologist Pasteur, did not exist.

Q: *So are you saying that observation was unimportant before the scientific revolution?*

A: No, not at all. Human survival, or for that matter, survival of other species, has always depended on accurate observation. The Paleolithic hunter who depended on migratory game and the women who gathered seeds had to have knowledge about when those food items would be available or they would starve. And later in history such events as the rise of the Nile had to be accurately observed. The same would be true of a non-human hunter or herbivore. However, humans mixed in other kinds of knowing techniques with their observational ones, and sometimes depended on non-observational techniques completely. The history of non-scientific medicine is loaded with techniques that derive from peoples' supernatural beliefs. Believers have prayed or made offerings to a whole variety of invisible beings to avoid illness. Hindu villagers have long made offerings to Sipahi-mai to avoid smallpox, while Christian villagers have prayed to a whole variety of saints to get cured of this or that. The scientific revolution simply put knowledge all on a naturalistic level that could be either observed directly or inferred from indirect evidence. And a much larger number of theories was produced. But despite mixing the supernatural with the natural (that which can be observed), the basis of culture has always been observation. Peoples who didn't observe well were replaced by those who did.

Q: *So what's so special about the scientific way?*

A: We became consciously aware of the significance of observation for getting knowledge, and set up rules for doing so. And probably the most basic rule is that if it couldn't be observed, either directly or indirectly, it wasn't scientific.

Q: *And is that all that is special?*

A: Well, I might throw in one other characteristic, though it is really only true of what we call the hard sciences, the fields of study of physical and biological events, but not humanity. That is, the practitioners are pretty good at prediction; they can foretell that something will happen and it will. Astronomy makes a good example. An astronomer can predict that there will be an eclipse or a meteor shower and it will be so. The sciences like economics, psychology, and anthropology are not nearly so good at prediction.

Q: *I think I have a general idea of what science is about, and now comes the question of its emergence. I think most of us think of it as European in origin. Could you say anything about that?*

A: Sure. It is conventionally considered to have begun about 1530, with Copernicus's theory that instead of the sun traveling around the earth, the earth travels around the sun. And though some claim that the scientific revolution lasted about two hundred years, the scientific way of explanation continues to the present day.

And yes, in all of the first two hundred years or so, science was being done by Europeans. Since then, it has spread and become established all over the world and can now be considered an international way. For instance, what we once called Western medicine we now call cosmopolitan medicine.

Q: *In those early days there was a lot of resistance to the new ideas, no? Especially from the Church.*

A: Yes, and it is not over yet. In the city of Vista near where I live, a Christian fundamentalist group has been able to challenge the teaching of Darwinism in the public school system just this year. But in the early days, the threat of science was taken more seriously and the Church, being much more powerful, could apply strong punishments for advocating new ideas.

The basic objections by the Church were that mankind was de-emphasized by the new way of thinking and its own version of the origin of things was challenged. As you well know, Christianity is built on an idea system which begins with the axiom that man is the most important creature in the universe. Along comes a way of thinking that begins by claiming that man's home base, Earth, instead of being the center of the universe, is merely one of many planets revolving around the real center, the sun, and later, that the sun itself is only one of billions of similar objects. And it ends by claiming that even among life forms on Earth, man is by no means central except for a very short time span. Science has been continually de-centering humanity and it was inevitable that an idea system which placed man as the be-all and end-all of existence was certainly being threatened. As you will have noted in my narrative, the last and perhaps most threatening scientific concept was evolutionism. The first, heliocentrism, is the basis of modern astronomy.

Q: *Could you please explain why the way of science is included in this work?*

A: Remember, I mentioned in the beginning that I would include the major occurrences in the history of mankind that need to be understood in order to understand modern man. I began with the simple manufacture of tools, without which no later tools or machines would have been possible. And then I included language, without which systems of complex learning could not exist, and then the domestication revolution, the urban revolution, etc. All these were occurrences unique to humankind, at least in the way or to the extent they were practiced. Now I come to idea systems, and I argue that the scientific way was also unique, at least to the extent it came to be practiced. It has colored the life of all mankind, whether the individuals know anything about it or not.

Q: *Do you mean to say that even the peasants of the third world, say in Africa or Latin America, are so influenced, and yet they know nothing about the system itself?*

A: Certainly. For instance, I will take a worldwide problem, one which particularly affects village people everywhere, population pressure. As we will discuss in a future chapter, one of the problems mankind faces is the constantly-increasing number of people. As an interesting irony, the other basic problem for human survival is the ecology of the earth. The increasingly rapid destruction of the earth's environment is directly related to population growth, which means there is a constantly-increasing pressure on the remaining usable territory.

How did we get all these people? The peasants of the world have long had a high mortality rate. They adjusted to this by having enough children to make up for the ones lost in the early years. Along comes science with its germ theory of disease and methods of combatting illnesses (clean water and penicillin) and before you know it, there are four surviving children instead of two. Soon there are one billion Chinese instead of five hundred million. The same thing happens with Indians, Africans, and others.

Or take the example of electricity, a discovery made during the scientific age. It has affected mankind everywhere, including the peasants of the world who have never seen an electric wire or light bulb. How? Through the transistor radio, which has been carried to almost every remote spot on earth that would support human life, establishing a communication revolution long before standard electricity was brought to the villagers.

Q: *So I take it we are going to discuss the various discoveries and developments of the age of science, and the great men involved?*

A: Not really. Remember, this is anthropology, not a "great man" version of history. Without denying that there were particular discoverers of important developments in cultural history, we anthropologists tend to emphasize the system. All developments take place in cultural systems, without which the particular events are unlikely. What I am saying is that particular occurrences take place when the culture has come to a certain point. Thus, we have already discussed the age of exploration and though we know that Christopher Columbus was the first navigator to cross the Atlantic to try to find the Indies, if he had not, some other European would undoubtedly have done so in the next few decades. And if Pasteur had not discovered bacterial fermentation, some other biologist would have done so in the nineteenth century. It is simply a different way of looking at events. I have just finished reading a good book called *The Discoverers*, which takes the reader from one great man to the next. This is the standard historical approach, while the anthropological approach would emphasize the significance of events and context. Thus, what is really important in the fourteenth century is that Europe was primed for a better communication medium, not that Gutenberg came along. The same could be said of the speculation about the origin of life forms in the nineteenth century, not simply that Darwin came along. As a matter of fact, the discovery of evolutionism is particularly relevant because it came to two men independently at the same time, Wallace and Darwin. The conclusion could be that Europe was ripe for this kind of idea. The opposite side of that coin is that a culture may not be ready for a new idea when it does come along and may fail to accept it. Thus, though Gregor Mendel published the first study of modern genetics in 1866, it was ignored by other scientists until the principles were rediscovered by three people independently thirty-six years later.

Q: *Do you mean then that the great men of history, like Darwin and Gutenberg, are of no significance according to anthropology?*

A: No, but I do think they have been over-emphasized in standard history, while the influence of cultural systems has often been neglected. But of course, before the nineteenth century historical events were only written emphasizing the "big men," primarily because they were paying to have it written. Who cared enough about slaves, commoners, or women to write histories about them? But these were the standard culture carriers. And even if someone from the lower classes "discovered" something, it would be unlikely that he would be given credit. Some "big man" would make the claim.

Q: *But the discoverers you talk about were educated people, weren't they? Wouldn't they be much more likely to make scientific discoveries than ordinary, uneducated people?*

A: Yes, the ones who could get an education would be much more likely to come from the privileged classes. There are very few peasants who became scientists. But of course, even the discovers were products of their cultures. Thus Newton, despite his earth-shaking theory of gravity, spent great amounts of time trying to prove the scientific validity of the Bible while Einstein, who modified Newton's theory, made no attempt to relate science to Judaism. This only means that the cultural matrix had changed in the two hundred and fifty years that separated them.

But there is another reason to take the cultural point of view when discussing science, which is that no matter who made the original discoveries, they affect everyone. Thus, if we ordinary mortals had never heard of Pasteur, we would still be affected by pasteurization, and if we had never heard of Faraday, we would still be able to operate our transistor radios. This is what I tried to show in the narrative—that you can take anyone's life and find all kinds of consequences of the scientific way, admittedly more in an urban center in twentieth-century America than in an Indian village, but even in the latter, science is there. So Wilhelm, Bertha, Henry, and Adolph all lived with the consequences of the way of science.

Q: *Another thing that interested me was your treatment of the interrelationship of science and technology. Is that characteristic of systems of explanation?*

A: Much more with some than with others, mainly, I think, because there is more application possible from science than from other systems of explanation. For instance, we can compare religion and science in this regard, and I will use Christianity, simply because I know more about it. As we know, men have tried to use Christianity for practical benefit from the beginning, particularly in the field of health. Christ was reputedly a healer, and there have been a great many saints since to which people have made offerings for healing. And men have tried to use their faith for other functions also, though perhaps not so much. People have prayed to win battles in many cultures. The trouble with an idea system like Christianity in this regard is that it is very difficult to prove cause and effect. Thus, a people like the Spanish conquistadors fighting the Indians might believe that they won their battles because they were chosen by God, but that would be hard to prove. However, the firearm was another story. It was very clear why people with firearms won against people with bows and arrows. So, technology was taken from science with a vengeance while it was rarely taken from religion except for curing. Maybe Moses did control the waters by opening the Red Sea for the Israelites, but real water control, whether in ancient times or in modern societies, has been done by engineers, using scientific methods.

Q: *It seems that several different classes of people had some ideas about science though, at least according to your narrative.*

A: Yes, that is true. By the nineteenth century, the notion of science and even quite a few of the findings were widely spread. And this can be explained by the fact that knowledge became democratized by one special bit of technology that was already in place when the first discoveries were made. By that I mean line printing which began in Europe about 1450. The famous "discoverer" was of course Gutenberg. Block printing had been going on far longer, particularly in the Orient. And there had even been experiments in line printing, but the real "breakthrough" occurred with the idea of making a character for each sound, and that happened in Europe where a sound-based writing system existed. Chinese, Japanese, and Korean were idea-based writing systems.

Line printing made it much easier to make many copies, and before you can say Gutenberg backwards, there were books all over and ideas were being disseminated to all kinds of people who had no such access in the day of the copyists. And then came the age of public education, the nineteenth century, and literacy became widespread. And before long all kinds of people were reading who had never done so before. Line printing was even modified to fit the remaining idea writing systems, and their literacy was greatly increased also. The day of the copyists and block printers was over, to be used only by artists.

Q: *And how did all the great change of printing affect science so much?*

A: It came at a time when new ideas were popping up all over the place, but even more important, copies of them were being sent all over. For instance, both Darwin and Wallace were stimulated by reading separately copies of *An Essay on the Principle of Population*, by Thomas R. Malthus. Also, everybody in physics, including Einstein, read Newton's publications. Another development during the era of scientific growth was the spread of higher education; and of course students always read the old masters which were by this time available in printed versions. New ideas were not merely emerging at a steadily-increasing rate, they were also being spread even more rapidly. And of course we now have the electronic media—radio, television, and computers, all consequences of the scientific age.

Q: *A lot of things you have mentioned appeared in the narrative, but perhaps it would be worthwhile to discuss some a little further. For instance, transportation. Why was the horse and wagon still being used in the age of automobiles?*

A: Things never change completely overnight. We anthropologists talk about something called cultural lag. Thus while it is true that the automobile was around on the streets of America by the beginning of the century, it was there in limited numbers only. And there were still things the horse could do just as well. The car, truck, and tank were operating in World War I, but so was the horse. There were still plenty of places in the mud of the Western Front where the horse was superior. For that matter, the horse was still being used in my boyhood in the 1930s, to pull autos out of the mud when they got stuck. That was in the country where all the roads were not yet paved. The same kind of places nowadays would be traversed by four-wheel drive vehicles, but of course all the important roads and streets are paved now. But everything was changing even then. My uncles were all getting Model A Fords even while they were working the fields with horses. And you will recall perhaps that before he migrated to the city, Wilhelm was working in the prairie district where tractors were being brought in. By the time I came back from World War II, the horse was practically gone except for races and riding in the park. By then my father was delivering milk with a truck. But the horse did manage to hang on through the 1930s, mainly because once it learned its route, it could do pretty well without guidance. Now of course one carries one's milk home from the supermarket.

Q: *I guess there was somewhat of a similar history with people transportation.*

A: More or less, although the electric tram got started a little earlier. Before I was around, they had horse-drawn cars. One of the problems in the crowded city was manure. But when I was a small boy the tram was the way to go—in the city. As you read, Bertha found it to be one of the great improvements of life in the city. The tram she rode was on an iron track, but later ones had inflated rubber tires to make lateral movement possible. And still later, the motorized bus was put on the streets and we continue to live with this machine.

Q: *Another specific—what was so important about pasteurization?*

A: It is one of the many ways we sanitize our food. The process was to heat the milk to a temperature less than boiling, to keep it palatable while killing the bacteria. It was based on the discovery of bacteria in raw milk by Louis Pasteur. This was one of the most important discoveries of scientific medicine because we then learned that sanitizing things was one of the key elements for healing wounds and otherwise keeping healthy. It is said that the other main discovery which made scientific medicine, particularly surgery, practical was the discovery of anesthesia. All kinds of medical procedures were possible if you could knock the patient out.

Q: *I take it that was why you put in the dentist's reconstruction of the discovery of ether and laughing gas. Was that really the way it happened?*

A: I believe so. I wanted to show that many scientific discoveries were not made in the classical way at all. Many of them were based on accidents or observations of unexpected occurrences.

Q: *Was the medical discovery really made by dentists?*

A: It is thought so, but because of dentists' low status at the time, it was difficult for them to convince the surgeons of the value of the new chemicals. In any established field, the majority of practitioners resist change, no matter how much they need it. Usually much more than necessity is required for people to accept a new idea. There is too much vested interest in hanging on to what is familiar, no matter how bad it is. A particularly interesting case is mercury, which was used to treat syphilis for about four hundred years, even though it poisoned the patients rather than healing them. And blood letting was done for at least two thousand years, even though it weakened the patients instead of strengthening them. It was of course replaced by blood transfusions, its exact opposite, once the medicos better understood the circulatory system. Before anesthesia, a good surgeon was one who was fast and strong. He didn't have time for the delicate touch with a wildly thrashing patient.

Q: *Then was nothing ever discovered deliberately?*

A: Yes, sometimes. But the accidental discovery has been much downplayed in the idealistic picture that is painted of science. Radioactivity, penicillin, and the cure for puerperal infection are some important accidental discoveries which come to mind.

Q: *But what about the classical method of science, discovering things in the laboratory?*

A: That happens, and perhaps more now than in the past, but even these days the main work in the laboratory is validation of theories which have already been posited. But of course one does not get a job to make accidental discoveries, so the methodical laboratory techniques are emphasized.

Q: *One interesting bit you put in was the tools of science—the micro-scope, the telescope, and the syringe. Many people think of science as a matter of such devices, no?*

A: I am sure they do, which is okay. After all, they are clear extensions of the long tool tradition of mankind, all the way back to Squint the Australopithecine. How could he ever have imagined that the crude chipping of stone tools would come to the electron microscope and the great radio telescopes, searching the universe for alien sounds? Both in their way are significant of another aspect of science which is that it has enabled us to "see" so much that is not visible to the naked eye, one within, the other without.

Q: *One other aspect of science is not done in the laboratory and lacks the control which scientists are so proud of. I am thinking of the Theory of Natural Selection by Darwin and Wallace. Neither of those men was a laboratory scientist, was he?*

A: No, both were in what we call naturalistic science, which is observation of events as they occur in nature. Most of the events in history cannot be put in a laboratory or otherwise reconstructed, so those who study them are compelled to study their evidence as it exists in nature. Darwin went around the world on the famous voyage of the Beagle, and Wallace went to Indonesia to collect specimens and to observe the animal forms there. And with this they came up with what many people think of as the most earth-shaking idea of the nineteenth century. But many other brilliant scientific ideas were derived from observing things as they occur in nature. Copernicus, Galileo, Kepler, Brahe, and the other astronomers viewed the universe—with the newly-developed telescope, it is true—but as it already existed. Geology, and later archeology, had to be field sciences. In the nineteenth and twentieth centuries, ethology, the study of living creatures in their natural environment, became very important. The zoo-based study has been almost completely replaced by the field study of mammal species.

The laboratory study gets most of the credit for being scientific because conditions can be controlled, but natural behavior will only occur among free animals. This is especially true of humans and is one of the principal justifications for anthropological field methods.

Q: *Perhaps the last question I have is about the use of animals for experimentation. Was this something special for Westerners?*

A: Probably, and it certainly made medical science progress much more rapidly than it would have otherwise. What would have happened if science had grown up in say Hindu or Buddhist culture is hard to say. According to Christianity, animal life was put on earth for man's benefit. Animals had no rights apart from serving human needs. It was thus almost inevitable that animals would be used insofar as they would help understanding humanity and its problems. The laboratory animal was practically inevitable, despite the fact that science itself grew up in a basically non-religious environment. Much was carried over from Christianity even when it lost its dominance over the scientific way. For instance, the homocentrism of Christianity prevented experimentation on humans in science. If science had emerged among the Aztecs, whose homocentrism fostered the taking of human life for ritual purposes, experimentation on humans might have been accepted.

And the other side of the coin is the Hindus. Their ideology, which stems from their notion of reincarnation, is that all creatures are important in their own right, and therefore shouldn't be used freely for experimentation. The Indian government passed a law to prevent further exportation of monkeys for scientific use. So the pattern of science has been guided overall by the ideology of the West.

Now let's move on to the great new production technique which was developed in the West, but which has become universal—industrialization. It has affected us all at least as much as science.

9

The Machine

Oliver

At one end of the cavernous room steam engines were tended by four men, two to fire the boilers and two to monitor the controls and gauges. A mechanic stood nearby, and a boy swept up litter. One of the engine-tenders carried an oil can and a rag to keep the moving parts lubricated. Steam hissed from pipes, preventing the pressure from building up too high. The power generated by the machines turned wheels which were encircled by belts which were connected to other wheels and belts which kept levers, presses, and other parts moving.

A pile of coal lay near the boiler doors, where the horse-drawn coal wagon had left it that morning. The firemen were grimy from the coal dust, except the areas around their eyes where they had squinted. One was shovelling coal back to the central pile from where it had spread in the delivery. The factory got coal almost every day and the draymen were not careful where they put it. The other fireman was feeding the machine.

Harold Driver put oil on a joint and wiped it off before any dripped on the floor. He turned back to his workmate, Oliver Levering, who was studying with great concentration a sheet of newsprint. Harold came close and peered at the print also.

"What does it say?"

Oliver just grunted, continuing to pass his finger across the line. Harold stared as hard as he could and recognized a kind of order in the print even though he couldn't read it. Like most of the other workers, he had not learned to read. There had never been either time or money. He had begun helping his father on the farm when he was seven or eight years old; and when they had lost the farm they were renting and had come to the city, his father had got him a job in the factory within a few weeks. At thirteen, he had been older than a lot of children who worked in the factories, but working twelve hours a day, six days a week had been exhausting. The only time he might have used for studying had been Sunday, and by then he wanted only to sleep. Besides, there wasn't enough money, nor any expectation that he should learn to read. Most people in the working class did not.

Oliver Levering was an exception, having learned some reading in the two or three years he had gone to school. His father and mother had made enough money then to be able to afford it. But when his father had lost his job, he had taken Oliver out of school and put him to work also. Parents would often let their children go to school as long as the parents were working, but then take them out when they lost their jobs. Oliver didn't know how to read very well, but enough to make out the articles in papers he found. He could also sign his name and write a little.

Harold leaned over the paper and spoke again.

"Come on, mate, what's it say? Remember, I found it for you."

One of the managers had probably thrown it away.

"Awright then," Oliver said, "Though if you think it's that easy, you don't know much. Reading's hard work."

"Aw, I know, mate, it's so hard you're going to ask me for some coppers to do it. But what's it say?"

Oliver pointed to a piece on the upper left of the first page.

"That's about how Colchester is becoming the center of the cotton industry, you know, the factories like this one."

"What'd they say, did they say there was going to be lots of jobs?"

"Naw, not that, just that Colchester is becoming the main place where all the spinning mills are. And that they are making a lot of cloth in Colchester, you know mate. But you know all that. Why ask me dumb questions like that?"

"Well, don't start getting so uppity. A person might think that just because you can figure some of the tracks on a piece of paper you're something extraordinary. Now, just tell me what's it say."

Oliver moved his finger over to the right, to another piece.

"This one is a little difficult to read. It's about those men I told you about before who are going around bashing up the machines, you know, I told you. They're called Nomers, which means no machines."

"I know you told me about them, but why would they bash the machines? What would folks do for a living if the machines were all bashed up?"

"Well, they hate the machinery. They think they are the instruments of the devil. They want people to go back to working in their homes. You know, like they used to do before everybody came to the city."

"But why would anyone want to do that?" Harold asked. "That don't make no sense. You know, when we lived on the farm me mum used to work at home weaving and me dad used to tell her all the time it wasn't worth the cost of keeping the loom repaired. And she almost ruined her eyes, she did."

Oliver couldn't concentrate on the reading and talk at the same time, so he just grunted. Harold's interest was caught by this time, so he paid no attention to the lack of response.

"And now here in the factory they make so much cloth, they have trouble getting rid of it. And it's cheap when you see it in the shop." He didn't mention that no matter how cheap it was, he and his usually didn't have enough money to buy any.

Oliver continued to concentrate on reading the paper. Whenever he figured the meaning of a phrase or sentence he said it aloud.

"Here it says they destroyed a steam engine and a lot of machinery over in Dunbridge."

"So they must have called out the coppers, didn't they. From what I've seen, the owners wouldn't let no blokes break up their machinery. Why even back on the farm they wouldn't let that happen. Once when some farmers were put out of their cottages so the owners could make bigger fields and cultivate with the new machines, some farmers tore down the fences. And they called in the militia. Why, I'll bet the owners of the factories wouldn't let some revolutionaries break up their machines here in the city."

"Well, you're right, mate. They did call the police, and they hauled a bunch of them off to Leading Gaol."

"Does it say what kind of sentences they got?"

"Blimey, mate, no. They don't sentence them that fast. Though you can bet that the magistrates won't be easy on them. Tampering with the factories is a serious offense."

The two men had been so preoccupied that they didn't notice the foreman approach. He was dressed like the workers but with newer and cleaner clothes. Behind him was a well-dressed man, the son of the owner, wearing a beaver hat and polished boots, and smoking a cheroot. The foreman spoke in an officious tone, emphasizing his supervisory function.

"What are you men doing? You think they pay you good wages to set around reading the paper?" He turned to the young man. "You see, sir, the kind of workers we get these days. They don't take any responsibility. You teach them something, like I taught that sod there the fine art of lubrication, and what do they do? The minute you take your eyes off them, they sit around entertaining themselves.

Harold picked up his oil can and wiped it with his rag, saying, "We was just taking a little rest, gov'ner."

Oliver put down the paper, and opening the boiler door, began to stir up the coals.

"Well now, there's no need for you to be acting so busy," the foreman said. "We seen how you was entertaining yourself already. No need to put on an act. Mr. Capstan here has seen it too. And it would be best if in the future you keep to your jobs. There's plenty to do." And he threw in the usual threat. "We all know there's plenty of souls who don't have jobs and would be only too happy to get an easy berth like you men. Imagine you, Harold Driver, come in here from the country and all you know is how to shovel manure and walk behind a plow, and you get first-class training on how to lubricate factory machinery, and a good wage for it. And you spend your time reading the newspapers." He turned toward the young man. "You see, sir, they don't show appreciation."

The owner's son nodded and blew out a stream of smoke.

"Just go on to the business, Cassidy."

The foreman got into his officious mode again. "Driver, you can go on into the factory and lubricate the joints. I'm sure they need it."

The lubrication man took his can and rag and went down the line, following the power belt. As soon as Driver was out of earshot, the foreman put his hand on Levering's shoulder.

"Just you lay off the boiler for a bit, Oliver. I'm sure it can keep the heat up for a few minutes while we discuss a matter for Mr. Capstan. Just come over here and sit down on this box."

Oliver looked suspicious, but closed the boiler door and sat down. Capstan looked off in the distance as if he wasn't concerned with the affair, continuing to puff his cheroot.

"Now Oliver," Cassidy began. "Mr. Capstan has come to me with an interesting proposition. I think it will benefit all who are concerned."

Oliver felt uneasy since the owners never brought propositions to the workers. And if they were going to cashier you, they did it through the paymaster at the end of the week. But there was little that he could do, so he listened.

"Oliver," Cassidy continued, "as you may know, Mr. Capstan comes in every four or five days to look over the factory, and he has noticed your daughter bring in your tiffin. He asked me about her several times and he wondered why she wasn't working. I told him you have another daughter and a son and both of them was working. So Mr. Capstan asked me if I thought you would like to get a job for Melissa. I think that's her name, ain't it?"

"Yes, gov'ner, she's Melissa, my second born, and as good a lass as you'll find. She be well nigh on fifteen. And a good help to her mum, I'd say."

"I'm sure she is and so it's surprising like that she's not working. I'm sure the family could use the extra money a strapping lass like her could bring in. Does that sound interesting?"

Oliver could not figure yet what was going on.

"Well, of course, Mr. Cassidy, and she was working until a couple of months ago. She had a job over at the Turnbull Works, but you may know that they laid off almost all the employees. They say they was bought out by a Scotchman who was going to put in all new machinery. Us don't know if it was right what was told but us workers generally don't. The owners don't need to tell us what they be doing."

Oliver had asked around where anyone was hiring and had only been able to find one place, but their wages were so low that it would hardly have been any better than her working at home, sewing shirts.

"You remember, Mr. Cassidy, I asked you if any work was available here and you said that we was full up. You know she has already had experience on the power looms. And she is a good lass, does what she is told."

"Well, Oliver, you might be in luck. Mr. Capstan here says he can find something here for your lass, even though it is true that we are full up. And he might even fix it up that she will get an hour or two off one or two days per week. Mr. Capstan would want the girl to be available for socializing during those times. He would make a room available for her to come to."

Then Oliver knew what it was all about, not that he shouldn't have figured it out sooner. The only thing the owners and managers were ever interested in from the lower class was their work or their women, and the cheaper, the better. Sometimes the managers told the women on the line to be ready at such and such a time at such and such a place and there was little they could do about it. If they refused for long, they would be cashiered. Oliver's wife, Hannah, had had several meetings with owners or their relatives before and had not even received anything for it but the right to keep her job. Cassidy interrupted Oliver's thoughts.

"Why, Mr. Capstan here is a real gentleman. He says he will be giving an additional sum for each time the girl comes, he says he would be giving two shillings—to the father, of course."

Oliver had no idea where else he could go for a job, and since his wife worked there too, what would they do without it? Besides, this was done all the time. It was a bonus that you were lucky to be able to get if they paid extra. He thanked the Lord that he had a good looking daughter. And Mr. Capstan didn't seem like such a bad sort.

"It seems like it will be all right," he replied. "Course I'll talk it over with the Missus. Let you know tomorrow." He hoped he didn't sound reluctant and that they wouldn't back out, because the more he thought of it, the better the deal sounded.

Cassidy turned and spoke in a low voice to the owner's son, then turned back to Oliver.

"Mr. Capstan says he will wait one day, but no more. Because after all, Oliver, you must know that there are a lot of girls that a man like him can get. But he's a nice fellow so he says he will wait until tomorrow.

Hannah

It was spitting soft snow, but the street was full, as it usually was on Sunday mornings no matter the weather. Sunday was the shopping day for most working people. Those who ran the shops and stands were anxious to get rid of whatever perishables they had and were willing to lower the prices. Much was left over from the week's stock of the better markets.

She pulled her tattered shawl around her shoulders and picked her way through the half-frozen piles of sludge, places that had accumulated garbage for months, the snow melting during the day and freezing again at night. Whenever she had to cross the street, she saw the familiar slush of manure, hot and steaming when first dropped, frozen later. The air was yellowish from the accumulation of coal smoke. She coughed periodically.

She could remember the clear, frosty air on the farm. When she would go out of the cottage in the morning, the air would come into her face, sharp, sometimes even cutting, but always clear. It had been a shock when they had first come to the city where everyone lit stoves with soft coal, turning the air first murky and then yellow. On the farm they had burned peat, which Oliver and his brother cut for them and the landowner. Here in the city the smoke bit her lungs, making her cough; everybody seemed to always have a cold.

The yellow fog accumulated most densely nearer the factory district because most of the smoke came from the chimneys there. Some mornings when they went to work there was a wall of smoke which they had to step through and then it would be as if you were inside the chimney. But she had got used to it as most did. What else was there to do? The landowners didn't need them on the farms anymore. They would rather use machines.

As she picked her way through the piles of slush and around the garbage and trash, her thoughts shifted to the inside of the factory, to the constant clicking and clacking which went on for the thirteen hours she tended the machine, and which had become a rhythm that dominated her life. On the farm there had been no special or constant noises. The sounds varied according to what one was doing or the time of day or year, and one paid attention to them because they meant something. Songbirds only sang in the spring, and even if you didn't know what time of the year it was by other signs or by a calendar, you could tell what time of year it was by the songs of the birds. And the sound of rain against the windows at night meant that the next day would be too wet for the men to plow and probably too wet to do washing outside; but it would also mean that the turnips or potatoes would grow faster. And even the sounds of work were meaningful and could be pleasant. The thwack of a hatchet when someone was making kindling meant that a fire would soon be burning and after that there would be hot porridge with milk and treacle or boiled potatoes with bacon grease; even the crackling of the fire in the evening was a sound to give comfort. But noises in the city, and particularly in the factory, not only gave no meaning to what was going on, they gave no comfort either, and after a while they came to dominate a person's being. It was a click and clack, constant movement of parts engaging and disengaging as cotton fibers became thread and thread became cloth. And since she was one of the workers charged with a given stretch of loom, she understood quickly that the repetition of sound was the primary means of realizing whether the machine was operating properly. Whenever the sound changed, she would try to localize it so she could rush to that place and fix the torn or slipped thread or machine part that had got askew, or call one of the mechanics for help. For she learned very quickly that disaster could occur if the power continued while the thread or cloth was not feeding right.

And the result was that the clickety-clackety of the workshop became her life rhythm. Long after she had left the factory and into her night's sleep, the sound of the moving parts of the machines kept repeating itself. Sometimes she would awaken in the middle of the night and the first thing she would think of was whether the machine noise was going in its proper rhythm.

Hannah did not analyze her perceptions in such a precise way. After all, she was working class and had never received any schooling. But she knew that life had changed in most ways when they had come to the city.

Horse drawn carriages kept passing on the street and most were far enough away that she didn't need to worry about them. But she had become so deeply immersed in her thoughts that she didn't notice one carriage which came careening to the side, and before she could get out of its way, it splashed muddy slush and manure on her. She jumped back and when she looked up, she could see the driver had a bottle in his hand.

"Get out of the way, wench," he shouted. "The street is for carriages."

She ducked into the entryway of a closed shop to try to wipe off some of the slush, feeling the cold from her wet skirt and petticoat. Her feet were already wet from walking in the snow and slush. She shivered, wishing she had a swallow of gin. A poorly-dressed working class bloke stopped outside the entryway and eyed her for a bit, then came into the sheltered area.

"Now here's the poor missus, out shopping for victuals for the family in this foul weather and she got dowsed by a drunken hackney driver. It don't pay to try to do good sometimes. Poor missus."

She could see that he was drinking too when he pulled a bottle out of his tattered coat.

"Here missus, this is what you need. Warm the innards with a swallow of gin."

She knew she shouldn't because that wouldn't be the end of it. No drunken bloke on the street was going to offer her some of his gin without expecting something in return. But she was so cold and dispirited that she ignored her judgement.

"All right," she said. "But just one." She knew he would try to get her to take more and then he'd be all over her. She could visualize the miserable shack he would lead her to.

He handed her the bottle and when she put it to her mouth, he put his arm around her. She swallowed fast and twisted away, saying, "Now that's all, there's not going to be anything else. You can see that I'm on the way to do the weeks' shopping, so just be off."

She tried to hand back the bottle but he refused to take it. She put it down and ran out.

"Sorry wench, thinks she's a queen," was his parting comment.

She pulled her shawl tight, and her bonnet down, and hurried toward the shopping area, clutching her coins and carrying sack in the other hand. She slipped on an icy spot and as she recovered she almost stepped on the carcass of a small animal frozen in the snow; she could not tell if it was a rat or a cat. She hurried on so she wouldn't have to look at it. Soon she came to the shopping area, where vendors had put up temporary roofing against the sides of warehouse buildings to give them some shelter from the weather. She came to a place where some people were warming themselves at a makeshift fireplace, feeding it with little bundles of sticks which they got from a vendor who had a cartfull. A donkey was harnessed to the cart, his head down in protection from the weather. She warmed her hands at the fire, watching some of the dogs who wandered sniffing under and around the stands, searching in the piles of garbage. The slush here was even dirtier.

Her wet feet were cold and she wished she were back at the living quarters, no matter how crowded it was. At least there would be a coal fire in the grate and a roof over her head, though the roof leaked in a couple of places. And she couldn't help worrying about the sick child,

Luke. Another woman came alongside and put her hands toward the fire.

"Ay, dearie, it's foul weather, ain't it? You'd think the good lord would have a little mercy on us poor folks, working all week shut up in the factories and on the one free day, dumping all this snow and filth on us, and freezing our poor fingers and toes."

Hannah noticed that at least the woman had gloves, though they were threadbare and worn through at most of the fingertips. She guessed that the woman also worked at one of the cloth factories.

"It's miserable to be out in such weather, but what else can a person do? There's the hungry mouths to feed at home and little enough to pay for them. Why a soul's lucky to get some real meat more than once a week."

Whenever Hannah had to fix the city meals, she could never keep from thinking of the meat they had on the farm. They had one or two pigs every year, and mutton once in a while. Whenever a sheep fell off a cliff or froze to death or was killed by dogs, the landowner had let them have the carcass. He would only eat meat from deliberately killed animals. She suspected that every once in a while Oliver would help a sheep along to its death so they could have fresh mutton.

But there was none of that in the city. Everything had to be paid for, and there were so many mouths that there was always a scarcity. And what you did get was high priced or something that no one but the working class would eat.

"So you are heading over to Leafy Lane, eh dearie, to buy some turnips and potatoes?"

Leafy Lane was the produce section in a weedy area along the river into which the vendors would discard the outer leaves and rotten parts of the vegetables. Potatoes and turnips were the mainstay most of the year, but especially in winter. The farmers kept them in root cellars after the cold weather came and many could manage to have some almost until spring. Hannah and Oliver had done the same on the farm for their own use.

"Us working class always needs potatoes or turnips," Hannah said to the woman. "Though with a onion thrown in now and then. A person has got to have some taste with boiled potatoes and turnips."

She didn't add a comment about salt because they used it so regularly she never thought of it. The other lady pulled off her remnants of gloves so she could rub her hands directly. She said, "Us didn't buy them gloves. Lord no, we got more things to get than a pair of gloves for shopping. Besides, the old man would box me ears for spending money on something like that. The old bounder wants all he can get for his gin."

Hannah knew what the finger-warmer was talking about. Few men in the working class didn't need their drink and wouldn't get ugly if they didn't get it. But it was a tiresome thing to talk about so she changed the subject.

"You been shopping already?"

It was obvious that she had since she was carrying a string bag which had some items in it.

"Indeed, missus," the woman said. "On the way back to the living quarters. Suspect that there will be several hungry mouths by the time I get back. And maybe the old man will even have brought back a snort for the old lady."

"I know I can find vegetables," Hannah said. "But tell me if there's someplace where I can find some meat without paying too much— some fatty bacon or sausage or even some pig's feet or ears—something that wouldn't cost more than a few pence a pound."

Hannah would like to buy some ham or a piece of mutton, but she knew that they would be far too expensive for her meager funds.

"I know what you mean, dearie, and I would like to help, but everything has gone up so much. There's just no cheap meat left in the market. If you want meat, you got to expect to pay. Them farmers don't raise the animals for us poor folks."

When Hannah had got a little warmed she said goodbye to the other woman and, braving the cold wind, left to do the stands. She found a vendor who had small potatoes at half the price of regular ones and got some turnips which were sprouting for a lower price. She felt so jubilant that she also bought two pounds of small carrots.

But there were no bargains in the meat section. She didn't bother to look at the stands where regular muscle meat was being sold. But even the section with the less desirable cuts had few bargains. In fact, there was little enough at any price. She could find no pig snouts or ears or even tripe. She did find one vendor selling pigs' testicles and almost bought some but finally refrained because Oliver wouldn't eat them. He believed they made a man make more babies and he didn't want any more. Hannah knew what was happening to all the small meat items. With the new grinding machines that had become available, the butchers were grinding them all up for sausage.

She found some fatty bacon at a lower price, which she got mainly for the drippings. Oliver didn't like to eat his potatoes without some grease or oil to put on them. They also used bacon drippings to put on bread. She liked jam on hers and when they lived in the country she would make it. But they couldn't get berries in the city. They were lucky if they got treacle once in a while.

She was determined, however, to get some meat, if for nothing else, just to make some broth for Luke. She longingly studied the carcasses that hung from hooks, but didn't ask the prices. She came to a stand where game hung from hooks, eviscerated but not skinned. There were partridges, grouse pheasants, and rabbits. The fat vendor wore a blood-spattered apron. He took a cigar out of his mouth and put it to one side.

"Ay missus, them's fat rabbits."

He plucked one off the hook and held it up so she could see the body, which he stroked with his fat, red hand.

"Not a sign of shot, missus. You can see that this rabbit was taken by snare. Them's the best kind, missus. They ain't full of shot, with their bones all mangled up."

She knew that the poachers brought in the game they caught in traps or snares, even though they would pay dearly if caught with it in the countryside. The landowners were always sending their gamekeepers out to get poachers, but despite the risk of being shot or sent to the work-house, the poaching went on. A good poacher could make more money at it than at regular farming. Much of the game came to the city markets. The officials did not prosecute the vendors, and the vendors never admitted knowing where the animals came from. Hannah reached up and felt the rabbit's fur. It was indeed undamaged.

"How much?"

"Ay, missus, for this fine beastie the regular price would be one bob, thruppence. But a man can see that you are a hard working mama, looking out for her little brood. So we'll sacrifice it for one bob, tuppence."

Her heart fell. Despite her continuous contrary experience, she always hoped something would be less. With her few knotted-up coppers, it was way out of reach. Without making a counter offer, she shook her head. He held the rabbit out further.

"Missus, it'll make a fine pie. And I think the old man would be grateful for such a fine piece of meat."

She looked around to see if there was anything else. He put the rabbit up on its hook and withdrew a mushy one, its fur stiff from dried blood. She knew immediately that it had been shot by a gamekeeper, and then hidden or found later by one of the drivers who sold it, along with others, to a traveling market buyer.

"Now here, missus," he said, "is another one and just as good, except it may have a few shots in it. But when the missus gets finished dressing it, it'll be as good as a trapped one. And at half the price, now that's reasonable, ain't it? We'll let this fine beastie go to the good missus for seven pence."

Even though that was a good price, she knew she only had five pence left. He would probably come down one penny more, but not two. She shook her head and started to move away.

"Now come on, missus, you know this is a good price. Us vendors know how hard it is to make ends meet but we got to make a living too. Even so, just for the little missus, this vendor will make it six pence."

By this time she was moving away on toward the beef section where sides and quarters hung from hooks, bloody with chunks cut out, and heads with tongues hanging out, arranged in a line. She passed them all, knowing full well that she couldn't afford any chunks of beef, continuing on down to the end where the bones were. Behind the stalls, boys were cutting and sawing bones on wooden blocks. In front were two stalls where adult vendors presided over piles of bones. On the fringes emaciated dogs skulked, trying to edge nearer the bones, but keeping wary eyes on the boys and men. Hannah came up to one stall and eyed the bone piles. The vendor, rubbing his hands to keep them warm, said, "Bones for the missus? These be first class bones, dearie, just right for a rich broth which a body needs to keep the chilblains out on these cold winter days. Good bones from prime beef. How much does the little missus want?"

Some of the bones looked a little dried out. In this kind of weather the butchers could keep them for several days before they would start to stink.

"How old be they?" Hannah asked.

"Ay, dearie, they is as fresh as a new day. Old vendor John, he who is offering these fine bones, sells only the freshest. Why if you had come thirty minutes before, these bones wouldn't be here. They was just cut up by that strapping lad you see there, Walter he be named."

He pointed to a boy of twelve or thirteen who did not bother to look up.

It was dark when she got to the neighborhood. During midwinter the days were short, not that it made much difference in such filthy weather. The only decent place was indoors. She went by the pub and thought of looking into the taproom to see if Oliver was there, but decided against it. He would not be happy to see her if he was drinking. And she certainly could not join him. She had no money left and he would have little enough for himself.

She continued until she got to the hydrant. Melissa was there, waiting in line to fill her buckets. There was ice around the standpipe where runoff water had frozen. Melissa was huddled, keeping her hands inside the threadbare muff for warmth. The girl saw her mother and put down the buckets.

"Mama, I came to get some water. There was hardly any left."

"That's a good girl. Now we can make some soup since I got some bones. I got them especially for your brother. How is he feeling?"

"Oh, mama, he don't look good. His eyes glitter and he coughs so much. I feel so sorry for poor Luke. He has never been right since he came back from the mines."

Luke had been sent to the coal mines in Hempstead two years before, along with many other boys and girls from their neighborhood. Most of his wages had been given to Oliver by the agent who had recruited him. The agent, who hauled workers there every couple of months, had said that Luke was fine for most of the time, a good worker, but he finally said that the boy was sick and several weeks later had brought him back. Luke had not worked since, and lay about the quarters most of the time, sleeping whenever he could under as many covers as he could get. But he rarely had any appetite, and continued to get thinner all the time. Hannah felt bad too, but what could she do? Everybody in the family had to work. They had trouble getting enough for food and rent as it was; and if one person was not working, there just wouldn't be enough.

"Has he eaten anything since I left?" she asked.

"Well, you know mama, there wasn't much in the house, but I found some crusts of bread and I heated up some drippings to put on them. But he wouldn't eat it. He just wanted some tea and you know we don't have any."

The line kept moving and when it was Melissa's turn, Hannah reached over.

"I'll take one, so we can get home soon. I want to make some hot soup."

They filled their buckets in turn and started back.

"Is your papa at the quarters?"

"He's there. Came back a while ago, plonked. Been snoring something terrible. In the other bed."

"And Catherine? She been helping?"

Catherine was the youngest and not yet working outside. She stayed home most of the time, though she collected rags and bones when the weather was good. Two children had died when they were very young.

As the two walked back, Hannah realized that at least when the weather was cold the smells weren't so strong. They passed an outdoor toilet and she could hardly smell it. And the place where the men pissed did not smell so much. She needed to go herself but put it off to the last. But when they reached the last toilet she gave her bucket to Melissa and went in. Then inside where it was warmer, the odor of the night soil filled the air. The landlord was supposed to have the cesspits emptied more often, but he ignored the complaints as long as he could. Hannah had used this kind of outhouse all her life, so she was used to it. But here there were so many people using one toilet. And on the farm the men would dig a new hole when the old one got partly full, and usually one toilet was used by only one family.

Their quarters consisted of two rooms in a larger building which had once been a storehouse, and which had been subdivided for renting to the working class. They were luckier than many who had only one large room, often occupied by five or six people.

Catherine was hunched down near the grate, poking at the smoldering coals, when they came in. In the far corner Luke lay on a pallet. A thin dog sat near the fire, but got up and moved farther into the darkness when they came in. The only light in the room was from the fire and a rushlight stuck into a container on the table that stood back from the fire. Three old chairs and two barrels for seating were spaced around the room. Clothes hung from hooks on the walls. A trunk which held their best clothes had been brought from the farm and put in the other room. Hannah guessed that Oliver was in that room, which was separated by a curtain. She and Oliver stayed there most nights while the children slept on pallets in the big room.

"How is my little boy?" Hannah said.

"He moves around often and groans," Catherine said. "He doesn't seem too good, poor little Luke." She put another small coal on the fire. "Mama, will I have to go to the mines also?"

Without thinking about it much she said, "We hope not, little Cathy. But if it is necessary, we know little Cathy will go just like Luke."

"Yes, mama, but if I go, will I have to take off all my clothes in the mine like Luke did?"

"We shouldn't think about things like that, little Cathy. We should think that we will never go to the mines. And maybe Jesus will look down on us and say no little girl will go to the mines again." And to get away from the dismal subject, she said, "Little Cathy, will you go and fix the rushes? The light is going out."

Catherine got up to get the rushes and dip them in the dish of drippings which they kept near the fire so the grease wouldn't congeal. The boy groaned in the darkness. Hannah went to his pallet and lifted the cover lightly.

"No, mama, it's so cold."

She tucked the cover in around the thin shoulders, aware of how much weight he had lost.

"How does Luke feel?"

"Just cold, and then sometimes hot. Is the fire going in the grate?"

"Yes, Luke baby. Little sister Catherine is watching it. So just sleep because Mama brought some good soup bones and she will make a hot soup. That will taste good, won't it?"

The boy turned over, mumbling. Hannah added, "And maybe tomorrow we'll go see the apothecary for some medicine."

When Melissa finished washing the dishes she carried the water outside and poured it into the drainage gutter. The steam rose. A pig that had been rooting in a nearby waste pile lifted its snout to take in the odor and came to check for scraps. The snow had stopped and it was a little warmer. Icicles were forming from the roof melt. With nothing on her arms, the girl shivered and returned to the house.

The rushlight was out and the fire in the grate was dying. No more coal would be put on until morning.

"You better get in with Catherine before she gets cold." Hannah told Melissa.

Hannah thought it would be better for Luke if the girls slept with him. That would keep him warmer. But he thrashed about so and he didn't want to be with anyone else. He just wanted more covers. She had got all she could from wherever she could, all of them old and worn. She would let the boy sleep with her if only Oliver would permit it. She heard Melissa get in with Catherine and then whispers as the girls settled down. Oliver got up to go outside, she hoped for the last time that night. He would go to the wall down the alley. She went also. They kept a chamber pot in the house for anyone who had to go during the night, but everyone went outside before going to bed.

She met Oliver coming back and followed him into the house. Without a word he went into the back room. She checked Luke's covers then the girls', then followed her husband. Oliver was sitting on the edge of the bed, still fully clothed. He looked more lively than he had when he had come from the room before, still groggy from drinking. The soup and bread had made a difference, as it had for everyone but Luke. The boy had hardly eaten any, despite her effort to feed him. Hannah had finished Luke's bowl. She sat next to her husband and put her arm around him and felt warmer than at any time during the day.

"Oh, Oliver, I feel so worried about little Luke. He's not getting any better, no matter what we do for him. He hardly ate anything tonight."

"I know, woman. It appears he has the consumption. It's the cold night air, they say. And more often than not when a body gets it, they're goners."

It bothered Hannah when Oliver was like this, not believing that a body could do anything about illnesses and the other problems of being poor. Not that she believed much could be done herself, but she hated hearing it. Oliver had been just that way when they lost the others, as if one just had to put up with whatever happened.

"But maybe some physic would help," she said. "I know that Mary Gordon gave some physic to her little sick Harold and he got well."

Mary Gordon was a neighbor whose young boy had had diarrhea and stomach cramps so that he couldn't keep food down, and after she gave him the drug, he had relaxed and slept soundly and kept his food down better.

"But where did she get this fine drug? And where did old man Gordon get enough to pay for it? They tell me that the drugs ordered by those physicians cost an arm and a leg."

"She got it from an apothecary. Their drugs don't cost so much as those from a physician."

"But woman, we don't have no money. We're lucky to have enough for food and rent."

She wanted to add "and drink," but didn't because that would only provoke him. And though Oliver was not the meanest husband, if pushed too far he would give her one, and that was his right. And she guessed that he didn't feel so guilty about Luke, that he felt that getting sick had little or nothing to do with being sent to the mines, and that it was expected.

"Maybe I could pawn something," she said. "It wouldn't have to be much if I went to an apothecary."

Oliver was taking off his boots.

"Maybe so, but I wonder what you have that any pawn dealer would look at twice. I mean, woman, think of it, we are in the working class and that means we don't have anything that's worth enough for a pawn dealer to look at."

She hated the idea, but she couldn't help thinking about the silver pin her mother had given her. Her mother had told her it had been purchased when her husband had still been a landholder, and that she should never part with it. She had never worn it or told Oliver about it, but what good would it be if they lost little Luke? She decided on the spot that she would take it to the pawn dealer the first day she had time.

Oliver took off his pants but left his shirt on. It would be too cold otherwise.

"Well, woman, maybe we'll be getting a few more quid soon," he said from under the covers. "I got a proposition today for our oldest."

She quickly took off her dress and got under the covers next to Oliver. Before she could say anything, he continued.

"Yes, indeed, a proposition. And the more I think about it, the better it sounds."

He continued as she expected. "Our lovely little daughter has captured the eye of one of the uppers. You have seen him, the son of the factory owner, Mr. Capstan. He comes in about once a week, all fancied up, you know. And he approached Mr. Cassidy to be the front man. He couldn't come to me direct, you know. The uppers don't do that. But he says to Mr. Cassidy that he would like to see our little Melissa every once in a while, about once a week I gathered, and that he would see that the family would be recompensed."

She knew what that meant, that Oliver would get whatever came in. And more likely than not it would disappear for grog. Not that it would be that much, she thought. She said with a sigh, "Ah that's the way it is, the men think just one thing about us women. And if they got money, they can get us easy. Did this Mr. Capstan say how much he would pay?"

"He was quite straightforward about it. Two shillings extra."

"You mean he would fix her up with a job and when she gave him the extra service, he would give the extra two shillings?"

"Well, it sounds better than what I hear most girls get. And at least it's steady. Why, you know I hear of girls who never had any arrangement. They just go when they're asked to, and it's usually mighty little when they do get extra.

"There's just one thing," he continued. "This Mr. Capstan says he needs to know in one day. Or at least that's what Mr. Cassidy says. And being a bloody Irishman, you can't never tell when he's telling the truth. Anyway, he's right when he says that the upper class have a choice of a lot of girls."

"One day? What's the bloke's hurry? Where does he think anybody is going? And what's the idea of telling me so late?" She got so irritated, she felt like jumping out of the bed, except she knew how cold it was outside the covers.

"Well I told him I would talk to the missus before we decided. And I didn't want to bring it up in front of the lass before we had talked about it. I mean I thought it would be best for you to explain it to her. It seems like it's women's business." He added, "You must remember, mum, that old Oliver took care of all the explanations and arrangements for Luke to go to the mines. Since he was a boy, I thought that was man's business."

She had guessed already that he had expected her to tell Melissa.

"But what if she won't go?"

He stiffened and raised himself partially. She cringed, almost expecting a blow. But he only replied, "What do you mean 'if she won't go'? If her Mum and Dad tells her to go, she'll go." And as if it was inevitable that she would refuse, he countered in advance, "What does she think she is, some kind of princess? She'll go alright."

She knew there was little possibility that the girl wouldn't go. She could run away but what good would that do her? There wasn't anyplace to go except to some other bloke. And besides, many other girls had been picked out for such service and it wasn't so bad. Sometimes the owner became quite fond of the girl and gave her gifts. Then she thought of Luke.

"And so can we use some of her wages to pay an apothecary's bill?"

Robert

Robert Capstan sat comfortably astride his hunter. He wore a bright orange coat, riding pants and boots, leather gloves, a white scarf, and an orange hunt cap. He carried a quirt in his left hand, and his right held the reins. His big brown horse was sleek from the hay and oats it received at the stables, and from the regular grooming and exercise. Robert looked as if he belonged there, along with the other men of property.

The other riders were strung out in front and behind, the men dressed like him and the few women sitting side-saddle in long skirts. At the front of the group the pack of hounds trotted slowly, their tails erect, their noses busy reading the morning scents. Periodically each dog let out a deep-throated yelp which melded with the others into a constant baying.

Interspersed were a few hunt workers—dog handlers, a bugler, and a couple of horse handlers. Most were riding hacks. Just behind Robert was the assistant hound master, holding a burlap bag with the terrier. It would be released to drag out the fox if the pursued animal found a hole that had not been plugged.

The retinue was moving across the open countryside at a steady trot. The hounds were on a trail, but not yet close. The scent of the fox was taking them toward a culvert at the bottom of the slope.

Robert moved to one side and held his horse back to let the others pass. He guided his animal onto a small hillock from which he could get an unobstructed view of the procession. It was quite a sight. At least once each season he got this feeling and that made the struggle well worth it. Though he might never be completely accepted as one of the landed aristocracy, none of the local gentry would now openly downgrade him and his. And his children would probably be accepted as if they belonged. In the meantime, all the local gentry and even most of the aristocracy were willing to accept his generosity. He believed that there had never been fox hunts on such a grand scale before he became established at Fairhaven Manor.

He saw Jeremy coming toward him. The young man rode his horse well, as he should, since he had learned while growing up. It came as naturally to him as sharp financial dealings came to Robert. But that was the nature of things, he thought, that the founder of a dynasty had to be strong in financial matters.

Jeremy rode up alongside him.

"A good hunt so far, eh what?"

"Yes, we only need to get a good run. And for that the hounds have to get up a fine fox."

"I'm sure they will soon. They're on the scent of one now. All we need is for the fox to bolt. And then there will be bedlam to pay." Jeremy pulled out a silver flask. "Fortunately, Jones handed me this before I left." He proffered it to his father. "Would you like to have one, sir?"

The older Capstan knew the younger was trying to establish a manly camaraderie with him, which did not displease him. He was too well ensconced in life by this time to need to be concerned with small breaches of protocol. However, he did not want a drink this early. He felt too satisfied with the ambience to have need of alcohol. He waved to his son.

"No, but you go ahead. I'll wait for a glass of port when we return."

Jeremy unscrewed the cap and took a good draught of whiskey, wiping his mouth with the back of his gloved hand when he had finished.

"I thought you would be riding with Miss Service," Robert asked Jeremy. "Where is she?"

He spoke of the daughter of one of the poorest of the aristocracy in the county whom Robert hoped would become matched with his son. Unlike the Capstans, the Service family had been established for many generations with a large estate. But the last two lords had succumbed to the racing sickness and had literally gambled the land away, selling it piece by piece to pay the debts. Now there was little left other than the mansion itself; and it was said that even that was heavily mortgaged. Young Jeremy could count on little or no dowry from the family, but he would be getting the daughter of an aristocrat.

"She's coming, though her horse is not very fast. And when I'm out on a hunt, I'd rather give it a good go, you know, sir—with the boys."

"Yes, yes, I understand that you young fellows need to let out some steam, but there are still social matters that need to be attended to. And getting a first-class spouse is one of them. It matters for the future, you must realize."

That was one arrangement that Robert Capstan had never managed, and though Amelia did all a good wife could, he frequently regretted that she came from the colonies. Robert had made his fortune dealing in cotton and had travelled in his early years, mainly to Egypt and the Americas, buying cotton for the continually opening mills. And it was in Carolina that he had met and married Amelia, the daughter of a planter he had dealt with for years. And though the planter was a wealthy property owner and his daughter a graduate of one of the best finishing schools, she was not English. And it was difficult enough to get into the upper class, even with all his wealth, without having a wife from the colonies.

"There goes old Bently," Jeremy observed, "which means that's the last of the riders."

Bently had been in the stable all his adult life, from the days of the original owners of the manor, the Desmonds. He had become an institution in taking the last position of the troupe except when he was called to help with an injured or lame horse.

"Don't you think we ought to get moving ourselves, sir? They might get up the fox any time now, if I'm any judge."

The front of the troupe had moved almost half the distance down the slope and would be at the edge of the culvert in a few minutes. Robert waved to Jeremy.

"Yes, I suppose so, but why don't you go on and join Miss Service and I'll be along shortly."

"Are you sure, sir?"

"Yes, yes, go ahead. Don't worry about me. I'll be along."

The younger man struck his horse on the withers while heeling it in the ribs and the black gelding jumped forward. Robert also moved his horse out, though more slowly. His mind was not on the hunt; instead he relived the events of the past as he seemed to do more and more these days. He could have gone on buying cotton for the rest of his life, but he knew he wanted to settle down in England and the only really respectable way to do that was to become one of the landed gentry. Since he wasn't born into it, he had had to buy his way in.

When he was in his early forties he had realized that the real money would come from processing the goods he was importing from the colonies, so he had bought the factory in Colchester. Under his control it made money fast, and then at a weekend at the home of his partner, Gormley, he had learned about the financial troubles at Fairhaven. He had known immediately that it was what he was looking for. It was true that the long- established gentry looked down upon upstart owners, but money usually prevailed, and in that he had no peer. The former owners moved to London and Robert took over and began modernizing Fairhaven.

There was a clamor from the hunters, followed by the sound of the horn, and the troupe was off in noisy pursuit. The fox had been sighted. Robert's horse responded quickly, hardly needing the quirt's sting. It had been through enough hunts to know what was happening and broke into a gallop. Robert stayed on his horse well, but took no chances in jumps or through wooded places. He had seen enough accidents not to want that to happen. He wished Jeremy would learn to control himself instead of making such a to-do of keeping up with the other men. After all, he would be the inheritor.

Robert gained on the troupe, which went alongside the culvert, while the dogs went straight in. He could see them slow down at a clearing on the north side, Jeremy and two of his friends in the front, gesticulating and speaking animatedly, their horses prancing. Robert joined them.

"The fox got away," Jeremy said. "It found an unplugged hole alongside that fallen log."

A group of men had gone out very early to plug all the holes where the fox might go, but evidently they had missed this one.

"Get the assistant hound master," Robert ordered. "That's what he was brought for."

Even as he spoke, the man came on his hack and dismounted. He spoke to Robert.

"No need to worry, sir. This one here will handle the fox." He set the bag on the ground and reached in to pull out a small black and white terrier who, though at first a little confused, quickly oriented himself. "These little Pete Harolds can handle any fox in the country, sir."

Robert knew the Pete Harolds were a special breed, developed just for the purpose of getting a fox out if it managed to get in a hole. They were named after a fox hunter who had bred them for that purpose and they were frequently a part of the hunt retinue on the estates. Robert had inherited his from the Desmonds.

The assistant hound master was a talkative old fellow and kept at it while he carried the dog to the hole.

"Yes, sir, they don't look like much, but them little devils is all heart. Once they head down a hole, that Mr. Fox don't have a chance."

As he got nearer the hole, the little dog became agitated and when he was set on the ground, he smelled the hole and then quickly jumped in. Genevieve, Jeremy's older sister, moved her horse between Jeremy and Robert. She was a striking girl with long black hair.

"This is the part I just hate," she said to Jeremy. "It's a lark riding in the freshness of morning and seeing all the colorful action. But when it gets down to the point of the whole thing, I wish I was somewhere else."

"Why don't you do like mother and not come?" Jeremy asked.

She scowled. "Well I certainly don't come to see a bunch of full grown adults, abetted by a pack of ferocious dogs, tear a poor fox apart. But what can I do if I'm ever going to marry? I have to be seen, you know that. And one can certainly meet people on a fox hunt. It's easy for you, since all the girls come after you. They know you will inherit the property. And I will get precious little."

Robert turned to them. "What are you two quarrelling about? We're here to participate in one of the real pleasures of the gentry, and you two go on like magpies."

The assistant hound master was on his knees at the hole, whistling. He turned toward the group.

"I think the little devil's got him. It won't be long now."

The scuffling and snarling from inside the hole brought the pack of hounds as close as they could get.

"Just keep back, ladies and gentlemen. He'll be out in no time. And when he does, I'll not be able to keep these hounds back."

"Oh, it's just awful," Genevieve moaned.

"So why don't you wait out of sight?" Jeremy asked her. "You don't need to stay here, you know."

The snarling sound got nearer. The two beasts in the hole, so close by relationship, had been committed by genes and learning to being lifelong adversaries. The tenseness in the humans, some of whom had dismounted, had become palpable. The rear end of the terrier came out first, the muscles of his haunches bulging with effort. The hound master and assistant beat the dogs to keep them from swamping the struggling animals. Then, with a supreme lunge, the terrier yanked free from the hole, the tail of the fox in his jaws, the fox turning to snap at his tormentor. When the fox saw the mass of churning animals that surrounded them, he gave a mighty rake with his jaws and tore the terrier's face. The terrier yipped and let go and the fox leapt free, jumping incredibly high, but when the desperate animal came down, forty jaws were waiting and the fox disappeared in the churning carnage of the dog pack.

Genevieve/Amelia

Genevieve descended the winding stairway with her younger sister, Matilda. She wore a blue velvet dress with four petticoats underneath. Her cap was of the same color and she carried a small bag for her rouge and powder. Her fourteen-year-old sister wore a white frock, a jacket, and a pink cap. They both carried a *reticule.*

Matilda turned to Genevieve. "How does it feel to be moist?" she asked.

Helen had damped down her chemise to make the top of the frock cling. "Oh, it doesn't feel so wonderful. But that's not why you do it. You do it so the young men will notice you. You'll be doing it yourself in a few years, when you start hunting a husband."

"Oh, it doesn't sound so pleasant. Even hunting a husband doesn't sound like much fun. Maybe I won't do it." She carried a little Japanese fan and waved it in front of her face as she talked.

Genevieve laughed. "You'll learn. Most young girls talk like that until they get older and find out that there's practically no other choice. Why do you think your parents send you to finishing school to learn needlework? It's so people will think you're cultivated. Why else would someone want to marry you, you goose?"

Their mother stood at the bottom of the stairway, speaking with the butler. Though they had done this many times before, and the staff had been told the particulars of this affair already, there were always some last minute changes.

Amelia wore a maroon velvet dress. "And you need to have the right wines with each course," she told the butler. "I explained all that to you yesterday. But if there's any doubt, you must serve the claret. You have permission to ask me anything, but do it discreetly."

Genevieve and Matilda stood to one side until their mother had finished. Genevieve was always impressed at how well her mother handled these gargantuan affairs, being from the colonies and all. Amelia turned to her daughters.

"Oh here you are girls, I thought you would never come. You know that a person has to be punctual at social functions." She nodded toward Genevieve. "And you in particular, young lady. After all, you know you will 'come out' soon."

That special ball, to be arranged within the next couple of years, was referred to constantly. Matilda was tired of thinking about it. She would prefer to be with her books and to play on the grounds.

"Oh, Mama, don't get started on that now."

Genevieve, knowing her sister's thinking, said quickly, "Is everything arranged, Mama? Can I do anything?"

"No, Hercules and Lena have it all under control. And I should hope they have had enough practice to do a hunt weekend without any trouble."

It was true the butler and the housekeeper were well practiced in handling the lower servants, but Genevieve knew that it was because her mother was in charge of everything, even if she was not conspicuous about it. Amelia said to Genevieve, "I hear that the end of the hunt bothered you. It isn't nice what they do to the foxes. Of course they do raid the chickens, but there are better ways to get rid of them than to have them torn to pieces by dogs."

"Oh, yes, Mama, and then after that, cutting off what was left of the poor creature's parts and handing them out to different people. You know, they wanted to give the tail to father, but he wouldn't take it. He had them give it to Gormley, since he hadn't been on many fox hunts, and he seems to get a great pleasure out of all kinds of country events."

"Yes, I know. Many city people are like that. They really open up when they get a chance to do country things."

Gormley was the engineer whom Robert had found in Colchester and whom he had taken on for his mechanical experience. The combination had been a good one and Robert had made Gormley into his junior partner.

"Oh, Mama, I don't know if I want to go on any hunts," Matilda said. "I just heard about them 'blooding' the son of that Earl Newmarket. I just wouldn't be able to stand that."

She was referring to the blood of the fox which they had put on the boy at his father's request, to get the child hooked on fox hunting. The earl was a thoroughly dedicated hunter.

Amelia, touched her youngest daughter's elbow. "Oh, I wouldn't worry about that. I've never heard of them doing it to a girl. And no matter what you see, your father is not that dedicated to the hunt. But if you are going to be accepted by the gentry, you have to act like you enjoy it. But enough about the hunt, it's time for the dinner and there are things to do. Why don't you two girls go meet some of the other people while I go to the grand room and see about the punch."

She turned to Genevieve. "You ought to go find that Mr. Harlequin. He just came by to pay his respects."

Then she said to Matilda, "And you, young lady, why don't you go and find your papa? I don't think you have seen him all day, what with you so busy with your books while he is tending to his affairs."

The two girls walked toward the fireplace where several people were standing, glasses in their hands. Amelia went toward the high arched grand room, where a cut glass chandelier shed light from the center of the room. She glanced up and the candles seemed to be well lit.

It was a grand mansion, even though the plantation house in South Carolina had not been inconspicuous. But how could she have imagined that she would become an English lady in the luxury of a traditional mansion? Robert had been well established in London when she first came over, but she had learned soon after that to live in high style one had to have a country place. And his steps for getting them established had gone like clockwork.

She greeted people as she continued, usually with a comment about the hunt. She thought there must be about thirty people, the usual for a weekend affair, and about the number that would fit comfortably at the dining table. Robert was standing to one side of the punch table, talking with the new guest, Mr. Warner, the cloth merchant. She reached the table where the punch and the appetizers were laid out. One of the servants brought clean glasses which he arranged around the bowl. She took one, inspected it, poured in a small amount of punch and tasted it.

"This doesn't have enough rum. Please add another bottle."

"Yes, madame. Anything else?"

"Yes, William, the plate of anchovies needs to be replenished."

"Yes, madame." The man turned to head for the kitchen.

As she watched him go, she realized she still felt uncomfortable. All the household servants in South Carolina had been black. No white man, even one from the hills, would work as a household servant. It had been hard for her to learn to give orders to white people, particularly when they had English accents.

She moved to join Robert who was near enough that she could supervise the addition of the rum when the footman returned. Robert stopped talking to let her join.

" Ah, Mr. Warner," she said. "I was told this was your first fox hunt. How did you find it?"

"Very interesting, though I'm afraid I did not contribute anything useful. But I must say I find your countryside very beautiful."

Robert took a drink and spoke. "I'm afraid, my dear, that we are having a boring talk about business, one that would not interest you very much."

"Oh, just go on. I shall be here for only a minute or so. I want to stay nearby so I can supervise the replenishing of the punch." She was not at all surprised. She knew that her husband used the country weekends for promoting the cloth business, constantly inviting men of business to the affairs. It was his way of using the country life for practical advantage, an ingrown trait of his. Both men held cigars.

"Since you are here, and since all your life you have been closely connected with cotton," Robert said to Amelia, "you might give us your opinion as to the final stage, how to sell the end product."

She found it intriguing that he would include her, even if only for a short while, since generally Robert and the other men kept business to themselves.

"That sounds interesting," she said.

"Well," Robert began, "you know that Mr. Warner is an international trader and he is considering taking on our cloth. And as you probably know, we and the other producers are making far more than we can sell in England. So we are looking for new markets. And Mr. Warner is considering expanding either to India or China. Both have very large populations and in both their hand weaving traditions are rapidly declining. They will need to buy cloth soon. But since Mr. Warner cannot expand everywhere at once, the question is where shall he start. I can see advantages and problems with both. So why don't you give us the woman's point of view, that of a lady who grew up on a cotton plantation and now is the lady of a family which is deep into industrial production."

"Oh, I didn't know I was getting involved in international trade policy. But it is an important matter, isn't it?"

"Yes, my dear, it may well affect the lives of millions, and will prompt the voyages of dozens or even hundreds of ships."

She could think little about either place except that in one the population had slanted eyes and the men wore pigtails, while in the other they had dark skins and wore large turbans; and that the English more or less ran those places, no matter the size of their area and their populations. But she heard more about India in conversations, so she said, "I guess I would have to choose India since the British have conquered that country."

"That is one reason, I grant," Robert said. "We certainly do have more control there, though I'm not at all sure that our traders make more money as a consequence. They certainly do not do badly in China."

"I do not see much difference," Warner said. "As long as we keep producing the vast amounts we are, and as long as we have trade dominance, we are bound to make money in my opinion."

"Yes," Robert agreed. "For a time we will do very well. The greatest threat in my opinion is if the Yankees start manufacturing their own cotton. And I hear they are scouting the British mills now." He touched Amelia on the back. "You see, Mr. Warner, we have an agent of the enemy in our camp."

She smiled and returned his pat with a touch of her fan. "But you know, my daddy and all the other planters sell most of their cotton to England."

"Yes, but the factories will begin in the north, in the true heart of Yankee-land."

She was pleased to see the footman returning with a tray holding the bottle of rum and the plate of anchovies.

"I must go watch over that affair," she said. "Just you gentlemen remember not to get too involved in your international discussion that you neglect to get to table in time for dinner. It's at seven-thirty. And we will have some real country specialties—turtle soup, lobster, lamb cutlets, and plovers' eggs in aspic, and for vegetables, your specialty, Robert, stewed parsnips. She hurried away to get her mind off the terrible boiled parsnips, wishing only that it would be hominy grits.

~

Q: *There is little doubt about the title of this piece, even though the narrative is more about lifestyle than about devices. Would you explain that?*

A: Sure. It's because this era is named for the technological changes, but their effects have gone far beyond technology, as is true of most great innovations among men. You will undoubtedly remember that the development of the steel ax permitted cutting the forests of the world and an expansion of agricultural man at the expense of foraging man, while when warfare became democratized, the peasants of one side could kill the peasants of the other with steel weapons. Technological innovations have always powerfully affected social patterns. Moreover, our species has invariably been attracted to more efficient technical devices, or as an American folk saying goes, "better mouse traps," and their adoption has caused major changes in most aspects of life.

Q: *The era is more traditionally known as the industrial age or sometimes the industrial revolution, no?*

A: Yes. This has been the latest profound change in culture, one which started a little over two hundred years ago, has affected everyone on the globe, and will undoubtedly be the way things will go for the foreseeable future.

Q: *Certainly you are not saying that all cultures are industrialized, are you? What about Africa, the Middle East, and parts of Asia?*

A: I am arguing that all these places have been strongly affected by industrialization and if the leaders of these countries would have their druthers, they would be fully industrialized. You will note in the discussion that follows that I will bring in an industrial aspect of India because that is where I did my field work for my Ph.D., in an industrial city of north central India. And believe it or not, with no direct encouragement from me that I remember, my son did his study for his Ph.D. in an industrializing community in Taiwan. It is simply that industrialization has become such a pervasive force everywhere.

Q: *But there must be some difference in the degree of industrialization in different countries. Everyone knows that the rich countries in Western Europe, as well as America and Japan, are fully industrialized, while the poorer countries in Africa and Latin America have much less industry.*

A: There is a difference, yes, but that's primarily because of the history of the different countries. Some got started earlier than others. But now all nations of the world are hell bent to become industrialized, though there certainly are serious obstacles for many. But unlike the way it was in the recent past, all peoples now that I know of believe it is the way to go.

Q: *Why is everyone so much in agreement? There have been men in the past who did not think that industrialization was so wonderful. And if one is to believe your description of the worker's life, it certainly wasn't so wonderful, at least in the beginning. Did industrialization finally improve the way of life of the majority?*

A: I don't think I ever implied that the changes in culture improved mankind's way of life in the sense of giving more absolute satisfaction to more individuals. About all one can say is that throughout history man has been attracted to new ideas and practices, and if they accomplished some goal better, he usually adopted them. So it must have seemed that domesticating animals and plants, and producing more food, would be beneficial to the individual. But in the long run this merely produced a large class of specialists which the farmer had to support and thus work harder. Yes, the lucky ones might have some gold ornaments, but at the expense of harder work to produce enough food for the goldsmith, the tax man, and the military conscriptor. As a matter of fact, the history of mankind has been one in which there has been a constantly-increasing proportion of non-producers of the basics, which the producers have had to maintain.

Or you can look at it in another way, taking one particular type of technology through time. Take transportation for instance. I now have two motorized vehicles—a station wagon and a pickup truck. My parents could afford one car late in their life. My grandparents had only horse-drawn vehicles, and once or twice in their lives they had a ride or two on a train. If you go back a few thousand years there was nothing but human legs to get you about. Now the question is, did this improvement in transportation make life better? I think there is no doubt that the means of transport became more efficient through time, but to get where and why? I am sure my own ancestors thought of their lives as just as good as I do mine. And one important thing I have learned from anthropology is that the people of simple societies, those who had to walk to where they wanted to go, were just as content as those who can fly all over the world and zip across freeways endlessly. In fact, the negatives of unlimited car travel are now fully recognized even though most people in the world still want such vehicles.

Once a technological innovation is developed in a culture, conditions are created to make use of it. People who have only their legs for travel simply adjust their lives so they do not need to go as far. Once you get cars, you create places to go. Now we go to malls instead of neighborhood stores and we live in the suburbs and spread out all over the countryside instead of in the central city. In fact, we have handed the central city over to the poor, though that doesn't keep them from wanting cars also. And we can go from country to country with efficient air travel. But how does that satisfy us any more than a horse and buggy did my grandparents or a new pair of moccasins did a tribal? The point is that it is impossible to prove that technological innovation improves the quality of life. Remember that practically all the tribal peoples of the world took desperate measures to maintain their simple lifestyles. Civilization was shoved down their throats.

Q: *So if this is so, why do peoples adopt technological innovations so enthusiastically?*

A: The only answer I can think of is that technological innovations create a powerful illusion which tends to be self-fulfilling. That is, individuals are conditioned to want cars as they grow up, and by the time they are able to get them, they realize that their culture has made it very difficult to live without them. The culture has expanded to fulfill the inchoate requirements of the innovation.

Thus, my grandparents lived with the expectation that they would be farmers like their parents and would live in the same area, and so they did not get any specialized schooling. I went to college and learned a field I had never even heard of, anthropology, and my son did the same, as well as getting a higher degree in business administration. We both went to college in distant places. So, in accordance with my grandparents' expectations, they spent most of their lives in the same rural area of their state and neither went out of the state to work or live. And because of my expectations, I left my home state very early and settled down in my fifties in a state two thousand miles away, and have depended on auto trips of from fifteen to one hundred miles one-way for work and living ever since; and my son has done the same while living three thousand miles away from me. Both of us also would go anywhere in the world by air for a variety of reasons. We both assumed in our twenties that we would have to travel far, mostly by auto, and we made life choices to fulfill that destiny. But at no time could it be proved that our life was better than that of my grandparents.

Q: *But surely your own personal history is exceptional, isn't it?*

A: To a certain extent, but I think my generalization that the motor vehicle has become a necessity in our culture and that it hasn't increased our life satisfaction is true, as is the fact that my grandparents in their horse-drawn vehicles and the tribal on foot got just as much pleasure from living as does the motorman, despite Thomas Hobbes.

Q: *So if technology does not improve things, why spend so much time studying it?*

A: I did not say it did not improve things, I said it did not give more life satisfaction to the individual. The improvement of technology though time has made mankind as a species more and more powerful. And so he has fulfilled the Bible's injunction, he has peopled the earth. But the presence of more people will by no means improve the lot of the individual, and it may make it worse.

Q: *But nowadays, we in the civilized countries have a life span in the seventies, while the less industrialized countries, and I assume the tribals, have average life spans only in the thirties and forties. Surely that is progress, isn't it?*

A: Ah, now we get to the crux of the matter—progress. I was wondering when that would come out. Okay, let's ask ourselves if living to our seventies is so much better than only living to one's forties. My belief is that it is only so because we are conditioned to believe it as we grow up. If we grow up in a tribal society we simply expect to die younger and make no invidious comparison. In either society, if we get sick, we take steps to continue life. But again I'll go back to my long suffering grandparents. I do not believe that they felt their lives were less satisfactory because they did not live as long as we do now. And I believe the same is true of the tribal and the peasant in the non-industrialized countries. No matter how long their life span, neither willingly exchanged his way for ours. But this discussion could go on at great length, and the chapter is about industrialism. The one clear-cut truism is that man adopts more efficient technologies because it almost always seems that they will benefit him. And when he starts out with an innovation, man rarely thinks of the unexpected consequences which usually turn out to be numerous. And so with industrialization. Though the negatives have been numerous, it is a more efficient way to process raw materials. And we cannot understand the species in the twentieth century unless we know how it happened.

Q: *Okay, but is industrialization the final greatest achievement? After all, we are now verging on the atomic age and perhaps that of computers. Don't those merit special discussion in a list of man's achievements?*

A: Well, you know that we historians, even loquacious ones of an anthropological sort like me, have to stop somewhere. And though I have no doubt that atomic energy will be very significant in the future, so far it has been a minor source of power compared to the fossil fuels. And as a method of storing information and communicating, the computer is a powerful force also, but still most information is transmitted through that primitive invention of the fifteenth century, the printing press. In the meantime, the forces of industrialization affect the lives of people all over the world, primitive and civilized.

Q: *Would you describe the technology of the process?*

A: Primarily, it solves the problem of processing raw materials more efficiently. Ever since he has been on the cultural road, mankind has been faced with the problem of making useful things out of the raw products he got by gathering or cultivating. He had to convert stones into weapons, animal skins into clothing, plant fibers into cloth or baskets, and grain into an edible state for his constantly-weakening teeth. And throughout the first four million years he did it on a piece-by-piece basis, and during most of this period he used his body as the source of energy. When he enslaved animals, he got a new source of energy and also captured some natural forces, mainly wind and water. But these were piddling compared to what was to come, the force for industrialization which was a consequence of advances in the knowledge of natural processes during the scientific and engineering revolutions. The primary breakthroughs were the increasing knowledge about gases and the recognition of coal as a fuel. Man invented the steam engine then systems of levers, pulleys, and belts, and harnessed the genie first into the power loom and later into machines for making everything he knew about. So today there are only a handful of items used worldwide that are made by simple human power. Even the remnants of the tribal societies mostly use industrially-made goods.

Q: *So thank the heavens above that we still have artists. At least this is one type of modern who still makes individual pieces by hand.*

A: Yes, and there is an intermediate kind of production, oriental carpets. Most of these are made in poorer parts of Asia, and only because Westerners, who are inundated with industrially-made goods, will pay high prices for hand-made items. The salary of the workers is very low, and child labor still continues. Also, some of the few tribals in the world eke out a precarious existence making by hand items for tourists.

Q: *I assume the other kinds of power resources followed steam.*

A: Quite right. After steam, men learned how to use electricity and invented the internal combustion engine. Both drive the industrial machines of our day, and steam power is almost gone.

Q: *And how did mass production get to be a part of all this?*

A: The machine is very fast compared with hand production; also, it has no feelings about its products. While the artisan could take pride in each item he made, this is irrelevant to the machine. It will turn out whatever it is programmed for. And the money men quickly saw the advantage in numbers—the more you produce, the more you can sell. As the money manipulators of the 1980s said about greed, mass production was good, no matter how boring it was to the machine supervisors, the workers. In fact, the profitability of industrial production was at least a partial cause of the new system of financial gamesmanship, capitalism. When the technology became available, wealthy individuals began to invest in factories and trade systems. Until the industrial era began, one put one's money in land. After that, investors were more likely to put their money in industry and trade. The hero of our narrative was a man in the middle. He made his wealth in industrial production, but used it to buy his way into the rural upper class. The values of the previous era still predominated. But as industrialism became progressively more intense into the twentieth century, land became less important. Nowadays you are rich when you have interests in industry. Even modern farming has become a form of industrialism in the fields, relying on power machinery as much as do factories. Moreover, the key to successful farming in the industrial countries now is the amount and complexity of one's machinery. Furthermore, mass production is just as important in farming as in industry. Biologists complain that there is a continuing loss of species of cultivated plants because modern farmers select only those which are best commercially and ignore the others, the ones pre-industrial farmers developed. So mass production is in while artisanship and individualistic production are hard to find except among artists.

Q: *You have frequently indicated that trade went along with industrialism as they used to say love and marriage went together. Would you comment on this?*

A: Yes. The technological base was only the beginning. It created the possibility of producing goods like never before. But as you will have noticed in the early occupation of Robert Capstan, the new machines created a large need for raw materials. You will remember that the original industries in England were weaving mills, and the two kinds of cloth they made were wool and cotton. And though you know that sheep are raised in cool England, cotton simply will not thrive there. It requires a long hot season, which is why Robert was buying the stuff in South Carolina. The British also bought much cotton from Egypt and other hot places. This points to another fact—the industrial countries developed the custom early of gathering the raw materials needed from all parts of the world. And though at one time it was worthwhile to have some raw materials in one's own country, as England and the United States did, it turned out that one could be quite a successful industrialist with practically no raw materials of one's own. One simply bought the raw materials elsewhere, processed them, and then sold them back to those same countries. The classic case is Japan, though the same is true of a number of other Asian and European nations. The idea we were taught in school, that having many raw materials made a country rich, simply is not true. International buying and selling became intricately bound up with making things industrially. And Britain was at first a leader in the selling game also. Industrial production requires it. Otherwise, the gain from mass production is negated. And again, Japan and several of the smaller industrial nations of Asia have streaked ahead of the pioneer, Britain, and some other countries of Europe. They have practically no natural resources, but plenty of hot-shot engineers, good workers, and salesmen.

Q: *So you are saying that industrialization necessarily includes international trade for buying natural resources and selling finished products as well as a special kind of financial system, is that right?*

A: Yes, I think so, though I don't know that the final verdict is in on the financial system. Industrialization got going with capitalism, which created a great degree of misery as well as wealth. But there was quite a bit of opposition from early on.

Q: *If life in nineteenth century England was truly as you portrayed it, I can see why. The workers' way of life seemed dismal indeed.*

A: I think it was. If anything, my portrayal of the way of the working class was too kind. Although the literary authors of the period spent little effort in describing it, what we do get is horrible. Some of the items I gathered in my research about the working class way of life are:

- Mothers and children worked twelve to fifteen hours a day under unsanitary conditions.
- Small children were treated cruelly to keep them awake.
- Men often sold their wives and children to the mills.
- Women and children worked up to fourteen hours in the coal mines, the children as young as nine years of age. Men, women, and children took off all their clothes to work in the mines.
- Children would be too tired to eat after a day in the factory, so parents would wash them and put them to bed.
- Few workers had coats or shoes to go out on Sunday or to find a new job.
- Six men would stay in one eight-by-ten room, three in a bed.

Q: *It really does sound terrible. Surely things got better.*

A: Yes, they did through the nineteenth and twentieth centuries, but only, I suspect, because it was forced on the factory owners. But we should not blame the English that much. They simply were the first. Industrial workers were treated pretty badly in the U.S. and other countries as well.

Q: *But now there are laws to protect workers, no?*

A: Yes, and like most other significant changes they were the result of angry protests. Wealthy classes have rarely given up privilege voluntarily. Even in the early days, there were organized protests and machine destruction by the Luddites. It is true that there were a few Utopian types who organized humane factories and communities. But probably the most significant protestors were the trade unionists and socialists. Through decades of agitation they gradually got improved conditions for workers.

Q: *As I recall, Karl Marx was one such protester, right?*

A: Yes, he and Engels developed their fanciful theory for the rise of the masses and the paradisiacal socialist world to come after seeing the miserable conditions in nineteenth-century England and Germany. Unfortunately, much of their theorizing was far from accurate, and it was never carried out as they anticipated by either the Russians or the Chinese. So we still don't know if Communism as they envisaged it would work. And though the trade union movement has been greatly weakened, it has left its mark. In the successful industrial countries we no longer have child labor and twelve to fifteen working hours per day.

Q: *If the system was so hard, weren't there other ways to go for mankind?*

A: It's possible, but I'm afraid the lure of improved technology is so great that few cultures can resist it. And there was resistance to industrialization until after World War II. One of the most famous voices was that of Mohandas Gandhi, the liberator of India. Presumably from his knowledge of the miseries of British industrialism, he turned totally against the way. He envisaged free India as a nation of craft workers, which he called *swadeshi,* and effectively blocked the industrialization of that country for several decades. It has not been until the twentieth century that his influence has been effectively cancelled and India has finally got on with the new way. And all other nations have got on the same bandwagon. I know of no other country which does not have a policy to industrialize as quickly as possible.

I might usefully insert my own personal experience with industrialization, even though it occurred after conditions in the factory were much improved, in the 1930s. I grew up in the working class in Indianapolis, Indiana, and graduated from Emmerich Manual Training High School, which was established to train factory workers. Like most Americans, I had no idea that there was a class system in my country and that I was part of the lower class. And so I never studied "shop" as all my friends did, which I now realize was part of the curriculum to train manual workers. And when I graduated from high school and needed a job, I went around to the factories until I found one which would hire me, a place which manufactured automobile mufflers. As a beginner, I was given a very monotonous job which I had to do by "piece work." This is work which is gauged by the amount one does, the number of pieces, instead of by the hour. I found the job very hard as well as monotonous, and quit within a few weeks to go to business school. There I learned typing, shorthand, and simple accounting, after which I got a job in an office. And despite the drawbacks, including very low pay, I found it more agreeable than the factory job. I should mention that most of the boys I grew up with, almost all of whom did take "shop" courses, ended up with factory jobs or other manual labor.

At the time I didn't mind so much the fact that the work was hard, but rather its monotonousness. And they say that is a continuing price the industrial worker pays even though his salary and the working conditions have improved. But in any event, industrial work certainly does not have the creative aspect that artisanship has. I might add that I went on to college afterwards and the closest I got to industry after that was to use the products and to study the social conditions of an industrializing community in India as an anthropologist.

The productivity seems to have always outweighed the disadvantages of this type of work, for cultures if not for individuals. And so until a better way of processing raw materials comes along, I suspect we will continue to rely on machine production.

Q: *I noticed that you made quite a contrast between conditions in the country and those in the city, and the worker's neighborhood certainly seemed dismal.*

A: I did that especially because the effects were very great, probably more than for any previous technological innovation. In the first place, when the boilers for the steam engines were fired up, a great demand for workers became apparent. Where would one get them but from the countryside? At the same time, machinery was being introduced into the farms and the need for rural hand labor was less. So there was one of the biggest population shifts in history, from the country to the city. Before the nineteenth century, the great majority of mankind lived in the countryside. By the twentieth century it had reversed in the industrialized countries, and nowadays there are fewer than ten per cent of the population in the rural areas, and power machinery has replaced workers on farms all over. This migration took place in North America also. My parents were both migrants to the city and with one exception that I know of—me—all their children and grandchildren have remained urbanites. I now have a small avocado farm, but it is my retirement home. Basically, I live from the pension I earned in city jobs, when I also lived in the city.

This movement from the agrarian countryside to the industrializing urban area has had enormous social repercussions. A population shift has even taken place where industrialization has been much less, in the third world. In places like Mexico, Peru, and Brazil, people are leaving the rural areas to live in crowded tenements in the main cities. Industrialization has finally turned the world into a place of cities instead of a place of villages and farms, controlled by a few cities.

Q: *And you say there was a considerable growth of population in the industrial area?*

A: Yes. Large families were the norm, even for those who migrated, at least for a couple of generations. Furthermore, there were new kinds of food and increasing medical knowledge, so no matter how dismal their lives, more people lived longer.

Q: *And another consequence has been to the environment?*

A: Yes. Industrialization has really been mostly responsible for the era of environmental degradation. Men had damaged their local environment before. Even the tribals polluted their immediate area. Trash heaps have been one of the primary kinds of sites excavated by archeologists. But there really weren't enough tribal people or a technology complex enough to affect roads, living sites, rivers, and air on the scale that was possible when factories became a reality and when there were vastly greater numbers of people.

Q: *The more you discuss it, the less desirable industrialization sounds. I had always thought it was a great step forward, is that not so?*

A: Well, it depends on what you think forward is. If you think producing a greater variety of goods for more people is progress, then this was progress. And of course the men of the nineteenth century, and most since, except for some "crackpots" like Gandhi, believed it was true progress. The men of the burgeoning industrial countries who affected public opinion really thought this was an era of great progress. And for them—the members of the upper class, and later the middle class—it was. But you also must remember this was the era when colonialism as a method of spreading "civilization" was thought to be quite all right. Nowadays, we do not think so highly of colonialism, and perhaps it is even appropriate to be somewhat critical of industrialization. But whatever our opinion, I suspect it is here to stay.

Q: *Can we now go on to talk about social organization? I gather that you think it was based on inequality between workers and supervisors.*

A: Yes, I'm afraid I would generally have to go along with Marx on that one, though not in all respects. The way I see it, all societies beyond the tribal are based on inequality, for the simple reason that some individuals are always more capable than others and they get a higher proportion of the goodies, social and material, which they then tend to pass on to their children. In the long run, this creates differences which we call classes or castes. And the more goodies there are, the greater the potential differences. So even though it is politically expedient these days to use the word democratic as much as possible, the fact is that there is a large number of people with a little and a few with a lot. Few social scientists would deny that we live in a class system. And the goodies which are unequally shared are primarily from industry.

Q: *But these differences are mostly a matter of education, aren't they?*

A: Sure, but I hope you do not think that access to education is equal to all in a democracy. The first thing people in a democracy do when they can pay for it is send their children to elite schools.

Q: *But I thought you just said earlier that you went to a high school for the working class. And now you have a Ph.D. and can write books. Doesn't that prove that there is no class system?*

A: I don't think so. I never said there was no mobility for the individual. And I was one of the few who got out of my class background and went on to get a higher education. But I can assure you, I was the exception. All my high school buddies went on to manual jobs, mostly in factories. And even more telling is what happened in the next generation. My son almost automatically went to college and got his Ph.D. also. And he is now preparing to send his children up the same road. In other words, I escaped from the working class, and since then my descendants have been in what we now call the upper middle class, primarily through higher education.

Q: *Another thing about the effects of industrialization on the social order is male dominance. It seems that men were the boss through that period, no?*

A: Yes, but that is nothing new. If you go back to the pre-hominid level, you will find that males usually have their way, at least among the higher mammals. And the only periods in hominid history when females have approached a level of equality have been in the stage of hunting and gathering and today, and the reason seems to be the same in both cases—the female has become a major producer in these two stages of history. In the foraging stage, the gathering done by the female provided the most food; and nowadays, in the age of push-button technology, the female can again produce just as well as the male. We are so given to moral explanations that we talk of various human rights, including female, as being a matter of morality, but there is also a basis in technology.

Q: *Why did you devote so much time to your description of life in the English countryside during the industrial era, since you say that the future of life will be in the city?*

A: The high life in industrial England was in the country estates even if real money-making was in the new factories and in commerce. It was a time of transition, and the English were just looking backward. Since then, the countryside as a place of high living has become less important, there and in all the newly-industrialized countries. But in those days the great status difference was the contrast between the urban working class and the gentry in the countryside. Thus while the factory workers had to make do with a few bones for soup, the upper class in the countryside could have plover eggs in aspic. And while the upper class could afford multitudes of servants in a great country house, the working class had to live several people to a room in a dingy tenement.

Q: *But conditions have certainly improved since then, haven't they?*

A: Yes, the working class in the most favored countries now lives better, one of the main reasons being that they are now considered to be consumers, and consumers have to have enough money to buy things. Also, more limits are now put on the power of factory owners, largely due to the socialist and trade union struggles of the recent past.

Q: *So what about the future? Could you say anything about that?*

A: Ah, well, predicting the future is a risky business. But I suppose we culture specialists can put in our two bits worth also. But let us save that for the final chapter.

The Machine

10

More

Harilal

A t eight thirty the corridors were already filled with people. Most were men, dressed either in *dhoti* or *pajama*, with loose shirts and a Nehru or Jinnah cap, both types from the Independence forty years before. White was the most common color. Most of the men carried cheap plastic briefcases. The few women, dressed in *sari* or *pajama*, usually passed in pairs. The pajama came to the West, along with the word, from India, although in the process it was changed to a garment for sleep. Many of the women carried sheaves of papers tied with wide red cords, an inheritance from the British period when the *baba* bureaucracy was established.

Harilal and his colleague, Zahur, maneuvered their way through the throng with a deftness born of long experience. This was the busiest time of day in the building, just following the department meetings.

Zahur would accompany Harilal for the five miles to the road to Bara-Imli, then Harilal would travel another two miles to an adjacent village district. Both were village-level workers.

As the field workers headed for their various assignments, Zahur asked Harilal, "What did you think of the new scheme?"

"Which do you mean, the one for men or the one for women?"

In the meeting that morning two new ideas had been brought forward, for the men the monetary reward for having their tubes cut was to be increased to 100 rupees, and for the women, the same would be offered for coming to the clinics for an IUD.

"I'm sure they would both like to have some extra money," Harilal continued. "But I still think most people who participate will be those who are beyond the child-bearing age, particularly the men. I mean, I have seen some coming into the clinic who could barely walk. Besides, I still think they gave up too early on the rhythm method."

The two men were outside by this time and were heading for the parking lot.

"It is certain that Muslim women, young or old, are not going to come into the clinics," Zahur said. "Even if their husbands would permit it, they wouldn't come. I would think some of the doctors would know that, particularly the Muslim ones."

Zahur was one of the few village-level workers who worked in a Muslim district, since he also was a follower of Islam.

"Why didn't you say so at the meeting?" Harilal asked.

"It wouldn't make any difference. The doctors and administrators from Deenpur never listen to us anyway, or at least they never change the program. It's already set when it gets to us."

They had reached the bicycle lot which was about one-third of the total parking space of their government building, even though four-fifths of the workers traveled by bicycle. Some who worked in the city traveled by bus, while the doctors and administrators traveled by car. Both men unlocked their bikes and put the chains in their baskets, along with the manila envelopes tied with red ribbon they had been give at the meeting. They threaded their way out onto the street and entered the traffic of Bismat Ganj. While the number of bodies was considerable in the provincial office building from which they had just come, the number and variety of people on the street was mind-boggling, like the center of most other cities in India. A thick swarm of people spread out from the sidewalks on both sides, filling about two-thirds of the street. Those nearest the wall on both sides were walking in one direction and another stream of people walked in the opposite direction. The next layer consisted mostly of bicyclists with some pedestrians mixed in. The bicyclists and pedestrians usually were able to avoid each other, but when two men collided, a noisy interchange usually ensued. If women were involved, there would generally be little disturbance since females did not speak out in public. Further into the middle of the street was the mixed conglomerate of vehicles pulled by men and beasts, as well as autos, scooters, and motorized tri-wheels driven by turbanned Sikhs, with upper-class women or well-fed merchants as passengers. There were even a few rickshas being pulled by men. Here and there thin-legged men pulled carts piled high with furniture or sacks of rice. Other carts were pulled by teams consisting of a man and a water buffalo, both in the same harness, the man in front guiding, the buffalo behind him, providing the power. The drivers of autos threaded their way through the dense crowd by constantly honking the horn. Pedestrians and bicyclists got out of their way, though slowly. Everyone including the drivers of autos was accustomed to this constant density, and accepted as normal that the more slowly-moving vehicles would move out of the way of the faster ones.

The two men pushed their bikes into the moving stream and began cycling. The din was so great and so constant that individual sounds could barely be picked out. However, the village workers and everyone else had no problem talking to one another. They simply raised their voices. The cyclists passed an intersection where a turbanned policeman was directing traffic with no conviction. When people crossed against his direction, he ignored them. At the next intersection a cow was standing in the center of the intersection, observing the traffic and placidly chewing her cud. Passersby merely moved around the animal, leaving a small space. Further along on one side men were pissing against a wall, positioning themselves so no one would see their penises, a capability Indians had developed from early on, since urinating outside was the norm, there being practically no toilets except in homes of the well off. Most women could urinate from a squatting position without being exposed. That particular spot must have been used for a long time, since a heavy growth of moss covered the bricks. Thin streams of urine flowed out to the street and the odor was high.

Neither the density of people or the constantly-changing sights provoked any interest in the two cyclists. Harilal had grown up in Deenpur and Zahur had come from a smaller town some twenty miles away. As they talked, they moved progressively farther out from the center.

"What do you mean, too early to give up on the rhythm method?" Zahur asked. "Practically no one was using it properly. What good was it doing?"

"I think anything that has worked so well in so many places must have something good about it."

He was well behind the times; the rhythm method had been replaced almost completely by the IUD and the Pill in the industrialized countries. He wouldn't have heard the old joke: What do you call someone who uses the rhythm method? A parent.

A group of dogs, most of them mangy, all of them cadaverous, were trying to make their way across the street, dodging the various animals, people, and vehicles. The dog in front was a bitch in heat, followed by several emaciated but still interested males.

"Now that's the way it is with the people in India too," Zahur observed. "They don't have enough to eat, but do you think that keeps them from producing more? Not at all, they keep reproducing no matter what."

"You better keep your eyes on that pack or they will be under your wheels," said Harilal.

Street dogs never attacked people in India, whether on bicycle or foot. They were too cowed for that. Boys were always throwing stones at them. But they could get in the way of cyclists and cause them to fall. This group made it across and slithered under some decrepit market stands, the males still following the female.

"Well, to go back to the rhythm method," Harilal continued, "this isn't England or America, this is India. I get tired hearing how well everybody does in Europe and North America all the time. And let's face it, the people in those countries are well educated. They're not a bunch of dumb peasants, like we have to work with."

Harilal still couldn't adjust to his job. After all, he had a teaching credential, but this was the best he could get. He could get a teaching job in a primary school, but that would be in a village also, and would pay even less.

They were nearing the bridge and traffic was thinning. Once they crossed the bridge they would be heading out into the countryside. Harilal was getting his usual anxiety. He was really becoming tired of village life. If only he could find something in the city.

"I want to stop and get a *pan* at that shop before we get into the country," he said. "Otherwise I'll never make it. You want one?"

Pan was ground betel nut in lime paste with spices, encased in a folded leaf. It was chewed slowly, causing the saliva to flow and turn red. People who had used the mixture for a long time had bright red mouths. Sometimes after taking several *pan* in a day, the inside of

322

Harilal's mouth was pink. Getting *pan* when he was going into the country was especially pleasant because he could then spit on the roadway. Some people even did it in town, but Harilal didn't like to see the big red blotches of spit.

"I mean some of the stories you hear about what people did are beyond belief," Zahur continued. "Even if you are an illiterate peasant, you wouldn't do some of the things that have been reported. That business about the beads really sticks in the throat, wouldn't you say?"

Harilal had also heard the story that someone had worked out a contraceptive string of beads which the woman was supposed to put up in her house and use for deciding when not to have intercourse. It had twenty-two white and six red beads, one of which she was supposed to move each day. The idea had been dreamed up because most of the women were illiterate and couldn't have read the same information on a piece of paper.

Chuckling, Harilal said, "I couldn't believe it when I heard that part about the woman complaining when she became pregnant because she had moved a bead each day and that when she was asked if she ever had sex on the wrong days she said she had sex whenever her husband wanted it, thinking that moving the beads would keep her from conceiving."

"So what good were the demonstrations, then?" Zahur said.

When the rhythm method was introduced into a village area, there would be demonstrations, usually on film, of how to keep track of the fertile days when one might conceive. And though it was one of the most difficult points to get across, a female voice would come on to say that the woman should not have sex on those days.

The vendor at the *pan* stand sat cross-legged at the level of his table top. Dozens of jars of spices sat with the basic ingredients. A mangy dog sniffed around the papers and garbage that littered the area around his stand.

Harilal felt more relaxed as soon as he began to chew. Zahur bought an individual paper-wrapped cigarette. As soon as he lit up, Zahur put the cigarette into the end of his clasped fingers to make a tube and sucked from the opening at the thumb end, the traditional method of smoking in that part of India. It kept the mouth from touching the end of the cigarette, and was perhaps derived from the traditional way of smoking the water pipe so that the mouthpiece could be taken by several men without having to worry about the problem of untouchability. Being a Muslim, Zahur was theoretically unconcerned about untouchability, but the Hindu idea had affected the Muslim community.

They moved to one side where they wouldn't be overheard by the vendor or his other customers.

Harilal spit and said, "Well, you know about the demonstrations. Most of the village people have little entertainment, so they come to see the movies to pass the time as much as anything. They might like to see something else, but even a doctor talking will do. But they also know the woman in the film is not really a villager, that she is an actress. No village woman would let strangers take photographs of her, much less take part in a family planning show."

"Certainly I agree," said Zahur. "But the government has to do something." He paused. "Though sometimes I think they exaggerate. After all, India is a big country and it is well known that some little European countries have much more dense populations than India— Belgium and Holland, for instance."

By this time the two were leaning on their bicycles in the shade of an old mango tree. The lower branches had been cut off and carried away for goat food. Harilal spotted some flies on a mango seed and contemplated sending a squirt of *pan* juice to splatter them, but refrained on the grounds that it was not genteel.

"Of course, it's a little easier to believe that the women can't see the color of the beads in the dark when their husbands come to bed," said Harilal. "But they could have looked earlier when there was still light. But it's my opinion that the light explanation was merely a ploy so the government would give them a free torch."

The Indians followed British usage by referring to the flashlight as a torch. Harilal wanted to squat but knew that educated men never did that, following the European way of sitting on a chair or bench or standing. Traditionally, Indians did sit on platforms or their rope beds, especially in the villages, but usually in the cross-legged position. That was one thing that Harilal liked about being in the village, the opportunity to sit in a cross-legged position.

"All these special methods to help village women remember when not to do it don't matter much anyway," Zahur said. "The man is the one who decides. If he wants to have his wife, he will take her. And if he doesn't have at least two good-sized boy children, he will want to make some more."

There was a steady procession of passersby, vehicles and animals going up the incline to the bridge. The pedestrians generally tried to keep to one side. A turbanned policeman was directing traffic. The two men idly watched the movement.

"It's true, and you really can't blame the men since a family has to have some boys. And since frequently one or two are lost to illness, the man can't take a chance by having only one, or even two, not to mention the problem of a man who has one girl after another."

They smoked and chewed for a bit, tired of thinking of the population problem. Harilal never even knew there was such a problem until he went to college. He thought that it was normal everywhere to have large families. Finally, Zahur broke the silence.

"What do you have to do today in the village? Are you still putting out publicity for the whole program?"

"I have a meeting with the village council leaders and I need to push the sterilization program. The last time the medical team came, there were only three; and if I don't get more soon, I'll certainly not get a promotion, and my bonus will be very little."

The government had instituted a policy of paying the village-level workers five rupees for each volunteer they got for either IUD insertion or sterilization.

"And what have you got lined up? Harilal asked. "Or are you just going to hang around the office smoking *bidis*?" These were the local cigarettes which Harilal knew Zahur smoked most of the time because he couldn't afford many paper-wrapped ones. He said it jestingly, even though he suspected that Zahur did loaf around a lot, not that he blamed his colleague. After all, it was difficult enough to sell family planning to villagers, but to Muslims!

Zahur took mild offense. "I work as much as anyone on village development projects, I'll have you know. But you try to convince some of the followers of Islam to limit their families and you'll know how hard it is. Anyway, I have a meeting also, with a group of *imams*. You know how hard it is if something is not explicitly mentioned in the Koran. Their answer always is 'If Allah had wanted us to do it, he would have told Mohammed.'"

"So what is your tack now?"

"All I know to do is claim that many new things have come into the world since Mohammed, like the Pill, IUD's, and sterilization. So how could Mohammed have known about them?"

"I understand that, though isn't the normal Islamic belief that Allah knows all, whether it existed before or later?"

"That is a widespread belief," Zahur answered. Though among the educated there is less willingness to take the Koran literally. Modernized Muslims think that many things have come since the age of science which would have been difficult if not impossible to know about before. I have trouble imagining that Allah knew about IUD's."

Harilal chuckled. "But those villagers are hardly educated. The majority cannot read—in any language." He picked up his bicycle. "But we had better get on the road or we'll miss our meetings."

"Achaa." Zahur got his bike and the two men walked their two-wheelers to the edge of the stream of humanity, along with the animals and mechanical go-alongs. They mounted as soon as it was practical and began pedalling up the incline and onto the bridge. The bridge was a long iron structure, put up during the British *raj* across the sacred Mother, she who began with the icy waters of the Himalayas, nurtured her people on the plains of Hindustan, and emptied out into the bay of Bengal. It was early summer, and sand flats dotted the middle of the river. On one a couple of emaciated dogs worried the remains of a human corpse while white-headed crows circled overheard; on another islet a couple of very large turtles picked over another mass of human remains. These bodies were the partially-cremated corpses of those whose relatives had not been able to afford enough wood to have them completely consumed. In another direction, vines snaked across the sand, protected by woven fences serving as windscreens. These were watermelon gardens; the peasants had taken advantage of the silt-laden soil as the river receded during the dry season. The roots could easily reach the moisture underneath. Life and death in Hindustan, Harilal thought as he pedalled steadily.

Auraat

The only light in the room came from the one open window. The only furniture was a trunk, some rolled-up mattresses, and two woven rope beds. On the walls a few pieces of clothing hung on pegs. On one bed a small figure lay huddled under a coverlet, from which could be heard light breathing.

The door opened and a small woman dressed in a sari entered, carrying a plastic glass. She came to the bed and stooped to lift the ragged coverlet. The girl was very slight, perhaps seven or eight years old. Leela opened her eyes and looked at her mother. Auraat put her hand on the girl's forehead. It was hot even though the child was shivering.

"How is my little pumpkin feeling?"

"So cold, mama."

"I know. It's the fever. The little pumpkin will have to get better, so she can go to school." Auraat put her arm behind the girl's back and gently lifted her. "Mama brought a glass of hot milk for the pumpkin."

The girl looked groggy as she stared at the plastic glass which Auraat put up to her lips.

"Now drink, little pumpkin. It's the only milk we'll have today and the pumpkin needs it to get her strength back."

The Misras didn't have their own cow, so she had had to get the milk from her neighbor, Radna. Radna had slipped it to Auraat without her husband knowing about it. He always felt they didn't have enough for themselves. Finally the little girl sipped some of the milk.

"It doesn't taste good, Mama."

"I put a spoon of sugar in it, little pumpkin, but I couldn't put more because even the brown sugar of the village is expensive. And what money there is has to be used to get the little pumpkin some medicine so she will get well fast."

The exertion of sitting up to drink the milk had tired Leela.

"Let me lie down, Mama," she said. When her mother pulled up the coverlet, she said, "Is there another cover? I'm so cold."

"I'll see, pumpkin." She knew that there wasn't another unless she gave her the one from her own bed.

She closed the door quietly and went to the other room where the cooking area took up one end. Her other daughter, Larki, was working with a slate and chalk, doing arithmetic. She was two years older than Leela.

"I thought you said you would be finished with that. You know it's time to get the *dal* on and fix the chapattis. Your father will be home before you know it and he gets angry if his food isn't ready."

Auraat expected to be back before Moonesar got there but the time at the tank was precious to her as it was to most women, and she especially wanted to talk to Radna this night.

"But the master said he wanted us to finish the exercises on percentages," Larki said. "And I'm almost finished."

"Well, you just put it down now. It's all very well to learn some numbers and writing, though when I was little, only the very rich ever thought of it. Even some of the big landowners would not let their girls go to school. Anyway, you will be getting married in another couple of years and you'll not need arithmetic then. You'll be doing like the rest of the village girls, tending the house and taking care of boy babies for your husband."

Auraat never forgot that she had no boy children, while there were the two girls. Moonesar would never let her forget that fact. But she couldn't help insisting that her girls do the right thing. Larki put her school things away carefully because they were precious, especially since she couldn't know how long she would have in school. Girls were always taken out of school when they were married and sent to their husbands' villages.

"Is Leela any better?" she asked.

"She's about the same. She needs some medicine. I hope your father brings some."

The night before, Auraat had asked Moonesar to let her take Leela to the government clinic, but he had become angry. "What do you think she is, a boy?" he had asked.

She had felt so ashamed, almost as bad as she had after the second birth when she had learned it was another girl. But still Leela was her little pumpkin, and if something happened to her, Auraat would feel even worse. So even though she did everything she knew how in gesture and action not to anger him, she had continued her plea.

"I know husband, and I'm so sorry we have two girls and no boys, but I've done everything I know to change it. You know that I go to the Shiva temple whenever I have a chance, to put flowers and water on the holy lingam. But it hasn't helped."

"I know, do I?" he had said. "I do everything I can to feed and clothe the family and the one thing a wife is supposed to do, to bear boy babies, you do not do. There must be something wrong with you, woman."

And then she knew the outcome was inevitable, he would get angrier and angrier and in the end he would strike her. She consoled herself with the thought that at least he wouldn't take the drastic measures she had heard about—throwing hot oil or kerosene on the unproductive wife and setting her afire. And she wished she had not started though what else could she do? If she had not begun, there would be no hope that Leela would get some medicine. If it had been a boy who was sick, she knew he would get medicine, with or without her pleading. But at this point she couldn't quit.

"I think there must be, husband," she had agreed. It's not natural to only have girl babies. But what else can I do?"

Two girls in the first births didn't seem like that many to her, but she was ready to do anything to placate him.

"There must be something else to do," he said. "After all, you know that it will only be a little while before the first one will have to be married. And after that the next. And where will the money for the dowries come from, little as it will be for a poor family like us. But you know that without something for the dowry and some kind of wedding, people will think we are just dogs."

"Oh, yes, husband, I know."

He had become fired up by this time. "And then if by some miracle you had a boy, when he grew up we wouldn't be able to get a bride for him from a respectable family. Did you ever think of that, woman?"

And so it had gone as all those discussions had since the births of the girls. Finally, she just bent her head and pulled over the end of the sari to cover part of her face. But this had made him even angrier and inevitably he had knocked her down. But he was a fairly good husband in this respect. He never struck her when she was down. He didn't even beat her with his shoe. She did not have the courage to bring up the medicine again.

She felt lighter as she walked barefoot between the mud-walled houses toward the tank. Although it was late in the day, there was enough time for a good bath and talk, especially with Radna. She counted on this event as the high point of each day, especially since she had to observe so many social restrictions. She kept her head down and partly covered as she walked, especially when she passed men. She greeted the women she knew, and when she passed the temple to Shiva, she bowed her head and with folded hands supplicated the god of reproduction. A monkey was eating the flowers in the shrine. She passed the school with the attached clinic building. Boys played soccer in the schoolyard. She approached the tank, an artificial pond which held water from one rainy season to the next. These tanks existed in almost all the villages and were the scene of much activity throughout the day, but especially in the evening. When Auraat approached, there were several women on the bank or in the water, well separated from everyone else. On the other side, water buffalos were submerged to various depths, and nearby, boys played in the water, while watching the animals. Farther on, a few men, bare to the waists, fished with thrownets. At the end of the pond the washermen stood knee-deep in muddy water, slapping the soiled clothing against anchored pieces of wood, their donkeys standing on the bank nearby. Crows passed frequently and kites circled, ever scavenging.

Auraat hurried down the bank toward the women's group and let her sari fall free, exposing her entire head, the only time she could do this in public. She greeted several women but kept looking for Radna who had said she would come earlier to wash some clothes. Auraat was pleased when she saw her friend toward the edge of the group, at a place where a flat rock had been placed for washing clothes. There were no other women near Radna and she was no longer washing clothes, but standing in water up to her waist, sloshing it over her head and shoulders, fully clothed, as were all the other bathing women. It was unheard of for a village woman to take off any clothing for bathing.

Auraat joined her friend in the water, pleasurably feeling the mud squeeze between her toes and the water rising on her body as she went deeper. Small fish nibbled at her legs. She sloshed water over her head and hair, letting it run down her body. Then, pinching her nose, she submerged her head and came up to let the water stream off. She did this several times, feeling the world of sickness and births and husbands fall back, leaving her in a kind of bliss that she rarely had during the day. When she came up the last time, Radna was watching her with a bemused expression.

"I thought for a while, little mother, that you had turned into a turtle and would not come back to the village people."

The two came out of the water and up on the bank where they began drying themselves with cotton cloths they had brought along.

"Are you feeling better now, little mother?" Radna asked. "You looked very anxious." Then she stopped and peered at the bruised place on Auraat's cheek. She put her hand over to touch it. "Does it hurt, my friend?"

"Oh, no, it's nothing. I just fell when I went out to pee last night." There were no indoor toilets and everyone had to go to a nearby field to urinate and defecate. The women tried to do it when there was no one around to see, and that had to be very early in the morning or late in the evening, before it got completely dark and dangerous.

"Ah, no, little friend," Radna said. "It's not necessary to tell lies to a friend. But remember, it's not so serious to be hit by one's husband. They are men and that is their right. And that looks like just a little blow."

Auraat wouldn't tell that she had been knocked to the floor. Many women were beaten by their husbands, and there was little that could be done about it, even if it became serious. And she had to admit that she deserved it, presenting her husband with two girls and no boys. But she also knew it would only get worse if nothing happened. And all she could think of doing was to ask her friend for advice.

"I know, dear friend, but I get frightened when he gets so angry. And I do not know what to do. I pray and go to the temple as much as I can but I do not know if the Lord Shiva can make the child into a boy or a girl. He is supposed to help wives to have children, but I have never heard whether he can select one sex or another. And if I were to have another girl, I am afraid to think what Moonesar would do. And on top of that, since the birth of Leela, I have not been able to get pregnant again. Moonesar has already brought that up. He said, 'It's bad enough to have girl after girl, but now no babies at all.'"

Auraat stopped suddenly and looked at her friend.

"He said that maybe I was bewitched. And maybe I am. All women can have babies, so why can't I? Do you think I am bewitched, Radna?"

The other woman had combed and tied her hair and now moved over to comb that of her friend who had been so occupied telling what had happened that she hadn't taken the time. Radna said, "Oh, no, dear, I don't think you are bewitched. Many women have girls instead of boys, but it's always the same. The husband and relatives get angry. You are lucky you don't have your mother-in-law in the house. She would really give you trouble."

"I know, I know. Fortunately, the mother-in-law is staying with Moonesar's older brother."

The image of the *churail*, the witch with feet on backward, she who had died in childbirth and who was committed through eternity to preventing other women from having happy births, stuck vividly in her mind.

The two women stood up and let the evening breeze help dry their damp clothes.

"And my little Leela is sick with the fever, and Moonesar has not yet got her any medicine. My little pumpkin," she murmured. "I know if she was a boy, he would have got it already."

That night, after serving Moonesar and taking some herbal tea to Leela, Auraat came back to the kitchen to eat some of the leftovers with Larki. Moonesar had not eaten all the chapattis and some of the spiced potatoes were also left. She squatted down by her daughter and began eating by tearing pieces from the chapatti with her right hand and picking up pieces of potato with them, keeping her left hand away from the food as she had been trained. She also had a little hot pickle which she put in her mouth between bites of potato and chapatti. The hot oiliness was one of her favorite eating sensations.

"After you are finished eating," she told Larki, "I want you to clean up the dishes."

"But Mama, I haven't finished my schoolwork yet."

At this, Auraat lost her patience. "I told you before that things in the household come before schoolwork. You must know by now that no one needs educated girls, that in fact many families are reluctant to let their boys be married to educated girls or at least they demand more dowry. And your main responsibility now is to get ready for marriage. Do you think anyone wants a wife who cannot cook and keep a clean kitchen?"

"No, Mama, I didn't mean anything. I'll finish cleaning up, but then can I do a little homework?"

"I don't mind that, but you know we have only one lamp and I'll need it for a little while. Fortunately, your father has gone out to the village center where there is light and he won't need it."

The village had got electricity a few years before, and all the people who could afford it got one or two light bulbs; but more important, a light had been installed on a post in the center of the village, just next to the government office where the TV set was located. So most nights men would watch the set or play cards under the lamp outside. There was even a separate section in the TV room for women, a sort of purdah section, though without the curtain. Most nights Moonesar went to the TV room or outside to play cards. The Misras had not been able to afford a light when the village had been electrified, so they still made do with a kerosene lamp.

Auraat got the lamp from the other room to use to go over to Radna's house. She went in the back to get to the kitchen where she knew the women would be. Radna's family had electricity in the kitchen, so the women generally stayed there after the meal, doing chores and talking. Radna's little son and daughter were with her. Auraat looked at her with envy, knowing then why the *churail* wished evil on those who had children. But she felt badly for having such a thought when her friend motioned her to come squat next to her.

"Have you eaten, little friend?"

"Yes, dear Radna. Moonesar has been fed and has gone out to join the men, and Larki is cleaning up so she can get on to finish her homework. She is a strange girl; she enjoys her studies like a boy. You would think she was going to be earning the living for the family."

"Girls are different nowadays. They expect more than we did. It's not enough for them to take care of the family. Many want the same things that boys do. Sometimes I think it is because of the television. They see those shows from America where women are supposed to have equal rights. And it gives them ideas." She was methodically pushing food into the mouth of her three-year-old boy who was obviously already well fed.

Auraat would have liked some of the *puri*, the deep fried unleavened bread, but controlled herself. A good housewife was supposed to have enough from her own larder. Anyway, she was here on another mission. Radna gave her the boy to hold and got up for a little packet of dried leaves. Radna's girl and her sister-in-law watched but made no comment.

"Give the little no-good to his auntie and come outside, dear friend," Radna said.

In order not to stir up the envy of the spirit and human evil-doers, it was the practice to refer to children with derogatory names, especially boys. The two women went outside and stood in the light of the doorway, but far enough away that their words could not be understood.

"Now this has to be given no more than an hour before he goes to bed. It's probably best to give it to him as a tea. Does he take tea before he goes to bed at night?"

"Not usually, but he often does take a glass of water. But perhaps I could tell him it was a medicine for making boy babies. Do you think he would believe that?"

"I don't know, but there are medicines for so many purposes. He might. You have to figure out something to get him to take it. And then he won't be able to resist coming to your bed. How long did you say it has been?"

Auraat hung her head. "It's three weeks now and if he doesn't come soon, we'll never have another child. And then we can't possibly have a boy." Then she added, "He did bring some medicines tonight for Leela."

Putting her arm around her friend's shoulders, Radna said, "I think it's a good night. Things might get much better soon. And remember after he takes it, you go to your bed and get ready. Men can't resist coming to women after taking that potion. Women have been using it for centuries.

Joe

He sat at the dining table spreading butter and marmalade on his toast. This was a custom he had picked up during his student days in Stuttgart. A man in his late thirties, he was dressed in western style pants but wore a loose Indian shirt, a *kurta*. The baby sat in a high chair taking pablum from Mahadevi, a svelte woman in her early thirties, dressed in a sari, her hair pulled back and wrapped in a traditional bun. She had a red stripe down the part of her sleek black hair, the traditional mark of a married woman. She gave the impression of efficiency as she alternately spooned the baby food into the infant's mouth and then wiped it with a cloth. The nanny stood by, assisting occasionally. Her job was to take care of the baby while the two adults were gone during the day, though she also helped to get them off each morning. As soon as they were gone, she could eat her fill and then tend to the baby. Despite being well-off, the Majumdars had no relatives in the house since theirs was a mixed marriage. Joe was a Christian and Mahadevi a Hindu. The wedding had taken place in the Anglican Church, and all the guests had been from Joe's side. No dowry had been given. Her relatives had not spoken to her since the wedding. She still considered herself a Hindu and went to the local temple frequently, as well as participating in the annual rituals. Joe went to church much less often, having lost interest in religion during his student days.

"What is your schedule today, Joe?" Mahadevi asked him. "Will you be out doing sterilizations again?"

"I've got three villages, and hopefully that will bring us up to our quota—that is, if the village-level workers have been doing their job."

"Does it depend so much on them?"

"Well, you know that it's not easy to convince illiterate villagers to let you cut down on their child producing capacity. They have been bombarded with audio-visual programs and speeches by local officials for years, but so far as I can see, it has had little effect. It's their superstitions."

"What do you mean superstitions?"

"You know, irrational, non-scientific ideas."

"Like what?"

"Ah, you know what I mean, like beliefs in evil spirits and ideas that you can get pregnant by propitiating gods or saints. They say the Hindus and Muslims up by Farrukpur go to the tomb of Hasan Baba for help in getting pregnant. And just recently I heard that a big rounded rock up north was being prayed to by Hindu women. They claim that the rock is growing, though we all know that rocks get placed by geologic action and not through internal movement."

"I think you are being too hard on them, Joe," Mahadevi said. "After all, they are just village people, not college professors. And besides, Christians can pray to Jesus or Mary, can't they?"

"I'm sure there are Christians who do believe in such things. But in the modern scientific world I don't see how an educated person can. But you should hear what these people say to one another when they come into the clinics. You'd be amazed. And they won't come in alone. Fortunately it's an operation which doesn't require complete antisepsis."

Mahadevi called the nanny to take charge of the baby, then poured another cup of tea for Joe and one for herself. A light smile flickered on her face.

"What the Family Planning Bureau needs is some kind of spirit that would keep women from getting pregnant."

"You make fun, but you know as well as I that this country is in serious trouble." Joe sounded a little exasperated. "A population of seven hundred million, and that is without Pakistan and Bangladesh. When I first started college, they counted all of India as having four hundred million.

"Now, Joe, don't start getting excited. You're doing your part. What else can be expected? And after all, despite the gloomy predictions of the economists, we are still feeding our people."

Dr. Majumdar got up and got his carrying bag from the inner room.

"Devi, you are always too understanding. Perhaps it's from those talk shows you are always hosting. You never want to antagonize people."

Mahadevi was a program organizer and host on All India Radio. Joe would drop her off at work, then he would head out to the village clinic.

"Well, it's true, they frown on oppositional interviewing at the station," she said. "But what good does it do anyway?" She put her papers into her briefcase. "Is the car working all right now?"

Joe received a mileage allowance for his travel to the village. Though it wasn't enough to pay for the travel, it did permit him to operate his own car, which seemed the absolute minimum for a man with a foreign degree. Everyone in Germany had a car, and it seemed to him that at least the professionals in India ought to be able to have them. He had an older Graham which always needed repairs.

"Yes," he said. "I had it fixed yesterday while I went to city clinics. It is going to need an engine overhaul soon, though."

Joe was paid by the number of sterilizations he did, and so could not afford to cut down on the number of clinics he visited. He usually managed three or four a day, and he let it be known that he expected the men to be waiting when he got there.

Mahadevi gave the baby a hug and then handed him over to the nanny.

"How's he doing on the formula?" Joe asked.

"He seems to be okay, and I'm starting him on solids now, so there shouldn't be any problems in the future. And if there is, I'll see Dr. Narayan.

They got in the small car and made their way into the street, Joe's hand hitting the horn almost immediately to scare back a group of water buffalo that a driver was taking down the street toward the river bank. From then on he was almost constantly on the horn, the mechanized dominant over the animate.

Without paying any attention to the continuous close calls that Joe maneuvered through, Mahadevi said, "When do you expect to be finished tonight?"

"Late, I suspect. We're having a staff meeting at four and I'll have to be there. It's about the progress of the program, and whether we should try something else."

"What about the women? I never hear you talking about them. I mean, they're involving in this too. To listen to you, one would think that only the men count."

Joe knew that Mahadevi had always been interested in women's rights, although it seemed to be getting worse lately. He felt it was inevitable that women would become concerned with the female cause when they got educated, and that had seemed to be a desirable mark of modernity at first. But lately the idea had not seemed so wonderful, especially in the kitchen and the bed.

"That's only because there has been more emphasis on it lately and because that is what I do. The operation for females has more complications and they like to keep them overnight. They go to separate clinics."

Joe kept to his driving, making a wedge through the mass of people, animals, and occasional vehicles without any letup.

"Incidentally, Joe," Mahadevi said, "what do you think about one of us getting sterilized? After all, we have our baby now and he seems to be quite healthy." She smiled lightly. "And he's even a boy, to make the Hindus happy."

He knew that both Hindus and Muslims emphasized boys, as well as almost all the agricultural peoples of the world. Only the people of the advanced nations welcomed both girls and boys equally, claiming that was one cause for their advancement.

Mahadevi continued, "You know that China has a one-baby limit. We probably need it here, too, but it seems that there's no way we'll ever be able to get our village people to follow such a rule. The only way you can get them to do something new is to make it a caste rule. But anyway, what about us? You know, I'd still like to go to England or America to get my Ph.D. in communication."

She had her Masters in English from Barnow University, but had got the idea of getting her Ph.D. quite a while before, shortly after she had started radio work. Joe was lukewarm about the idea. After all, it did entail a lot of disruption of their family life.

"You know," he said, "I don't mind. But there are a lot of problems with it, even apart from the cost. I mean what will you do with the baby?"

"Of course it's a time like this when I wish the family hadn't broken off. Then there would be no problem, my sister or mother would take care of him. Of course that's only because your parents are Christians. I presume your mother wouldn't want the baby."

Joe bristled. "I resent that. Christians like children also." Of course, he knew that she meant that since Christian families tended to separate when the children married, they didn't take over children so easily as traditional Hindu or Muslim families. He continued, "But she's not so well, you know. And I don't think I would suggest it."

He turned the corner and barely avoided hitting a bicyclist. "Some of these people don't take any precautions," he said in a raised voice. But he quickly came back to the problem at hand. "Don't you think your parents are about ready to bury the hatchet?"

"Oh, no, I don't expect them to ever to that. After all, we are Brahmins, so it was a real blow to their caste status for me to marry a Christian."

Joe had no trouble remembering that he had started talking to her but she certainly had made no effort to cut it off. And it wasn't that she was a completely traditional girl when he met her. She was already going to the coffee shop with other girls. But still, he knew that her family was traditional even if well-to-do, but this hadn't stopped him. However, in discussions like this one, he still felt guilty. Her family would have arranged a good marriage within the caste with a well-educated boy. Even the dowry would have been reasonable.

They had reached the radio building and Joe parked in the lot. "Do you have an appointment right away?"

"No, but it's time for me to get started. I have that script on 'The Green Revolution' to get finished. They will start shooting next week. But what about you? Won't you be late?"

"I've got a little time," he lied. He was sure his orderly, whom he had to pick up on the way, would be waiting, as would the men at the clinic. But he felt his time was more important, and he was particularly concerned about this issue. "I hate to talk about it, but what if we lost our child? You know that if the woman is sterilized, there's no way to make her fertile again, and even for the men there's no more than a fifty-fifty chance that the tubes can be reattached."

"I have thought about that also, but I believe little Varma will be all right. We have the best pediatrician around and you are a doctor, so the best medical attention is available. I don't worry about that. And you know I've always wanted to have a foreign degree. So I guess it's my responsibility to not have any more babies." She reached for the door. "I must really be going though so why don't we think about this today and we can talk more about it tonight."

Joe knew that she felt embarrassed about showing her feelings in public, that although people of the same sex could hold hands, people of the opposite sex could not, but still he always thought she could at least touch him with her hand when they parted. He didn't expect a western kiss, but at least a touch. But she did not, and before he knew it, he was on his way, first to pick up Ahmed, his medical assistant, then on through the pulsing streets, across the bridge, and into the country. While maneuvering through traffic, he kept his eye on the rising heat gauge, irritated that he had to drive this old car with all its problems.

Joe parked the Graham under a neem tree which had not yet been denuded by villagers, and walked to the one story brick building which served as the medical clinic, one side for outpatients, the other for more extensive treatment. No one was on duty at the outpatient side. The nurse and drug orderly came there only once a week to serve the line of people from several nearby villages. On the surgery side the door was ajar and just inside the village-level worker sat at the desk, working on a report. Two older men squatted in front of the building.

When Joe entered the room the village worker got up, holding his report. There was only one desk in the room, but it was understood to be for the doctor when he was there. Joe put his bag on the desk.

"Now, Mr. Vaidya, where are the patients? I hope you're not going to tell me that those two old fellows out in front are all we've got."

Vaidya, who had quickly moved to the front of the desk as Joe sat down, said, "We're supposed to have one more, but he hasn't come yet. I'm still hoping that he won't cancel."

Joe was not able to control himself completely. "Now I'm just not happy with another couple of old fellows. I'm sure you know what the goal of this program is, to limit births. And every time I come, you've got one or two old men for the operation, and what good is that? Those old fellows are not going to have any more children anyway. No wonder you can convince them to come in. They get the fee for nothing."

Vaidya looked properly contrite. "Well, you know, Dr. Majumdar, it's not easy to convince these people to be sterilized. They have all kinds of crazy ideas about it. Some of them think they will have trouble urinating. Others think you're gong to castrate them. Of course that makes sense to them since that's what they do to the farm animals. But the real reason is that they worry that they will lose their living children and will have no one to take care of them when they get old."

"That's all true, Vaidya, but you know that I have heard all those things before. So what about the cash incentive? Doesn't the fact that they'll receive twenty dollars help change their minds? I mean that's what it was planned for. Are you telling me the cash incentive doesn't make any difference?"

All of a sudden Joe felt a weariness. It seemed that the villagers were totally uncooperative, and when you added that to the laziness of the village workers, the situation seemed impossible. He sat down abruptly and opened his drawer for a cigarette. He was trying to cut down on his smoking, but there were times when it got him through a difficult situation.

"Dr. Majumdar, I—"

Joe cut him off. "That's enough, Vaidya. You just get out and see about the man who was coming." He turned to his assistant. "And you, Ahmed, get the room ready for surgery."

As Vaidya walked out, Joe gave a parting shot. "And if you have no luck with him, just talk someone else into coming. Remember, our position depends on the number of people we get to come in."

~

Q: *The meaning of this chapter is pretty apparent. This one is about population control, right?*

A: Yes, something I and quite a few social scientists, demographers, geographers, and others think is one of the most serious problems humankind now faces. The other serious problem is environmental degradation, although the two are closely interrelated. Environmental degradation or pollution can very easily be looked at as a problem of numbers. It is fashionable nowadays to claim that pollution is a result of bad values, particularly the Judaeo-Christian idea that nature exists exclusively for human benefit and that it is okay to exploit nature. Many westerners seem to believe that tribal peoples lived in total harmony with nature and refrained from exploiting or polluting the environment, that their supernatural beliefs prevented it. It can just as easily be argued that the technology of the tribals did not enable them to do it easily; and even if their technology had been like that of industrial man, there were only about one fiftieth as many people in North America. And if we now had one fiftieth as many people, factories, and cars in the U.S., what kind of pollution problem would we have? I suspect the air of Los Angeles would be clear as a bell. But the day of the tribals is past, and we now have to face the pollution of industrial man, who is of course more numerous.

Q: *So are you saying that this problem has only become serious since man went through the industrial revolution? That population increase is only recent?*

A: Yes, Though population increase among humans is nothing new, it is only since the nineteenth century that it has become very serious. Earlier we had a good margin for error, but that has diminished greatly. If we are not careful, we might breed ourselves out of existence and destroy much of the earth in the process.

Q: *I have two questions about all this. The first one is, don't the other species have this problem? And the second one is, what is the history of population increase, from the earliest times to the industrial and scientific revolutions?*

A: So far as I know, no other species has been as successful as ours. The only one I can think of are the dinosaurs, who became very numerous, but then died out completely. However, overpopulation is not one of the theories of why they died out. The latest widely-accepted explanation is that the climate changed.

Though there have been various animals who have done very well, their numbers have been invariably kept down by predators or by competing with one another for scarce resources. Thus some rodents, like lemmings, have the ability to increase their numbers greatly one year to the next, but it seems when they reach a certain density they take off on destructive migrations which bring their numbers down again. Others, such as rats, may get into heavy competition within the species and start killing one another or failing to reproduce.

In fact, though many people think the theory of natural selection is based on aggressive superiority of animal species, the real cause for success as a species which Mr. Darwin advanced was reproductive success. Animals which reproduce more than their competitors became the inheritors of life. So small or even minute creatures may be more efficient at reproduction than the big, aggressive animals. Thus, ants and fleas have no survival problems as species, while lions and tigers are in deep trouble.

The exception to the rule is *Homo sapiens*. As a species he has steadily increased his numbers until he has filled almost all the land areas on earth and much of the water and air, and his numbers have increased enormously. Man has been able to vanquish the big predators (lions and wolves) and hold the small ones at bay (bacteria and rats). In a sense, pardon the pun, he has made a monkey out of Darwin by proving that reproductive success could be a negative characteristic.

Q: *Wow, and I thought you were in favor of Darwinism.*

A: Oh, I am. As I have said earlier, I believe his theory was the most significant idea of the nineteenth century. But Darwin was too much of a scientist to have taken offense at a modification of his concept. And I have a feeling he might well agree with this modification if he were still around.

Q: *So the other animals still survive as a species by means of reproductive success, while for man this is a negative characteristic. Then to the second question—how did this happen through time? When did all this growth of population take place? Surely it hasn't all been since the industrial revolution.*

A: No, there have been several stages. I will not try to provide numbers, which are by no means rock solid anyway, but I will offer a theory of what the stages were and what caused the increase. And just to give an idea of the enormity of the increase, I will give round numbers for the beginning and end. It has been estimated that in the hunting and gathering period as represented in chapters one and two, there was a total of one million people on earth, and at the end of our story, say 2000 A.D., there will be more than five billion. That is a five thousand-fold increase.

Q: *That is indeed impressive. So how did this happen? What were the stages?*

A: It seems that the main cause was improvements in technology. Whenever mankind invented something which made him more efficient in solving some human problem, he produced more, particularly food, and increased his numbers to gobble it up.

In the nineteenth century, we believed that progress was the inevitable consequence of civilization, and that there would be ever more material comfort and control of nature. We also thought that political systems were getting better and better. Now we are not so sure of all this, and rightly so. It is true that there were steady improvements in technology, but that these made the pleasures of life greater is hard to prove. This is one important lesson I learned from anthropology and its study of primitives. In our earlier years we were taught that the life of the tribal, whether a gatherer or a cultivator, was hard and unpleasant, an idea described graphically by the philosopher, Thomas Hobbes. But once we got to look at the way of life of tribals, this was not at all evident. There was a lot of companionship, ritual, entertainment, leisure, and usually enough nutritious food for tribal man. That he had fewer mechanical gadgets and a shorter life span was of no consequence. Man didn't miss what he didn't know about and accepted the existing life span as normal. Even the highly-touted freedoms of modern democracy would hardly have made things better. Further, the tribal did not have to pay income tax for the multitudinous contradictory and ill-planned projects of elected officials; he was not subject to conscription for wars he knew nothing about, and went to fight skirmishes only when he felt like it; he did not have to worry about the rat race or keeping up with the Joneses in gadgetry; and he had more freedom and leisure than anyone since. So what advantage would there be in being able to vote for one of two inept or crooked politicians? No, I'm afraid despite all we've been told, the progress of culture has entailed a loss of life quality.

Q: *You're really coming down hard on modern society. If it's so bad, why has man done it?*

A: It is true that man has chosen to go the technological way time after time. When the idea of the domestication of animals came along, or the idea of living in the city with zillions of others, or using steam power for making things, the given cultures have chosen almost invariably to do it, even though the consequences very often have been negative, if not terrible. The hunters and gatherers undoubtedly had food of better quality than that of the domesticators, and the conditions of living were just terrible for the majority during the early part of the industrial revolution. It seems that men couldn't resist a better mouse trap. And there were almost always seemingly clear-cut advantages in production. Men who had been cultivating with a digging stick were inevitably attracted to a plow pulled by an animal. And men who had been gathering wild products were almost always attracted to domesticated plants. The pygmies of Central Africa had a varied and sufficient diet of wild products, but when they learned about planted bananas, they had to have some. Civilized men have been no different. Everywhere in the world men have chosen industrial manufacture over hand production. The modernist would probably say that those were all rational choices, they did help in the greater production of those goods. And that is true, though no one has yet proved that more is better for life satisfaction. And there are always so many unexpected consequences. So the plow facilitated larger landholdings and ultimately the displacement of farmers, while those who came to the new industrial cities were forced to live in some of the worst conditions in history, while the diet of the pygmy deteriorated even while he was being displaced by the banana cultivators.

But no matter what it does to the quality of life, it seems inevitable that men will take over more efficient technologies, and those societies that do not take them over fast enough are eliminated by those that do.

Q: *But what has this got to do with population increase?*

A: Each time men invented new methods for production, there were more goods for less labor per unit. And each time, the producers had more children who survived and ultimately eliminated the advantage of the surplus production. So numbers increased, but leisure and life satisfaction for the majority did not, so that now at the end of the twentieth century we have the most advanced technology of any people before, and at the same time we have starvation on a scale which probably has never been greater. Oh yes, we have some countries which did well, but in Asia, Africa, and Latin America there are millions of hungry people. More goods, including food, are being produced in these places, but there are also many more mouths.

Q: *So what have these technological events been that produced the increasing population?*

A: I tried to think of the major events of history and came up with the following, though there may well be more.

1. The revolution of tool making. This was not a biggie, because man was still a hunter-gatherer, but it must have at least enabled man to start displacing his relatives, the apes, and he must have started keeping more of his children.

2. The domestication of plants and animals. There was more food available and children could even be used for farm work. We get some direct evidence for the increase in this stage from archeology. The first fixed settlements where more people lived have been found.

3. The urban revolution, when large numbers of people lived in cities and in which there is clear-cut evidence that many more goods, including food, were available. This is the first stage of culture in which production is stored and controlled by the ruling class.

4. The discovery and spread of the plants of the New World. The increases in food supply in both the tropics and temperate zones enabled much larger populations to exist.

5. The industrial revolution. The new method of factory production permitted much larger populations in the cities, even if the goods were very unevenly distributed.

6. The scientific revolution. New knowledge in medical practices and agriculture permitted great increases in food and survival rates. There was more to eat and people didn't die so early.

Q: *So you are saying that each of these advancements in technology brought a great increase in population which largely negated the advantage?*

344

A: Yes. If man the domesticator had remained at the same population level as man the gatherer, he would have had an enormous increase in food and other goods. And if some of the consequences of the scientific revolution had not been spread throughout the world, people in the traditional societies would have stayed at their earlier population level and the extensive under-nourishment we now see in Africa, Latin America, Asia, and some other places wouldn't be so apparent.

Q: *You seem to be blaming it all on the increase in family size rather than the deficiency in production or distribution. World leaders usually seem to blame the poverty of their countries on the lack of modern methods of agriculture and other production, or else it is claimed the goods are not distributed evenly.*

A: Yes, that is true, because limiting family size is not usually a good political ploy. Most peoples want to exert their own controls on the number of children they will have and keep, while the same people expect outside help for more food and other goods. There are some differences between cultures, but overall, people expect to be free in their family business. And surely there are distribution and production problems, but in each instance if the family size had not increased when some new technology was introduced, there would be more than enough to go around.

Q: *So it seems that in order to stop this perpetual increase, it is necessary that each man cut down the size of his family. Is that such a new idea?*

A: No, not at all. Birth control is as old as life itself. Remember that according to the theory of evolution, all species produce more young than are needed for replacement. The surplus is eliminated by predation and competition within and without the species. Some simpler types of animals, like insects, fish, and reptiles have enormous numbers of excess births. They have a built-in capacity to lose great numbers and still manage to succeed as species. Fish lose the great majority of their eggs and hatchlings. You have probably seen film of the large number of baby sea turtles that are lost to carnivorous birds before they get to the protection of the water. Still the sea turtles managed, at least until man got into the act on a mass scale, pilfering turtle eggs as well as killing off adults. But all this decrease by animals was not due to any interest in population control. As with all kinds of behavioral changes as described by the evolutionists, the controls went into effect automatically.

Q: *So what about man? Surely he does not have this capacity to lose such a high proportion of young.*

A: True, but he could lose some young and still replace or increase the numbers slowly. But of course the other option is not to have the excess young in the first place. There are even processes among the other animals in which births are limited automatically when conditions become unfavorable. Thus when rodents get overcrowded, they often lose their sexual urge or fail to get pregnant.

Q: *But what about deliberate efforts not to have young? Has this been widespread?*

A: Yes, in one way—infanticide. Quite a few animals will deliberately kill some of their young. Some fish do. I raise koi, which is a species of carp, and the adults eat both their eggs and baby fish. And lest you get the idea that this is a completely destructive act, I must assure you that the carp is a very successful species. Among mammals, in a number of species the male will kill the young. Male housecats will kill baby kittens if they get a chance. So will lions and even some species of primates, man's closest relatives.

Q: *And although in many cultures it is against the law, I know that people also sometimes practice infanticide. There would of course be no law against the practice if it didn't happen. Would you say it is universal to all societies?*

A: Perhaps not all, but certainly the vast majority. This is our direct animal inheritance, which will probably never be eliminated. But of course man being the tinkerer he is, he doesn't stop here, as do the other animals. He tinkers with the body to help with this problem, and this cannot be considered to have come from the animal inheritance. Rather, abortion and all the other methods to prevent births are products of man's complex learning and his culture.

Q: *I take it this is widespread also. But the most basic method to avoid births you haven't mentioned, the one recommended by the anti-abortionists and others—abstinence from sex. Doesn't man refrain from sex to avoid having children?*

A: Yes, but not very much. Special sects of religious devotees refrain, and in the normal population of all societies there are taboos and prohibitions. In many patriarchal societies girls are supposed to be virgins until they get married, and there are certain practices which cut down on pregnancies, though they rarely eliminate them. Many tribal societies had a practice of prohibiting sex during pregnancies or when the mother was nursing, and these made pregnancy less likely, though this didn't eliminate it totally. But in all societies I have heard of, people had sex more often than was necessary for producing the desirable number of children. And you know why as well as I do—because the sex act gives the participants pleasure. As with the other animals, people usually have sex for fun, even in those societies which claim that the exclusive function of sex is to have babies. So in almost all societies there are more children born than are wanted. And quite a number of ways have been figured out and passed down on how to avoid the excess, infanticide and abortion being two basic ones.

Q: *What about the rest of the methods, the ones which are put into action before impregnation?*

A: There are quite a few recorded through history although of course the majority have been devised only recently, because the knowledge base and mechanical sophistication of mankind became much higher since the scientific revolution. I think of them as being of three kinds: mechanical, chemical, and biological. Undoubtedly the most widely used mechanical device to prevent impregnation has been the condom, which was reported as early as the 1600s in Europe, and has had a new lease on life in the twentieth century to help prevent venereal diseases. Before that, the only methods I know about are infanticide and abortion, practiced by the Greeks, Romans, other early historical peoples, and tribals. A more recent mechanical device has been the IUD, also used to keep the sperm from reaching the egg. Another kind of mechanical obstacle to conception is surgery, which became significant during the period of the domestication of animals, ten thousand years ago. Although it is a very primitive sort of surgery, castration, or removal of the testicles of the male, was quite effective in preventing births in animals and men. In more recent times when surgery became one of the mainstays of medicine, we got sterilization of both males and females, in which the child-producing elements were removed. This has become quite significant, since it does not prevent satisfactory copulation, but absolutely prevents conception. It is, of course, the main method discussed in this chapter's narrative.

The chemical category may have existed before in the form of plant spermicides. At least I have heard of quite a number, particularly among tribals, although I have not heard of any which were proved effective. However, when we get to modern times, we find many chemical devices to prevent pregnancy. Undoubtedly the most significant has been the "Pill," the hormone extract taken orally by females to prevent impregnation of the egg. There have been others of less importance.

Q: *And what has been the most significant in the biological category?*

A: Actually, there have been far fewer effective biological methods. The one that has been used most widely, though not with great success, has been the rhythm method. You will remember it from the narrative?

Q: *Oh, yes, the one in which the woman failed to count her beads correctly. I don't hear of it so often nowadays. Has it been replaced?*

A: Yes. It was based on a technique to figure out when the woman was fertile so she would avoid having intercourse during that time. But it was never really effective, as I can personally testify. The Roman Church approved it by deeming it a "natural" method, whatever that means. But it was so ineffective that a large proportion of Catholics used other more effective methods, notably the Pill. And I don't really know of any other truly biological method to avoid conception.

Q: *It seems then that there are plenty of ways to cut down on births. I wonder why there have not been more consequences.*

A: There have been in the urbanized, industrial societies, because the population in these is more highly educated, and thus the individuals know more about the methods. It also seems there is an automatic decrease in interest in children with advanced urbanization. The rural society is the one where large numbers of children are wanted. Thus the countries of the third world are the leading child factories. In urbanized cultures like those of Europe, Japan, and the U.S., people are more interested in other things besides families. In fact, some in Europe have even come to a non-replacement rate. Generally, though, urbanized married couples want two children. But the "as many as possible" rate of third world rural countries is long gone.

Q: *One thing that you haven't really talked about, though you treat it as if it takes place automatically, is the increase.*

A: As I mentioned, people, like all other animals, will normally have more children than they need to replace the population. So all they have to do to increase is to stop using birth controls, and the increase will automatically take place. As a matter of fact, we have a society, fortunately small, which does do this in modern America. The Amish, a dissident Protestant sect, prohibits many modern practices, including the use of contraceptives. And since they lose as few children as other Americans, their families can become large indeed. The average number of children in an Amish family is twelve, which is therefore assumed to be the normal number for any well-provisioned women with good medical resources who do not use birth control.

Q: *Then why is it that the Amish have not increased all over the place, replacing other Americans who have only two to three children per family? The Amish are a relatively small sect, aren't they?*

A: Yes. But they keep losing children to the outside world. Many young people cannot take the strictures of Amish life and go into the great outside. In each generation a sizeable proportion of those twelve per family is lost. The Amish keep enough to replace themselves, but not to grow. But we have learned through their practices that if contraceptives are not used, the average family will have twelve children. But of course in most of the other families of the world, there are far fewer who grow to adulthood. It is thought that the average family in India, Pakistan, and Bangladesh, which certainly have increasing populations, has approximately five children. But of course fewer of them survive into adulthood.

Q: *All of this gives a pretty good sketch of what happened through history except for one last matter. What about government programs in general? When did thinkers and government leaders become aware of the population growth problem?*

A: Anyone who thought about it at all considered the growth of population desirable until the eighteenth and especially the nineteenth centuries. Until the nineteenth century there was always room for expansion. Until the discovery of the New World there was only a little problem in the centers of civilization, but then the Europeans began expanding into the territory of the tribals who died off at a great rate, leaving much new territory to be taken over. Following this was the age of colonization when European powers exploited the remaining territories. But by the nineteenth century, all the habitable areas were taken over, and for reasons connected to European influence, the native populations began to grow at a great rate. And thinkers began to worry about the world population. The most significant of these was a man named Malthus who wrote an essay called *Essay on the Principle of Population* which claimed that human populations invariably rose faster than the food supply and that their numbers were kept down by famine, disease, and war. As I have indicated, these factors haven't kept populations down overall, since populations have always increased when technological innovations, particularly those concerned with food and health, occurred, but I will agree that the increases have contributed greatly to famine, disease, and war, and still do.

Q: *Okay, so much for the thinkers, but what about the government leaders?*

A: Governments invariably operate on a basis of nationalism, the concept that policy should primarily be what is good for the nation. Other peoples' interests are not equally considered, much less thinking about population on a global scale. So up to the nineteenth century, the official policy of all nations was to have more citizens. Then it was recognized that resources were limited and that some nations might do better with fewer or at least no more citizens. But since an automatic slow-down in numbers was going on in the industrial countries, no population control was needed, with one exception, Japan.

The Japanese began industrializing and urbanizing in the middle of the nineteenth century, and for a long time they were content to expand their population. But after World War II they came to the realization that they didn't have much territory for the number of Japanese there were. They instituted a government program of medical abortions and practically stopped the increase. But soon, so much of Japan was industrialized and urbanized that the automatic decrease went into effect and a government program was no longer necessary.

The other two nations that became very concerned about the increase of their population were China and India. These countries were still based on a rural lifestyle and there was little automatic decrease in the villages. China instituted a "one child-one family" policy and put much government effort and expenses into it, offering both carrots and sticks. If one cooperated fully, one could receive many benefits, especially financial. If a family failed to cooperate and exceeded the one child limit, there would be punishments, including social harassment and transfer of spouses to distant locations. And, as is usual whenever a new program is introduced into a society, there were unexpected conflicts. Perhaps the major one in China has been the fact that old people would traditionally be taken care of by the son. But since births are evenly divided between male and female, if the first (and only) child was a girl there would be no one to take care of the parents in their old age. Sons were more highly prized than daughters for some other reasons, but the old age problem seemed to be the primary objection to daughters if only one birth was allowed. Thus, it has been reported that if the firstborn was a girl, she might be killed at birth. But with the western attitudes of sacredness of life dominating international circles, this is hardly admitted officially. And there were other strategies to get around the one-child rule, particularly if it was a girl. One of the latest international ploys is for the married couple to seek sanctuary in the U.S. as political refugees, claiming they have been tortured or harassed for breaking the one-child rule. And being ethnocentrists, Americans naturally apply their own values to other cultures. Though the one-child policy has reduced the increase rate, it has not induced all parents to have only one child, even those who have stayed in China.

Q: *That leaves us with India. What kind of program did they have, and how successful has it been?*

A: I should inform you here that I have been particularly interested in the Indian case because I did my original field work there in the early 1950s and have tried to keep abreast of events in that country.

First, India is mostly a rural country, and the population increase has been high ever since colonial times. It seems that a few simple health improvements were introduced, probably the most important being cleaner water, vaccinations, and antibiotics. Also, some new agricultural techniques and some industries have been brought to the country, making more food and goods available. So though the child mortality rate is high, it is less than it was before. But a process called cultural lag has been in effect, which is that when conditions change, a given society usually continues its old practices for a while. All creatures are reluctant to change, a phenomenon which we call behavioral inertia. So Indians have more or less continued to produce the same number of children as before, even though more are surviving to adulthood. It has actually been calculated by social scientists that the average number of children desired by an "average" rural family was pretty accurate for what was needed—five. Indians, like most agrarian peoples, are male oriented and need sons to take care of them in old age. So if under old conditions five children would be born, half would be girls, leaving 2.5 boys, statistically speaking. And if half were lost through childhood illnesses, there would only be 1.25 remaining. But when conditions improved in the last two hundred years, the average family ended up with, say, two boys and two girls remaining, which is quite a hefty increase rate, especially for a country with an already large population. So India also became concerned after World War II and started many birth control programs.

Q: *I see. And obviously you have been describing one of these in the narrative. How effective have they been?*

A: Not very. India has a very complex and deeply-entrenched traditional society, and short of having a revolution resulting in an authoritarian government, it is hard for them to counterbalance the inertia of tradition. And India at independence opted for a "democratic" government, though there have undoubtedly been many counter forces to the free choice of individuals. I think that the greater, though far from complete, success of the Chinese is due to the fact that their government is much more authoritarian.

Q: *I noticed in the narrative that the authorities in India relied on carrots more than sticks to get compliance. Is that a cause of their relative lack of success?*

A: Partially, I think, though there were other reasons. Obviously, the financial reward for letting oneself be sterilized was a carrot. But of course, they got around it to a considerable extent by having their older men be operated on, men who had finished fathering children. The interests of high government officials are usually quite different from those of the standard citizenry. And when it comes to family matters, the average villager will be far more likely to follow traditional values than those promulgated by government officials. Population control is an idea that exists among demographers, economists, and other social science types, but having children for one's old age is the primary concern of the villager. So if the rewards and/or punishments are not large enough, the villager is unlikely to change.

Q: *Now that you have sketched out the big picture, a lot of things that occurred in the narrative are clear. But there are still a few questions. One which is of interest to all of us women is, why is there such a great emphasis on boys in this kind of society?*

A: As I mentioned in an earlier chapter, the emphasis on one sex or another is closely correlated to the significance of the sex in the production of goods. Societies where the male is the most important producer will tend to be more male focused. In the agrarian society, the male is the cultivator, so he gets the prestige. The same is true of the herding society, because the male tends the animals, the true source of wealth.

Q: *But the woman is the producer of children, the most prized possession, no?*

A: Yes, but women bear the children in all types of societies, and balanced against that fact is the fact that the male is the strongest. So in social points the woman loses in the agrarian society. She only gets lifted closer to equality when physical strength is no longer important and she produces food and goods on a comparable scale with the male, as in an industrial society. Whatever else happens, the woman does

352

not make many points for bearing and rearing children, even in societies where children are highly desired.

Q: *So that must be why the Indian villagers were less concerned about the health and education of their girls.*

A: I am sure it was. In male-focused societies girls are invariably second best, and their chief responsibility is to produce more boy babies. And of course the girls were taught this so intensely in their early years that they acted it out when they were adults. We in the West are very fond of claiming that each person has a right to make up his own mind, but in fact, we are all brainwashed so early that we are scarcely aware of it. So the village wife in India thinks of herself as a boy producer, while the middle class wife in the American suburbs thinks of herself as having the right to choose what she wants.

Q: *That's interesting, particularly in reference to the wife of the doctor in India. She even thought of leaving her child behind while she went off to get a higher education. She had values like many American wives, didn't she?*

A: Yes, to a certain extent. She already had a college degree and was working as a professional. Like many others of her class, she had already taken on a lot of western values. For that reason, she had married a Christian, something a traditional girl would never do.

Q: *I presume that is why her Hindu family had cut her off.*

A: Yes. The usual method in India and elsewhere to enforce social conformity is to ostracize the wrong-doer. And it usually works. In this case it did not.

Q: *I was interested too that Joe and Mahadevi, unlike the villagers, were satisfied with one child. They really took population control seriously.*

A: Perceptions are different according to class level as well as other status positions. Once you get people educated and in professional jobs, they no longer care about large families as much. One to three children will do. They set other goals for themselves, like Mahadevi wanting to get a graduate degree overseas. That would be a goal that a village girl would never be able to consider. And so she remains a keeper of the house and producer of children.

Q: *And since we are again comparing the middle-class woman with the villager, let me take up a few other matters that I did not completely understand about the village wife. First, was her belief that the gods and spirits would become involved in childbirth common with village folk?*

A.I would say so. Until we got into the area of scientific knowledge and secularization, mankind generally relied on supernatural powers to solve many problems that have since been turned over to secular specialists. So that nowadays in the west if one is not having success in having a baby (and even westerners usually want one or two), one goes to a fertility specialist. But this has happened fairly recently, even in western countries. Before that, and in places where western scientific knowledge has not got to the majority, people still rely on the supernatural for getting and keeping children. India has a variety of such beliefs. And as do most peoples of the world, ordinary Indians realize that man and woman have to copulate for the woman to get pregnant. But they don't know much more, and so when there are problems connected with birth and raising babies, they have a variety of traditional supernatural beliefs to help. A woman can pray to the gods, the most special one being Shiva, who is represented in a Hindu shrine in the form of a stone penis. She also has to avoid evil influences if possible. One such is the spirit being known as the churail, a woman who died in childbirth and who now has wings and her feet on backward, and whose mission is to bring evil to living mothers or pregnant women. Mothers also fear the evil eye, envious women who can harm their children by looking at them. It is for this reason that mothers in many cultures make disparaging comments about their children, making them sound so undesirable that even a person with evil power will not harm them.

Q: *They certainly seem to work hard at it. I presume the potion she planned to give her husband was of the same category.*

A: Well, it obviously had the same goal, to help produce a boy baby, but it's hard to know whether to put such a practice into the supernatural category. People all over the world have worked out procedures to help with the problems of life, and one of these is herbal medicines. Probably most often these are not thought of as supernatural items. Plants and animal parts are often considered to have magical properties, not because they are connected with some spirit, but simply because they are thought to work without any clear-cut perceived cause. Most of us use many substances like aspirin in this magical fashion without really knowing why they do what they do. Incidentally, the Chinese were also very much involved with aphrodisiacs and other medicines from plants and animal parts. Most peoples of the world must have been, until we got to the era of statistical testing.

Q: *One other ethnographic question of interest to western women is why is it so difficult to get girls married in India?*

A: It's not so difficult if one is well-to-do. Marriage is a major undertaking and is expensive to the families, but especially to the girl's family because of the dowry system. Money has to be given to the boy's family, the amount arranged beforehand and reflecting their social status. If the amount is small, the union is considered of low quality. If there are several girls and fewer boys, it can be a heavy drain on the family resources; and, of course, if there are more boys, the family will gain. It's a complex process which the Indian government made illegal a long time ago, but which still goes on. In fact, that business of setting fire to the wife has been reported as a method of getting more dowry.

Q: *Ah, the poor Indian village woman. She really has a rough time of it from a western woman's viewpoint.*

A: Yes. Although there are some advantages for the woman in that system, there are probably few western women who could tolerate the strictures, even if they were "in love."

Q: *They don't have much freedom, do they?*

A: No, not in public. It's a system you have probably heard of, called *purdah*, which prevents them from going about freely outside the house. That is why the visit to the village tank is so important. It was the only time Auraat could really let her hair down, and it probably served the same function, only more important, as the coffee klatsch in American culture, or the telephone gossip session.

Q: *But despite all, there were signs of change coming in the village.*

A: Yes, as everywhere. Even in the villages they are now getting electricity, radio, TV, films, and government programs for all kinds of change. But of course, change always comes first to the city, and fundamental kinds affect the middle class first, which is why I wanted to show a little bit of the lifestyle of Joe and Mahadevi. They would be part of the small but growing middle class of India, and would have more and better material comforts, like Joe's old car and their refrigerator, and quite a few different concepts. Having learned English, they have absorbed quite a bit of Western rationalism which has displaced many traditional beliefs. Thus, many baby matters are settled in the western way. So Mahadevi feeds her baby on a formula instead of breast feeding him. But this is standard in many parts of the world. The people who change first are the educated middle class. And nowadays they are the ones who direct the programs of cultural change.

But of course they still have far to go unless they become industrialized and urbanized, in which case the automatic population decrease will go into effect. But the increase is rapid nowadays, so any delay will put them and the rest of the world in greater jeopardy.

And so, shall we move on to look at the second and related threat to the continuance of mankind—environmental degradation?

11

The Harness

Most of the hill country had been covered with forest, large trees that had grown mostly untouched by human hands for one to two hundred years. The patches with lower growth had been made into fields by the Shawnee, Wyandot, or Miami, then abandoned after the second or third crop because the soil would not produce another worthwhile harvest. The men had done the clearing, ringing the trees with stone axes until the 1750s, when considerable numbers of steel axes began coming in. The Indians had heard then that a new kind of man, one with a light skin, had come and was trading axes to the tribesmen on the frontier for beaver pelts. From there the axes would move from one tribesman to the next, traded for corn or deer hides or salt, whatever was in surplus in each settlement. The tribesmen saw a few other items—Venetian beads, other metal objects like flat discs with raised marks and images of men on them, and some new harder kinds of pottery and pottery you could see through. They had also heard of a new kind of weapon, a metal stick with a hole in it which belched smoke while hurling a small object forward so fast you couldn't see it. And there were some reports of the kind of men who had brought these things. They had come into the forest from the east, wearing leather clothing or the new kind that was made from plant fiber, and they always carried the smoking belchers. And on the big river to the west were similar men, though among them there were also some who wore long black robes of the fiber stuff, and wide black hats instead of the fur headpieces or stiff cornered hats of the eastern traders.

With the steel axes the tribesmen had been able to cut forest patches faster, which gave them more leisure time for hunting or going on raiding trips against other tribes. They left most of the lighter field work to their women.

Herman Hofmann knew little about what had happened in the Indian days. He had been a ten-year-old when they had come from Pennsylvania in the wagon. There were places where the Indians had camped, clearings with blackened stones in circles where they had fires, and broken pieces of pottery and some arrowheads. And he had heard of a village to the south, near the Ohio River, but most of the Indians had gone west of the Mississippi. On newly plowed land he would pick up stone arrowheads sometimes in the spring after heavy rains. However, they didn't interest him much. Despite the fact that the new territory was called Indiana and the growing town to the north, Indianapolis, it was as if the Indians had never existed except in stories at the fireplace at night.

It was still dark when Herman came into the all-purpose living room where Katie was working in the cooking area. Herman was dressed in homespun, his pants held up by suspenders. He put a wide-brimmed hat on and went out of the log house to the animal barn. Otto, his oldest at seventeen years, was already there, harnessing the horses. The cow and her calf were in one corner in a separate stall. The five half-grown pigs and the sow were at the far end of the small log building. Chickens, perched on partitions and other places where they could get footing, clucked sleepily. Some farm tools hung from hooks or leaned against the walls. In another corner a corn crib stood half full next to the section used for hay, which was almost empty. The horses ate corn as Otto adjusted their harnesses. He was a sturdy young man, dressed like his father, his face and the back of his neck burned rust red. He didn't look up as Herman entered.

"Did you feed the other animals?" Herman asked.

"No, I didn't know I was supposed to. Mom said she wants to feed the cow when she comes to milk. And I didn't know if you wanted to give the pigs anything now. I thought you were going to run them up under the oaks and wait until tonight to feed them so they would be sure to come back."

Pigs could get wild quickly if they weren't penned when they weren't foraging. But Herman hated feeding them what little corn they had when there were acorns out in the woods.

Herman's new wooden shoes hurt his feet as he walked over to the pig sty. He had come up to slop the hogs the night before and when they had mobbed him, he had kicked the sow so hard, he had broken his shoe. Luckily he had an extra pair of wooden shoes. He couldn't afford to buy another pair of leather boots, and he used the ones he had for trips to town. He walked over to look at the pig he had kicked. He could see the bruise where his shoe had landed, but the sow looked all right. She lifted her nose and sniffed at the bearded man.

"Goldarn hogs, man wonders why God made them so mean. Seems like the best things to eat are the meanest."

"I'd rather have deer meat any time," Otto answered.

"You still planning to go over to the watering place to try to get a deer?" Herman asked him.

Otto had finished harnessing the horses and he walked over to where Herman was standing by the pigpen.

"Yah, I brought the gun. It's primed and loaded."

He reached over to where it was leaning against the wall.

"I'm trying one of the new balls I made the other night."

The deer were the last of the big wild animals in the region. When the family had first arrived, there had been some turkeys, bear, and even a few wolves, but the wolves were all gone and the only bears left were those in the Salt Creek Marshes. There were not many turkeys for that matter, and few deer. But Otto kept track of the deer that remained and managed to get one or two each year. Herman had never been much of a hunter and was happy to leave it to Otto.

"You'll have to be leaving soon, won't you? Once the sun gets fully up, you'll not see any."

"Yah, it's time." Otto headed for the door. "I'm finished with the harnessing. So I'll go and see you up at the North Hill Woods."

The North Hill Woods was the last of the virgin forest. In the other woods original trees were still scattered, but about half of the sixty acres had already been cleared and made into fields or pasture.

Herman followed Otto out to watch him head down the hill toward the creek. A half mile upstream there was a pool where animals came to drink. The boy planned to hide in the brush to wait for deer.

The father looked up at the lightening sky in the east. Reddish wisps of cloud hung over the landscape, smoke from the fires of men clearing the forest. Soon the trees which he and Otto were cutting would be set afire, too, adding to the red tint. There were still sizeable woods, but fewer and fewer big trees. When he had first come there had been hickories so high you couldn't see the squirrels in the top. But trees that big were few now except in the North Hill Woods and they would have that down in a couple of weeks.

At least, he thought, there was no need to worry anymore about losing children. He remembered when Anna, now fifteen, had wandered off just twelve years ago and it had been twenty-four hours before they had found her. She was curled up under an overhang, her eyes wild and staring. They told stories about the first pioneers coming in before much of the forest had been cut when there were still bands of Indians passing through the country and children would be lost and never found again.

Herman looked with satisfaction at the corn in the hill field and next to it the pasture, surrounded by rail fence. His thoughts were broken by the sound of voices, Katie and Anna coming up to get water and milk the cow. He watched Anna go to the well carrying a wood bucket. Anna pulled the well bucket up and over the stone wall that encircled the hole. Herman had dug the well with the help of the Ottmeiers from across the valley, and together they had built the wall around it to prevent children or animals from falling in. One still heard about a child or animal drowning after falling into an old well or after climbing on the wall and falling in. Anna poured the water into her own bucket and brought it along to the animal barn to meet her mother.

Katie was short with coal black hair and a sharp, intelligent face. She was wearing a long homespun dress, belted at the waist. Her hair was pulled back and tied in a bun. She wore nothing on her head, but would put on a bonnet when she went out in the garden later. All the country women tried to keep their skin as light as possible. Anna was dressed like her mother, though she wore her hair loose, hanging on her shoulders.

Katie entered the barn, carrying a bucket for the milk.

"Did you see Otto leave?" Herman asked her.

"Yes. Think he'll get one? You know we could use some fresh meat."

"Can't say. They get scarcer all the time. I think it's because we haven't had enough rain. The deer like it very green. But he's a good

362

shot, so if there's one around, he's likely to get it."

"I hope so. If he does, I promise we'll have deer stew tonight. I would think you'd like something besides ham hocks with your turnips too."

"Yah, it wouldn't be bad to have a little change."

Anna stood next to her mother as they talked.

"What's Anna doing now?" Herman asked.

"I'm teaching her how to milk. It's time for her to learn."

"Yah, that's good. She's getting to be a big girl now."

It wouldn't be long, Herman thought, before there would be young men around, and not long after that would come the arrangements for a marriage. And then she would need all the household skills she had learned. And milking the cows was one that every farm husband expected of his woman.

"Put the water down and come over here," Katie said to Anna. She stood next to the cow and her calf. The calf was tied so it couldn't reach the cow. The cow moaned quietly, the calf watching and straining its rope. The girl joined her mother.

Katie walked past the cow and untied the rope, but held it fast. The calf tried to strain forward but without success. Katie was surprisingly strong for such a small woman.

"Here, you take it," she said to Anna. "I'll keep holding on this time, just to be sure the calf doesn't get away.

Herman had moved behind them to watch.

"I can help," he offered.

"No, I want the girl to learn without depending on any men. I know you can hold it back, but she's going to have to do it herself."

"She's got plenty of time."

Katie showed her independence then.

"She may, but I don't. The sooner I can give some jobs over to her and the other kids, the better. Then maybe I'll have some time for myself before nine o'clock."

It was true that she worked all day and as long as she could at night before her eyes were too tired. The last jobs were sewing and patching, now with the factory-made cloth which they bought in Helmutberg a couple of times a year. The cotton had particularly been a big improvement over homespun. The wool cloth had been too hot during the warm days of summer.

"Now I'll get started, and when the milk is flowing you can try. You won't get as much at first because your hand is not used to it. But it will get stronger soon. First we have to give the cow hay and let the calf start the flow.

Katie put an armful of hay in front of the cow, and quickly tied the back two legs together. Then she let the calf pull the rope until it could reach the udder. It began to suckle hungrily. The cow looked back briefly, but then returned to munching the hay. Katie waited just a few seconds, then pulled the calf back to tie it again. She had to use more force than she had at first since the young animal had tasted the milk. Katie tied the rope to the same post as before so the calf couldn't reach the udder but could still touch the cow with its nose. Then Katie pulled the log stool up and sat facing the udder. With a strong clasp she put her hands around two teats and began to squeeze rhythmically. Two white jets of milk streamed out with each squeeze, hitting the inside of the bucket which she had placed between her legs against the stool. The cow looked back and jerked her leg, but the tie held and she could not kick forward.

"Don't ever forget that tie," Katie said. "Or she'll knock the bucket over—or even hit you. Just remember she wants to give milk to her calf, not to you."

"I'll remember, momma. You can't blame her for wanting to feed her own baby, can you?"

"Remember, girl, cows were put on this earth to make food for people. They may not know it, but we do. And so it's not worthwhile worrying about the cow's feelings." She took her hands off the teats and, getting up, pulled the girl to the stool.

"All right, now you do it. And don't worry if not as much milk comes. You don't have the strength yet."

Anna began squeezing. The cow looked around again, but returned to the hay. Smaller jets of milk streamed into the bucket. A cat stood nearby, watching the process closely.

"There's that cat that has learned how to drink milk," Katie said. The cat would open her mouth if someone directed a jet of milk at it and would swallow as much as she could, getting thoroughly doused in the process. But since Anna was just starting, her mother did not interrupt her. Anna continued doggedly until her mother took over. She stopped when she decided there was still enough left for the calf, then released the young animal. It hungrily grabbed a teat and suckled noisily. Anna watched it.

"Will it have enough?"

"It should. We need the calf, so we want it to grow right. We'll start it on some mush as soon as it will take it, to go along with the milk."

"But Dad sold the last calf, the one that Bossie had before she died."

They had had two cows, Bossie and Speckle, and one or both had usually had milk flowing. But Bossie had died from some disease despite all that Herman had done to keep her alive.

"That calf of Bossie's was a bull and we don't have enough cows to keep and feed a bull," Katie answered. "We can use the Ottmeiers' bull. This one is a cow, and we need it to replace Bossie. But that's enough questions. Just do what your mother says and we'll take care of the rest." She turned to Herman. "Are you coming in to eat breakfast before you go?"

Before Herman could answer, a shot rang out from the direction Otto had gone.

"Maybe he got one," Katie said.

"Can't tell," Herman replied. "If there was no sign of deer around, he might have shot at something else. These days, a man who goes out for deer is lucky to come back with anything."

"Breakfast will be ready when you come in," Katie said. "Unless you're going down to see what Otto got."

"No, we'll wait until he gets back. No use taking the wagon down there unless he got a deer. Just got to let the hogs out and take out a load of manure. Otto ought to be back by that time also. Are the other kids in the house?"

"Marie is working on breakfast and Hans is probably looking at that reader or picture book he got from the Meier boy."

Hans was thirteen and Marie eleven. Little Henrietta had died when she was three and Bertram, the firstborn, had died in the cradle before he was one year old. It wasn't a bad family, Herman thought, half boys and half girls. And they had lost only two. Besides, they were well-behaved kids. The only funny one was Hans and his books. Herman could sign his name, but reading was too difficult for him to try if he didn't have to. And Katie was about the same. They did get readers for the kids sometimes, but all except Hans preferred to play when they weren't working. Hans had taught himself to read already, just from those lessons given by the traveling teacher who had stopped by for a few weeks a couple of times.

Katie and Anna went back to the house as Herman let the hogs out, prodding the sow with the manure fork. He had been careful this time not to kick her and lose this pair of wooden shoes. He wiggled his toes from the pain, deciding he would have to wear his boots when they went up to the woods. He turned back and began shovelling the steaming manure into the wagon. When it was full, he mounted and sat on the board seat and drove it to the field. The horses had plenty of strength this early, and pulled the wagon along with little strain, but with enough to make them fart frequently. Herman paid no attention to the odor or the sound, watching to keep them on the track. The field where he was taking the manure was on a slope, and he had to negotiate carefully at a couple of places where fair-sized gullies had washed through. He was surprised since the field had only been cleared about six years before and had been planted in corn twice and in wheat three times, and he had left it fallow one year. The clay soil where he threw down the manure was reddish. It was a good thing, he thought, that they would have the north woods field cleared by next year because they would need it. There were many mouths to feed and more fields would be required. When he had shovelled all the manure out, he stopped to take out his bag of chewing tobacco. He put a small quid in his mouth.

Otto was coming up the hill when Herman arrived. The father could see the squirrel hanging from his son's belt and figured there would be no venison.

"Didn't see any, eh?" Herman asked Otto when he came within hearing range.

"No. No sign, just this squirrel that I shot on the way back. Cutting on a hickory. Something's happening to the deer. Maybe it's dog packs."

Since the wolves were gone, there had been an increase in the number of dogs that had gone partly wild, hunting in packs at night.

"No," Herman said. "It's the weather. It's changing. Not enough rain."

"It's one of the new kind of squirrels, the red ones. They've got the color of a fox. They call them fox squirrels."

"Well, put it on the table and come on in to eat. We got to get up there soon. I want to get the fire started before noon."

Otto put his dead animal down on the hand-trimmed log table they used for game and meat and other farm produce before taking it into the house. He waited for his father to wash his hands at the basin on the end of the table, then did so himself. The two men went into the log house.

Inside, Katie and the girls were busy putting the knives, forks, and bowls of food on the table, which was made the old-fashioned way with recesses carved into the top board for each place setting. At Herman's place there was a long knife and a drawer full of loves of brown bread. Herman sat down, followed by Otto, and then the smaller children, taking their regular places. Katie sat on a separate chair and they all bowed their heads as Herman spoke, "Bless us oh Lord for these, thy gifts...."

When the blessing was finished, they all raised their heads and Katie went back to the cooking area. Herman took out a loaf of bread and cut thick slices for everyone. Then the bowls and plates of food were passed around—fried eggs, thick sliced bacon, fried potatoes, and a bowl of hot grease into which slices of bread were dipped, or which was poured into the plate concavities and sopped up with bread. Herman and Otto sprinkled salt generously on their eggs and potatoes. The bacon had already been made quite salty to preserve it. Katie placed cups of hot tea, which the adults would drink with brown sugar and the children with sugar and milk, at each setting. After everyone was served, she joined the rest of the family at the table.

Herman and Otto went together to the north woods, both riding on the wagon seat. Otto had brought the gun, putting it on the floor in the back.

"You figure you might still get a deer?" Herman asked him.

"No, it's too late now. But we might come across another squirrel or two so we'd have enough for a meal. We'll be going by that big hickory that wasn't cut. And there's lots of nuts in the top. If there's any more squirrels around now, they'll be up that tree."

Just before they reached the woods, they had to go across a big gully.

"Look there," Otto said. "A big snake crossing the road."

Herman slowed down. "I see it."

It was a long indigo snake, one they sometimes called a blue racer. There were many stories about it, and particularly about how fast it could move.

"You ought to shoot it," Herman said. "It might bite somebody."

"Aw, dad, it's not worth using the powder and shot. They're too hard to make. I can kill it with a long pole."

Otto jumped down and, picking up a stick, ran ahead of the horses. The snake moved fast and had almost reached the rail fence when

Otto hit it. It writhed in pain and he hit it again and again until the convulsions became slower and slower.

"You got it," Herman said. "That's one dadgum snake that won't be biting nobody or sneaking into henhouses again. They say them's very poisonous."

Otto picked up the reptile with the stick and draped it, still moving with barely visible convulsions, over the rail fence.

When they reached the cut over area, they stopped next to a pile of firewood that Otto would take back to the house for cooking, and, when winter came, for heating. This was the only part of the cut trees they would save. The rest would be burned so by next spring they could plant corn in the ashes.

Some of the logs were lying where they had fallen, others lay in piles where the men with the horse team had dragged them. The two men had cut for two months after they had finished the spring planting, building scaffolds around some of the very large trees so they could cut the trunks where they were thinner. It was difficult to imagine the amount of ax work that had gone into downing the monsters. Now, after four months, they were dry enough to burn. After the winter's snow, the field would be planted in corn or wheat or seeded for pasture.

As the father and son bent to pick up the logs, a shadow crossed the field. Both men looked up to see a flock of thousands of birds crossing in front of the sun, their calls so frequent that they made a steady sound.

"Passenger pigeons," Otto said. "Heading for the Salt Creek Forest."

"Yah," Herman answered. "Don't see flocks like that much any more."

"I hear they catch them over on the Salt. They land in flocks so thick they break the branches. There's men who knock them off with sticks at night. They put them in barrels and take them to Helmutberg to sell. Say they get a nickel apiece for them."

"Just as well get rid of them. If they get into a wheat field when the grain is ripe, they can really tear it up."

The birds passed. The men filled the wagon and Otto started back.

"Come on back for the other load as soon as you can," Herman said. "In the meantime I'll go to the northwest corner to clear out some of that thicket. I don't want the fire to get across to Meier's woods."

Herman and Otto collected dry brush and sticks to make a stack to start the fire. Otto had already returned for the second load of wood and had left the wagon by the house afterward. He had returned with his ax, two dogs following. Herman got out matches he kept in a metal container.

"Them sure makes it a lot easier, don't they?" Otto said.

"Sure do. When we first came, we had to start all our fires with a smoldering piece of wood. It was a bother to have to fix something that would burn the wagon when we burned those first woods."

They had only been able to buy sulphur matches in the last ten years at the stores in Helmutberg.

Herman struck the match against a log cross section and lit some dried grass at the bottom of the fire stack. A wind picked up the flame and it spread rapidly up the pile. He stepped back, and the two of them began feeding the stack with dry pieces of wood. The wind continued to spread the fire to the first small limbs, then to the nearest logs. The men began to feel the heat and moved back. As the fire grew, a couple of rabbits skittered out. A few songbirds flew, followed by quail.

"Should have brought the gun," Otto said. " Might even be a fox."

Soon there was a towering sheet of flame, and smoke streamed up into the sky.

Katie

She put on her best petticoat and dress and shoes with heels, even though she might have to get out before they reached town. But they only got to Helmutberg every month or so. It was only six miles, but with all the hills, the trip took at least two hours. If there was any trouble along the road, it would be much longer. Herman had found out at the beginning of the week that Father Bremen was coming to the church the next Sunday. Then it had started to rain and continued day after day for almost the whole week. Herman had decided they would not be able to make the trip, but then late Saturday a brisk wind from the north had cleared the skies. Katie had waited until that night, and after Herman had lain with her she brought it up. She was surprised when he had agreed to go without much pushing. They had decided to leave Otto and Anna at home and take the two younger ones.

Now, as she dressed, she felt almost as excited as the children. Otto was out harnessing the horses to the wagon. Katie put several items into her carrying bag, got her shawl, and went to the girls' room on the ground floor. Marie was almost ready; she also wore her best dress. Marie had already combed her hair, but Katie combed it again.

"I know you will get mussed up on the ride, but it's best to start off fixed up." She looked at Anna, who watched the preparations. "Anna there is getting to be very pretty. It won't be long before the boys start to notice her."

"Aw, mom, I'm going to be a sister like I told you."

This was still difficult for Katie to understand. While she knew some girls wanted to become nuns, somehow it always seemed that hers would get married and have families.

"You still got time to think about it," she said.

Katie noticed a button missing on Marie's dress.

"Anna, get the needle and thread and fix that," she said. "You know Marie can't do it very well yet." All her girls would learn to sew, beginning as soon as their fingers were nimble enough. That and cooking were certainly the most important abilities a girl could take with her when she got married. Anna went off to get the needle.

Katie called upstairs, "Aren't you dressed yet, Hans? You know that Mass begins at nine o'clock and it will take us at least two hours to get there."

The family didn't have a clock, but Katie and Herman were very good at estimating the time when it was necessary, which was only when they went to town for an event like Mass for which there was a set time. There was no need for a clock at the farm, since everything occurred according to the time of the sun. The Helmutberg parish wanted to get a bell but that wouldn't help country people like the Hofmanns who were too far away to hear it anyway.

When there was no answer, Katie called again. "Now you get down here right away, Hans. I want to check to see if you're dressed all right."

Finally a voice came down from the loft.

"I'm coming mom, I was just finishing one part of my book."

She wondered how he could get so interested in whatever he had to read, which wasn't much. She knew he would read the same book over and over. It bothered her a little, since she couldn't read the books herself and she knew the church disapproved of many. If only one of the fathers would stay in Helmutberg longer and she could get in to see him alone.

But that was just a passing thought in the flurry of getting ready.

"Otto is already bringing the wagon around and we'll be leaving in a few minutes," she warned.

She went out to the toilet the last thing before starting off. As she was walking from the house, Anna came out of the outhouse. It was a

370

typical split-log structure with a polished wood seat piece with a hole inside. Papers were kept in one corner for wiping. Katie often wished she could do like the men and go off into the woods or orchard to pee. But women couldn't take the chance of being seen. So she would grit her teeth and go inside the smelly place.

Katie always liked it when they went to town and she could sit in the front of the wagon with Herman. She could see better, but even more important when they got closer to town, others could see her. She was the mother of the family. The children sat on temporary split log seats behind their parents.

Herman handled the horses easily, and seldom had to use the whip. The horses knew that he would permit no skittishness. The first part of the trip went along the creek that ran below the house and was level. Katie knew that part would be easy, even with the rain they had had. But when they went up the first hill, she could see that the road was slick, though the horses managed it by digging in their hooves. When they went down, Herman held the wagon back with the hand brake. In the very slick places he held the brake pole so tight that the back wheels slid instead of turning.

"I'm not sure this was a good idea," Herman said. "Probably would be better to have waited a week, to let the road dry out some."

"But we get to go so seldom," Katie said. "And one of the fathers only comes every three or four weeks. If we keep these children at the farm any longer, they'll never learn the faith."

"I know, but it won't do to get washed away in the Salt just because of one service."

She knew he was talking about the ford across the Salt River, which was risky after a heavy rain. And it seemed the river was getting worse. She didn't remember people talking about it so much in the early days, and she still remembered what a beautifully clear and shallow river it had been when she was a girl. Now, if there was any rain at all the river would become muddy and high.

"Maybe we'll meet someone else and we can go together, Katie said hopefully.

"We might. The Ottmeiers try to get through whenever there's a Mass. Or someone else."

They met no one the rest of the way until they came across the top of a long hill. At the bottom lay the Salt River, high after the rains. Next to the river sat a wagon. As Herman held the horses and rode the brake, Katie could hear the children talking. She looked around to see them standing up, holding the sides of the wagon, looking down the hill.

Herman recognized the others from a distance. It was the Herberts, who were surely also going to the parish Mass at Helmutberg. Most of the people in the hills there were of German ancestry, having come into the area overland from Pennsylvania or Cincinnati, or directly on paddlewheelers up the Mississippi and the Ohio. The only others in the hills were the Kentuckians, who had come from eastern Kentucky and West Virginia. They were not Catholics and did not go to the Helmutberg church. The Germans had built the log church as soon as they could get enough men together.

Herman got the team on level ground and brought the wagon alongside the Herberts' buckboard. Katie had wanted a buckboard for several years, but Herman had held back because it wouldn't carry as many people as the wagon, and also was not as sturdy. The Herberts could manage with one since they only had two children. Thelma held the baby, and the other child rode between the parents. Herman stopped and wrapped the traces around a post that stuck up from the side of the seat.

"Howdy, folks, going to Mass?"

"That's where we was heading," Billy Herbert answered. "You and the young ones too, looks like?"

"Just decided last night. I figured earlier the roads would be slick and the river high with all the rain. Don't know if it was a good idea, now. How's the river look?"

"You can see that it's pretty high," Billy answered. "There's been several logs washed by since we came. If a man was hit by one of them in mid-stream, he could be knocked clear off the wagon."

Just then, as if to illustrate Billy's point, a big oak came careening down the river, its roots in the air. It hadn't been cut, but had been washed off a slope or undercut by the current. It bobbed along in the main channel, going by surprisingly fast, lodging against a jam of logs downstream from them.

"A man sees a lot of big logs nowadays when the river gets high," Herman said. "Too bad they ain't logs for building, but at least every one that gets washed out is one less to cut and burn."

The water was thick and brown from the mud that had washed off the hillsides along with the trees. Katie looked at Thelma Herbert.

"How's little Frederick? Is he sleeping?"

"He likes to ride in the buckboard," Thelma answered. "Sleeps real well."

"That's good, and it's not far now. Once we're across the river, it's only another mile and a half. I know our kids are looking forward to it. They don't see other kids very often on the farm."

"I'm not sure we'll get across," Billy said. "That river is running fast and this buckboard is lighter than the wagon. Might tip over. And I wouldn't want to get hit by one of them big trees that are washing down."

"This is one time when a man is glad he has his wagon," Herman said. "This one was put together maybe not as strong as the old Conestogas, but still stout."

Herman had sold his original wagon, which was made for cross-country travel, to a man who was going west, and had bought a farm wagon with the proceeds. It wasn't as sturdy as the original, and you couldn't cover it, but it carried a lot more goods.

"Well, I don't think I'll chance it with the buckboard," Billy said. "I think we'll go on back. We can go to the church at the next Mass."

Katie turned to Herman. "Can't we take them across? They came all this way. And I'm sure Thelma and the boy want to go."

"I don't know why we can't," he said, then turned to Billy. "You want to go across with us? I'm sure the wagon will take everybody. Just make it heavier and keep the current from carrying it down."

Billy considered. "The only problem is what to do with the horses," he said. "If we can't get the buckboard across, we might leave that, though I wouldn't want to lose it. But I couldn't take a chance on losing a good team of horses."

"Well, why don't we just take the horses along?" Herman suggested. "You could unhitch them and ride one across trailing the other. I don't think it would be a good idea to tie them onto the wagon until we're across. We could put the buckboard over there behind that brush. No one would see it."

"I appreciate the offer, Herman, but I don't think it's worth the chance. We do our evening and meal prayers at home, and I figger that God don't expect us to lay our life out on the line just for one Mass. You sure you want to try it? After all, you got them two young ones. They swim?"

"Naw, but I figure that with this wagon, we won't have any trouble." And with that he eased the horses forward.

Katie turned to the children. "Now you heard your Papa. You just hold on tight. We don't want to lose either of you because you ain't holding on right."

"Just head more upstream," Billy called to Herman. "Then if the wagon slips some, it'll still be on the regular track."

The wagon slipped into the water and rose on the wheels as the horses pulled it forward, putting their hooves down carefully to keep their footing. Herman stood up, hauling back on the traces. He was a strong man, and the strength of his arms pulled the horses' heads up. Some sticks and a washed out bush floated against the wagon. The water rose until it was just under the floorboards. Waves sloshed up through the cracks.

"Pull up your feet," Katie said to the children. "Put them on the seat logs."

In a mixture of excitement and tension, they obeyed, holding the sideboards tightly. None spoke.

The wheels dropped and the wagon floated for a second. Herman took the ends of the traces and whacked the horses' withers, yelling, "Yah, yah, giddap!" The animals churned the bottom and the wagon wheels came back into contact with the gravel. They were almost in the middle when a good-sized log came hurtling toward them. Herman held the horses back to let it pass, then, whacking the animals again, made the final lunge. The horses pulled hard and for a moment the river shallowed. It seemed they would mount to the other side rapidly when the animals dropped deeper and in an instant the wagon was off the bottom again. Herman flogged them hard, yelling. For an instant the horses seemed to be swimming, only their heads and part of their necks showing. Katie clutched the side and pulled her feet up. Herman held fast and when the horses touched the other side of the hole with their feet, they clawed onto the gravel and pulled the wagon up. After that the water became shallower and the wagon pulled up on the bank.

Each of the worshippers genuflected and then everyone began moving into the aisles and out the door in family groups, the men first, followed by their wives and then the children. There were thirty or forty adults, each pair with anywhere from two to five children. The parishioners were already talking about putting up a board church, now that the sawmill had opened.

The Hofmann family was one of the first to go out since they had been one of the last in. The priest was waiting at the door.

374

"Glad to see the family," he said. "Hope the rest of them are all right."

"Two oldest stayed home to watch over the place," Herman said.

"Just give them my best. That's Otto and Gertrude, isn't it?"

"Otto and Anna. Yes, thank you, father."

When they were outside, Katie said, "I see Beatrice Ottmeier and her daughter over in that group. I think I'll go over and join them. The kids can come along with me or go off and play with the others."

"All right," Herman agreed. "but remember that we can't stay too long. We got to get across that river again."

Herman filled his pipe and lit it, then walked over to the men's group standing under the big oak they had left when they had made the clearing for the church. He knew everyone there, all men who had come in the last twenty to forty years and a few of their sons. They were dressed in their best homespun but without their work hats, the sunburn on their faces and necks clearly apparent. Where their hats usually sat on their foreheads, a clear line of white could be seen. The backs of their hands were also deeply burned, and their joints thick from grasping the heavy tools of clearing and cultivation.

Harry Biesanz called, "We knew you'd come through, Herman. No high water would keep Herman Hofmann from coming through. River was high, though, we hear."

"Seen it worse, though that current was grinding out some real holes. Thick as paste, the water. It's changed since the early days. Seems like every year the rains make it come up higher."

Herman smoked his pipe with pleasure. He had got some tobacco from Carpenter, the Kentuckian over the next hill. None of the Germans grew tobacco. One of the others, Georg Meister, said, "I been noticing that even the little cricks are getting bigger. Why it used to be that there was never no problem crossing the little crick below my house. It didn't even have a name. Now there's times when it pours down the ravine."

"Maybe it's like what the father says," Biesanz said. "That God tests us. Don't want us to take everything for granted."

"What'd you think of that sermon he give today," Herman asked. "About how everything was created to make life better for humans."

"Well," Meister said, "if that's so, what's God have to make it rain and make the rivers so high just when we're going to Mass? That don't look to me like much help."

"It's like the father says," Herman explained. "A person don't know the reason for everything all the time."

Ewald, a man who usually kept quiet at these talks, spoke.

"As for me, I just can't see what kind of help it is to make the river come up when the people of the parish are trying to get in to church. What kind of help is that?"

"Who knows the exact reasons for everything?" said Biesanz. "But it must be like the father said today, that God made the cattle and the fish and the fowl of the air and gave man dominion over them all. And he said that God gave them all to men for meat."

"Well," Herman said, "that all sounds good, but why did he have to make rivers flood? It don't sound much like the Salt, what the father describes. In those early days the rain just fell like a mist and made things grow. Until everybody got so wicked and God made them forty days and nights of rain, and flooded everything. Now that don't sound like the rains here. I sure ain't planning to build an ark to save the family."

"Aw, Herman," Biesanz said. "That stuff is all over. That was the ancient times over in the Holy Land. These are modern times when we're going to farm the United States and have progress."

~

Q: *You must surely expect to discuss this title, since it is on the cryptic side, no?*

A: Perhaps, though I suspect you have some idea about what I was aiming at. It's not all that cryptic, although I will admit that it is pretty far from what I started out with. On the outline for this chapter I called it "Cutting the Forests and Fouling the Air and Water." This has been one of mankind's major problems. The other, of course, has been his reproductive rate. And of course the two are related. Men could do a lot of forest cutting and fouling the environment, but if there weren't so many people, it wouldn't matter so much. Anyway, the above sounded pretty long for a chapter heading in a book which is supposed to be readable as well as meaningful. So I racked my brain and came up with a short version, "The Harness," which I suppose has some meaning to you even without any elaboration.

Q: *Yes, you seem to mean that men were trying to harness nature.*

A: Yes, very good. It is always satisfying to me when a reader understands one of my titles, especially when I think it is a little original and apt. But the title especially fits here because it also refers to one of the significant activities these pioneers were engaged in—harnessing horses. In order to harness nature, you had to harness horses—at least during most of that part of man's history in which he was trying to control or conquer nature.

Q: *And what part of history was that?*

A: The true period of trying to control or harness nature came after the domestication of plants and animals. You undoubtedly remember the chapter "Slaves," when men and women were in the business of taming the plants and animals for their own use. That was the beginning of taking control, and from then on most of mankind became "harnessers."

Q: *Are you saying that during the four million years of prehistory that preceded the period of domestication man did not try to take control?*

A: As usual, my response is an academic waffle. Man the hunter-gatherer certainly tried to use those parts of nature which were of benefit for supporting life, but in that respect he was no different from the other animals. They of course got their sustenance by gathering or hunting also. They gathered what seeds, roots, and berries they could, as well as killing what grass-eaters they could get for meat. But the exploitation of nature during this long period was a piddling affair compared to what happened after the domestication revolution. Then man the cultivator and herder took off in a big way, which kept getting bigger all the time in exploiting not only the animals and plants, but also the water, minerals, and even air and of course in our own time he has even gone beyond Earth. And so we ended up in the era of pollution.

Q: *Sounds like a real problem, just as the expansion of population became one, and by the same kind of people. That is, the same cultures that made slaves of the plants and animals also became the mighty reproducers that started with one million and have ended up being five billion.*

A: Yes, that's us, and where we will end no one knows.

Q: *So I suppose we ought to know how we got into this fix. And since in the last chapter you described how we got into the population fix, now I guess we ought to know how we got into the pollution fix. Can you give us a history of that?*

A: I thought you'd never ask. Once some plants and animals were domesticated, the basic need was for more sunlight. You know that plants change sunlight, water, and minerals into nutrients which animals can eat. Most plants are eaten directly by the animals, including man. Some of these plant-eating animals are subsequently eaten by other animals, also including man. So we eat beef from cattle which eat grass and pork from pigs which eat corn. But almost all these plants and others which man has domesticated need at least five hours of direct sunlight each day, so once the domestication revolution took place, man needed fields with more sunlight. But he also needed considerable amounts of water and where water falls abundantly, trees take over. The trees shade out the smaller plants. So man begins to cut trees to make fields to grow his sun-loving plants. And that was the beginning of the great era of deforestation, a version of which was going on in Indiana in the narrative, and the last version of which is going on now in the rain forests of the Amazon, Asia, and Africa.

Q: *So you are saying that the ecological destruction going on in Brazil is nothing new?*

A: Absolutely not. Deforestation has been going on for ten thousand years. We who criticize the Brazilians for denuding their forests went through our own forests in very fast order much earlier. But now that the fields of North America, Europe, China, and India are in crops, many of us, being the lousy historians that we are, think they were always this way. But the forests of eastern North America were so full of tremendous trees, growing so thickly, that children could get lost in them and never be found again. And you may remember that in the folklore of Europe the really scary place was a deep, dark forest. This was based on the reality that Europe had forests, if not as tremendous as those in the Amazon, at least very full of imposing trees.

Q: *But if that was ten thousand years ago, people had nothing but stone tools. How could they cut forests of big trees? Nowadays in the Amazon, as we so often see on TV, they cut the trees with power saws.*

A: That is a good observation. It is true that there were nothing but stone tools in the beginning of the deforestation period, but that didn't last long. Archeologists tell us that the age of metallurgy began about five thousand years ago. But for two thousand years the only metals man could smelt were copper and bronze, and these were not fantastic for cutting big trees. Even so, bronze age pioneers went up the Danube basin on foot and probably into England and points north by boat, always carrying along the plants and animals that had been domesticated, and they had to clear some forest. But then about three thousand years ago somebody figured out how to forge iron and that made all the difference.

The iron ax is no doubt the supreme deforestor of history. The power saw pales by comparison. Apart from cutting down the cedars of Lebanon and other stands of trees in the Middle East, the iron age peoples headed north, cutting as they went. Once men learned how to forge iron, they learned that it was a common metal and that it kept its edge much longer than anything they had previously. Archeologists have identified the iron age people of Europe as the Halstatt and La Tene Cultures, village people who depended on agriculture and animal husbandry. They had to have been clearing forests, as their descendants continued to do. And of course when the Euros spread over the world after 1492, they took the steel ax along and began clearing forests elsewhere. The final phase of Euro-cutting in the New World is that going on in the present day in the tropical rain forests. There, after displacing the Indians, the Brazilians got busy cutting down the forests so they could graze cattle on the grass which grows in the sunlight.

Q: *And so it seems it was the Euros who did all the cutting down of forests.*

A: Not all, but a lot. You will remember I said that iron was originally forged in the Middle East. The earliest culture which was using it was that of the Hittites in the region of modern Syria. But from there, it diffused everywhere, replacing copper, bronze and stone tools. It traveled east and south. Iron was carried through Persia, India, China, and Japan, and all the less well-known places along the way. When the Euros first encountered them, the Japanese were making a very high-quality steel, which is an alloy of iron and carbon, to use in swords for their samurai and as implements for their farmers. They had, of course, already cleared their lowland forests for rice fields. The Chinese also began using iron long ago, and have cleared parts of their country so thoroughly that there is no evidence left of what the original vegetation was like. And in India, too, men had cleared the Ganges basin, plus many other areas where domestic plants would thrive.

Q: *You also mentioned the spread to the south—what happened there?*

A: Most of the great forests of central Africa were downed by the iron ax. Anthropologists have discovered that a veritable caste of iron workers existed in many parts of Africa. There has also been a number of side effects that have intrigued anthropologists. Africans have a high incidence of an illness called sickle cell anemia. And without going into the complete details of the condition, it is thought that having half a condition which is called polymorphism provides immunity to malaria, which is carried by mosquitoes who breed in abundance in the stagnant waters of cut-over forests. Also, sleeping sickness, an African illness, is spread by the tsetse fly, which breeds in cut-over forest areas. But the benefits of cutting the forests were the same as elsewhere, that African villagers could grow sun-loving plants, in this instance bananas, yams, and various seed crops.

Q: *Now I see why you chose Indiana for the narrative. You wanted to illustrate a recent period of deforestation, no?*

A: Yes, and also because I experienced that hill region when I was very young, very pleasurably in fact, but I did not understand what was going on ecologically. It has only been after fifty years of reading anthropology and history and knowing what happened in the place of my boyhood's pleasures that I feel like I understand what happened from the days of Herman and Katie to the beginning of the twenty-first century. And I want to explain that history in some detail if that is all right.

Q: *Sure. It's always satisfying to get a personal perspective of a process that is going on globally.*

A: Before I do outline what happened in Helmutberg, let me explain how this is a case of retrospective anthropology, an illustration of the value of study and reading for reasons apart from such mundane goals as getting a better job or a promotion. I understand that American culture has emphasized from the beginning the idea of knowledge for a purpose. And they say we are living in the practical generation. But it is my opinion that knowledge can and perhaps ought to be an end in itself, if we are to claim that mankind has any special characteristics. Moreover, much thoughtful analysis can only come after long reading and study, at least of historical events. And so this is a case of retrospective anthropology.

Q: *That is an interesting idea. But what happened in Helmutberg?*

A: As you know, the Euros landed on the east coast of North America in the 1600s. They very quickly began to displace Indians and establish farms, which of course requires cutting down trees.

Q: *Were there no clearings made by the Indians?*

A: Yes, they were cultivators too, though of a less intensive kind than the Euros. Most of the cultivation was in what has been called the slash-and-burn technique, which I referred to in the beginning of the narrative. They would clear patches in the forest by girdling trees and setting them afire after they dried out, and then they would plant in the cool ashes. That story we heard when we were children about

Indians burying a fish in a hole and then planting seeds sounds like nonsense. The fish would be worth more as food than the corn.

In any event, after two or three years, the cultivator would go to another place to clear a patch, since the ground would have lost most of its fertility. In the meantime, the cleared patch would start growing up, first in brush and then in forest. It was a low-intensity form of cultivation which worked without destroying the environment, but only with a low population density.

Q: *You are saying that the Indians didn't have as many people as the Euros? How did they keep their reproduction rate down?*

A: Perhaps you have forgotten from the last chapter that all people had methods of keeping family size limited, the most common before the twentieth century being infanticide, abortion, and intercourse taboos. The Indians practiced some variations of these. Anyway, they were doing well enough on their own until the Euros showed up, and from then on it was all downhill.

And even while the Euros were displacing the Indians, they were already sending their scouts and surveyors (Daniel Boone, George Washington) into the wilderness. And as soon as the last of the Indians were killed off or forced to move west, the pioneers came in with their covered wagons, horses, and harnesses. And that was what Herman and Katie were doing in southern Indiana. And like other Euros before them, they saw the forest as their primary impediment, and with their sharp axes and crosscut saws they went at it. Moreover, they planted their farms in European style, using, among other implements, the moldboard plow, which went deep and made a furrow while turning the soil over. It contributed significantly to erosion. The Indians had mainly used a digging stick which caused no erosion. Then the Euros planted wheat, oats, rye, and corn in rows.

Q: *I thought corn was a crop of the American Indian; and you have been emphasizing that the Euros did everything their own way. Where did they get the corn?*

A: I am sure you remember from Thanksgiving lore that the pilgrims were helped to survive in the first couple of years by the Indians, and in particular that the Indians helped them either get or grow Indian foods. That is, of course, why the holiday includes turkey, which presumably the Indians helped the pilgrims hunt or gave them some birds. But it also included corn and pumpkins, both of which were Indian crops. The biggie was of course Indian corn or maize, which must have helped more than anything else in those early days.

But of course people are not usually appreciative of gifts, particularly from those of other cultures. So getting corn or anything else from the Indians did not slow down the displacement efforts of Euros. As soon as they were well enough established to organize militias, they started raiding Indian villages. In fact, one of their regular methods of driving Indians out was to burn their corn fields, just as later the Euros killed off the primary food animals of the Plains Indians, the buffalo.

The Euros took corn over with a vengeance and grew it everywhere they could, using it not only as human food in the Indian way, but also for their animals. And unfortunately, it is a crop which, when planted in the Euro fashion in hill country, particularly contributes to erosion. That was one of the reasons the Salt River in the narrative was so muddy.

Q: *So what happened in Helmutberg after Herman got the forest down and the area well-planted?*

A: Well, he and his descendants continued for several generations growing their crops and families and taking over new methods as they became available. The log houses, for instance, were covered with boards when sawmills were set up. Also, a flourmill was set up on the Salt River. And all the large wild animals were killed off, the forests that remained turned into second-growth woods, and the cleared fields continued to erode.

It was about this time that I showed up, in the early 1930s, a small boy on vacation at Grandma's farm, one of the new generation of city kids. My father was one of the first of the Hofmann clan to make the migration from the country to the city, as was my mother from another rural area. This migration was to turn into a flood, ultimately depopulating a large part of the countryside. The farm with its wood-burning stove, outdoor toilet, well for water, and lack of electricity was a real backwoods place compared to the conditions in the city where I grew up. As I went about the farm trying to catch lizards on rail fences or frogs in creeks, I hardly noticed the eroded fields and grown over brush areas and did not know that all kinds of large wild animals once lived there, not to mention Indians.

But others had noticed, in particular, the eroded gullies. This was the middle of the Great Depression and make-work projects had been set up throughout the land. One of these was the Civilian Conservation Corps. This was a brainchild of Roosevelt's New Deal to put young men to work. They lived in camps in the country and worked on improvement projects. One project was to build catchment dams in the gullies to slow down the erosion. I used to see such dams all over when I walked around in the hills.

But then I and the C.C.C. boys all went off to World War II, and nothing was the same afterwards. My vacation days on the farm were over, the C.C.C. camps were closed, and the farmers began abandoning the hill region. The era of agribusiness was beginning, but in Indiana that was only on prairie land. Those scrabble fields in the hills were no longer worth the effort. The remaining farmers sold the last great isolated trees for high prices and then went off to prairie farms or retired.

I am told that the Hofmann farm and most others in the hills have been bought by wealthy city people as country homes. The woods are growing again, gradually restoring the forest. Also, game specialists are re-introducing some of the wild animals, notably deer and turkey, that were there during the days of Herman and Katie. It is not exactly full circle, since there are no Indians left, nor is there any likelihood that there ever will be, but ecologically it is a great improvement.

Q: *I take it that elsewhere in the world it has been different. At least the media keep talking about the destruction going on in Africa, Asia, and Latin America. What about that?*

A: Of course it is always easier to blame others than to accept blame oneself. Moreover, when the temperate zone forests were being cut, there was little ecological awareness. The Euros thought it was perfectly normal to cut down forests. They had of course cut down most of their own quite a while before, and they had adjusted to the new conditions by the time industrialization took over and almost everybody headed for the city. The Euros even evolved a relatively harmless way to use their hill regions. They generally made their up-and-down terrain into pastures, as well as developing good systems of using animal wastes. Switzerland is a classic example.

In the tropical countries they have gone at their rain forests much like we did our temperate zone forests, and perhaps even faster, since they now have power equipment to do it with. Erosion and leaching of the soil is going on now at a great rate where the rain forest has been cut, and whether they will let it grow back, no one knows.

Q: *Evidently you believe that deforestation is the most significant ecological problem, what about the others you mentioned?*

A: Most of them are products of man's movement to the cities, industrialization, and the scientific revolution. The water problem, though, was largely a consequence of deforestation. Forests with their leaf mold store rain water. Once the trees are cut, the leaf mold washes away and the water runs down, carrying large amounts of soil. Muddy rivers are the result, ultimately carrying the soil into the sea. And floods become more destructive. It is no accident that the Mississippi was called the Big Muddy or that the big one in China was called the Yellow River. You will remember that the Chinese cut down most of their forests a long time ago. They of course set themselves up for some of the worst floods in history. And like others before and after, they tried to correct the problem by building great dikes.

Mankind created another problem with his water, however—that of fouling it with wastes and chemicals. Water of course moves very easily while soil and things imbedded in it stay put longer. Thus, it probably came naturally to use water to get rid of wastes. Cleaning oneself in streams or lakes was inevitable and cleaning clothes came just as naturally once men invented them. Apart from these, though, the use of water to get rid of wastes only became serious after urbanization and industrialization. What Herman and Katie did was of very little consequence in this regard, and of course the Indians had even less impact. But my family were city dwellers and contributors in a serious way to the pollution, in this case of the White River, which ran the length of Indianapolis. My first awareness of pollution was of this river. I remember that the only fish which could live in it were carp and catfish, both of which can manage in highly-polluted water. I was pleased to learn recently from relatives still in that city that most of the river has been cleaned up since I left. Cities dumped their wastes in rivers all over the world. Until the 1900s, many infectious diseases were carried in the waters of polluted rivers.

But man the despoiler also dumped the leftover products of his industrial revolution into the rivers of the world and ultimately the oceans. As we know, during the last four hundred years there has been a revolution in many areas of knowledge, one of which was chemistry. And as man learned more and more about substances, he used them more and more in his manufacturing procedures, dumping the wastes into the nearest rivers. The White River in Indianapolis had so much industrial residue in it that the fish tasted like kerosene. Other rivers have become so fouled that fires would burn on their surfaces and new diseases from the dumped chemicals occurred in many places.

Even in the countryside, pollution by chemicals took place, though not in Herman's day. But in the era of agribusiness the use of chemicals became so widespread that great areas of land and the waters into which they drained became fouled.

Q: *You seem to indicate that there has been some improvement in controlling polluting chemicals. Is that so?*

A: Actually there has been, in my lifetime. We in the industrial countries have become more aware of what we are doing and there has been increasing control of polluting activities. Though this has been far from the case in the countries which are trying to catch up in industrialization. They have been much slower in trying to control their dumping practices, since their populations have continued to grow rapidly. And more mouths to feed do not cause people to get more persnickety about pollution control. So there is still a lot of chemical pollution going on in the waters of the world.

Q: *So is that about it, in pollution, I mean?*

A: No, there is one other biggie which is the most recent. Herman and Katie wouldn't have known what you were talking about if you had mentioned air pollution. Up until the twentieth century, air was thought of as free and clear. Now, of course, we know better, especially if we live in Los Angeles or Mexico City or Tokyo. In any of these places one's eyes burn, the air smells of chemicals, school children are not allowed to play on smoggy days, and old people are at health risk. But except for the country which began the industrial revolution, England, this never happened before the twentieth century. The factory system with its belching smokestacks began in England and so did the fog/smogs. But the worst was to come when men discovered oil and invented the internal combustion engine. The automobile became the second greatest air polluter and the air of the cities became foul indeed.

Q: *But even that has improved in recent times, hasn't it?*

A: They say so. I read that there are less air alerts in Los Angeles than there were decades ago. And it may be so. Even in London the famous "killer fogs" no longer take place. There is certainly more awareness of the problem and more effort to correct it. It is like most other kinds of ecological destruction. The industrialized countries are more aware of the problem and are trying to do something about it, while in the poorer countries there is less such awareness and effort. And while the urbanized, industrialized countries are lowering their reproduction rates, the village countries of the world are still growing babies at a great rate. And to me it seems that the reproductive rate is the key to survival of man as a species.

Q: *It sounds sort of bleak to me. It's a far cry from the idea that man is forever, which we seem to have been taught in our earlier years.*

A: I guess it is natural that man hopes to continue forever. That is merely a group manifestation of the individual drive to survive, which we share with all the other animals. But if there is anything we can learn from history, it is that continuance of individuals and species is only temporary. Forever-ness is a mental set, not a reflection of reality. But anyway, I am sure that we as a species will try to use all the resources we can to continue. And though I am far from optimistic for the long run, I will admit that we have learned a few things. Unfortunately, other things have become worse.

Q: *And so with that not so positive note, shall we shift to clearing up some things in the narrative? For instance, I was interested in your treatment of your birthplace, Indianapolis, Indiana, and particularly the names. Could you clarify that a little?*

A: Sure, because it is something I became aware of only after long study of anthropology and history. The names mean city of Indians and state of Indians. And the interesting thing is that there are no Indians in the city or state, or at least none in identifiable communities. Furthermore, none of my teachers in primary or secondary school ever said anything about how the names came to be. I presume now that the names were given because there were lots of Indians in both the state and what became the capitol city, Indianapolis. And I now know that the militia and army killed Indians with a vengeance and those who survived had to go west, eventually ending up in Oklahoma Territory, which became the state of Oklahoma. It is the typical history of people who lose wars, and it has occurred all over the world repeatedly. The only real anomaly is the names. But that was taken care of in a typical fashion also. One simply did not talk or teach about it and so I, and I am sure most others, never wondered about it. My only problem was that I later studied anthropology and came to consider history a highly-biased procedure for explaining the past.

Q: *The settlers seemed to have been mainly self-sufficient, though they were getting some trade goods also, no?*

A: Sure, the pioneer society was merely an extension of the core society, which was by this time going hell-bent into the industrial revolution. So factory-woven cloth was replacing homespun, iron axes and cross-cut saws from the iron foundries of the east were coming in, and even matches got to the early settlements once they were invent-

386

ed in 1827. And as I mentioned, not too long after the first sawmill was set up, the settlers could build with boards instead of logs.

Q: *Another thing about the settlers that was interesting was the size of their families. Were there really that many?*

A: Well, as you know, the pilgrims started with a few hundred and by Katie and Herman's day there were twenty million Americans. Most of that number came from internal reproduction, since the major immigration came in the latter part of the nineteenth and the early part of the twentieth century. Agricultural people are generally great reproducers. The population of the U.S. only began slowing down after we were well along in urbanization. My own recent ancestry is significant. My grandparents, the descendants of Katie and Herman, had twelve children. My parents had four, and I had one. It's not quite this neat if I figure in my sisters and my maternal grandparents, but there was a steady decrease in the number of children through the generations. Now I believe the average number is less than two.

Q: *I guess it is because children were useful then. I noticed that both Katie and Herman depended on the help of their children.*

A: Yes, farm children were generally useful to the family before the first public schools were established in the 1870s, and moreover, they were counted on for one's old age. Remember, this was long before there were any old age programs run by the government. My grandparents, and I am sure the great majority of the old people of previous generations, were taken care of in their old age by their children. The two government programs which greatly reduced the usefulness of children were universal education, which kept them busy in school and in homework; and old age insurance and retirement funds, which made old people financially independent of their children. Once these were in place and people moved to cities, there were fewer and fewer children born.

Q: *Another characteristic of the family seemed to be the dominant role of the father.*

A: Yes, this was a continuation of the Euro peasant pattern of a male-oriented family with the primary producer, the male, in charge. In a sense, this kind of family was like the Indian village family, and for the same reasons. You probably remember that they emphasized children, too, and the father was expected to be in control, and was even allowed to hit his wife or children. Another common custom was the emphasis on marriage. And of course this was logical because a society cannot have many children who will contribute during the parents' lifetimes if the younger people don't get married and stay married. All these things changed as the city took precedence over the country and as the peasant was replaced by the factory worker.

Q: *The early frontier certainly had its problems, didn't it? Was the forest really such a dangerous place?*

A: Writers up into the late twentieth century still referred to it as the forest primeval or the howling wilderness, and there is little doubt that there were sources of danger. Children could get lost, though statistically such an occurrence probably wasn't so important. And Indians were not always friendly, though I believe they generally were at first. But when it became clear to one group after another that the whites were intent on taking everything, they sometimes retaliated. In general, though, the Indians were usually terrified of the whites, usually well in advance of their actual appearance. The things they heard about whites, which were generally true, were enough to scare them. And in the early days there were some wild animals which might have attacked humans, but they were killed off fast. But accidents did undoubtedly happen. People were drowned, there were fires, and trees fell on them. Moreover, there was little medical help, and what there was wasn't so wonderful at that time anyway. And finally, the frontier people had come from settled areas and a forested place was scary just because it was different. So they worked mightily to civilize the country, killing the wild animals, cutting down the great trees, and beginning the fouling process which we today are heir to. And the process was justified by the homocentrism of the Book of Genesis. These people believed that all was created for their benefit.

Q: *One of their customs we have inherited—that is the food they ate. Isn't that so?*

A: I think so. Remember these people were from north Europe and this is one of the heaviest meat-eating areas in the world, at least for settled people. The nomadic Eskimo and the Plains Indians perhaps ate more meat, but they were highly-specialized hunters. Most nomadic peoples ate many more vegetable products. Although they inherited the plants and animals of the Middle East, the Euros concentrated on the animals. Just recently I learned that the ideal middle class meal in nineteenth-century Britain consisted of five courses: soup (undoubtedly with a meat stock), fish, meat, desert, and savory (a dish of stimulating flavor for the end of the meal). No vegetable dish was included.

The most popular animal product for all classes was probably cow's milk, which the Euros drank and processed as cheese and butter. But they did not forget Elsie's brother, Elmer. Beef became a food eaten in constantly-greater quantities as the Euros prospered. But they ate pigs in large numbers also, particularly in the form of bacon and sausage. Another domestic animal which was consumed in large quantities was the chicken and its eggs. The Euros also learned how to fatten their animals well with grain. And when they got maize from the Indians, they could make their animals even fatter. And this is the kind of food that Katie and Herman were eating. It wasn't too bad for the physically active life of the farmer, but when men came to the cities and took up a more sedentary life, it spelled cholesterol, obesity, clogged arteries, and heart attacks. That is one bit of inheritance we are trying to fight our way out of today, but it is difficult. Too many people are addicted to burgers, french fries, milk and ice cream.

Q: *But they also ate a lot of bread, didn't they? I was especially interested in that bread drawer and the father cutting a piece for each person. Was that a peasant pattern?*

A: It certainly was. Bread was the mainstay for the Euro peasant. The families who could afford it often substituted meat. But when you couldn't afford anything else, you got by on bread. The French Revolution broke out and Marie Antoinette lost her head reputedly because when the French peasants and workers demanded bread, she said "Let them eat cake." That particular way of cutting the bread in the narrative I learned from seeing a very good documentary film on French peasant life called "Farrebique." The kind of table with the eating places scooped out of the top wood slab was also portrayed in that film. I do not know if American settlers had the same kind of table, but it is possible that some did. But it is so peasant-ish that I took literary license and gave it to the Hofmanns. Incidentally, the English and German countrymen were just as dependent on bread, and these countries still are. We in the land of processing have shifted a bit and gone to soft white bread, particularly as hamburger buns.

Q: *What about reading? Since there was no public education yet, many didn't learn, did they?*

A: No, it wasn't until my generation that reading became common. My parents learned to read, though they left school after seven years, probably to help on the farm. But until they came to the city, there were few books available. In fact, one of the popular "books," which was kept in the outdoor toilet and which was pored over because there was nothing better, was the Sears and Roebuck catalog. And then, too, the Hofmanns were devout Catholics and that religion has always been suspicious of books, and justifiably so. They tried to keep subversive books out of the hands of the young, as Hans in Helmutberg and Henry in "The Way of Science" learned.

Q: *I guess we have done enough on the "despoilers," though I have one other matter to ask about, which also concerns religion. Would those people really discuss sermons like they did in front of the church?*

A: They certainly would. I remember watching my uncles and other men standing in front of the country church, discussing in great detail the points the priest had made in his sermon. They were trying to relate the events and descriptions of what they had heard to their own lives in Helmutberg, which of course wasn't easy. After all, how much did their lives in the hills of southern Indiana resemble the lives of semi-nomadic tribesmen in the deserts of the Middle East, much less totally mythical accounts of the creation of the world as in the Book of Genesis? And they had even adopted a totally new life value, that of progress, in contrast to the early Jews and Christians, who saw all existence as a process of degeneration.

And so that's how he did it, our hominid ancestor, both positively and negatively. But I suggest that for our final talk we sum it all up and take a peek at the future, anthropologically speaking, that is.

392

12

Beyond 1999

Walter Lansing settled down in the comfortable seat of synthetic material. The room was ordinary enough, like an office or meeting room, neutral in decor except for two large glass screens on one wall, surrounded by lights of different colors. Two more chairs and a low table stood in the center. Lamps were strategically located between the chairs. Pads and pencils lay on the table.

He laughed inwardly that he was continuing to think in old imagery, trying to find any familiarity he could. It was almost as if he were trying to convince himself that the old world still continued, that we were not in an entirely new era, dominated by very different creatures. They had appeared cruising at a thousand feet, at first in the late evenings, but eventually at any time of day, vanishing whenever the military sent fighters or missiles aloft, but then reappearing later. Eventually they had released clouds of gas, and finally they landed. It was not long before it became clear that they intended to take over the planet.

There was music in the background, Stravinsky, he thought. Also a pleasant, slightly musky odor permeated the air. The room temperature was ideal.

The music faded and the lights around the screens flickered. A cursor appeared and began moving across the screen, leaving words behind. A soothing female voice repeated the words audibly.

"How do you do, Mr. Lansing. My name is Moma and I am here to welcome you."

Walter felt totally cooperative, no matter what had happened. Of course, in the back of his mind he guessed that much of his attitude was a consequence of their manipulation. It was no accident that the ambiance was ideal. After all, considering whatever else they knew, which was a lot, they surely knew that Stravinsky was his favorite composer. Also, there was little doubt that he was not getting the same treatment as the rest of the people of the world. But he simply felt too good to fight. Moreover, he had long recognized their superiority. So he decided to go along, at least for a while.

"How do you do, Moma?" he said. "I take it you are going to be my interviewer?"

"Yes, and does it bother you that I am electronic?"

"No, it seems most natural. After all the technological marvels I've seen since your kind took over, I would hardly be surprised at anything. But even we *sapiens* had developed quite a few electronic devices in the last century."

He decided to try a little levity. After all, their treatment of him so far had been amiable enough, not at all like the treatment of most other earthlings that had not been eliminated. They were being used mostly as laborers, servants, and service people for their robots.

"It also doesn't bother me that you have taken a female voice. As you know from my dossier, I had a strong fondness for the female of my species during most of my life."

"Oh, yes, we are quite aware of that. We think we should do everything we can to make you comfortable, since we will be spending a lot of time together. You have the information we want; and since we have not yet developed a method of extracting information directly from the brain, we need to depend on a cooperative subject."

Walter considered that the last comment meant the aliens seemed to be flexible in their choice of methods. After all, they certainly had no compunction against using force. There had not been many direct confrontations between their robots and the earth military, but when there had been, the aliens had used overwhelming force. But that had only been in the beginning when the men of earth had no idea how absolutely superior the aliens' technology was.

A green light flickered and the soft voice of Moma came on, along with the words on the screen.

"Since we have tried to make everything as familiar as we can, we have selected Standard American English as the medium of communication. Also, of course, the music, odors, and sights will be as familiar to you as we can make them. All this will be handled by our Department of Illusions. It is really no problem since we have done it in one new world after another.

"One thing that may need explanation is my name. The Department of Illusions selected this one since it is close to the most pleasing sound for most in your language. We made it into Moma because we thought the word Mom might be confused with usage of the term for mother in the transcript of our talks. And you will undoubtedly not be surprised that all we say will be put on tape."

"Okay," Walter agreed. "And in order for me to reciprocate by keeping this informal, you can call me Walt, the abbreviated form that most of my friends and relatives used."

The bank of green lights went off and a series of pulsations of different colors began to flicker. Walter quickly became aware that the pulsations were synchronized to the arrhythmic beat of the "Rite of Spring." After a while the volume went down and the green light became brighter. The cursor reappeared on the super screen and words appeared, accompanied by the voice.

"If that last piece pleased you, I suggest we get started."

"Sure," Walter agreed, waiting to see his word on the screen. "But I would like to get a little clearer idea what we are going to do."

"I will try to explain. Basically, we are going to talk about how your species became the temporary dominants of your planet. We will depend primarily on your memory of what occurred, because you are one of the older members of your species with a still-active intellect, and presumably with a non-impaired memory."

Walter laughed inwardly. It was true that he had managed to get to the end of the second decade of the twenty-first century in relatively good health. He was almost one hundred years old and had seen the most sweeping change he could have imagined—the conquest of earth by extra-terrestrials. And here he was cooperating with them.

"Okay, I understand that, but why me?"

"We decided on you because you belonged to the profession of anthropology which by what we make out has concerned itself with the broadest study of your species in time and space, and has exhibited the least amount of bias in its studies. It was felt that men of your profession were the least ethnocentric and would give the least skewed version of history. We need this kind of perspective, even though it is not the kind of history that people teach their own citizens."

Walter agreed with that, though he had thought many times that when anthropologists drifted away from the truth, they tended to do just the opposite from most historians—they took the side of "the others" rather than emphasizing the achievements of their own culture.

"But surely you will get information from other earthlings, those from other fields of study, won't you?"

"Oh, yes. We have robot analysts researching every aspect of your culture, but particularly your printed works. You earthlings are one of the few kinds we have discovered who have developed a way to freeze messages—with printing, and more recently with electronic tape. And however primitive the methods are, the books and tapes will undoubtedly help. We will also interview some of your surviving specialists—economists, psychologists, political scientists, and others. But the core of our study will come from the anthropological viewpoint, because we see this discipline as a unifying force, even if it is relatively recent and lacks scientific rigor."

Well, no matter that these creatures had gobbled up the planet as if there were no other places in the universe, Walter thought, they certainly had the capacity to make one feel good. How could he have resisted such an approach? Still, there were a few questions.

"If it isn't too impertinent," he said, "I would like to know why your kind are doing this. Why would they want to know how our species developed since they are obviously superior to us in so many ways?"

Walter was impressed with the quickness of the reply. It seemed no matter what the question, Moma never hesitated. The electronic device, if that's really what it was, obviously already had a vast amount of information which it could plug in to almost instantly.

"You may imagine that since we escaped from our own world and started cruising the galaxy, we have encountered quite a few planets in other star systems, many of which contained some kind of life. So, like many explorers, including a few of those on your own planet, we were curious about how different beings got to their various stages of development. No matter that the forms we discovered were inferior to us, we felt that we might learn something which we could use for the development of our own way of life. You should remember that the study of mankind in your profession began in this way."

He realized then that it was almost a direct parallel to the early development of anthropology, when the first research workers began their studies of extinct cultures and those of recently-conquered primitive peoples. It seemed that this was a kind of extra-terrestrial anthropology, invented independently. He mentioned this to Moma.

"Yes, it is true," the voice answered. "We came up with a methodology much the same as that of your profession, and for the same reasons. Just as you people began exploring your world, we began exploring our universe. And in both instances, different kinds of beings were encountered. Of course, the variety we discovered was far greater. Still, there were many parallels."

"Very interesting," Walter said. "But I am now the informant, while you are the interviewer."

Moma's lights flickered for a moment.

"I might mention one more parallel which should interest you," the voice said. "But then we should get on with it. As you know, your own profession really got started only after your ancestors, the light-skinned variety, had basically conquered the world. They called it the Age of Discovery, but it could just as aptly be called the Age of Conquest. After three to four hundred years, your ancestors had imposed their way on almost the entire world and had drastically changed the way of life of all the less-complex cultures, right?"

He puzzled for a moment over how different Moma's point of view was from that of traditional historians.

"That's certainly not the way we learned it in school, but I am afraid you are right." He began to see where Moma was taking him and said, "And you are going to say that we began to study the remnants of tribal cultures all over the world, in what we called 'salvage ethnology.' After our tribal people were completely conquered and their old way of life effectively destroyed, we decided to study what we could of the old ways. Our anthropological patriarch, Franz Boas, pushed this idea so hard that almost all his followers did nothing else. They studied tribe after tribe by interviewing the old men who could remember what it had been like before the beginning of reservation days. I enrolled in a couple of classes at the tail end of the career of one of Boas's disciples, Alfred Kroeber. But by the time I got into the field, we were doing studies of village people because the old men of primitive cultures were getting harder to find."

He stopped speaking, struck by the parallel. He was now the old man and he was about to pour forth all that he could remember about life before the Takeover to their version of an ethnologist, Moma, the electronic interviewer. She would be the twenty-first century counterpart of Clark Wissler, Morris Opler, and Robert Lowie.

"I think this may be time for a break. As you know, an electronic device has no need for rest periods, but life forms do. And since you people have developed a custom of 'taking a break,' I suggest we discontinue for a bit. Why don't you get up and stretch? Some coffee and cake will be here in a moment. I believe that is what you light-skinned variety tend to take at such times. You should be fresher afterwards."

Then the screen faded slowly.

~

Q: *What was that all about? In most of the previous chapters, the title suggested fairly well what the subject was going to be. But an old man talking to an electronic interviewer hardly gives a clue to what I consider you mean to be a summary.*

A: I understand your confusion. In this last interchange I would like to tie things up, a weakness of mine. Other people do the same thing, which they frequently call a summary. Anyway, here in the remaining time I want to go over three matters and any others you may want to ask about. I want to summarize the history of man from an anthropologist's point of view; then I would like to explain why we did not include a number of occurrences in man's history; finally, I want to make a wild guess as to what the future holds for the species. I know that is risky business, but since so many professions try to foretell the future, more often than not with very poor results, I see no reason why an anthropologist cannot do the same. After all, his guess would probably not be much worse than that of an economist, weather forecaster, geologist, or religious pundit. And the fact is that from earliest times, man has tried to peer into the future.

Q: *So are you saying that the future of mankind is likely to be domination by extra-terrestrials?*

A: Possibly, but if you don't mind, I would like to talk about that at the end of this final discussion. I would like to do the true wrap-up or summary first, then make a stab at what it all means, then talk about why we did not include some other events in man's history. And it seems to me that we would then be poised to discuss what the next chapter might be or where mankind is heading—okay?

Q: *Sure, since you are leading the discussion. I am very interested in the alien factor, but I can wait. So the summary?*

A: All right. Life is believed to have started about three and a half billion years ago and evolved from then on through all the pre-human species we know of, both living and extinct, until about five million years ago, when the first hominids evolved on the plains of Africa. The significance of the numbers is that mankind in any form has existed for only a very short period of earth's history—one seven-hundredth, in fact. That would mean that if life began two years ago, the first hominids appeared yesterday. There have been multitudes of species that have lasted much longer than man. And as we will discuss when we talk about the future, man can still be replaced by other living forms on earth.

For better or worse, the first primate ancestors appeared in Africa as upright tool-makers about five million years ago. Most of the rest of our knowledge about Australopithecus is based on speculation or inference. Then, after two to three million years, man's ancestors escaped from the tropics, still as hunter-gatherers, but we infer that they had better shelter, clothing, and fire. We speculate that they also had evolved a rudimentary language. Finally, some one to two hundred thousand years ago, physically modern man appeared, still dependent on hunting and gathering, but with a fully-developed language.

Then around ten thousand years ago came the breakthrough of animal and plant domestication, which made possible much larger populations, as well as more freedom from scarcity, but also more work. Within a few thousand years, a second revolution occurred, which was the development of cities, places where much larger numbers of people could live close to one another, in which milieu a multitude of social and technical innovations were invented.

Apart from endless wars and political rearrangements, nothing much of worldwide significance happened until the rise and spread of European man in the Age of Discovery and Conquest. Though many places retained some of their pre-European characteristics, the mark of Euroman was deep, more like a tattoo than a skin painting. And apart from technological and social innovations, European man also spread his religion to almost all parts, in conversion and derivative beliefs and customs.

Two other significant cultural complexes spread worldwide by Euroman were science and industrialization. Science was a new way of understanding and describing the universe, and industrialization was a new way of producing goods, the most effective devised so far.

Throughout this whole saga, man chose new ideas because they solved one life problem or another. Unfortunately, there were often unexpected consequences. For instance, man settled down in fixed places, villages, because it was important for him to stay put while he was farming or tending animals. But as an unexpected consequence, he soon faced the problems of wastes and infectious diseases, neither of which bothered hunting and gathering peoples very much, since they left their garbage behind when they moved camp. And though he became more productive as a domesticator and later as an urbanite, he also set up the basis for great social inequities. The era of rich and poor, slave and free, subject and ruler, conquered and conqueror began. Anthropologists discovered that among hunters and gatherers, there was a process of primitive generosity that caused the less capable hunters and their families to receive food from the more capable ones. Relief was automatic, and there were no rich people.

One of the most significant unexpected consequences to man's progress was population increase. From a hominid who numbered less than a million (Australopithecus), he became a species of more than five billion, the most numerous large animal on earth. Basically, this was a result of improved technology. Each time some improved method for production occurred, mankind increased his birth ratio over his death ratio so that the surplus was basically used up. I am not saying that each individual figured this out for him or herself, but it happened because there seemed to be less threat of starvation, and the methods for limiting births were neglected. This occurred over and over until the modern era, when the advanced technological cultures are, for the first time since the beginning of the Age of Domestication, having the same amount or fewer babies than deaths. In the poor countries, the increase in population still goes on.

The other great problem is the one which began at the same time, and that is the destruction of the environment, particularly the accumulation of garbage, pollution, and other kinds of environmental degradation. This has become steadily worse as the numbers of people increased.

Q: *Isn't it true, though, even with the problems, that life has become steadily better? There has been progress in the human way, hasn't there?*

A: As I have said earlier, it is unlikely that there is more life satisfaction to individuals in successive stages or in different cultures. You can ask yourself if there is more satisfaction for the working class in a modern industrial state than there was for hunters and gatherers in a primitive society. Anthropologists have learned that people in primitive societies like their way just as much or more than we do in modern society. The fact is that people of all cultures like what they are used to, what they were taught as they grew up.

Q: *But isn't it true that primitive people have always been attracted to new things from modern societies? Didn't bow hunters invariably want guns, and don't peasant villagers want bicycles and transistor radios?*

A: Yes, but in almost all instances they want individual items, while expecting to keep the main pattern of their way of life. The Eskimos originally wanted guns and outboard motors, but were not interested in European marital customs, legal systems, or religion. And the Indian villager who gets a bicycle or radio still expects to keep his own social order and artistic traditions. Basically, what less-developed people want is the technology of the advanced people. Unfortunately, much else comes along with the technology, and before they know it, the borrowers are changed in unexpected ways. Their family, political, artistic, and religious structures, and even their languages go if they take over too much of another people's technology.

Q: *But even within a society people are usually interested in a "better mouse trap," are they not?*

A: Yes, I have no doubt that new technological devices have an inherent attractiveness to most. But I think that despite the hoopla in a production state, there is no evidence that improved technological devices make the quality of life better. Even what we are doing right now, writing on an electronic word processor, does not enable us to write better than if we wrote with a pencil on a tablet or on a typewriter, though once these devices are available, we want them. We simply see what emerges technologically as more desirable than what we are used to, which is what keeps technology in constant progressive change.

And this brings me to the point of all this change. Progress has continually occurred in technology, but in the other parts of culture there has been no such clear-cut gain. So men are, more often than not, uninterested in changes in religion, family systems, political systems, or other non-technical aspects of culture. However, whether we like it or not, when we change our technology, we inevitably bring change to other aspects of our culture.

Q: *So that's what we can conclude in man's five million year evolution, that we have progressed in technology, which has brought some changes about in the other aspects of culture.*

A: I think so, as I suspect most of my colleagues do also. And so I suggest that we go on to the next item on our agenda.

Q: *You mean the events in history you did not include, such as wars? You did mention some small wars, such as the* Homo erectus *and Cro-magnon's defeat of other hominids, and the wars of the city-states. But the great wars of mankind such as those of the Greeks against the Persians, the conquests by the Romans and the Mongols, and the great wars of modern times, the World Wars, were not included.*

A: As you have already seen in the narrative of this section, the kind of history we have here is one which is designed to give an extra-terrestrial anthropologist an idea of how man became the dominant species on earth. It doesn't purport to explain everything that occurred in man's past. And let's face it, would it matter for some "others" to know about either the Greeks or Persians, much less which conquered which, compared with knowing about the domestication of plants and animals and the development of cities? Even warfare in general has not been that important except as a means of wasting a lot of resources. Of course, many people got killed, but not to the extent of affecting either population growth or man's steady progress in technology.

Q: *But there were great shifts of power as a consequence of warfare. Weren't they important?*

A: Of course they were to the people involved, but not to mankind generally. The Aztecs of Mexico and the Inca of Peru were destroyed as powers by the Spaniards, as was the Roman Empire by the barbarians. But apart from those who died in the takeovers, the people survived and the technological progress of mankind continued, inevitably shifting to the conquerors each time. Science and industry emerged among the descendants of the European barbarians with knowledge that came to them through the Greeks and Romans. For instance, all the barbarian peoples of Europe got writing systems from the Greeks or Romans, without which both science and industry would not have been possible. Remember that anthropology is a study of man done with the widest brush strokes. These particular topics are those I learned when I became an anthropologist, and were developed through 150 years of study by my predecessors.

Q: *I suppose we might as well go on to a discussion of the future. What will happen from an anthropological viewpoint?*

A: Let's begin with the best scenario, as it is put by various analytical pundits these days. First, there is absolutely no doubt that there will continue to be progress in technology, and at an even faster rate. Industrial production will continue to turn out ever more goods which those who can get them will consume as fast as they can. Perhaps the most futuristic of production techniques will be the use of robots, which is merely more sophisticated machine use. There will be a continued growth in electronic devices to control and exploit other knowledge, particularly the computer. And no matter that it is not currently in favor, nuclear sources of power will be developed. Finally, there will be interplanetary travel. However, unless there is some kind of completely unexpected breakthrough in space travel, we will not get out of the solar system. Thus, life for most humans will not get better, but it will get more complex.

Q: *Your best scenario doesn't sound all that wonderful. Is there no way we could improve the quality of our lives?*

A: As I told you before, we seem to be destined to keep improving our technology, which does not in itself make things better. For instance, in warfare there has been constant progress in the ability to kill. But what difference was it to be burned to death in a firestorm in Dresden or Tokyo or to be skewered by a Paleolithic warrior on a stone spearpoint?

I must say this conclusion, which I came to rather late in my life, has bothered me also. I have wondered how we could really improve our lives, and I finally came up with a provisional answer, which is that since it seems inevitable that tools will continue to get more efficient, we might as well continue to use those which do help on a given task. Thus, it makes sense to use a word processor even if you learned to write on a typewriter.

But we must avoid taking over "things" just because they are new and we must always expect unforeseen consequences. This has not been easy in the past, and the only way we can avoid some of the mistakes like those we made in the past is to be ready to modify or even abandon innovations if the consequences are too serious. For instance, the automobile was a useful "thing" to have been invented, but the pollution it caused has been terrible. If we had kept our eyes on the development of the machine, we would have done quite a few things to have kept pollution in check—restricted its horsepower, kept lead out of gasoline, limited ownership, and built up public transit systems. But we just muddled along until we were choking in the big cities and now we are belatedly doing some of these things.

Q: *That sounds reasonable, but it also sounds like the kind of recommendation one would expect in a materialistic culture. Isn't there anything we can do besides selecting better "things"?*

A: Let's remember that the crux of the human way is tools and we will never get away from that fact. But there was something else developing through those five million years which we can now use far more than we do. Our ancestors did not just take over new tools, they took over the ideas of the tools, mainly how to make and use them. And they messed around with a lot of other ideas. For instance, men developed systems of philosophy, religions, science, art, and much more, all of which were fundamentally idea systems. And they embodied them in one of their languages, of numbers or words. It's all right to think of man as a tool-using animal, but he is also an ideological animal, a creature of ideas. And so it seems to me that in the future, we need to concentrate far more on our ideologies, our thought processes, if we want to improve our life quality. The supreme act of humanness is creative thinking. We need this far more than we need to consume more and more goods if life quality is our goal.

Q: *That makes the best scenario sound much better. I am then almost ready to hear the worst scenario, which I presume is the takeover of the world by aliens, right?*

A: That could happen, though there are still some other possibilities which could take place from forces now on earth. For instance, the two main problems of unforeseen consequences of technology are not yet solved. The population bomb, as it has been called, is still not defused. Fortunately, in the industrial nations the numbers of children are much smaller, mainly because adults are more interested in their own affairs and frequently have independent old age systems. But among the less-developed countries there is still a powerful drive to have children, particularly for help in old age. Of course, though having many children may help some individuals in their old age, it aggravates the problems of the society. One recent idea is that the people of the less-industrialized countries will automatically limit their own families as they industrialize and urbanize, as has happened in the industrial countries. But it is not at all certain that all the poor nations of the world can be quickly brought up to the industrial level of the West. The only other possibility is for the governments of poor nations to try to brainwash their people to limit their family size through direct rewards and punishments. This has already been tried in many places and has not been very effective. The only country that has made any real headway has been China, but its population has continued to grow anyway. More authoritarianism is obviously needed, even though this is anathema these days in the Western countries with their efforts to push their concept of human rights onto other peoples.

Q: *And the other problem, environmental degradation?*

A: It looks a little better. Many countries have got on the band-wagon to save the environment and there has been some progress, par-ticularly in the developed countries. And though there are serious problems, like that of the hole in the ozone layer and the continuing destruction of the rain forests, we might yet halt or slow the pollution of the world, particularly if we can stop populations from increasing.

Q: *And is that the sum total of what man can do to his world?*

A: No, not quite. Although it is less probable now that the Cold War is over, it is still possible for *Homo sapiens* to do to each other what the aliens did to *Homo*, which is to "nuke" him, gas him, or dump pathogens on him to the point of obliteration, all of which he has done to his human enemies before on a small scale. The one hopeful sign is that since the Americans "nuked" the Japanese, the major pow-ers have not used those methods again, though of course they still keep the weapons. However, dissident less powerful countries do use or threaten to use these forces on one another, which causes one to fear a scenario like that which produced World War I.

Q: *Gee, I hope that concludes the terrestrial threats to man's future?*

A: Unfortunately, not quite. One which is important but has been put into the background by man's homocentrism is the ongoing com-petition with other species. We have told ourselves so often that we are the dominant species on the planet, that many of us come to believe that the others don't count. For instance, man has created an "endan-gered species list" on which he includes most of the big animals that he is capable of eliminating. But there are also "unendangered species," many of which he thinks of as pests, but has no way of cut-ting down their numbers, much less eliminating them. Most of these are small, they have short life spans and large numbers of young, and usually eat all kinds of foods. Flies, cockroaches, rats, and mice quick-ly come to mind. These creatures not only evolved lifestyles that have enabled them to survive in nature generally, they have also adapted to man's environment. And there is no expectation of eliminating them other than by poisoning the whole earth and killing off everything. Many have increased their numbers exponentially by utilizing man's environment.

I used to have a "cockroach lecture" which pointed out that this much-hated little guy originally lived in the leaf mold of tropical forests, but found that man's garbage piles made a good substitute and his transport devices were just fine for hitchhiking. From the cockroach's point of view, the greatest thing to come along was the sewer. The cockroach could travel in these in comfort and have water and food available at all times. And when the era of nuclear confrontation would come, the cockroach had a perfect bomb shelter. In fact, I imagined a scenario of what would have emerged after an all-out nuclear exchange between the great powers.

Q: *Don't tell me, I can imagine it myself. It would be the cockroach, right?*

A: Yes, that would be most likely, since no matter how many of them got incinerated on the surface, the great majority would have been underground as they usually are, and after the earth had cooled off, they would come up. And with antennas probing the airwaves, they would soon locate the great new food supply, corpses of humans and other animals who had been on the surface.

Q: *That is indeed a frightening scenario. And I suppose you would claim that others from underground might be there also?*

A: Yes, the rat and mouse and of course all the creatures of decomposition—bacteria, worms, beetles, etc. In fact, that is another type of creature which not only continues to compete for earth space but at the same time makes the earth inhabitable for man—those which change the body parts of plants and animals into soil, and which I have called "the gnawers." Without the creatures of decomposition, the bodies of the dead, plant and animal, would accumulate, and all living things would suffocate under the weight of corpses. It was put graphically by the biologist Edmond O. Wilson, who said, "What would happen to men if the insects of the world were eliminated?"

And the answer: "All men and other living forms would soon die off."

"And what would happen to the insects if man were to be eliminated?"

Answer" "Nothing."

In other words, they don't need us but we need them. From this point of view, the earth is little more than a huge compost bin.

Q: *This is indeed a different point of view about mankind. But I thought anthropologists always considered man as the paramount species, and now it seems they see other creatures as being clearly important also, if not the most probable inheritors of life. Is that so?*

A: Well, sort of. Perhaps I push this idea farther than most of my profession, but I think it is clear that any thinking person who can put his homocentrism into perspective has to recognize that the dominance of his species is not as total as he would like to think, and that some modesty is in order. And when you include the bacteria and viruses as biological competitors, you have a formidable group indeed.

Q: *Okay, we can now look at them with more respect. But are you really suggesting that some of this group will probably be the inheritors of life? After all, we humans can control the insects and even most of the bacteria and virus with our chemicals and other techniques. We can even get some insects to combat others for our benefit.*

A: It is true that in recent times we have marshalled an impressive array of defenses. But there are still some real problems and there is one force which all these creatures depend on for their continuance— their short life spans and consequent much faster rate of mutation. And we have not yet learned to counteract that.

And yes, I would guess that one of the lowlier, less-differentiated creatures is much more likely to be the inheritor of life on earth than is man. After all, the remotest mammalian ancestor of man was the tree shrew, a small, undifferentiated creature about the size of a small rat. Any self-respecting dinosaur, whose type had been dominant for more than 200 million years, would have considered that diminutive mammal very insignificant. So if man is to be replaced, a small, inconspicuous creature like a cockroach, rat, or bacterium makes a more likely candidate than one of the big mammals on the endangered species list.

Q: *Your scenarios are certainly not reassuring. And we of course thought that anthropology, the study of man, would emphasize the importance of man's culture. Is man doomed? And are you sorry you became an anthropologist?*

A: Well, no, we are here and we have done pretty well by the cultural way, and I am still impressed by man's achievements. After all, we are the only species that got to the point of being able to encapsulate knowledge, as well as reproducing ourselves so successfully that reproduction has actually become a problem. And we can also consider how precarious our dominance is. Furthermore, I have no doubt that, like the members of any other species, we will continue to do everything we can to maintain ourselves; and our cultural way gives us some fair-ly effective weapons.

But when we talk about one earth, we need to keep in mind that rats, mice, cockroaches, crows, bacteria, and virus are also included.

I sometimes think that our primary problem is that we Westerners inherited an ideological system which set us off from the rest of nature—Christianity. Our creator formed us after all the other crea-tures were created and then informed us that they were made just for our benefit, that is, according to the sacred book. The Hindus and Buddhists are taught that the soul can transmigrate from one creature to another, that our grandmother might have been an insect in anoth-er life. So the believers of those religions see other forms of life as more than mere food for humans, or pests to be destroyed with no com-punction, or laboratory animals that can be experimented upon for perceived human benefit. But I doubt that any number of all-life lovers such as myself will change the Western trend.

Q: *So can we go on to the scenario that opened this chapter, that of aliens taking over? Is that what you think is most likely?*

A: Instead of answering that immediately, let me give a little his-torical perspective. Man is a very imaginative creature, and long before the era of astronomy, men were fascinated by the skies, creating both mythological and empirical theories about the universe. In the various ideologies extraordinary conditions existed in the sky and affected man's life on earth. The afterworld was more often than not a place in the sky. And then men in ancient Mesopotamia got the idea that movement in the sky influenced life on earth. And the mythology of man was enriched by creatures that came from this wondrous place, the heavens, particularly in what were called origin myths. Some of these creatures went back and forth between sky and earth. The Greek and Germanic pantheons had many such creatures, but so did other religious systems. There were otherworld spirit beings which con-tributed to the downfall of the two great American civilizations, Aztec and Inca, because the Spanish conquistadors were thought to be their incarnations. And so it was perhaps inevitable that in the age of writ-ing, imaginative authors would see sky creatures and aliens coming from other worlds. And thus was born the era of science fiction.

In my early years I was taken by a classic, H.G. Wells's *War of the Worlds*. He imagined from the primitive state of astronomy in the late nineteenth century that aliens would come from the planet Mars. And it is particularly interesting how Wells solved the alien threat imaginatively. The Martians in their space ships were unbeatable by humans, but just when the situation seemed hopeless, they started dying off. It was discovered by men that they were being infected by bacteria to which they had no immunity. So even then, at the end of the nineteenth century, the imaginative writer, Wells, recognized the significance of the "lower orders."

Nowadays we find it less likely that other creatures will come from within our solar system. But that hasn't kept imaginative writers from bringing in aliens from beyond. They simply skip the technical details of how their creatures got here. But in any event, men are still very intrigued by "sky creatures."

And there is of course a small minority of the world population who really believe that aliens have come to our planet, the flying saucer people. And I think there is a real possibility that some may have or will come. Moreover, just by getting here, their technology will be so far beyond ours that they will have no trouble taking us over.

Q: *But why do you believe there are such creatures?*

A: Without being convinced that anyone has seen or interacted with aliens on flying saucers, I accept the scientific explanation of the universe in which there are millions of millions of stars, around many of which there could be planets, on some of which life could emerge. So I find it easy to believe that there are other forms of life on other worlds.

Q: *But even granting that, why do you assume that they would want to take us over?*

A: For that answer, we need go no further than our own planet. Its history consists of one variety of human displacing another whenever biological or technical superiority occurred. Many previously unknown life forms were eliminated by man—the mammoth, the wild horse in North America, the giant buffalo, the giant sloth, the moa of New Zealand, the passenger pigeon, etc., etc. There is evidence that Neanderthal was eliminated by our own species, and it is possible that Australopithecus was wiped out by *Homo erectus*. The European discoverers wiped out the Tasmanians in Australia, all the tribes of southern South America, most of the Indians of California, and others. Those they did not wipe out, they engulfed or put on fractions of the territory they used formerly.

Q: *It sounds terrible, compared with what we are taught in our early schooling. The only hope I can imagine is that we will discover the aliens instead of them discovering us. Is that likely?*

A: Again, that is grist for science fiction, though I find that possibility unlikely simply because of the vastness of the universe and the statistical probability that some other creatures will develop a more advanced technology more rapidly. The other hope I see is that the challenges of space travel outside the solar system are so daunting that neither we nor other creatures will break out in the foreseeable future. And in the meantime, we *Homo sapiens* can continue on our cultural way.

And I am pleased with that idea and one that comes from it, that there will still be a place for anthropology—at least for a while. And if we do hark to some of the words from the science of man, can we not hark to some others, to cease practicing the unbridled homocentrism and ethnocentrism of the past? In that way, we might even learn something from one another, which might help if and when we will have to face the aliens.

INDEX

Order Form

Telephone orders:
619-728-8123. Have your Visa or MasterCard ready.

Fax orders:
619-728-6002

Postal Orders:
The Hominid Press
Arthur Niehoff
Box 1481
Bonsall, CA 92003-1481, USA

Please send the following books. I understand that I may return any for a full refund — no questions asked.

_____

_____

_____

Company Name: _____

Name: _____

Address _____

City / State / Zip _____

Sales Tax:
Please add 7.75% ($1.00 per book) for books to California addresses.

Shipping:
$2 for the first book and 75 cents for each additional one. (It may take three to four weeks.)
Air Mail: $3.50 per book.

Payment:
❏ Check
❏ Credit Card: ❏ Visa ❏ MasterCard

Card number: _____

Name on card: _____

Expiration date: _____